THE CIVIL SERVICE COMMISSION
1855–1991

The Civil Service Commission was created in 1855 and became the key institution in the development of the British civil service. Its work was primarily the recruitment of civil servants by fair methods, treating all qualified applicants equally, and using open competitions wherever practicable. It was held in high esteem not only in the United Kingdom but also in many other countries throughout the world which, in many places, modelled their methods of public service recruitment on its pioneering work. It continued until 1991, when most of its work was devolved to over 3,000 recruitment units in government departments and executive agencies.

This book describes the gestation, growth, development and eventual demise of the Commission and includes a number of in-depth case studies. Using source material such as official files, many only recently available for research, together with other records and evidence to official committees, the book provides a biography of an institution. It shows how the department was formally organised and there is a particular focus on how it actually worked on a day-to-day basis. With three in-depth chapters on the chronological development of the Commission and seven case studies of themes or issues that reveal methods of work and influences on its activities, this book uses file-based research more extensively than any other history of a British government department.

The Civil Service Commission 1855–1991 reveals insights into civil service recruitment and makes a major original contribution to our understanding of the practice and politics of public administration.

Richard A. Chapman is Emeritus Professor of Politics in Durham Business School. He previously taught at Carleton University, Canada, and the Universities of Leicester, Liverpool, Birmingham and Durham. He is a Foundation Academician of the Academy of Learned Societies for the Social Sciences. His previous books include *Ethics in the British Civil Service* (1988), *The Treasury in Public Policy-Making* (1997) and *Leadership in the British Civil Service* (1984).

BRITISH POLITICS AND SOCIETY
Series Editor: Peter Catterall

Social change impacts not just upon voting behaviour and party identity but also the formulation of policy. But how do social changes and political developments interact? Which shapes which? Reflecting a belief that social and political structures cannot be understood either in isolation from each other or from the historical processes which form them, this series will examine the forces that thave shaped British society. Cross-disciplinary approaches will be encouraged. In the process, the series will aim to make a contribution to existing fields, such as politics, sociology and media studies, as well as opening out new and hitherto-neglected fields.

THE MAKING OF CHANNEL 4
Edited by Peter Catterall

MANAGING DOMESTIC DISSENT IN FIRST WORLD WAR BRITAIN
Brock Millman

REFORMING THE CONSTITUTION
Debates in twenty-first century Britain
Edited by Peter Catterall, Wolfram Kaiser and Ulrike Walton-Jordan

PESSIMISM AND BRITISH WAR POLICY, 1916–1918
Brock Millman

AMATEURS AND PROFESSIONALS IN POST-WAR BRITISH SPORT
Edited by Adrian Smith and Dilwyn Porter

A LIFE OF SIR JOHN ELDON GORST
Disraeli's awkward disciple
Archie Hunter

CONSERVATIVE PARTY ATTITUDES TO JEWS, 1900–1950
Harry Defries

POOR HEALTH
Social inequality before and after
the Black Report
Edited by Virginia Berridge and Stuart Blume

MASS CONSERVATISM
The conservatives and the public since the 1880s
Edited by Stuart Ball and Ian Holliday

DEFINING BRITISH CITIZENSHIP
Empire, commonwealth and modern Britain
Rieko Karatani

TELEVISION POLICIES OF THE LABOUR PARTY, 1951–2001
Des Freedman

CREATING THE NATIONAL HEALTH SERVICE
Aneurin Bevan and the Medical Lords
Marvin Rintala

A SOCIAL HISTORY OF MILTON KEYNES
Middle England/Edge City
Mark Clapson

SCOTTISH NATIONALISM AND THE IDEA OF EUROPE
Atsuko Ichijo

THE ROYAL NAVY IN THE FALKLANDS CONFLICT
AND THE GULF WAR
Culture and strategy
Alastair Finlan

THE LABOUR PARTY IN OPPOSITION 1970–1974
Prisoners of history
Patrick Bell

THE CIVIL SERVICE COMMISSION 1855–1991
A bureau biography
Richard A. Chapman

THE CIVIL SERVICE COMMISSION 1855–1991

A bureau biography

Richard A. Chapman

LONDON AND NEW YORK

JN
425
.C43
2004

First published 2004
by Routledge
11 New Fetter Lane, London EC4P 4EE

Simultaneously published in the USA and Canada
by Routledge
29 West 35th Street, New York, NY 10001

Routledge is an imprint of the Taylor & Francis Group

© 2004 Richard A. Chapman

Typeset in Baskerville MT by
Newgen Imaging Systems (P) Ltd, Chennai, India
Printed and bound in Great Britain by
Antony Rowe Ltd, Chippenham, Wiltshire

All rights reserved. No part of this book may be reprinted or
reproduced or utilised in any form or by any electronic,
mechanical, or other means, now known or hereafter
invented, including photocopying and recording, or in any
information storage or retrieval system, without permission
in writing from the publishers.

The publisher makes no representation, express or implied, with
regard to the accuracy of the information contained in this book and
cannot accept any legal responsibility or liability for any errors or
omissions that may be made.

British Library Cataloguing in Publication Data
A catalogue record for this book is available
from the British Library

Library of Congress Cataloging in Publication Data
The Civil Service Commission 1855–1991: a bureau biography/
Chapman, Richard A.
p. cm.
Includes bibliographical references (p.) and index.
1. Great Britain. Civil Service Commission – History. I. Title.

JN425.C43 2004
352.6′3′09410904–dc22   2004002093

ISBN 0–7146–5340–3 (alk. paper)

CONTENTS

Series editor's preface   ix
Preface   xii
Acknowledgements   xiii
Note on terms used in the Civil Service Commission   xiv
List of abbreviations   xv

1 Introduction: the Civil Service Commission   1

PART I
The rise and fall of the Civil Service Commission   9

2 The period from 1855 to 1920   11

   The creation of the Civil Service Commission 11
   The first meetings of the Commission 18
   What the Commission did 24
   The expanding role of the Commission 33

3 The period from 1921 to 1951   41

   The MacDonnell and Leathes Reports 41
   Experience during post-First World War reconstruction 45
   Waterfield and the Method II system of selection in
     post-Second World War recruitment 49
   The problems of conscientious objectors 54
   The scientific civil service 58
   Fairness and efficieny in personnel management 59
   Change, development and achievement 62

4 The period from 1952 to 1991   66

   From 1952 to 1968 66
   From 1969 to 1991 73
   The demise of the Civil Service Commission 82

PART II
Competition, confidentiality and complacency   91

5 The growth of working relationships   93

*Relations with the Treasury 94
Relations with schools and universities 103
Relations with other government departments 111
Contacts outside the civil service 115*

6 Setting standards in the civil service   125

7 The case of Arthur Creech Jones: clerk in the
   Civil Service Commission   140

8 Centenary celebrations   156

9 The effects of Fulton   175

10 Administrative culture   194

*Women and the civil service 195
Publications by officials 203
The work of scholars 211
The administrative culture 215*

11 'Bias' in selection   220

*The selectors and their social attitudes 221
The educational system 226
The nature and content of the selection system 230
Publicity, liaison and visits 234
'Bias' in selection 241*

PART III
The Civil Service Commission in British public administration   247

12 The Civil Service Commission: a bureau biography   249

*The Civil Service Commission – a central department for recruitment 249
Recruitment: examinations and competitions 253
Perspectives of accountability: the social and political environment 257
Bureau biography 259*

Appendix: Civil Service Commissioners 1855–1991   264
Bibliography   270
Index   277

SERIES EDITOR'S PREFACE

The history of what is now called Human Resources Management is not a much-studied topic. This is perhaps a surprising omission. Despite all the suspects rounded up to account for Britain's comparatively poor economic performance in the third quarter of the twentieth century, this one seems to have largely escaped scrutiny. Even the British civil service sometimes managed unaccountably to overlook this important topic; for instance, the extensive contingency planning which preceded the First World War somehow ignored the issue of industrial manpower. Yet, as this example bears testimony, at a macro-level Human Resources Management can have a material effect on how well a nation stands the test of war. At a micro-level it helps shape the replication and retention of knowledge, the corporate values, the internal culture and management structures of a firm or organisation. Not only does it shape the potentialities of these organisations but it also, as Richard Chapman shows in this study, can reflect what they feel themselves to be.

To be fair, some aspects of the history of this field have received more attention than others. Training is one example, though more often through the prism of policy than in terms of its application within a given organisation or its relationship to other aspects of Human Resources such as grading, remuneration, recruitment or retention. It is important, however, that these other aspects also receive due attention. Richard Chapman's study of how the Civil Service Commission discharged one of these functions, recruitment, for nearly 150 years is therefore very much to be welcomed.

Contrary to the apeing of what they take to be business methods by the devotees of New Public Management, the Civil Service Commission was instead an example to be followed. It established its requirements and sought to shape the way they were met by its supply agencies in the schools and universities almost from its inception in 1855. In a sense it might thus be seen as of a piece with the various clarifications of the boundaries and routes into other professions that were also being established in the mid-Victorian era. Arguably, however, the combination of the more or less monopolistic position of the CSC as gatekeeper to entry to the civil service, and the powerful patronage of its support in the Treasury, gave it considerably greater leverage than that of cognate bodies in other professions.

At the same time, it reflected the liberal rationality of the age of Gladstone. Service to the state was an indivisible function, even if the discharge of it was, after 1870, to be organised into different classes for grading purposes. However, those best suited for that service, it seems to have been assumed, were likely to come from the great Public Schools and the ancient universities of Oxford and Cambridge, an assumption which reflected convenience as much as prejudice and which was arguably defensible in the context of the late Victorian era, but decreasingly so as the twentieth century wore on.

The result was a meritocratic elite of somewhat narrow social formation. This did not prevent, however, remarkable adaptability. Over the life of the CSC the concept of the state underwent a number of changes and its range of functions waxed and waned. It might be argued that the civil service nevertheless stood the test, not least during two world wars, remarkably well. In the post-war years, however, increasing criticism came to be voiced. By the 1980s, the decade of the lampooning of Sir Humphrey in *Yes, Minister*, it had become a truism that 'Whitehall failed to attract the rich mixture of human skills it needed, relying overmuch on a single if refined stream of generalist graduates'.[1] If that was true, then the fault clearly lay with the CSC. What would-be reformers wanted was not a single point of entry to an unified civil service, but instead a multiplicity of entry points to the much more differentiated service which, through the hiving off of functions into executive agencies, was already in the 1980s beginning to emerge. Specialisation of function implied specialisation of recruitment, a process which, as Chapman points out, had already started in the 1960s and even then was beginning to undermine the *raison d'être* of the CSC.

It could, of course, be argued that the would-be reformers of the 1960s onwards chose the wrong target. It was not the mid-Victorian architects of the CSC who produced the type of state, and consequently Civil Service, they railed against, but those who adapted the system to meet the exigencies of war in the Edwardian period and after. Indeed, it could be said that among the intentions of Northcote and Trevelyan was the creation of a narrow policy making elite, which is after all not so dissimilar from the objectives of the current masters of the ship of state. Those who litter their speeches with metaphors of mapping and steering imply a policy making elite who pass on down to operational cadres the targets and performance indicators by which governments now choose to be judged. The difference is that much of their policy making elite, unlike that of Northcote and Trevelyan, has not been selected by competitive examination, but instead been parachuted in as special political advisers.

Indeed, in some ways they represent a replication of the patronage system which mid-nineteenth century reformers regarded with such disapprobation. Nor do they have the pragmatism, or humility, to reflect with W.D. McIndoe

> Government is concerned with people and events. Even at home both are only partially predictable; abroad, they can take us completely by surprise. This element of the unforeseen and unforeseeable commonly

receives less attention, in discussion of the machinery of government, than it deserves. But it provides one of the best tests of a Government's resilience and flexibility, and, even if our system has the defect of providing insufficient opportunity for the discussion of long-term issues (which often turn out to be very different when the time comes) it usually manages to react reasonably quickly and effectively to the shorter-term problem (the nature of which is generally unmistakable). In a sense this means no more than that we conduct the business of government pragmatically. But we are a pragmatic people.[2]

Pragmatic generalists were arguably well-suited for this model of governance. But it is a model no longer in fashion. Change, however, has not been without its downside. The importation of special advisers has certainly provoked concern in recent years linked to what the House of Commons Select Committee on Public Administration has euphemistically called 'unfortunate events'. One consequence has been the warning of the First Civil Service Commissioner in June 2003 that

> As departments recruit more people from outside to senior positions, it is essential not only to make sure the Civil Service benefits from their skills, experience and different ways of doing things, but also that they understand the core values which underpin the work of the service.[3]

It was, if anything, the CSC that inculcated those core values and made them common. This history is a salutary reminder that the process of recruitment is about far more than simply fitting the right men – and eventually the right women – to the job. Historians need to pay attention to it because it plays an important role in shaping the entire organisation. And tinkering with a system of recruitment is, as recent concerns highlight, rarely likely to bring the consequence-free benefits that the CSC's critics in the 1980s fondly assumed.

Peter Catterall
8 September 2003

Notes

1 Peter Hennessy, *Whitehall* (London: Secker & Warburg, 1989), p. 725.
2 PRO/PREM11/4838, W.D. McIndoe notes, 'Organisation of the Cabinet and its Committees', c. January 1964.
3 Preface by Baroness Prashar to Civil Service Commissioners, *Report for the Period 1 April 2002 to 31 March 2003* (London: Office of the Civil Service Commissioners, 2003).

PREFACE

My research project on the Civil Service Commission, which is the basis for this book, had its origins in the two biographies of senior civil servants which I wrote in the 1980s. These were on Sir Percival Waterfield, *Leadership in the British Civil Service* (1984) and on Sir Edward (later Lord) Bridges, *Ethics in the British Civil Service* (1988). Those two biographies, like this book, were primarily the result of a detailed study of files in the Public Record Office.

Like those two biographies, this book contains no dramatic revelations or intimate details about personal relationships. It is, however, hoped that the book provides a readable record of the work of a very important department of government. It is also hoped that it makes a contribution to understanding the practice of public administration in Britain.

The material presented has had to be selective because a very large number of files have been read in the Public Record Office – not only in the Civil Service Commission class but also in the Treasury and other related classes. Because it has been selective, many interesting facts and other details that could have been recorded have been excluded. It should, however, be noted that the value of reading nearly 3,000 files is that they provide a broad understanding of the subject matter; therefore what is presented here is both a fair representation of what is available and is conditioned by the accumulated experience of reading many files that are not referred to in the text.

Each chapter is largely self-contained (i.e. does not assume prior knowledge from earlier chapters): although they are arranged in a logical and designed sequence they do not necessarily have to be read in the order presented. This means that terms used and individuals referred to are explained when they first appear in each chapter – but a brief glossary and a list of abbreviations are provided for quick reference when desired.

I hope that readers will feel that the project has been worthwhile and that they get as much enjoyment from reading this book as I have from doing the research and writing it.

Richard A. Chapman
May 2003

ACKNOWLEDGEMENTS

I wish to record my thanks to the following institutions and individuals for research help received in various ways. The University of Durham appointed me to a Sir James Knott Foundation Research Fellowship 1995–96; the Leverhulme Trust appointed me to an Emeritus Fellowship 1997–99; the Economic and Social Research Council awarded me a research grant (R 000 237 383); Nuffield College, Oxford, appointed me Official Visitor for some weeks in 1996–97; and Durham Business School gave me office accommodation, facilities, the status of Honorary Research Fellow and friendship and understanding.

The following archives were used for access to the papers stated: the Public Record Office – now the National Archives (where the staff were extremely helpful, especially Jeremy Harley); the London School of Economics Archives (the Robson Papers and the LSE Council records); Rhodes House Library, Oxford (the Creech Jones Papers); the Hartley Library, University of Southampton (the Palmerston Papers); the British Library (the Gladstone Papers); the Robinson Library, University of Newcastle-upon-Tyne (the Trevelyan Papers); the London Metropolitan Archives; Trinity College, Cambridge Library (the Stanley Leathes Papers); and the Mitchell Library, Glasgow (for Official Publications). An earlier version of chapter 6, 'Setting standards in a new organisation' was published in Richard A. Chapman (ed.), *Ethics in Public Service for the New Millennium* (Aldershot: Ashgate, 2000).

Many people have helped me by answering questions and donating old copies of the reports of the Civil Service Commissioners. These included: Sir David Bailey, Dr Andrea Duncan, Dr Kathleen Prior, Mr David A. Wooff and Professor Maurice Wright.

My special thanks must be expressed to the following who read parts or the whole manuscript in draft and made helpful comments: Dr F.H. Allen (chapter 11); Professor J.A.G. Griffith (chapter 8); Nevil Johnson (chapter 4); Keith M. Reader (chapters 2, 3, 6, 7, 8, 9, 10), Professor Peta Tancred (chapter 10), Dr Duncan Bythell, Dr Barry O'Toole and Dr Peter Catterall. The responsibility for the final manuscript is, of course, mine alone.

NOTE ON TERMS USED IN THE CIVIL SERVICE COMMISSION

Open competitions are open to all candidates, both within and outside the civil service, who satisfy the prescribed conditions of eligibility.

Limited competitions are confined to people already in the civil service; the conditions of eligibility vary, but usually require the completion of a prescribed period of service.

General Service grades are employed in all or most departments on a similar range of duties, usually with common salary scales and conditions of service.

Departmental/Agency grades are staff employed in one department, or executive agency only, on duties special to that department or agency.

Certification is the procedure of issuing a certificate of qualification for a particular individual; the certificate is issued to the employing department and is an assurance that the individual has satisfied the Commissioners in terms of health, knowledge and ability for a particular situation.

Nomination is the naming of a particular person for a position (or the naming of a person to compete for a position): usually nomination was the alternative to open competition; in many cases it was based on previous employment, often temporary, in the civil service.

Fast stream: the civil service fast-stream development programme is a training and development scheme for very able graduates. In recent times this recruitment scheme has included recruitment to the General fast stream (for the Home Civil Service, Diplomatic Service, European fast stream, Science and Engineering fast stream, Clerks – House of Commons/Lords and Legal Officers (Europe)) and certain other opportunities in specific government departments.

ABBREVIATIONS

AC	Administrative Class
ACCA	Association of Certified and Corporate Accountants
AT	Administration Trainee
APM	Assistant Provost Marshal
BBC	British Broadcasting Corporation
CA	Clerical Assistant
CIB	Central Interviewing Board
CISSB	Civil Service Selection Board
CO	Clerical Officer
CO	Conscientious Objector
CPB	Central Probation Board
CSC	Civil Service Commission
CSD	Civil Service Department
CSSB	Civil Service Selection Board
CRO	Commonwealth Relations Office
DCM	Distinguished Conduct Medal
DFC	Distinguished Flying Cross
DSO	Companion of the Distinguished Service Order
E and AD	Exchequer and Audit Department
FSB	Final Selection Board
GPO	General Post Office
HC Deb.	House of Commons Debates
HL Deb.	House of Lords Debates
HM	Her Majesty
HMSO	Her Majesty's Stationery Office
ICA	Institute of Chartered Accountants
ICI	Imperial Chemical Industries
ICS	Indian Civil Service
ILP	Independent Labour Party
IPA	Institute of Public Administration
LCC	London County Council
LMA	London Metropolitan Archives

ABBREVIATIONS

LO	Liaison Officer
LSE	London School of Economics (and Political Science)
MC	Military Cross
MP	Member of Parliament
NIIP	National Institute of Industrial Psychology
O and M	Organisation and Methods
OBE	Officer, Order of the British Empire
PRO	Public Record Office
PSA	Property Services Agency
QT(s)	Qualifying Test(s)
RAF	Royal Air Force
RIPA	Royal Institute of Public Administration
SDC	Special Departmental Class(es)
TMA	Treasury Medical Adviser
UAB	University Appointments Board
UK	United Kingdom
USA	United States of America
WOSB	War Office Selection Board
YMCA	Young Men's Christian Association

1
INTRODUCTION: THE CIVIL SERVICE COMMISSION

The intention of this book is to provide insights into how a department in British central government actually worked and consequently to add to knowledge about the practice of public administration in a particular context. It discusses and explains the gestation, growth, development and eventual demise of the Civil Service Commission. It also outlines and considers, in as much detail as possible, a number of themes and specific problems (some of them controversial) that illustrate how the Commission worked.

Most books that have been written on the work of government departments – certainly the books in the 'Whitehall Series'[1] and the 'New Whitehall Series'[2] – have concentrated on explaining the responsibilities of particular departments and giving an account of the departmental structure and organisation to achieve given aims and objectives. That emphasis was primarily the result of constraints placed upon authors: the books could not have been written without official co-operation and approval, and the approval was given, with conditions, to ensure that nothing was published that might be embarrassing either to the government of the day or to the British civil service. The editor of the 'Whitehall Series' was Sir James Marchant, a nonconformist minister, who had a wide range of interests and was a tireless social worker.[3] In 1924 he approached several heads of departments with a view to securing contributions to the series. Warren Fisher, then Head of the Home Civil Service, after being consulted by the permanent heads, adopted a distinctly cool attitude. He believed purely historical accounts would 'make dull and unpalatable reading unless the author touched on matters of controversy, and in such cases it might well be desirable for any Civil Servant invited to contribute to the series to refuse to do so'. It should be clearly understood that the authors of the books 'must limit themselves to plain unvarnished narrative'.[4] The volumes of the 'Whitehall Series' began to appear in 1925 and were, in fact, written by retired civil servants. They were indeed largely confined to unvarnished narrative, but were useful, if only to a limited academic extent, because, for people who wanted to know about government departments, there were no serious alternatives.

After the Second World War the 1945 Labour government tended to think that government had been too secretive in the past. This attitude was helped to some extent by certain academics who worked in Whitehall during the war, whose understanding of it had improved as a result, and who had become more or less accepted by career 'insiders'. It was also helped by the Institute of Public Administration (which was formed in 1922, received the title Royal in 1954 and went into administrative receivership in 1992).[5] The Chancellor of the Exchequer, Sir John Anderson (later Lord Waverley), who had been heavily involved in Machinery of Government issues during the war,[6] became the Institute's President in 1944 and it received its first Treasury grant in 1948. These circumstances led to the Institute proposing in 1949 a revision of the 'Whitehall Series'. The 'New Whitehall Series' was authorised by Sir Edward (later Lord) Bridges, then Head of the Home Civil Service, but only on condition that the books were written in departments under the guidance of each permanent secretary so that – to quote Bridges – they could be 'satisfactory, consistent and unembarrassing'.[7]

The 'New Whitehall Series' therefore updated the contents and approach of the earlier series. Again, for people who wanted the information, there was no alternative. Some of the academics who became temporary wartime civil servants (such as K.C. Wheare,[8] H.R.G. Greaves[9] and Oliver Franks[10]) published thoughtful and reflective lectures or articles after their return to their universities, but these were based on experience rather than academic research. This meant that there was still a large gap in the literature – a gap that was generally recognised by academics but not thought important by officials. There were attempts to fill the gaps (e.g. by T.A. Critchley[11] and William A. Robson[12]), but for one reason or another they achieved only limited success.

Meanwhile, historians, researching before the liberalisation of access to records in 1967, sometimes studied periods or topics within central government and produced well-received scholarly books. For example, Emmeline Cohen,[13] Geoffrey K. Fry,[14] Henry Roseveare,[15] Maurice Wright[16] and others, made valuable contributions to the literature, but they were not able to cover more than selected periods or aspects of departmental work. Moreover, they tended to present little on what public administration specialists would now recognise as the political activity within and between departments. Other contributions to the literature, for example, by K.M. Reader,[17] Louis Moss[18] and Dennis Bird,[19] resulted from encouragement to celebrate significant anniversaries of departments, but these, like the Whitehall books, were written by officials and intended to be consistent with the 'unembarrassing' requirements as expressed by Fisher and Bridges.

It is not surprising that, together, this field of public administration literature was often thought to be incomplete or inadequate. Scholars from the United States (e.g. Hugh Heclo and Aaron Wildavsky[20]), where the social sciences developed apace, especially after the Second World War, introduced new methods of research, including interviewing officials, and these methods were later continued with more journalistic flair by others who focused on contemporary institutional structures and attitudes (e.g. Anthony Sampson,[21] Peter Hennessy[22] and Peter Kellner and Lord Crowther-Hunt[23]).

In addition, there have been books by scholars who, by one means or another, have sought to focus on particular periods in the history of departments, using published and unpublished documentary sources together with all other available evidence, such as evidence presented to committees and commissions, and interviews with officials both serving and retired. Authors who used this approach included Jill Pellew,[24] Colin Thain and Maurice Wright[25] and Richard A. Chapman.[26]

Further insight into the history of government departments has been provided by the numerous memoirs and accounts by officials, often retired, who have reflected on their work and tried to find a rationale for patterns of experience and influences on personal behaviour. These included George Mallaby,[27] Alix Meynall[28] and Antony Part.[29]

All these approaches have made valuable contributions to understanding the work of particular departments and of British public administration, but their readers have sometimes thought that there was more to be known than had so far been revealed. Such thoughts have, from time to time, been stimulated or justified by the expressed anxieties of officials to prevent unrestrained research, and to prevent the publication of findings even after projects had been 'approved'.[30]

This history of the Civil Service Commission builds upon the approaches outlined and considers various sources of information, but its main source is the files available in the Public Record Office. Although such files have been used in preparing some of the books mentioned above, the concentrated use in this way of large numbers of files was first used to present biographical studies ('bureau biography' as termed by Professor J.M. Lee[31]) of Sir Percival Waterfield[32] and Lord Bridges.[33] The books on Waterfield and Bridges were sufficiently well received for this much larger project, the history of the Civil Service Commission, to be conceived as viable. There are, however, differences between using the files to write a bureau biography of an individual or to write the history of a department. In particular there may be reservations about presenting the history of a department as a biography. Perhaps two examples from the literature may be mentioned here. In 1959 Charles Cooke wrote *Biography of an Ideal*,[34] to celebrate the diamond anniversary of the United States Federal Civil Service; and in 1972 J.E. Hodgetts and his colleagues published *The Biography of an Institution, the Civil Service Commission of Canada 1908–1967*.[35] A characteristic of these two books is that they focused on themes or individuals to present a study of an organisation. Neither book was a comprehensive and detailed historical study of its subject, but each is valuable in presenting insights into how a particular important organisation evolved, how it was motivated and how it went about its daily work. This present book therefore combines features of a bureau biography which is based on archival resources, and a biography of an institution which concentrates on themes and individuals. It should be noted that information has to be selected; not all the available detail can be included; and sadly, for one reason or another, on some important and interesting themes there is insufficient detail to sustain an acceptable account. Two good examples of this are that there is hardly any information about the appointment of Commissioners or about recruitment to the security services.

There are advantages and disadvantages in adapting the bureau biography approach to write about a department. In the case of the Civil Service Commission the main advantages are that the department had a limited existence: it was created in 1855 and abolished in 1991. There is also the additional attraction of studying a department mainly concerned with providing an operational service within government (for most of its life its policy guidelines were the responsibility of the Treasury). Fortunately, as a result of the Public Records Act 1967, which made files available after 30 years – previously it was after 50 years – most of the Civil Service Commission files destined for preservation are now publicly available; in addition, early access has been approved for some of the others. As much of the work of the Civil Service Commission was not highly sensitive for reasons that would justify extended closure[36] (i.e. beyond 30 years) there are few files remaining closed for longer periods. Nevertheless the Civil Service Commission was an extremely significant department, at the centre of government, with important responsibilities that extended way beyond its specific functions. The Commission in fact played a major role in the development of the unified civil service, a feature of British public administration that became admired and copied in numerous other countries.

The main disadvantages of using the bureau biography approach are related to the physical and other constraints of keeping public records. It is generally understood that the Public Record Office preserves only about 1 per cent of files from government departments, so that much material that might subsequently be regarded as valuable is destroyed before scholars can see it. In any case, even in a well-developed bureaucracy there is much that is not fully recorded, and it is not uncommon to read that reasons for a particular decision or course of action were at the time explained only orally. Some officials have been better than others at recognising what should be preserved in the interests of future historians, and in writing and preserving documents in ways that scholars best appreciate. In any case, it should be remembered that the workings of government are not designed for the benefit of historians: there is a job to be done and ways of working are designed for that purpose and not for others.

The task of reading the files for the purpose of writing a history is not as straightforward as may at first appear. Files in the Public Record Office have survived after officials have weeded through them and departmental records staff have decided they should be kept. By the time they are accessible to scholars they may have been reorganised more than once – sometimes a number of files on a related topic are amalgamated and given a general title which does not necessarily reflect the richness of the contents of the original files. Consequently it is unwise to depend upon the computerised catalogue for this purpose: the catalogue has other uses, of course, but dependence on it for selecting files for study may result in a seriously misleading account and to conclusions quite different from what actually occurred. There is no scholarly and reliable alternative to reading all, or as many as possible, of the files themselves. This is no easy task. Before the invention of typewriters the main records of decisions were handwritten drafts, often heavily amended, of letters that were subsequently copied for despatch. Decisions may have been recorded, but reasons frequently were not. For this project, nearly 3,000 files were read in the Public Record Office at an average rate of about six per day.

The use of files for the purpose of writing a history therefore has to be undertaken with care and the benefit of experience. It also has to be supplemented by other source material. What can be said, however, is that this approach is evidence-based and other scholars can check the details if they so wish and, perhaps, offer alternative explanations or interpretations. Fisher and Bridges might not be happy if they were able to read it – one sometimes feels that they could be easily embarrassed – but they have long since passed away and attitudes and expectations change with time. Whether they would approve or not, this study presents the evidence even where previously it might have been censored as embarrassing; it tells the story of the Civil Service Commission and it presents a great deal of new information about the actual working of a key department in British central government. In doing so, it contributes to our knowledge of the administrative culture, the closed politics of Whitehall and the British ethos of public service in the twentieth century.

After this introduction the book is divided into three parts. Part I contains three chapters written on a mainly chronological basis. The first focuses on the period from the creation of the Commission and goes up to the reconstruction work after the First World War. The second continues until just past the reconstruction period after the Second World War and the end date marks the retirement of Sir Percival Waterfield, under whose leadership major changes in recruitment were introduced. The last covers the period from Waterfield's retirement up to the demise of the Commission as a department of government. The pattern of evidence in the files seems to suggest first, a period of creation, enthusiasm and achievement; then a period of consolidation and success; and finally decline and abolition. The most significant factors in determining this evolution were, without doubt, exogenetic: whilst developments within the organisation were by no means unimportant, the factors really important in determining change, development and reform originated, as with so much in the practice of public administration, from the social and political environment. This is seen in the contexts of the three chapters in Part I, but it is also to be seen in the seven chapters in Part II.

The thematic chapters in Part II are intended to give more detail and insights into the actual working of the Commission as a department of government. Although the Commission was an independent department (with the Commissioners themselves being appointed by Orders in Council), for reasons of financial and political accountability as well as historical and practical convenience, for most of its life it came within the ambit of the Treasury. It had relationships with all other departments and those relationships could each have been considered in detail, but this was impractical because of constraints of space. Chapter 5 considers these relationships, with special attention to the particular contacts with the Treasury. Chapter 6 examines how the Commission set high standards in recruitment and consequently achieved its internationally important reputation not only for efficiency in its operational roles but also in the development of the unified civil service within the context of the British system of government. These chapters are followed by three case studies, on the case of Arthur Creech Jones, the intentions to celebrate the centenary of the Commission and the consequences for the Commission of the investigations and report of the Fulton Committee on the Civil Service. The topics in each of these chapters are presented with as much detail as possible, so that the actual working of the department, as well as its relations with other departments and with individuals, can be appreciated in the context of the attitudes and pressures of the time. The history of any department of government contains much human interest (more than was ever reflected in the Whitehall Series and the New Whitehall Series), as these chapters demonstrate. Chapters 10 and 11 explore the ethos of the Commission through its administrative culture and through a consideration of bias in selection. Any institution has its own culture, developed from its purpose, its staff, its work experience and its reactions to particular events and pressures; and this is well illustrated by the chapter on allegations of bias in recruitment – not because the Commission intentionally engaged in unfair practice but because it was so often accused of doing so, and there are valuable insights to be gained from considering how it reacted to such criticisms.

The concluding chapter (Part III) presents reactions and conclusions. The story of any department of government has unique features, and the distinctive characteristics of the Civil Service Commission are considered here in as much depth as possible. It was a department with a record of significant achievement; the standards it set were high; it was the keystone of the unified British civil service; and it attracted admiration from numerous other countries of the world. Its work did not have a high political salience and it was not generally involved in matters of state security. Nevertheless its work had to be conducted in a context of confidentiality, and it had to respect the requirements of competitive selection procedures. One of the consequences of these aspects of its work was, perhaps, that it developed a degree of complacency and other-worldliness that might have been criticised more publicly in a political or administrative system more open than in Britain.

Notes

1 For example, Sir Edward Troup, *The Home Office* (London: Putnam, 1925); Sir Edward Heath, *The Treasury* (London: Putnam, 1927).
2 For example, Sir Frank Newsom, *The Home Office* (London: Allen & Unwin, 1954); The Rt Hon Lord Bridges, *The Treasury* (London: Allen & Unwin, 1964).
3 *The Times*, 22 May 1956.
4 PRO/T163/85/G1824, Warren Fisher to Chancellor of the Exchequer, 9 December 1924.

5 Richard A. Chapman, 'The Demise of the RIPA: An Idea Shattered', *Australian Journal of Public Administration*, 52(4), 1993, 466–74.
6 See J.M. Lee, *Reviewing the Machinery of Government 1942–1952: An Essay on the Anderson Committee and Its Successors* (London: J.M. Lee, 1977).
7 PRO/T222/504.
8 K.C. Wheare, 'The Machinery of Government', *Public Administration*, 24, 1946, 75–85.
9 H.R.G. Greaves, *The Civil Service in the Changing State* (London: Harrap, 1947).
10 Sir Oliver Franks, *The Experience of a University Teacher in the Civil Service* (London: Oxford University Press, 1947).
11 T.A. Critchley, *The Civil Service Today* (London: Gollancz, 1951).
12 William A. Robson (ed.), *The Civil Service in Britain and France* (London: Hogarth, 1956).
13 Emmeline Cohen, *The Growth of the British Civil Service, 1780–1939* (London: Allen & Unwin, 1941).
14 Geoffrey K. Fry, *Statesmen in Disguise* (London: Macmillan, 1969).
15 Henry Roseveare, *The Treasury: The Evolution of a British Institution* (London: Allen Lane, The Penguin Press, 1969).
16 Maurice Wright, *Treasury Control of the Civil Service, 1854–1874* (Oxford: Clarendon Press, 1969).
17 K.M. Reader, *The Civil Service Commission, 1855–1975* (London: HMSO, 1981).
18 Louis Moss, *The Government Social Survey: A History* (London: HMSO, 1991).
19 Dennis L. Bird, *The Civil Service College, 1970–1995* (London: HMSO, 1995).
20 Hugh Heclo and Aaron Wildavsky, *The Private Government of Public Money* (London: Macmillan, 1974).
21 Anthony Sampson, *Anatomy of Britain* (London: Hodder & Stoughton, 1962).
22 Peter Hennessy, *Whitehall* (London: Secker & Warburg, 1989).
23 Peter Kellner and Lord Crowther-Hunt, *The Civil Servants: An Inquiry into Britain's Ruling Class* (London: Macdonald & Jane's, 1980).
24 Jill Pellew, *The Home Office, 1848–1914: From Clerks to Bureaucrats* (London: Heinemann, 1982).
25 Colin Thain and Maurice Wright, *The Treasury and Whitehall: The Planning and Control of Public Expenditure, 1976–1993* (Oxford: Clarendon Press, 1995).
26 Richard A. Chapman, *The Treasury in Public Policy-Making* (London: Routledge, 1997).
27 George Mallaby, *From My Level* (London: Hutchinson, 1965).
28 Dame Alix Meynall, *Public Servant, Private Woman* (London: Gollancz, 1988).
29 Antony Part, *The Making of a Mandarin* (London: Deutsch, 1990).
30 PRO/BA1/74.
31 J.M. Lee, review of Richard A. Chapman, *Ethics in the British Civil Service*, in *Public Administration*, 67, 1989, 110–11.
32 Richard A. Chapman, *Leadership in the British Civil Service* (London: Croom Helm, 1984).
33 Richard A. Chapman, *Ethics in the British Civil Service* (London: Routledge, 1988).
34 Charles Cooke, *Biography of an Ideal: The Diamond Anniversary History of the Federal Civil Service* (Washington, DC: US Civil Service Commission, 1959).
35 J.E. Hodgetts, William McCloskey, Reginald Whitaker and V. Seymour Wilson, *The Biography of an Institution: The Civil Service Commission of Canada 1908–1967* (Montreal and London: McGill-Queen's University Press, 1972).
36 *Open Government*, Cm 2290 (London: HMSO, 1993).

Part I

THE RISE AND FALL OF THE CIVIL SERVICE COMMISSION

2

THE PERIOD FROM 1855 TO 1920

The British civil service dates from 1855. Previously there were departments of state[1] and there were distinguished civil servants[2] but, as the MacDonnell Royal Commission observed in 1914, there was 'no unity of organisation, no regularity of recruitment, and (save in the expenditure of public money) no common principle of control. Moreover there was not any limitation...on the appointment of public servants by political patronage'.[3]

The most important single factor in the development of a unified civil service was the creation of the Civil Service Commission in 1855. Largely as a result of its efforts, by about 1920 there was a service – 'a competent, zealous and upright body of public officers'.[4] By then the Commission had established itself as an important department of government, with a set of well-developed principles on which it operated. It grew in stature both within the British system of government and in terms of its international reputation. This first substantive chapter presents details of its creation and development up to, approximately, the reconstruction period after the First World War.

The creation of the Civil Service Commission

The creation of the Civil Service Commission laid the foundations of the modern civil service. Its establishment in 1855 and its work during its formative years were the result of four major influences. These were the growth of competition to replace patronage; changes in recruitment elsewhere, especially for the Indian Civil Service (ICS); the influence of a small group of leading personalities; and the need to rectify administrative inefficiency. More extensive accounts of these have already been published,[5] but it should be noted that these influences did not operate in isolation from each other. They were inter-related and the significance of their individual and combined effects varied from time to time.

Patronage was the established method for making appointments to positions in government in the early nineteenth century. Appointments were made as an exercise of privilege: patronage was, in effect, part of the emoluments of political office. Under this system civil servants could sometimes benefit by obtaining from ministers appointments for their sons or relations. It was sometimes argued (as in evidence to the Playfair Commission, 1874–75) that this helped produce a body of trustworthy civil servants, animated by a certain *esprit de corps* and by useful official traditions.[6] In theory, patronage could be wisely and honestly exercised, but its consequences could also result in administrative defects, contrary to the public interest, unless measures were taken to avoid them. An important reason for this was that patronage did not have zeal for public service as one of its main motivating features. To whatever positions were vacant, sufficiently able and hardworking men, who would be expected to be a credit to their patrons, could in theory be appointed. In practice, however, this was often not the case and, as Peter G. Richards has shown, patronage could provide 'obvious opportunities for corruption, peculation, undercover influence and power-seeking of various kinds'.[7]

Middle-class radicals – whose significance had grown as a result of the industrial revolution and puritan attitudes associated with 'the onward march of the nonconformist conscience' (in the words of Richards)[8] – felt that much that they believed to be wrong in government was primarily the result of patronage. This middle-class attack was based on the assumption that it was the landed aristocracy who exercised patronage, in their own interests; it was, in fact, part of the aristocratic system of government (as with the Army and Navy) and it was both inefficient and indefensible. Consequently, in the early nineteenth century there were demands for reform which resulted in legislation: for example, to extend the parliamentary franchise and to create a form of elected local government (the Reform Act, 1832, and the Municipal Corporations Act, 1835). It now seems unsurprising that if the electoral arrangements of government were being reformed, the administrative institutions had also to be considered for reform. Moreover, the widening scope of central government, resulting from the Poor Law, Factory Acts and grants to schools, emphasised the need for a better, more professional, standard of public servant to ensure that the new legislation was properly put into effect.

During the earliest years of the nineteenth century, a start had already been made towards making the civil service of India more professional. Haileybury College had been founded in 1806 to provide suitable education for young men nominated to join the civil service of the East India Company. It was a pioneering endeavour in preparing individuals for public service and was supported by, among others, Lord Grenville (who had held a number of positions in government and was Prime Minister in the Ministry of the Talents 1806–07). Indeed, according to the historian G.M. Young, Grenville's speech in the House of Lords in April 1813[9] showed that he was the first man to see that public administration was a liberal profession to be entered by way of a liberal education.[10] From 1813, when the Company's charter was renewed, residence at Haileybury became a pre-condition of appointment as a writer (the cadet grade) in India. In fact, the record of the ICS was particularly important in the pre-history of the Civil Service Commission in two respects. First, it provided experience of overcoming recruitment problems and eliminating, or at least reducing, patronage, which made it a good example for at least partial adoption elsewhere. Second, it included the report by T.B. (later Lord) Macaulay, the statesman and author of the popular *History of England* (published in five volumes, between 1848 and 1861). Macaulay's report contained the core philosophy not only for the ICS but also for the Home Civil Service.

The East India Company was formed in 1599 for the purpose of trading with the East Indies, and British sovereignty over India was effectively established by 1757. At the beginning of the nineteenth century the directors of the Company were, however, still making appointments to its civil service by private patronage. Although a form of open competition was recommended as early as 1813, Grenville's suggestion was not adopted at that time, but as a move towards it the Charter Act of 1833 laid down that the directors should nominate annually four times as many candidates as there were vacancies, from whom one should be selected by competitive examination.[11] This system of limited competition was never effectively operated, but the Charter Act of 1853 made it clear that appointments were to be thrown open to a form of competition.[12]

A committee was then appointed by the President of the Board of Control (for India) to advise on the best method of examining candidates. Macaulay was the chairman; the other members were Lord Ashburton (who had been an MP and Secretary to the Board of Control 1841–45), the Rev Henry Melville (an evangelical who was then Principal of Haileybury College), the Rev Benjamin Jowett (of Balliol College, Oxford) and John George Shaw Lefevre (then Clerk Assistant to the House of Lords). The report[13] was brief, but to the point; Macaulay wrote it himself during the first week of July 1854 and it was signed in November.[14] The report recommended that Haileybury should cease to be maintained as a higher education college for the ICS; that there should be a broad general education (indeed, the best education that the country provided) rather than a specialist training for ICS recruits (specialist education was to be required later); that recruitment should be by open competition in order to select the best available candidates on the principle that the examination 'should be so conducted as to ensure the selection of candidates with thorough, and not merely superficial knowledge' (in the hope of defeating the crammer); and that appointment in the first instance was to be subject to a period of probation.

Macaulay was the son of Zachary Macaulay, a leading evangelical and philanthropist, and he became acceptable in Whig circles through the friends he made during a brilliant career at Cambridge. In 1830, when he was 30 years of age, Lord Lansdowne provided him with the pocket borough of Calne, to get him into Parliament. In 1832 he made a formidable speech in favour of the Great Reform Bill and, having made his mark, he was appointed Secretary of the Board of Control. He then defended the new India Bill in the House of Commons and became a member of the Governor General's Council, and as a result he sailed to India with his sister, Hannah (Macaulay never married). In India he met C.E. (later Sir Charles) Trevelyan; they became close friends and Trevelyan married Macaulay's sister in 1834.[15] Macaulay lived with the Trevelyans after their marriage, and when they returned to England they all again lived together in 1839 and 1840. The Trevelyans then moved to Clapham and Macaulay took chambers in the Albany.[16]

Trevelyan had spent four terms (i.e. two years) at Haileybury before going to India in 1826 when he was 19 years of age, he was a writer in the Bengal Civil Service. After two years there he accused a senior member of the Indian Service, Sir Edward Colebrook, of taking bribes from natives. After an enquiry, Colebrook was sent home in disgrace. On 21 January 1840 Trevelyan became Assistant Secretary (the most senior official) at the Treasury. When Macaulay wrote his famous report on the ICS he completed his rough draft on Friday 7 July 1854, wrote it out fair on Saturday and read it to his brother-in-law on the Sunday. Trevelyan, he found, 'was well pleased'.[17] Jowett was a Fellow of Balliol College (he became Regius Professor of Greek in 1855 and was elected Master of Balliol in 1870). He was the dominant personality in the Oxford of his time,[18] exercised considerable influence on his contemporaries and was a close friend of Macaulay. He was a constant visitor to Trevelyan's London house in Westbourne Terrace, where Macaulay would also be present because he was again living with them.[19]

Although the ICS was so important in the pre-history of the Civil Service Commission, developments elsewhere in the British empire should not be overlooked because they contributed to the climate of reform. In South Africa, for example, a Commission was established in 1847 to improve the organisation of and regulate admission to the civil service. It reported on the sad lack of standards and system that it found. As a result of its recommendations, rules were published on 23 January 1850 for the future regulation of the civil service of the colony. These included the appointment of a Board of Examiners, whose duties were laid down in a Government Notice of 29 January 1850.[20] Meanwhile, Governor Patrick More O'Ferrall, the first civil governor of Malta, proposed as early as 9 November 1848 that recruitment to the Maltese public service should be subject to an examination, and open competitive examinations were introduced in 1857 by More O'Ferrall's successor, William Reid.[21] It seems unlikely that these developments in relation to those in Britain were merely a coincidence. More O'Ferrall worked in the Treasury, where Trevelyan was, before going to Malta, and the report on the Colonial Office (see below) by Trevelyan and others had been submitted in 1849.

Within Britain, too, reforms elsewhere were relevant to experience in public administration. Reform in the universities began around the beginning of the nineteenth century. In 1787 there had been purification of the system of election to Fellowships at Trinity College, Cambridge: Macaulay, who became a Fellow of Trinity by competitive examination,[22] noted in his report that the College offered about four fellowships annually by open competition. W.E. Gladstone, Member of Parliament for Oxford University, helped sponsor the university reforms and later, as Chancellor of the Exchequer, commissioned the Northcote–Trevelyan inquiry.[23] At Oxford, the School of *Literae Humaniores* (Greats, as it is often called) was established, which soon outstripped the other schools in numbers and attracted a significant number of students who later became Indian or Home civil servants.²⁴

The influence of individuals, growing democratisation, demands for more efficiency in government and experience of developments at home and abroad, were important influences contributing to a climate which was conducive to more specific public service reforms. From the late 1840s there had been a series of investigations into the work of various departments of government. These included the Treasury (1848), the Colonial Office (1849), the Board of Trade (1853), the Department of Practical Art and Science (1853), the Poor Law Board (1853), the Privy Council Office (1853), the Colonial Land and Emigration Office (1853), the Board of Ordnance (1853), the Office of Works (1854) and the Post Office (1854). Trevelyan, in his capacity as Assistant Secretary at the Treasury, was active in all these inquiries, and Sir Stafford Northcote (later Lord Iddesleigh), then a young gentleman of conservative views who was one of Gladstone's private secretaries, was involved in most of them. The reports from these inquiries have many recommendations in common: examinations should precede appointments, which should in the first instance be probationary, and promotion should be strictly according to merit. The report on the Board of Trade specifically mentioned the need for 'a central Board of properly qualified examiners... without whose certificates no persons should be placed on the public establishments'.²⁵

By 1854 reports had been produced on at least 11 government departments. The Northcote–Trevelyan Report therefore had a 'finale' aspect. Indeed, Trevelyan himself said he had brought the result of 14 years continued labour to a distinct issue.²⁶ As already mentioned, it was Gladstone, as Chancellor of the Exchequer, who commissioned the inquiry, which was to look at the conditions common to all the public offices, in order to achieve a more efficient service. Northcote was seconded to this inquiry, which was paid for from the Civil Contingencies Fund, on a full-time basis. The report was signed on 23 November 1853 and presented to Parliament in February 1854.

The recommendations in the Northcote–Trevelyan Report were directed to achieving three objectives. These were:

1. To provide, by a proper system of examination, for the supply of the public service with a thoroughly efficient class of men.
2. To encourage industry and foster merit, by teaching all public servants to look forward to promotion according to their deserts, and to expect the highest prizes in the Service if they can qualify themselves for them.
3. To mitigate the evils which result from the fragmentary character of the Service, and to introduce into it some elements of unity, by placing the first appointments upon a uniform footing, opening the way to the promotion of public officers to staff appointments in other departments than their own, and introducing into the lower ranks a body of men (the supplementary clerks) whose services may be made available at any time in any office whatever.²⁷

The report said the civil service did not attract the ablest men, but instead it was sought after by the unambitious, indolent and incapable. This was because the work was comparatively light and there was provision for retirement in the event of bodily incapacity. The result was that the service suffered both in internal efficiency and in public estimation. The effects of the patronage system meant that the best men were not chosen for office (though in many offices some kind of examination system operated) and even when able men were appointed nothing was done to make the best use of their talents. Also, since it was a fragmentary service, promotions were made only within departments.

It suggested that the best method of getting good civil servants, and of making the most of them after they were recruited, was to train young men carefully selected by examination and whose permanent appointment would be confirmed only after the satisfactory completion of a short period of probation. In order to ensure that the examinations would be carried out in an effective and consistent manner throughout the service, the report recommended that a Central Board of Examiners should be established, 'composed of men holding an independent position, and capable of commanding general confidence'. It would be imperative that candidates for admission to any appointment should obtain a certificate from the Board of Examiners. The examination should be a competitive literary examination, plus an inquiry into the age, health and moral fitness of the candidates; and arrangements should be made for holding examinations in various parts of the United Kingdom. There should be a proper distinction between intellectual and mechanical work; and for the intellectual positions the examination should contain an extensive range of subjects and should be open to all persons of a given age and on a level with 'the highest description of education in this country'; there should be a lower standard to test for the more 'mechanical' clerkships.

Once in the service, the recruit should be on probation, with advancements of salary dependent on certificates of punctuality and satisfactory service. The recruit should also be transferred from one department of the office to another so that he would be given the opportunity of making himself master of the whole of the department's business; then his promotion should depend on merit and not seniority. The report also mentioned pensions or superannuation which, it was stated, was already receiving separate consideration by the government. Appended to the report, and published with it, was a letter from Jowett in which he outlined a scheme of four 'schools' or subjects of examination.

The Northcote–Trevelyan Report might not have had the impact it had – or, rather, it might not have been acted upon in the way it was in the years immediately after its publication – without the growing awareness of administrative inefficiencies, the focus of attention from the Administrative Reform Association (founded in 1855) and, in particular, the revelations of incompetence in the Crimean War. Dispatches from W.H. Russell, war correspondent of *The Times*, drew attention to the sufferings of British troops; there were debates in Parliament, and at the beginning of 1855 a Select Committee of Inquiry was established 'to inquire into the conduct of our army before Sebastopol, and into the conduct of those departments of the government whose duty it has been to minister to the wants of the army'. The report of the committee was published in June 1855 and constituted a severe indictment of the administrative chaos which it found.[28] Articles in magazines and pamphlets also emphasised the need for administrative reform.[29]

The Northcote–Trevelyan Report had envisaged its suggested reforms being embodied in an Act of Parliament but a different procedure was followed. The Queen's speech on 31 January 1854 referred to a plan to be laid before Parliament to improve the system of admission and thereby increase the efficiency of the civil service.[30] There is evidence that a bill was prepared,[31] but there was a change in ministry and the important move to set up the Civil Service Commission was embodied in the Order in Council of 21 May 1855. Dorman B. Eaton, writing in 1880, argued convincingly that had the original plan, for an Act of Parliament, been followed, the reform would have been defeated: the Order in Council therefore represented progress in a reform programme that was recognised as being fatal to patronage.[32] The first debate on the subject did not take place until some weeks after the Order in Council was made, and the vote at the end of the debate was against open competition, leaving the Civil Service Commission responsible for the introduction of a procedure less rigorous than open competition, involving the continuance of nomination.[33]

The Order in Council set up the Civil Service Commission with Sir Edward Ryan as Chairman, and two other members: Lefevre and Edward Romilly. The Trevelyan Papers, however, show that within official circles it was known who the three Commissioners would be as early as February 1855.[34] Ryan, a great friend of Macaulay, was educated at Trinity College, Cambridge, had been Chief Justice of Bengal and in 1855 was Assistant Comptroller General of the Exchequer. He was regarded by Macaulay as 'the most liberal of judges', but Macaulay thought it 'absolutely incredible' that he had saved nothing, though he had been in India for ten years and his salary was £8,000 when he left.[35] From time to time Macaulay dined at Ryan's, sometimes with the Trevelyans, and Ryan would, with others, take breakfast at Macaulay's. Lefevre, who also knew Macaulay well, was elected a Fellow of Trinity College, Cambridge in 1819, had been a member of Macaulay's committee on the ICS and was Clerk Assistant to the House of Lords; he became Clerk in 1855 and was Vice-Chancellor of the University of London 1842–62. Romilly, who had been MP for Ludlow 1833–34, and from 1836 was one of the Commissioners for Auditing the Public Accounts, was, in 1855, Chairman of the Audit Board – he withdrew from the Commission on 26 November on grounds of health and pressure of work in his department.[36]

The Order in Council, which appointed the Commissioners, also became the key document in the constitution of the Commission. It required that all young men to be appointed to any department of the civil service, before being admitted to probation, should receive a certificate of qualification from the Commissioners.

17

The procedure became known within the civil service as certification. It required the Commissioners, before granting a certificate:

1st To ascertain that the Candidate is within the Limits of Age prescribed in the Department to which he desires to be admitted;
2nd To ascertain that the Candidate is free from any physical Defect or Disease which would be likely to interfere with the proper Discharge of his Duties;
3rd To ascertain that the Character of the Candidate is such as to qualify him for Public Employment; and,
4th To ascertain that the Candidate possesses the requisite Knowledge and Ability for the proper Discharge of his official Duties.[37]

The first meetings of the Commission

The first official meeting of the Civil Service Commissioners was on 4 June 1855. They met at Ryan's apartment at the Exchequer Office and received a letter from Trevelyan, which they read; they also read the Order in Council, 21 May 1855, which appointed them.[38] The practice they adopted was to meet every day, including Saturdays, to review certificates, testimonials and examination papers of candidates, to approve drafts of letters and to meet people. They usually met at Ryan's apartment; sometimes they met at Lefevre's apartment in the House of Lords. Their first meeting in their own office, 11 Manchester Buildings, Cannon Row, Westminster, was on 11 June 1855; and their first examination was held there on Saturday 30 June. By September their work had developed so much that the space at Manchester Buildings had become quite inadequate. Trevelyan, therefore, motivated by Ryan, wrote to Sir George Cornewall Lewis, who was Gladstone's successor as Chancellor of the Exchequer suggesting that Gateway House, 4 The Sanctuary (leading to Dean's Yard, Westminster) would be well suited to the Commissioners' needs. As soon as they moved to Gateway House (10 October 1855), and had more space, they confirmed to the Treasury an earlier request they had made for more staff.[39] By 1900 the Commission had moved again, to 68 Victoria Street. In 1902 they transferred to much more splendid and spacious accommodation in Burlington Gardens (though it should be noted that the Commission had, for examination purposes, been using the Examination Hall in Burlington House since 1859).

Once there was agreement to set up the Civil Service Commission, one of the first tasks was to appoint someone responsible for the examinations: early in 1855, before the Order in Council, this position was referred to as the paid Commissioner of the Examinations Board. Jowett appeared to be the obvious person to take this on (especially in view of his letter published with the Northcote–Trevelyan Report), but he declined. Jowett suggested the Rev Frederick Temple, who was then Principal of the teacher training college at Kneller Hall, Twickenham and who later became Archbishop of Canterbury

1896–1902. Temple was approached in February 1855 by Trevelyan, writing on behalf of Gladstone: this was a matter of seeing whether Temple would be prepared to be recommended to Lord Palmerston, as the appointment was the responsibility of the Prime Minister. When Temple also declined, Jowett, A.P. Stanley (who was a leading churchman, a graduate of Balliol College, Oxford and, in 1855, a Fellow of University College, Oxford) and B. Price recommended Theodore Walrond, Fellow of Balliol College. Trevelyan therefore wrote to him on 27 February 1855.[40] Stanley, in particular, recommended Walrond to Gladstone in the strongest possible terms. Walrond, he said, was 'a man of sound and high principle', had 'great power of application', 'strong sense and sound judgment' and 'remarkable firmness and presence of mind'. He was 'an excellent scholar', 'with long experience...in tuition and examination'. It seems that Jowett had already mentioned the possibility of this position to Walrond, which probably explains why Walrond was able to reply immediately, by return of messenger, that if the offer were made to him he would feel it his duty to accept.[41] Consequently Walrond became one of the two full-time Assistant Examiners at the Commission. The other Assistant Examiner, Edward Headlam, Fellow of St John's College, Cambridge, had also been suggested (by Jowett) for the post of Secretary to the Commission.[42] The Assistant Examiners were responsible, not for the actual work of examining, but for the selection and supervision of examiners, the maintenance of standards and the co-ordination of methods and results.[43] Walrond became Secretary to the Commission in 1863 and in 1875 was made one of the three Commissioners. Headlam later became Director of Examinations and a new Assistant Examiner was appointed in 1876: G.G. Butler, of Trinity College, Cambridge.[44] Another Fellow of Trinity College was appointed Assistant Examiner in 1890: L. Blaikie.[45]

The procedure for appointing the Secretary to the Commission was important at the outset, and subsequently became more important: the first Commissioners were determined that the appointment should be theirs alone.[46] The Order in Council gave responsibility to the Commissioners to appoint 'Assistant Examiners and others', 'subject to the approval of Her Majesty's Treasury'. The Treasury was also responsible for presenting to Parliament an estimate for the remuneration of the Secretary and other staff. On 28 May 1855 the Commissioners wrote to Lewis for clarification of responsibility for the appointment of their Secretary.[47] Lewis in turn consulted Palmerston. It was agreed, as proposed to Palmerston by Lewis, and in accordance with the Commissioners' wish, that the appointment of the Secretary should be left to the Commissioners, but it was also agreed that the Commissioners should be told privately that the government would 'wish to come to an understanding with them as to the choice...before his appointment is made'.[48] It had occurred to Lewis that Goldwin Smith, one of the Secretaries of the Oxford Commission, would be a fit person; Horace Mann, then employed in the Census Office, had also been recommended. Lewis saw Ryan at 1 o'clock on Saturday 2 June and told him of the procedure agreed with Palmerston.

As a result of these discussions and agreed procedures, when the Commissioners met on 18 June 1855 they considered the qualifications of 17 men (including Walrond) and appointed James Spedding to be their Secretary; but in November Spedding resigned his post in order to devote himself to his literary commitments. Spedding, who was unmarried, served in the Colonial Office from 1835 to 1841, but devoted himself to the study of Francis Bacon: his 14 volumes of Bacon's works were published between 1857 and 1874. He was offered, but declined, the professorship of Modern History at Cambridge, but accepted an honorary fellowship at Trinity College. He occupied chambers in Lincolns Inn Fields but later moved to Westbourne Terrace; he died in 1881 after being knocked down by a cab (an accident, he said, that was the result of his own carelessness).[49] Spedding was succeeded by his friend John G. Maitland on 14 November 1855. Maitland was a Fellow of Trinity College, Cambridge, a barrister at law and had already served the Commission as an examiner. When Maitland died in 1863, he was succeeded by Walrond on 7 May. Walrond was succeeded by Horace Mann on 10 December 1875. During this time the Order in Council of 26 April 1862 was promulgated. It confirmed the procedural arrangements and declared expressly that the Commissioners had power 'to appoint from time to time a Secretary and such Assistant Examiners and others'.[50] This was further confirmed by the Order in Council of 5 February 1870 which referred to the 1862 Order as an existing and therefore unrepealed Order. In July 1887, however, the procedure was changed and, on Mann's resignation, J.S. Lockhart, Fellow of Hertford College, Oxford, was appointed Secretary by W.H. Smith, then First Lord of the Treasury.[51] There are no records to explain why the procedure was changed, though it was the opinion of Sir George Dasent, a Commissioner from 1887 to 1892, that taking the appointment away from the Commissioners was 'a very good thing'.[52] Dasent's evidence to the Royal Commission on Civil Establishments indicates that he did not have a very high opinion of some of the staff in the Commission, and he believed that 'no one who was not a very able man could fill the place of our secretary'.[53] In a note of his memories G.G. Mennell remembered Lockhart as 'an amiable sufferer from ergophobia: he was usually absent on private affairs'.[54]

The procedure for appointing the Secretary became a matter of considerable importance in 1903 when the Commissioners intended that Lockhart should be succeeded by Richard Howlett. Howlett, a barrister at law, who was then Assistant Secretary, had worked in the Commission since 1862, and had ably deputised for Lockhart during his prolonged and increasingly frequent absences. He was known in the Commission as 'the man with the pen', owing to his ability to imply that candidates and correspondents, high or low, were fools or worse.[55] The Treasury instead decided that S.M. (later Sir Stanley) Leathes should be appointed. W.J. Courthope and Lord Francis Hervey, the Commissioners at that time, protested,[56] and when the Treasury did not concede, the matter was referred to the Law Officers of the Crown. In particular the Commissioners had argued that:

> the appointment by the Treasury...of a person unacquainted with the business of the Commission, without consulting the wishes of the Commissioners, must necessarily impair the efficient work of the Commission, and disappoint the reasonable expectation of officers within the department who are thoroughly competent to discharge the duties of the post.[57]

The Treasury did not at first agree with the Commissioners that the matter should be referred to the Law Officers of the Crown, but changed their mind when the Commissioners warned that the post of Secretary required certification and they were prepared not to do this in the circumstances presented by the Treasury. The matter therefore went from the Treasury Solicitor to the Law Officers without further consultation with the Commissioners. On 30 May the Attorney General and the Solicitor General gave their opinion that the right of appointing the Secretary was with the Treasury. The Commissioners then demonstrated misleading features in the Treasury Solicitor's case to the Law Officers. A.J. Balfour, then First Lord of the Treasury (and Prime Minister), referred the matter back to the Law Officers but they saw no reason to modify their opinion. Later, by joint consent, the matter was referred to the Lord Chancellor who decided against the Commissioners, but not in favour of the Treasury: in his opinion the appointment lay with the Crown (and therefore, presumably, with the Prime Minister as representing the Crown). A Crown appointment did not require a certificate from the Commissioners, but further action had to be taken to secure Leathes' pensionable rights. This was resolved by placing the office of Secretary under section 4 of the Superannuation Act 1859, which empowered the Treasury to make pensionable provision in specified circumstances.

Many years later, in 1950, Sir Percival Waterfield, then First Commissioner, commented to the Director of Examinations on Leathes' appointment: 'Interesting to see the happy go lucky way in which our predecessors used to be appointed!' The Director of Examinations queried where Leathes came from and what his qualifications were. Waterfield replied that Leathes certainly did not come from the Treasury: 'I am pretty sure he was a Cambridge don...(GGM has some amuzing stories to tell of the opposition that his introduction ab extra provided from the old hands who had hoped for the job!). Ask someone to go to the London Library and look up his record in Who Was Who?'[58]

It is difficult now, without access to either the personalities involved or to the records, which have not survived, to add to these details of Leathes' appointment – though it seems relevant to add that Balfour (who, like Leathes, was educated at Eton and Trinity College, Cambridge) is unlikely not to have known Leathes. In later years it became known that he had painfully survived a campaign in the Commission to make his position untenable.[59] The controversy associated with Leathes' appointment illustrates the significance of a development that has not yet been mentioned: the Superannuation Act, 1859. With certain exceptions, this stipulated that no person should receive a pension unless he had 'been admitted into the Civil Service with a Certificate from the Civil Service Commissioners'.[60] Its effect was to greatly strengthen the position of the Commission and of those who wished to extend its power.

When the first Commissioners were appointing their Secretary they also appointed other officers. As their Registrar, with the duties of Chief Clerk, on 9 June 1855 they selected Mann. The appointments of both Registrar and Secretary were to be held during the pleasure of the Commissioners: this helped establish the Commission as an independent department. They arranged for temporary clerical assistance from the Law Stationers; additional temporary assistance of a more professional kind was provided by the Rev Dr J. Woolley, Admiralty Inspector of Schools, and William Spottiswoode, of Balliol College, Oxford. The Treasury had to approve not only these individual appointments but also the pay for each position.[61] As Dasent later put it, everything the Commissioners did was subject to the approval of the Treasury.[62]

The influence of the Treasury was evident in various ways (considered further in chapter 5), but in the early years of the Commission it also served as the channel for the political appointment of a number of Commissioners, as a few examples will illustrate. It has already been mentioned that Edward Romilly, Civil Service Commissioner 1855, had previously been MP for Ludlow. Herbert W. Paul, Civil Service Commissioner 1910–18, was the Liberal MP for South Edinburgh 1892–99 and for Northampton 1906–09; he was also the author of a number of books including a Life of Gladstone.[63] Leathes, in particular, had reservations about Paul, whom he found to be a very pleasant colleague, 'but not strong enough to take any responsibility'.[64] Lord Francis Hervey, Second Civil Service Commissioner from 1892 and First Commissioner 1907–09, was the brother of the Marquess of Bristol, had been Conservative MP for Bury St Edmunds 1874–80 and 1885–92 and was a Fellow of Hertford College, Oxford. Lord Strafford (Viscount Enfield), First Commissioner 1881–88, had been MP for Tavistock and MP for Middlesex before being called to the House of Lords in 1874.

Some of the senior staff in the Commission, who were not required to take open competitive examinations before appointment, appear to have been unusual characters or had interesting experiences. David Beveridge Mair, Director of Examinations 1913–33, was an eminent mathematician and Fellow of Christ's College, Cambridge. He had the advantage of believing only what he could prove (which led to difficulties when faced by questions – say, of candidates' characters – that could only be a matter of opinion).[65] Mair had a rather reserved and hermit-like personality with, according to his wife, 'an infinite capacity for silence'.[66] When he retired he became an enthusiastic nudist; after his death Mrs Mair married her cousin-in-law and became Lady Beveridge. J.L. LeB. Hammond, who succeeded Leathes as Secretary in 1907, was a well-known historian and journalist who had been an active politician. In the case of C.G. Nelson, in 1907 Strachan Davidson, then Master of Balliol College was, apparently, asked by

Hervey (who had been educated at Balliol), to recommend a suitable man for the position of Assistant Examiner. Davidson, without knowing what the job entailed, wrote to Nelson to see if he would like the job. Nelson had a short interview at the Commission and was appointed forthwith, before the result of his Greats examination was known.

In the period immediately after the establishment of the Commission, its power was more limited than may have appeared at the time or, perhaps, in retrospect. True, the 1855 Order in Council required certification of appointments: the Order did not require open competition, though open competition was practised in selection for some departments of government. The system that actually began from 1855 was either the examination of nominated candidates or, more generally, a form of limited competition. The type of limited competition had already been indicated but not implemented for the ICS in the Charter Act of 1833 and had also been suggested by Palmerston in September 1855. Palmerston recognised that competitive examination on 'the great scale recommended by some would never answer' but instead suggested that three candidates should be chosen, to be examined at the same time, and in the same way, and the best of the three should be appointed. His argument was that

> By such an arrangement the Government would retain in its hands the right and power of selection, while the Public would have the advantage of...the appointment of the best of three instead of the mere passing muster of the one who might be only tolerable mediocrity.[67]

This, in fact, became the frequently used procedure up to the Order in Council of 1870.

It was the 1870 Order in Council that enshrined the requirement for open competition and gave the Commission real power. By 1869 it was recognised by Trevelyan and others that Ryan and his colleagues had been so skilful and successful that much of the earlier resentment, hostile motions and remarks in the House of Commons, had disappeared. He wrote to Gladstone in that year, following the report of a Select Committee, that all signs of opposition to the Commission had gone, as had sarcastic comments in the press. The new system had become highly popular and the time had come for requiring the adoption of competitive examinations and taking decided action on the classification of the civil service to ensure a more perfect division of labour.[68]

Whereas the Order in Council of 1855 may be regarded as the basic document for creating the Commission, the Order in Council of 4 June 1870 may be regarded as the key document for creating the unified civil service. In preparation for the Order in Council the procedures between the Commission and the Treasury are of some interest. R.R.W. Lingen, Permanent Secretary in the Treasury, received drafts of proposals and regulations from Walrond; he would offer comments, there would be re-drafts and further comments before ministers were involved. The Chancellor of the Exchequer had already given general approval but it was left to officials to work out the details before formal approval was given: the Civil Service Commission's role was to provide the details, but it was clearly understood that nothing could be done until the Treasury had approved the regulations. Instead of writers (i.e. the lowest grade of clerks) being hired on a short-term basis from the Law Stationers, the Commission was to maintain a register of qualified men who had passed the relevant examinations and who would be available when departments needed them. Departments therefore had to be quite clear what qualifications were required in particular positions so that the Commission could recruit for those categories. Salaries were also standardised and approved by the Treasury after consultation with departments. The Treasury made it clear that the most important distinction between classes was 'the nature of the duties to be performed and the more or less temporary character of the engagement'.[69] The 1870 Order in Council was, therefore, a very significant factor in the creation of classes in an increasingly unified civil service. It also marked a strengthening role for the Treasury – for the Treasury made it clear in a letter to writers, circulated on 15 November 1870, that payment of writers employed through any other procedure would not be sanctioned. To ensure that there was no misunderstanding the Treasury required the word 'certified' to be used in relation to clerks certificated for particular positions and 'registered' to be used in relation to writers eligible for general employment in whatever department their services were needed.[70] The unified civil service, which can be traced back to the 1870 Order in Council, was, however, advanced much further by the Order in Council of 1876 (which followed the recommendations of the Playfair Commission). The 1876 Order laid down rules for recruiting to the service-wide class of Lower Division clerks and for promotions from it to the Higher Division.

By 1870 departments had, of course, already acquired considerable experience in providing the Commission with criteria for appointments. Because the procedure from 1855 involved the Commissioners in approving nominations and running (mainly) limited competitions, their power and duties were limited. Departments were independent of each other and intended to remain so. Heads of departments retained what nowadays may be called the powers of hiring and firing. Therefore the Commissioners worked by persuasion, encouragement and careful reasoning – as is illustrated in the letters they sent to heads of departments about criteria for particular posts and the subjects to be included in their examinations (this is discussed further in both the next section and in chapter 5). The Commission, as a department of government, from its beginning set a good example to others by using open competitions to recruit its own staff: open competitions being the term for competitions open to anyone who applied and met the criteria in the regulations issued by the Commission after discussion with the department(s) concerned.

What the Commission did

The Order in Council of 15 May 1855 required the Civil Service Commissioners to ascertain that a candidate for a position satisfied the criteria required by the department for appointment. As a result, on 12 June 1855 the Commissioners approved a circular letter to be sent to departments about the rules and arrangements for appointments to junior positions in the various departments.[71] Resulting from this, the first procedure the Commissioners developed for recruitment involved departments notifying the Commission of a nomination, at the same time directing the candidate to attend the Commission at a specified time with documents confirming age, health and character. If the documents were satisfactory the candidate would then, at a later date, be examined in relevant fields according to the job specification of the department. The Commission was to pay examiners at a rate of 3 guineas per day. All these details were approved by the Treasury. It is important to note that from the beginning the Commissioners were concerned to approve only candidates who met all the criteria for appointment: age, health, character and ability. Satisfactory evidence had to be produced on all criteria. Furthermore, successful candidates were certificated on probation – and the wording was significant on the certificates: 'qualified to be admitted on probation'. Even after certification and the satisfactory completion of probation, it was made clear that positions were held at the pleasure of the head of department.[72] The Commissioners, from the outset, took their own role in probation very seriously. They expressed this on a number of occasions, including their Third Report: 'we regard as necessarily complimentary to the system of competitive examination the period of six months' probation and the rule of promotion from class to class by merit'.[73]

From this early base, the work of the Commission rapidly expanded. As a result of the circular letter to departments, the ability requirements that emerged for junior clerkships (17–25 years of age) were good handwriting, correct spelling and arithmetic. Clerkships, in addition, required précis and English composition, plus requirements necessary for positions in particular departments. By the end of February 1856, 1,078 candidates had been examined and 676 certificates granted.[74] From the beginning, competition was encouraged, though many posts were filled by nominations approved by the Commissioners: the Second Annual Report records that there had been 34 competitive examinations for junior situations – and the Commissioners made a detailed analysis of the educational and family background of the successful candidates.

An important development occurred in 1857 when the Commissioners were asked by the East India Company to conduct examinations for writerships in the Company. The British government consented to this expansion of work beyond that envisaged in the 1855 Order in Council. Then, in 1858, Lord Ellenborough invited the Commissioners to assume responsibility for the competitive examination for writerships in the East India Civil Service.[75] This responsibility in fact laid the foundation for the recruitment of graduates and became valuable experience for the Commission to run competitive examinations for the Home Civil Service and for recruitment to other 'superior' positions requiring comparable knowledge and abilities. The Commissioners referred, in 1861, to John Stuart Mill's 'Considerations on Representative Government' because his views on competitive examinations were, they said, 'in entire unison with our own'. Indeed, they said that in their opinion (echoing Macaulay's philosophy) superiority in academic attainments implied 'the like superiority in some moral qualities, such as self-denial, regularity, perseverance, and energy'.[76]

Competitive examinations had received further support in 1860, from the Select Committee on Civil Service Appointments, to which the Commissioners gave valuable evidence. By 1860 the Commissioners had dealt with a total of 13,491 nominations, plus 3,529 competitors for 974 situations: they had issued 6,587 certificates and had rejected 2,287 candidates in non-competitive examinations. In the year 1860 there were 80 competitive examinations for 196 situations. The Commissioners had recommended that a fee should be payable by candidates, and the recommendation was endorsed by the Select Committee. Another recommendation, accepted first for appointments to the Treasury, was for a preliminary test examination, to act as a sieve, to remove from the main competitions candidates who were well below the required standard for appointment. Within a few years this procedure was adopted by other departments. The Commission also had to set clear standards and a policy to deal with the increasing number of frauds brought to their attention, especially those involving misrepresentation of age but also, later, misbehaviour in examinations. They said: 'we consider it so important to check the growth of these frauds, that we intend to bring all similar offences in future before the proper authorities with a view to legal proceedings against the parties implicated'.[77] Aspects of this experience are considered further in chapter 6.

The most significant single advance for the growing importance of the Commission occurred in 1870 and was the result of the Order in Council signed on 4 June. This reflected support for the work of the Commission from the political environment. In April 1856 there was a resolution in the House of Commons affirming support for competitive examinations. This was re-affirmed in 1857 on a motion by Lord Goderich and further supported by the Select Committee (1860) under Lord Stanley's chairmanship. Palmerston approved the recommendations.[78] The Commissioners drew attention to these experiences and support, and in their annual reports argued strongly in favour of more open competitions. The 1870 Order in Council consequently required that appointments to all situations in all departments of the civil service should be made by this means. The Treasury decided that appointments should be divided into two classes. Positions in Class I were to be filled by candidates of a high order of educational attainments; Class II was for younger entrants, with less extended acquirements. The order of merit would be used to enable candidates to express a preference in which department they should be appointed. The competition for Class I was similar to the examination for the ICS, except that the upper age limit was to be 21 instead of 24, and there was to be a preliminary test examination in elementary subjects. For ten vacancies in the first three Class I competitions there were 141 candidates.[79]

Examinations for Class II were for candidates between 16 and 20 years of age. These examinations involved a preliminary test in handwriting, spelling and arithmetic, followed by geography, English history and bookkeeping. The Class II competitions were held in London, Dublin and Edinburgh. For 95 vacancies in the first four competitions there were 738 candidates.

There were also other competitions such as for appointments of Second Class Assistant of Excise and the outdoor service of the Customs department. For these positions examinations were held in the three capital cities and also in major provincial towns, so that residents in different parts of the United Kingdom might be as nearly as possible treated equally as regards opportunity to compete. Other competitions were for junior clerkships, sorters and telegraph messengers in the Post Office. Between 1 July 1870 and 30 June 1872, 10,065 candidates competed for 1,995 posts of this nature.

Meanwhile the Commission acquired other responsibilities. One of the most important was the result of the Army reforms, led by Edward Cardwell, Secretary of State for War. Following the recommendations of the Royal Commission on Military Education, Cardwell asked the Commissioners to assume responsibility for the entrance examinations for the Royal Military College at Sandhurst, the Royal Military Academy at Woolwich and also for the examinations for admission into the Army by direct commissions.[80] From these increasing responsibilities the Commission acquired considerable experience. Sometimes, as a result of the design of examinations for departments, new classes of position were developed: class was an increasingly accepted term for positions which had common requirements for entry and conditions of service.

Following the Order in Council of 4 June 1870 it was agreed by the government to organise a body of occasional assistants, 'Temporary Writers'. These were to replace the services of temporary staff hitherto supplied by the Law Stationers. This arrangement was promulgated by a Treasury Circular in November 1870; special rates were to apply. The Commissioners were to recruit these people: examinations were held weekly in London, less frequently in Edinburgh and Dublin and occasionally in other towns. This established a 'Register of Writers'. From August 1870 to 30 June 1872, 3,985 candidates presented themselves and paid a fee of 5 shillings. The Commissioners also organised a very efficient and economical class of boy writers (14–18 years of age) at 4 pence per hour. Up to 30 June 1872 they had 836 applicants and at that time there were 90 in actual employment. In addition, the Commissioners also organised a similar register of temporary messengers – to recruit pensioners from the armed forces and the Royal Irish Constabulary. The total number of all types of cases dealt with by the Commission in the 12 months covered by the 1872 Annual Report was 15,619. Fees paid by means of stamps (to the Inland Revenue Department) during the half year ending 30 June 1872 amounted to £2,360.[81]

It is clear from these details that the Commission had become a busy and increasingly well-regarded department. The year 1870 was very significant because, as a result of the Order in Council, the Commission was becoming, in some respects, and within policies decided by the Treasury, a department of personnel management. Moreover, with the register of temporary assistants it performed some of the functions of a clearing house for staff, and these attributes were extended as the Commission became an office for re-allocating redundant staff. There were refinements over the years. An Order in Council of 12 February 1876 (following the report of Sir Lyon Playfair's Committee which emphasised the distinction between routine and intellectual work) created a Lower Division of general clerks who could easily be transferred from one office to another. One of the main objects was to make it possible for clerks to be selected, not just to fill vacancies reported by departments, but in anticipation of expected vacancies, so that such vacancies could be filled as soon as they occurred. Also, as the new Lower Division was common to all departments, redundant staff could be moved from one department to another without the need for a fresh examination or certificate.[82] After an Order in Council in 1890 the Lower Division became the Second Division.[83] In the period from February 1876 up to the end of 1892, 489 clerks had been transferred between departments.[84]

The number of candidatures dealt with by the Commission had risen to 15,342 in 1875; and the number of letters received and despatched had risen to 147,350.[85] By 1884 examinations were being held at 23 centres throughout the United Kingdom and the number of applicants was very large in proportion to the number of appointments available. For example, there were 30 candidates for every vacancy for a Telegraph Learner in the Post Office. Running these examinations required a large-scale organisation to inspect and hire accommodation, engage invigilators, prepare and distribute the examination papers and supervise the examinations. In London there were numerous examination centres including, for example, the Albert Hall, Westminster Town Hall, Holborn Town Hall and Westminster Palace Hotel.[86] New examinations were frequently required: an example from 1883 was the need for a riding test. The ICS required that no probationer should be appointed without satisfactory proof of his ability to ride; so all selected candidates faced a new test. This was easily provided because the good relations that had developed between the Commission and the Army meant that the riding examinations were conveniently arranged with the Superintendent of the Royal Academy Riding Establishment at Woolwich.[87] The Commission also conducted examinations outside the United Kingdom. For example, in 1884 the Lieutenant Governor of Jamaica suggested that the Civil Service Commission should assume responsibility for examining for clerkships in the Jamaica Civil Service, with tests being sat in Jamaica – from 1885 the examinations for Lower Division clerkships in the Home Civil Service were used for this purpose.[88]

Following the reports from the Playfair (1875) and Ridley (1886) Commissions on the civil service there was reorganisation and a reduction in the number of superior appointments required in the Home Civil Service. Indeed, in 1894 there were only 24 competitors for ten posts in Class I of the Home Civil Service.[89] A public announcement was therefore made that Home Civil Service Class I examinations would in future be held jointly with the examinations for the ICS. Consequently the last separate examinations for these posts were in January 1895.[90] In 1905 the rationalisation went further, with an announcement that there would be a revised scheme of examination for the ICS which would apply also to Clerkships (Class I) in the Home Civil Service and for Eastern Cadetships (in the Colonial Services).[91]

A new rule, laid down in 1884 and implemented from the following year, gave Lower Division clerks the opportunity to choose the department where they would serve. In 1885, 137 candidates were allocated to their preferred departments whilst 89 were assigned to offices other than those preferred.[92] This helped reduce the rigid departmentalism as far as the Second Division was concerned, especially as it drew attention to the need for standardised conditions of service because clerks were preferring to work in departments with longer official hours so that they could earn more pay.[93]

The Commission, from its beginning, paid considerable attention to the probation records reported from departments. As already mentioned, this was an important part of the selection procedure, as indicated in the Northcote–Trevelyan Report and re-asserted by the Commissioners; but it was also important to the Commission as a useful indicator of the effectiveness of its selection tests. By 1894 the Commission reported that 129 recruits had failed probation; 95 were allowed further trials, satisfactorily. The main grounds were health (89) and inefficiency (31). Another revealing analysis by the Commission related to the backgrounds of applicants for the Upper Division of the Home Civil Service and applicants for the ICS. They found not only that the recruits for the two services were similar in terms of education and family background, but also that they did not differ from recruits to the learned professions: for the Home Civil Service all 11 recruits had attended public schools, ten went to Oxford and one to Cambridge. For the ICS there were 62 appointments in that year: 24 had completed a full university course, four had not completed a full university course; 29 had, in addition to a university course, been specially prepared for the examinations; and five had relied solely on special preparation.[94]

The volume of work continued to grow up to the First World War. In 1898 the Commission dealt with 38,732 candidatures,[95] in 1913 it dealt with 64,828,[96] in 1900 it received 148,504 letters and despatched 205,843 letters and 11,146 certificates were granted.[97] Opportunities for standardisation in the examinations for various minor positions were also taken to good effect. The Commissioners discussed some of these (e.g. for positions as Housekeeper, Office Keeper and Messenger) with departments and with the Treasury, and as a consequence the requirements were harmonised.[98]

As the volume of work increased and as the Commission grew in size, it developed regulations and developed practices that were both sensitive to the political environment within which it operated and were increasingly bureaucratic (in the technical or Weberian sense), thus reflecting aspects of fairness that had to be implemented in practice. Two examples illustrate this. As a result of regulations made under the Order in Council of 4 June 1870, personnel from the armed forces were able to deduct from their age time spent in the forces, thus giving them an advantage over candidates in competitions who had not served. This reflected sensitivity to demands from elsewhere in public service and to political pressures.[99] A second example reflected the need for equity in applying regulations. The Post Office required women candidates to be at least five feet in height, but from time to time there were requests for flexibility in applying the rule and requests for exceptions to be made in marginal cases. The Commissioners argued that

> to a minimum prescribed by regulations there can be no exception, and...a candidate who is perhaps only one-eighth of an inch below the standard had no more right to examination than a girl whose age was one day below the lower limits.
>
> ...It would of course be quite useless to establish a margin of allowance in such cases, for the lower limit of such a margin would only become the fresh minimum which, when applied with the necessary strictness, would lead to appeals like the one now under consideration...[100]

The growth in the Commission's work saw a continuing need to increase the efficiency of the office, and in this context technological advances became important. This is well illustrated by the introduction of the typewriter and the telephone.

In the nineteenth century letters and minutes were written by hand. Copyists usually wrote out a fair copy from the (often heavily amended) draft and the draft was kept as a record when the clean copy of the letter or minute was sent. Sometimes it is now difficult to read the original draft, not only because of the hand-written amendments but also because of abbreviations known within the office but not widely known outside. These difficulties were somewhat alleviated by the invention, around 1870, of the typewriter machine, whose operators were at first called typewriters, to differentiate them from copyists. The Remington Company, gunmakers, had the tools for making such machines economically and the inventors approached them to undertake production. The public service, however, was not quick to buy the new inventions.

On 21 November 1888 the Commissioners wrote to the Treasury explaining that they had been lent a typewriter by Remington and found it would save some money on copying costs. They sought authority to buy one (it cost £20.19s.0d); this was approved. Early in 1890 they requested authority for a second typewriter, as the benefits of the first had been clearly proved, and, with only one machine, work was still being sent for copying. Soon there were applications from departments for the Commission to select and certificate typists (at first these were men, but later women; some departments preferred boys). Some time later, on 17 March 1894, the Treasury issued a Treasury Minute to regularise the situation throughout the civil service and to enunciate a policy.[101]

The minute said that women typists had proved themselves to be 'an efficient and economical form of labour'. It was not difficult to acquire proficiency in using the machine; proficiency could be gained in a few years, and as the work was purely mechanical, payment was to be on a modest scale. The amount of simple copying required in the civil service was, however, in the opinion of the

Treasury, not great; and it was thought the class of women typists would not be very numerous and they did not anticipate the total would much exceed 100 in the civil service. The Treasury recognised that there were difficulties in employing women for this work because in some instances the copying was of a nature that must be left to men; in other instances it was difficult to find the separate rooms which a female staff required. The Treasury then outlined the rules for employing women for such work. These required the employment of women to cease after marriage; pay would begin at 16s a week (at age 18), rising to £65 a year (at age 23); they would be entitled to certificated sick leave on full pay as long as the absence together with ordinary leave (two weeks) did not exceed six weeks. T.L. Hedley, who joined the staff in 1909, recalled that some years after his appointment it was decided to try the experiment of employing female typists in the Commission. Two girls were employed and kept segregated from the rest of the staff. He added: 'The success of the experiment led to its extension – after a time.'[102]

Another technological advance, slow to be adopted, was the telephone. In November 1902 letters from the Treasury suggested that it would be a considerable convenience if the Commission could be placed on the Government Telephone Exchange. W.Y. Hayes Fisher (later Lord Downham), then Financial Secretary to the Treasury, even offered that the Treasury would be prepared to authorise the expenditure. Lockhart replied that it 'might lead to difficulties'. So much business was done by the Commissioners themselves that an officer answering the telephone on a complex matter might feel the need 'to refer to the Board, or to see the actual papers relating to a particular case'. The Commission dealt in a judicial way with a large number of individuals and 'to attempt to deal with such questions on the spur of the moment would not only cause much disturbance in the work of the Department but could probably lead to confusion and misunderstanding'.[103]

Nevertheless in January 1903 it was agreed that telephone communication could be established with the Treasury. Then, in October 1903, it was discovered that the Commission had been placed on the public telephone exchange. This caused consternation because the Commission began receiving unwelcome calls, so it was decided on 14 October 1903 that the telephone would be disconnected. Later it was agreed that the telephone, then in the messenger's room, should be removed and placed in a closed box (to be provided by the Office of Works) with the bell ringing in the messenger's room. Incoming calls were received by the messenger in the hall if he heard the bell: he then searched for the officer required who had to rush to the box in the hope of catching the call before it was cut off.[104]

By 1911 the instrument had been sufficiently accepted for the Commission to ask for a telephone on the public exchange – staff in the Commission were being inconvenienced because the Treasury refused to answer the telephone before 10.00 a.m. It was hoped, however, that the Commission could be ex-directory, to avoid constant and vexatious enquiries from outsiders. S. Cassan Paul, then Assistant Secretary, also hoped for a switch into his own room because he had 'to waste a good deal of time in the course of the day in going backwards and forwards from my room to the box'. The box later became known as the 'silence cabinet' and could be used by officials when they wanted to make a call outside the Commission.

In May 1911 the facilities were expanded to include an internal switchboard. This required Treasury approval of expenditure and resulted in a Treasury enquiry implying that there should, in consequence, be a reduction in the number of messengers. Nevertheless the general attitude within the Commission continued so that in 1934 it was minuted 'The nature of our work is such that we are anxious to keep the possibility of communicating with the Civil Service Commission by telephone as entirely out of sight as possible.' The London Telephone Service agreed to publish their name in the directory, without the number, though with a note to the effect that they were ex-directory.[105]

During the Commission's formative years the office was simply structured to carry out its limited functions, but the early distribution of duties lasted, with modifications and some changes in titles, throughout its life. The structure was rather rigid and relationships tended to be formal: communications were usually by note or memorandum. The Secretary, who was also the establishment officer, was responsible for branches dealing with correspondence and records. This involved preparing competition regulations in consultation with the Treasury and other departments of government, the handling of press advertisements, distribution of information about competitions (including links to schools, career exhibitions and conventions), the receipt of application forms, correspondence with candidates, the maintenance of records and statistics and the department's central registry. Under the Secretary there was an evidence and assignments branch responsible for the collection and examination of evidence of nationality, health and character; the branch also issued certificates of qualification in respect of candidates found eligible for appointment, and assigned successful candidates to departments. The establishments and accounts branches dealt with the department's staff training and welfare services and all aspects of office services (such as typing and messenger services, accommodation and equipment and office cleaning). The Director of Examinations was responsible for the general policy and conduct of examinations, the arrangements for setting and marking of written examination papers and the selection of examiners and interviewers – extensive use was made of outside examiners and interviewers who were paid fees. Within this directorate all the details of the physical control of examinations were the responsibility of the Chief Superintendent of Examinations. When the Civil Service Selection Board was created in the late 1940s it operated as a separate directorate within the Commission, headed by the Chairman of the Board who was a Commissioner, and closely associated with it was a research unit consisting of a small team of psychologists.[106]

There was an important development in 1910, when a new method of selection was introduced for recruiting Managers of Labour Exchanges – created as a result of the Labour Exchanges Act, 1909. It was in fact selection based on competitive interviews, though it was presented with sensitivity as 'tests...such as men of business use in the choice of their employees'.[107] The purpose was to assess attainments of more importance than could be examined by the then well-established processes of written competitions. The interviews were to test 'special experience and capacity in dealing with practical affairs'.[108] In recognition of the sensitivities associated with selection processes, other than written examinations where candidates were identified only by numbers, the Commissioners felt it necessary to emphasise more than once that 'political and other undue influence was completely ruled out in these proceedings'.[109] Selection by competitive interview was soon extended beyond meeting the needs of Labour Exchanges: by 1913 the method was used for Assistant Inspectors in the Inland Revenue, Assistant Official Receivers in Bankruptcy and various other positions.[110]

This development was important for recruiting Labour Exchange Managers, but it extended much further. Leathes, the First Commissioner, chaired the interview boards; later he chaired the Treasury Committee[111] set up as a consequence of a recommendation of the MacDonnell Royal Commission[112] to examine the suitability and methods of the Class I examination. It noted that the Consultative Committee of the Board of Education had, in May 1916, recommended a *viva voce* examination, and the Leathes Committee was unanimous in so recommending. They said that a *viva voce* examination should be 'a test, by means of questions and conversation on matters of general interest, of the candidate's alertness, intelligence, and intellectual outlook, his personal qualities of mind and mental equipment'.[113] As such, they said it was better than any other sort of test.[114]

Because of the First World War, open competitions were suspended for recruitment to the main civil service classes: this was a consequence of the government's general policy of not making permanent appointments in the civil service of men of military age. Open competitions continued, however, for categories of staff outside this restriction; there was a greatly increased demand for temporary staff; and competitive interviews were extended further. The war and its aftermath led to new problems and challenges for the Civil Service Commission; some of these will be considered in the next chapter.

The expanding role of the Commission

When the Civil Service Commission was created it was on an experimental basis. There was no general support from all parties in Parliament. The Commission was created by an Order in Council, not an Act. The Commissioners were unpaid[115] (though they held paid positions elsewhere in government). Before 1855 there was no general plan of examinations for recruiting staff, any system that did exist applied only to individual departments.

The Commissioners were appointed through patronage, though it cannot be doubted that they were successful. The importance of their work was reinforced by the Superannuation Act, 1859, which made the grant of their certificates an essential condition for a pension. Their early work mainly consisted of examining candidates nominated singly to single posts: there was no rule requiring competition either open or limited. Nevertheless the practice of competition was initiated and spread. The Commission itself set a good example in 1856 when 46 candidates competed for four clerkships in its office, and in 1858 when 22 candidates competed for one clerkship.[116] In 1859 there was a public advertisement for eight writerships in the India Office.

Open competition in the Home Civil Service became a requirement, however, after the Order in Council of 4 June 1870. From that time the Commission expanded into new areas of public sector recruitment and consolidated its position by developing principles for guiding its activities. These principles originated from a combination of the Macaulay Report on the ICS and the Northcote–Trevelyan Report on the Home Civil Service, but the essence of the principles was publicly stated from time to time and nowhere more clearly than in its Thirty-fifth Report (for the year 1890). That report said:

> The primary object of our competitive examinations is to select the best qualified candidates for appointment to the Public Service. In framing schemes of examinations applicable to different appointments the special requirements of each Department have first to be considered, and the Order in Council of June 4th 1870 accordingly directs that the rules applicable in each case should be settled between the Civil Service Commissioners and the authorities of the Department concerned, subject to the approval of the Treasury. While settling these rules to meet the requirements of each case we do not fail to observe that our higher examinations exercise indirectly a considerable influence on the education of the country, and we endeavour, therefore, to secure that the schemes of examination shall follow as far as possible the general lines of education in Universities and Schools and conform to the standards there established, and that in all cases they shall be of a character calculated to encourage sound and liberal methods of preparation.[117]

Together with the written examinations on these lines the other tests should not be diminished in significance: these were the tests for age, health and character. Aspects of these responsibilities are considered further in chapter 6.

In some respects the Commission acquired the functions of a clearing house for supernumerary staff. The volume of work in government departments changed from time to time, as national and international developments dictated. This was particularly evident following a war – as in 1905–06 when clerks became supernumerary in the Admiralty and War Office – and in these circumstances the Commission would re-assign staff to other departments.[118]

Once staff were re-assigned or loaned on a temporary basis the Commission was consulted to resolve anomalies about conditions of service. For example, could clerks on temporary duty carry forward leave allowances earned in another department in a particular year? Much depended on whether a transfer was to suit the convenience of the public service, and on the good nature of the departments concerned; but by October 1904 these questions had become sufficiently common for the Commission to produce a form, suitable for clerks on temporary service, reporting details of leave that had been taken or was due.[119]

From the earliest years of the Commission it emphasised justice, fairness and impartiality in doing its work. One aspect of this was reflected in its concern to provide examination centres throughout the United Kingdom; some aspects of this will be considered further in chapter 5. There were frequent petitions to the Commission for more local examination centres: sometimes for convenience of access (it was noted in 1894 that candidates in Inverness had to travel to Aberdeen for examinations, the better part of a day's journey); sometimes there were local or regional jealousies (such as between the Isle of Skye and the Isle of Lewis); sometimes there were language difficulties (candidates from Aberdeen experienced difficulties in understanding the pronunciation in Edinburgh during dictation examinations).[120]

Another aspect of fair treatment related to the candidatures of members of the royal family who were examined for the Army. Many European princes were related to Queen Victoria and were keen to be trained for the British Army. Such candidates were examined in the same subjects as any others, though arrangements were made for the examination to be conducted under special supervision apart from the normal public examination centres; also details of the results were not published in the normal way.[121] Similar arrangements were made for Prince Philip, now Duke of Edinburgh, when he applied to join the Royal Navy in 1939. Lord Louis Mountbatten was looking after the Prince's interests while he was a pupil at Gordonstoun, and made it clear that 'Prince Philip should not only appear before the Interviewing Board but that it is most important that he should not be given the impression that he is bound to be taken in any case'. In fact, unlike the marks for other royal personages, Prince Philip's are now publicly available: his marks ranged from 47 out of 150 for English to 380 out of 400 for interview.[122]

There were also numerous occasions when the Commission had to act in a quasi-judicial capacity, and it was useful to have an ex-Chief Justice of Bengal as one of its first Commissioners. Interpreting the nationality rule could be an area of considerable complexity – the normal requirement being that an applicant for a civil service position should be a natural born British subject and the child of parents both of whom were natural born British subjects. An example illustrates this well. Constantine Joseph Nomico was born in London 1910; his father was born in Zante after the island had been handed back to Greece in 1864 by the British government. Nomico's grandfather and great-grandfather were, however, born in the Ionian islands during the period of the British protectorate: the Commission had to decide whether Nomico's father could be regarded as a natural born British subject.[123] As a result of cases like this, the Commission produced a two-page statement that it felt should resolve most doubtful cases.[124]

By the end of the period 1855–1920 the Civil Service Commission was well established and respected, not just in the United Kingdom but also overseas.

There were requests for examinations to be held in Australia and New Zealand.[125] Numerous requests for information came from visitors or by other means. In the first ten years of the twentieth century these included representatives from Natal, South Africa; Siam; the United States; Perth, Western Australia; Canada; Cairo, Egypt; Victoria, Australia; Transvaal, South Africa; India; Austro-Hungary; China; British Columbia, Canada; Norway; Hungary; Malta; and Belgium.[126]

It was during the years 1855–1920 that the Commission became the keystone of the unified British civil service. This unification was one of the objectives outlined in the Northcote–Trevelyan Report. By examining nominated candidates the Commission was checking on the quality of appointments in departments. It set its own standards but also, largely through informal means, it persuaded others to observe good practice in the various departments of government. An internal memorandum approved by the Commissioners on 24 March 1887 stressed that young men were not entering the service of any particular department. It said 'it has almost become part of the Law of the Land that all clerical vacancies throughout the bulk of the service belong to the general public'.[127] Such sentiments are to be found over and over again in relation to specific cases. For example, R. Howell, of the Commission, wrote to the Board of Trade on 5 October 1903 about P.L. Edwards (whom the Board felt was unsuitable because of his lack of competence in French): 'A clerk in the Second Division is a member of the State Service *not* a Departmental service and no arbitrary standards can be set up by any Department in relation to him.' Edwards' 'services cannot be dispensed with on account of his ignorance of a foreign language'[128] and 'The finality of assignments…is a matter respecting which the experience of this Department is decisive'.[129]

Notes

1 See, for example, Henry Roseveare, *The Treasury: The Evolution of a British Institution* (London: Allen Lane, The Penguin Press, 1969); Jill Pellew, *The Home Office, 1848–1914: From Clerks to Bureaucrats* (London: Heinemann, 1982).
2 See, for example, E.N. Gladden, *A History of Public Administration* (2 vols) (London: Frank Cass, 1972); E.N. Gladden, *Civil Services of the United Kingdom 1853–1970* (London: Frank Cass, 1969); Samuel McKechnie, *The Romance of the Civil Service* (London: Sampson Low, Marston & Co., no date – 1930?).
3 *Royal Commission on the Civil Service: Fourth Report of the Commissioners* (MacDonnell Report), Cd. 7338 (London: HMSO, 1914) chapter 1, para. 1.
4 Ibid., Introduction, para. 14.
5 For example, Sir Edward Blunt, *The ICS: The Indian Civil Service* (London: Faber & Faber, 1937); Emmeline Cohen, *The Growth of the British Civil Service, 1780–1939* (London: Allen & Unwin, 1941); reprinted by Frank Cass, 1965.
6 PRO/CSC3/177.
7 Peter G. Richards, *Patronage in British Government* (London: Allen & Unwin, 1963), p. 17. See also Edward Hughes, 'Civil Service Reform 1853–5', *Public Administration*, 32, 1954, 17–51.
8 Richards, *Patronage*, p. 35.
9 *Parl. Deb.* vol. 25, cols. 709–52, 9 April 1939.

THE PERIOD FROM 1855 TO 1920

10 PRO/CSC5/1381, Young to Sinker, 30 September 1953; 'Sir Charles Trevelyan, Patronage and Competition in the Civil Service'.
11 3 and 4 William IV, c. 85, clause ciii.
12 Blunt, *The ICS*, p. 46. See also R.J. Moore, 'The Abolition of Patronage in the Indian Civil Service and the Closure of Haileybury College', *The Historical Journal*, 7(2), 1964, 246–57.
13 PRO/CSC2/13 contains the original, signed copy of the report. Reprints include *The Civil Service, Vol. I, Report of the Committee 1966–68* (Fulton Report), Cmnd. 3638 (London: HMSO, 1968), Appendix B.
14 G.O. Trevelyan, *The Life and Letters of Lord Macaulay*, vol. II (London: Longmans, 1883), p. 380.
15 PRO/CSC5/1381. See Also Roger Ellis, *Who's Who in Victorian Britain* (London: Shepheard Walwyn, 1997).
16 *Dictionary of National Biography*, vols. XII and XIX (London: Oxford University Press, 1917).
17 Trevelyan, *The Life and Letters of Lord Macaulay*, vol. II.
18 Noel Annan, *The Dons: Mentors, Eccentrics and Geniuses* (London: Harper Collins, 1999).
19 Geoffrey Faber, *Jowett: A Portrait with a Background* (London: Faber & Faber, 1957).
20 Cape of Good Hope, *Report of a Commission Appointed by His Excellency the Governor to Enquire into and Report upon the Existing Condition and Regulations of the Civil Service in this Colony*, G100-'83 (Capetown: W.A. Richards & Sons, 1883).
21 Godfrey A. Pirotta, *The Maltese Public Service 1800–1940: The Administrative Politics of a Micro-State* (Malta: Minerva Publications, 1996); PRO/CO158/143, O'Ferrall to Grey, 9 November 1848 and Grey to O'Ferrall, 6 December 1848.
22 PRO/CSC5/1381, Extract from Stanley Leathes' Address before the Civil Service Commission Convention, Philadelphia, PA, 15 September 1926; see also PRO/CSC5/99.
23 The Committee was appointed by a Treasury Minute dated 12 April 1853: PP. 1854–55, vol. XXX, p. 375.
24 Sir Ivo Elliott (ed.), *The Balliol College Register 1833–1933* (Printed for private circulation, 1934).
25 *Reports of Committees of Inquiry into Public Offices and Papers Connected Therewith* (London: HMSO, 1854).
26 Trevelyan to John Parker (a joint secretary to the Treasury) 14 March 1854. Quoted by Jenifer Hart, 'Sir Charles Trevelyan at the Treasury', *English Historical Review*, 75, 1960, 106.
27 The report has been reprinted on several occasions, including K.M. Reader, *The Civil Service Commission, 1855–1975* (London: HMSO, 1981), Appendix 2, and Fulton Report, appendix B.
28 See G.W. Keeton, *Trial by Tribunal* (London: Museum Press, 1960), p. 40.
29 See, for example, 'Administrative Reform – The Civil Service', *Blackwood's Magazine*, 78, 1855, 116–24; *Our Government Offices* (London: James Ridgway, 1855 – no author given).
30 *Parl Deb.* 3s., vol. 130, col. 4 (31 January 1854).
31 PRO/CSC2/41, letter to Chancellor of the Exchequer, 1 January 1862; PRO/CSC8/4, Ryan and Lefevre to Gladstone, 1 January 1862. See also PRO/T1/6362B.
32 Dorman B. Eaton, *The Civil Service in Great Britain* (New York: Harpers, 1880), p. 207. See also *Parl Deb*, 3s., vol. 132, cols. 1305–7 (5 May 1854), and vol. 141, cols. 1415, 1420 (24 April 1856); and A. Lawrence Lowell, *The Government of England*, vol. I (New York: Macmillan, 1908), p. 156.
33 *Parl Deb*, 3s., vol. 139, cols. 675–745 (10 July 1855).

34 Trevelyan Papers: CET 18, C.E. Trevelyan to T. Walrond, 27 February 1855.
35 Thomas Pinney (ed.) *The Letters of Thomas Babington Macaulay*, vol. III (Cambridge: Cambridge University Press, 1981), pp. 152, 183.
36 *First Report of Her Majesty's Civil Service Commissioners, together with Appendices*, PP. 1856, vol. XXII.
37 Reprinted in Reader, *The Civil Service Commission*, appendix 3.
38 PRO/CSC8/1.
39 Trevelyan Papers: CET 52; PRO/CSC2/33; PRO/CSC8/1.
40 Trevelyan Papers: CET 18.
41 Trevelyan Papers: CET 18, Walrond to Trevelyan, 27 February 1855.
42 Trevelyan Papers: CET 18, Trevelyan to Jowett, 6 June 1855.
43 John Curgenven, 'Theodore Walrond: Friend of Arnold and Clough', *Durham University Journal*, 44, 1951–52, 56–61.
44 PRO/CSC8/5, Minute of 1 May 1876.
45 PRO/CSC8/7.
46 PRO/CSC2/33.
47 PRO/CSC8/1.
48 Palmerston Papers: PP/GL/LE 20, Lewis to Palmerston, 29 May 1855; Palmerston to Lewis, 31 May 1855.
49 *Dictionary of National Biography*, vol. XVIII (London: Oxford University Press, 1917).
50 PRO/CSC8/4.
51 PRO/CSC3/180.
52 Sir George Dasent, evidence to the Ridley Commission, 1888, quoted in 'Appointment to the Post of Secretary in the CSC', PRO/CSC3/23.
53 *Second Report of the Royal Commission to inquire into the Civil Establishments of the different Offices of State at Home and Abroad, with Minutes of Evidence, Appendices etc.* (Ridley Report), C. 5545 (London: HMSO, 1888), Q. 15,254.
54 PRO/CSC5/1381, G.G. Mennell, June 1953.
55 Ibid.
56 PRO/CSC3/23, 26 March 1903.
57 'Appointment to the Post of Secretary in the CSC', PRO/CSC3/23.
58 PRO/CSC3/232.
59 PRO/CSC5/1381, G.G. Mennell, June 1953.
60 22 Vict., c. 26, s.xvii.
61 PRO/CSC2/33, PRO/CSC8/1.
62 Ridley Report, Q. 15,105.
63 PRO/CSC5/1381 and *Dictionary of National Biography, 1931–1940* (London: Oxford University Press, 1949).
64 Trinity College, Cambridge, archives: Add. MS c. 36.26, Leathes to Jackson, 11 July 1910.
65 PRO/CSC5/1381, G.G. Mennell, June 1953.
66 Lady Beveridge Papers, draft fragments of autobiography, J. Mair to WHB, 10 December 1907, quoted in José Harris, *William Beveridge, A Biography* (Oxford: Oxford University Press, 1977).
67 Palmerston Papers: Add. MSS. 48,579, fo. 142.
68 Trevelyan Papers: CET 54, draft of letter to Gladstone.
69 PRO/CSC2/54, Stansfield to Civil Service Commissioners, 15 October 1870.
70 PRO/CSC2/54, C.W. Stronge to Civil Service Commissioners, 22 December 1870.
71 PRO/CSC8/1.
72 *Fifteenth Report of Her Majesty's Civil Service Commissioners, together with Appendices*, C. 197 (London: HMSO, 1870), PP. 1870, vol. XIX.
73 *Third Report of Her Majesty's Civil Service Commissioners, together with Appendices* (London: HMSO, 1858), PP. 1857–58, vol. XXV.

74 *First Report.*
75 *Fourth Report of Her Majesty's Civil Service Commissioners, together with Appendices* (London: HMSO, 1859), PP. 1859, vol. VIII; *Thirteenth Report of Her Majesty's Civil Service Commissioners, together with Appendices* (London: HMSO, 1868), PP. 1867–68, vol. XXII.
76 *Third Report.*
77 *Ninth Report of Her Majesty's Civil Service Commissioners, together with Appendices* (London: HMSO, 1864), PP. 1864, vol. XXX.
78 *Thirteenth Report of Her Majesty's Civil Service Commissioners, together with Appendices* (London: HMSO, 1868), PP. 1867–68, vol. XXII.
79 *Seventeenth Report of Her Majesty's Civil Service Commissioners, together with Appendices*, C. 672 (London: HMSO, 1872), PP. 1872, vol. XIX.
80 *Fifteenth Report.*
81 Ibid.
82 *Twenty-first Report of Her Majesty's Civil Service Commissioners, together with Appendices*, C. 1867 (London: HMSO, 1877), PP. 1877, vol. XXVII; *Twenty-sixth Report of Her Majesty's Civil Service Commissioners, together with Appendices*, C. 3245 (London: HMSO, 1882), PP. 1882, vol. XXII; *Thirty-fourth Report of Her Majesty's Civil Service Commissioners, together with Appendices*, C. 2721 (London: HMSO, 1880), PP. 1880, vol. XXI.
83 *Thirty-fifth Report of Her Majesty's Civil Service Commissioners, together with Appendices*, C. 6412 (London: HMSO, 1891), PP. 1890–91, vol. XXVI.
84 *Thirty-seventh Report of Her Majesty's Civil Service Commissioners, together with Appendix*, C. 7126 (London: HMSO, 1893), PP. 1893–94, vol. XXV.
85 *Twentieth Report of Her Majesty's Civil Service Commissioners, together with Appendices*, C. 1587 (London: HMSO, 1876), PP. 1876, vol. XXII.
86 *Thirtieth Report of Her Majesty's Civil Service Commissioners, together with Appendices*, C. 4753 (London: HMSO, 1886), PP. 1886, vol. XX.
87 *Twenty-eighth Report of Her Majesty's Civil Service Commissioners, together with Appendices*, C. 4039 (London: HMSO, 1884), PP. 1884, vol. XXI.
88 PRO/CSC3/143; *Thirtieth Report.*
89 *Thirty-ninth Report of Her Majesty's Civil Service Commissioners, together with Appendices*, C. 7888 (London: HMSO, 1895), PP. 1895, vol. XXVI.
90 PRO/CSC3/249; PRO/CSC3/278.
91 *Forty-ninth Report of Her Majesty's Civil Service Commissioners, together with Appendices*, Cd. 2656 (London: HMSO, 1905), PP. 1905, vol. XXIII.
92 *Thirtieth Report.*
93 PRO/CSC3/218.
94 *Thirty-ninth report.*
95 *Forty-fourth Report of Her Majesty's Civil Service Commissioners*, Cd. 271 (London: HMSO, 1900).
96 *Fifty-eighth Report of Her Majesty's Civil Service Commissioners*, Cd. 7479 (London: HMSO, 1914).
97 *Forty-fifth Report of Her Majesty's Civil Service Commissioners*, Cd. 702 (London: HMSO, 1901).
98 *Forty-sixth Report of Her Majesty's Civil Service Commissioners*, Cd. 1203 (London: HMSO, 1902).
99 *Forty-fourth Report.*
100 *Forty-eighth Report.*
101 PRO/CSC3/204, TM 8896/93.
102 PRO/CSC5/1381.
103 PRO/CSC3/325, JSL to Treasury, 23 December 1902.
104 PRO/CSC5/1381, T.L. Hedley.
105 PRO/CSC3/325.

106 'Memorandum on the functions and organisation of the Civil Service Commission' in *Sixth Report from the Estimates Committee, Session 1964–65, Recruitment to the Civil Service*, HC 308 (London: HMSO, 1965), pp. 1–5. See also K.M. Reader, *The Civil Service Commission 1855–1975*.
107 *Fifty-fifth Report of Her Majesty's Civil Service Commissioners*, Cd. 5751 (London: HMSO, 1911).
108 Ibid.
109 *Fifty-seventh Report of Her Majesty's Civil Service Commissioners*, Cd. 6913 (London: HMSO, 1913).
110 *Fifty-eighth Report*.
111 PRO/CSC5/89; *Report of the Committee appointed by the Lords Commissioners of HM Treasury to consider and report upon the scheme of examination for Class I of the Civil Service*, Cd. 8657 (London: HMSO, 1917).
112 MacDonald Report, Recommendation 22.
113 *Report of the Committee upon the scheme of examination for Class I*, para. 36.
114 Ibid. para. 29.
115 PRO/CSC3/173; PRO/CSC3/127.
116 *Thirtieth Report*.
117 *Thirty-fifth Report*.
118 PRO/CSC3/260.
119 PRO/CSC3/318. See also PRO/CSC3/195 and PRO/CSC3/201.
120 PRO/CSC3/150.
121 PRO/CSC3/144.
122 PRO/CSC3/282; PRO/CSC10/4830.
123 PRO/CSC5/96.
124 PRO/CSC5/100. See also PRO/CSC5/120.
125 PRO/CSC3/176.
126 PRO/CSC3/33.
127 PRO/CSC3/177.
128 PRO/CSC3/257, 7 October 1903.
129 PRO/CSC3/257, 22 October 1903.

3

THE PERIOD FROM 1921 TO 1951

Changes in the nature and scope of government during the early years of the twentieth century had important implications for the work of the Civil Service Commission in two ways. First, there was a significant increase in the volume of work. Second, there were changes in the nature of that work. The purposes of government changed in the early years of the twentieth century as a result of such legislation as the Old Age Pensions Act, the Labour Exchanges Act and the National Insurance Act. This legislation required the creation of new, or the extension of existing establishments. In addition, the Commission had to cope with unprecedented problems resulting from demobilisation and post-war reconstruction. Traditional methods of recruitment, involving academic examinations, were inappropriate for applicants who had served in the armed forces. The MacDonnell[1] and Leathes[2] Reports will be considered next, because they were of lasting significance for the work of the Commission. There will then be a discussion of selected details of recruitment problems and developments in the early 1920s. After the post-1918 reconstruction experience, the Commission had a period of stability. This was followed by more dynamic change in the period of reconstruction after the Second World War, which included the development of the Method II system of selection and the creation of the scientific civil service. The period from 1920 to 1951 – the latter date marks the retirement of A.P. (Sir Percival) Waterfield as First Civil Service Commissioner – may be seen as the heyday of the Commission. It had its difficulties from time to time, and some of these will be considered in subsequent chapters, but the period from 1920 to 1951 was, in general, characterised by mid-life maturity and achievement.

The MacDonnell and Leathes Reports

The MacDonnell Royal Commission on the Civil Service reported in 1914. It was, as its Minority Report explained, the outcome of a feeling that, as a quarter of a century had elapsed since the last review of the principles on which the civil service was organised and recruited, it was time to re-examine those principles and the practice that had developed.[3] Compared with the Playfair Committee of 1874–75 and the Ridley Commission of 1886–90, the MacDonnell Commission was a more wide-ranging and prestigious inquiry. While the main effects of the earlier inquiries were to confirm and recommend refinements to existing practice, the MacDonnell Commission had a more rigorous and evidence-based approach, which led to significant changes in the way the Commission went about its work.

Three of MacDonnell's recommendations must be mentioned here. First, MacDonnell regarded with satisfaction[4] the development of competitive interviews to appraise the fitness of candidates in terms of their character and intelligence, and recommended 'most careful examination' of the new procedure.[5] They noted that *viva voce* examinations had been used for the Indian Civil Service up to 1891, and that the Civil Service Commissioners had found them useful for assessing a candidate's 'readiness, self reliance, and moral courage'.[6] The MacDonnell Commission found that the introduction of a *viva voce* examination for recruitment to what they called the administrative class (instead of the First Division, as termed by the Ridley Commission) was either strongly supported, or at least approved, in evidence from senior academics in the universities of Dublin, St Andrews, Liverpool and Wales. They noted, however, that the First Civil Service Commissioner, S.M. (later Sir Stanley) Leathes, who had used the procedure for assessing candidates when recruiting Managers of Labour Exchanges, 'did not commit himself to approval of it'.[7] In fact, Leathes' evidence shows not that he had doubts about the integrity of the procedure but that he was concerned about what others would think of it. Indeed, he said he was 'absolutely' satisfied about the sufficiency of the interviews as a means of assessing candidates' 'outlook upon life, their intelligence, and experience and knowledge of men'.[8]

Second, they noted that certain academic witnesses thought the syllabus for recruitment to the administrative class gave 'undue weight to the studies most commonly followed in the older universities' and that students in modern institutions were handicapped by this. To deal with these first two matters, the MacDonnell Report recommended that the Treasury should appoint a committee of specially qualified persons to examine the suitability and methods of the Class I examination.[9] This recommendation led in 1916 to the appointment of the Leathes Committee, which reported in 1917. Some of the evidence received by the MacDonnell Commission was particularly significant on the question of alleged bias in selection for the Administrative Class, and this will be considered in chapter 11.

Third, the MacDonnell Commission was sympathetic to the extension of employing women in the civil service: 'in self-contained sections, accommodated separately from male clerks, and working under the supervision of their own female officers', 'in accordance with the recommendations of the Playfair and Ridley Commissions'.[10] The MacDonnell Report, which recommended that there should be a return to the practice of having three Commissioners, as in the Commission's first 15 years, also recommended that 'the staff of the Commission should include one or more women of experience in a position to advise the Commissioners with respect to the recruitment and employment of girls and women'.[11] From 1918 it became normal practice to have at least three

Commissioners. Women were first employed as clerks in the Post Office in 1875; later they were recruited as typists (designated female typewriters); the first woman was recruited to the administrative class in 1925.[12] Aspects of the employment of women will be considered further in chapter 10.

The Leathes Report, on the scheme of examination for Class I of the civil service, was the product of a Treasury departmental committee, chaired by Leathes as First Civil Service Commissioner.[13] It will be remembered from the previous chapter that in 1903, in somewhat controversial circumstances, Leathes was appointed Secretary to the Commission. He became a Commissioner in 1907, apparently on a decision by the Prime Minister,[14] Henry Campbell-Bannerman (who had been a student of Trinity College, Cambridge, from 1853 to 1858).[15] Leathes was First Commissioner from 1910 to 1927. He was educated at Eton and Trinity College, Cambridge, and had been a Fellow of the College from 1886 to 1904. He was an author of considerable achievements. He contributed to, and was one of the editors of the Cambridge Modern History, and among his other writings he wrote a pseudonymous book *Vox Clamantis* (1911)[16] as well as three volumes on *The People of England* (1915, 1916, 1923). He never married. For some time after leaving Cambridge he lived in the Temple, and afterwards shared, with the Rev J.A. Nairn, a house in Maidenhead.[17]

By the First World War, the scheme for recruiting to Class I of the Home Civil Service involved a competitive examination which, at that time, was intended for candidates who had completed their university education. It consisted of a choice of 38 papers, with maximum marks for each, and candidates were required to select subjects with total maximum marks up to 6,000. For example, the list included Lower and Higher Mathematics, each with a maximum of 1,200 marks; Latin translation, 400 marks; Greek History, 500 marks; Roman History, 500 marks; Chemistry, 600 marks; and Political Science, 500 marks. No credit was given for superficial knowledge: 'mere smatterers', to use Macaulay's term, were therefore discouraged.

The Civil Service Commissioners wrote to the Treasury on 25 July 1916 drawing attention to the MacDonnell recommendation for a committee to re-examine recruitment to Class I. They said they believed that 'such subjects as language, literature, and history, are on the whole and for the most part of young men, the best preparation for the Higher Civil Service'.[18] They stressed the need for action to be taken on this matter so that details of the new scheme should be ready after the end of the war, for implementation following the period of reconstruction. The Leathes Committee was, in fact, appointed by a Treasury Minute, dated 16 November 1916.

The Leathes Report rehearsed the theory expounded in the Macaulay Report (1854) on the Indian Civil Service. This had emphasised the value of a liberal education, rather than a specialist education, and the importance of competition. As already explained, the Commissioners had followed the theory of Macaulay, and as a consequence had adopted the emphasis on classics and mathematics, as followed in the universities; but by 1916 there had been a considerable expansion in higher education, with civic universities being founded, and new subjects being introduced. In addition, the Consultative Committee of the Board of Education, in their 1916 Interim Report on Scholarships, had made recommendations for civil service recruitment, which included the introduction of a *viva voce* examination. Leathes and his committee colleagues felt that as a consequence of these and other developments it had become increasingly difficult to treat all candidates justly. They stressed that any scheme of recruitment at the post-university level should be designed to select 'vigorous, sound, well-educated men of good intelligence',[19] and they argued that 'the examination should be adapted to the chief forms of general education'.[20] One consequence was that they wished to see more value attached to subjects such as history, economics, law and politics; all of which, they recognised, provided suitable knowledge and training for the civil service.[21]

The Leathes Report recommended that all candidates should be required to write an essay and take a test in English (including a précis). They should be examined on both contemporary subjects (social, political and economic) and on general principles, methods and applications of science. They should also be required to translate from a modern foreign language. Indeed, significant emphasis was placed on foreign languages. The Committee said:

> To acquire a modern language for reading and translation purposes should not be a difficult task for any well-educated man; it can be done in leisure time with a little assistance. We trust in course of time all our candidates will be prepared to offer two modern languages up to a useful standard.[22]

In addition, the Committee strongly recommended a compulsory *viva voce* examination in 'matters of general interest', to test a 'candidate's alertness, intelligence, and intellectual outlook, his personal qualities of mind and mental equipment'.[23] Apart from these compulsory subjects, candidates would be required to be examined in a number of optional subjects chosen from a list of 59.[24]

It is not surprising that Leathes' reputation in the civil service was as an enthusiastic advocate of selection boards. He had pioneered them for recruiting Managers of Labour Exchanges, and he stated on one occasion that his experience as chairman of numerous selection committees had taught him 'how quickly one gets a definite impression of a candidate in a short period of conversation and observation'.[25] Some leading academics, however, expressed reservations about the weight given to the *viva voce* test in civil service examinations. Professor Herman Finer was one of these. Other reservations were expressed by the representatives of civil service staff associations, who extolled the advantages of open competitive written examinations.[26]

The combined effect of the MacDonnell and Leathes Reports was considerable. The Leathes Committee owed its existence to MacDonnell's recommendations. As a result of its work, compulsory subjects (Part A), including a foreign language and an interview of 15–20 minutes, became part of the selection system for the administrative class. There was also an extension to the list of optional subjects for examination. The recommendations in the MacDonnell and Leathes Reports could not, however, be immediately applied after the First World War because of the problems facing the civil service during the period of reconstruction.

Experience during post-First World War reconstruction

After 1914 there were no annual Class I examinations because the university education of potential candidates had been disrupted and the question of age limits had to be reconsidered. A committee of six officials was therefore set up, chaired by Viscount Gladstone, to consider recruitment to the civil service after the war. Leathes was a member. The committee, which reported on 30 October 1918,[27] recommended that in the two-year reconstruction period recruitment should approach as nearly as practicable to open competition. In fact, reconstruction competitions lasted longer than expected. Normal competitions for the administrative class only resumed in 1925, for the clerical class in 1927 and for the executive class in 1928[28] – this skewed the age distribution of staff, resulting in problems for departments in later years. The Gladstone Committee recommended that the Commission should sift the applications for Class I; there should be a qualifying examination, similar but easier than proposed by the Leathes Committee; and a selection board would review the applications on the basis of the written evidence. There should then be interviews by a selection board.

For Class I, the Gladstone Committee made detailed recommendations for the selection board procedure. The board would be chaired by the First Commissioner, with two or three other members, appointed by the Treasury, who 'must be good judges of men for the particular purpose in view' and who should also be 'men intimately associated with the universities though not necessarily engaged in actual teaching'. The procedure introduced, detailed in an Order in Council dated 18 December 1918, in effect provided for competitive selection without competitive written examinations. The Treasury approved 16 men to serve on the panel of interviewers. They included A.L. Smith, Master of Balliol College; A.D. Lindsay and H.W.C. Davis, two Fellows of Balliol College; Will Spens, Tutor of Corpus Christi College, Cambridge; A.C.G. Heygate, formerly Master of Eton College; J.H. Clapham, Tutor of Kings College, Cambridge; and John Murray, Member of Parliament for Leeds (West) and formerly a Tutor of Christ Church, Oxford. The Commission contacted 24 departments to get information about Class I vacancies.[29] Leathes took the leading role in the selection process, inventing an 'elaborate and highly artificial scheme...of marking for the final order', so that all aspects of the candidate's record and performance were taken into account. Nevertheless, Waterfield, one of Leathes' successors, facing similar circumstances in 1944, regarded it as 'far too subjective and unreliable a process' for it to be repeated after the Second World War.[30]

disabled veterans

A committee was also set up, chaired by Sir Malcolm Ramsay, to recommend to the Minister of Labour arrangements for the recruitment of disabled and demobilised men for temporary employment in government departments. This committee reported on 30 July 1919.[31] Applicants completed a form and were interviewed. In London, one member of the selection board represented the Civil Service Commission: W.F.C. Kelly, a Barrister-at-Law, was initially nominated by the Commission as their regular representative. Later, a further representative of the Commission was nominated: Col. C.M. Ducat. The Commissioners felt they did not have the resources to nominate additional representatives, though the Ministry of Labour wished to ensure that there was a Commission representative on all its recruitment boards for disabled and demobilised men. The Treasury issued a circular to departments[32] directing them to recruit disabled men as temporary assistants (such as clerks, messengers and porters). The chairmanship of the boards was taken in turns, but Kelly observed that others adopted his own method of interviewing. Kelly and Ducat wrote weekly reports for the Commission and those reports now provide a valuable record of their work.[33]

By 4 September 1920 Kelly estimated that he had personally interviewed nearly 10,000 candidates in the previous year. Sometimes a candidate who had been rejected by one board later presented himself before the other board; he would use his experience from the first interview and was passed by the second, quite unaware that his second application form would eventually find his first in the registry. Sometimes their names would be slightly altered. There might be other deceptions: for example, 'tuberculosis' would become 'asthma'. The requirement, following regular Commission procedure, for three referees was particularly important as a check.

Kelly reported that he had more than one Oxford or Cambridge 'double first' who was only too glad to avail himself of a Grade II or III clerkship. He commented that the experience of looking into ten or 12 thousand pairs of eyes revealed a good many tragic histories. Three examples illustrate his experience:

> In one of the earliest days of the Board's existence a man was shown into the room, a captain in rank. He was a striking figure, very tall and good looking but weather-beaten. He had been a real 'soldier of fortune', his entire career a romance.
>
> His age was about 47, and he had served or taken part in every kind of war or political disturbance in the last 25 years and more, Boer, Indian, Turkish, Russian, Japanese, Greek, not omitting revolution in Central American republics. In the late Bulgar–Turkish war he had been the representative for a cinematograph company and had taken pictures from both sides. In the late war he had been condemned to remain at home, his commanding figure and sang froid having evidently singled him out for an APM in a south coast town. Now he was down and out. He told his story and we did our best for him. At the end of the interview he stood up and said: – 'Now that you have been so kind I will tell

you exactly how I stand.' He plunged his hand into his pocket and a handful of pawn-tickets fell on the table. 'My Estate – mortgaged', he said. A writ for £80 followed. 'My liabilities'. Next a photograph, a snapshot evidently. 'My home', he said, handing it for inspection. We saw two caravans standing forlornly on the edge of a swamp.

'If I don't pay a deposit to my grocer (who had issued a writ) before the week's out I shall be sold up.'

He had a wife and six children 'at home' and his grocery bill alone came to £30 per month. In the end we found him something to carry him on and save the caravans. There were tears of gratitude in his eyes as he shook hands with us with the hand of a colossus.

. . .

A young fellow . . . nicely dressed, clean, smart and well-to-do looking – applied for a clerkship. He was only just 23 years old but had lost a leg in his first engagement. For some weeks he had been in the Army Pay Corps, but was leaving in a few days. He could not be taken on as a clerk, but he asserted he was a good typist, speed 80 words per minute, which he adhered to in spite of our scepticism; so, to give him all the chances we could, we sent him down to be tested. His form was returned marked 'No speed' and we told him it was impossible to engage him in that capacity. Then it all came out. He had lost a leg, had an invalid wife, and a baby at home – and nothing to go on with. Then he burst into tears. It was a much more painful sight to witness than to describe. After all he was only a boy, and he felt his handicap deeply. We sent him down to the allocation officer to see if he could find him a messenger's job, but I doubt if there were any immediately available.

. . .

Another pathetic case was that of a man who had lost a leg before the war. Someone had blundered in sending him before the Board at all, for he had no military service.

He looked very pale and ill and shabby and had been out of work a long while. He was married, and obviously in very low water indeed. The outbreak of war had ended his civilian employment, yet he was an experienced clerk and had also served in a clerical capacity in the Arsenal and in one of the Government offices during the war. Had he been an ex-soldier he could have been recommended for a clerkship without any doubt whatever.

Alas! We could do nothing for him. We had to tell him that only ex-soldiers, overseas or disabled men, could be considered.

He did not 'grouse' as so many do when they are turned down, but got up quietly and nodded. 'Well', he said, 'that is as it should be. They faced all the danger. Thank you gentlemen. I am sorry for taking up your time.' He turned and went out. We now saw he was in rags: the joints of his artificial leg had worn through his trousers.[34]

In the reconstruction period, the Commissioners and their representatives sometimes had difficult tasks, as represented by these cases. The experiences, however, illustrate the political environment in which the Commission operated. If departments refused to accept disabled ex-service men because they were untrained to office work, the government would experience difficulties from the commercial firms it had pressured to accept disabled ex-soldiers, even if not quite up to their requirements. The basic task of the Commission was to implement the recruitment policies of the government in this context. It also had to set an example of good practice.

The task of running civil service examinations was also, at times, enormous during this period. For example, in 1920 the Commission had to plan for 9,000 women and over 15,000 men to take the examinations for temporary staff in the clerical class.[35] The task was more difficult than running open competitions for normal circumstances. This was because the established practice depended on assessing university or school work; but it seemed unfair to use this approach when there was a long interval, caused by the war, between full-time study and taking civil service examinations. Consequently it is hardly surprising that the Commission was interested in exploring new approaches to testing its candidates. Leathes wrote to various government departments in 1920 explaining an experiment with new psychological tests and seeking co-operation to compare the performance of candidates so recruited with their subsequent work performance. The research was carried out by Professor C.E. Spearman, who was attempting to find out whether clerical work needed a high standard of 'general intelligence'. The research expenses were paid half by the Commission and half by Spearman himself. Some of the responses from departments were critical: whereas Spearman was interested in developing tests to assess intelligence it was suggested that the most important qualities needed for the lower grades of clerical work were accuracy and application. Nevertheless, the result of the research was that the correlation of scores on the 'psychological test' was better in terms of the subsequent performance of clerks in departments than any (individual or combination) of the educational tests.[36]

A few years later the Commission became interested in extending its experience of using psychological tests. On 21 January 1924, D.B. Mair wrote to Dr Cyril Burt about this. Burt was interested in comparable experience in the United States civil service and after his return from the USA he had discussions at the Commission. Officials there were particularly concerned about the low correlation between the departmental estimates of the efficiency of shorthand typists and their performance in the civil service examinations. On this particular problem Burt suggested the Commission should contact Dr C.S. Myers, Director of the National Institute of Industrial Psychology. The Institute, however, would charge for any investigation they undertook and it was agreed the cost

(100 guineas per calendar month) would be debited to the cost of the Commission's shorthand typist examinations. Leathes took a personal interest in the research project and made himself available to meet the researcher, Miss Winifred Spielman. The research took longer than expected, but Mair, writing for the Commission, had to explain they could not pay more, so after March 1925 the Institute was working without further payment. In fact, the Commission later decided they could afford more funds for this research, and the research was extended to 1928.[37] According to C.G. Nelson, writing in 1943 as Assistant Commissioner and Director of Examinations, the tests designed by psychologists were later abandoned because 'they did not seem to add anything of special value to the written examination'.[38]

Nevertheless, academic developments in personnel selection methods, and the problems facing the Commission in the post-war reconstruction period, affected its day-to-day work. These factors also contributed to a reconsideration and sharpening of the purposes of some of that work. One aspect where this was clearly apparent was the requirement for the Commissioners to examine the health of candidates before issuing their certificates. In 1924 G.G. Mennell explained to Dr A.E. Russell that the purpose of the medical examination was to ascertain whether or not the physical condition of the examinee justified a reasonable expectation of continuous effective service in the post sought till the age of 60: 'the Commissioners cannot be satisfied with less, but need not require more'.[39] A good relationship developed with Russell who was very helpful to the Commission in providing guidance in layman's terms, free of charge, so that the Commission's staff could interpret information in reports from other doctors.[40] Further aspects of the arrangements for medical examinations are considered in chapter 5.

Waterfield and the Method II system of selection in post-Second World War recruitment

Leathes retired on 31 December 1927 and Stanley Baldwin, then Prime Minister, recommended to the King on 9 November that R.S. (later Sir Roderick) Meiklejohn should succeed Leathes as First Commissioner. Meiklejohn was at that time Deputy Controller of Supply Services in the Treasury. His 12 years as First Commissioner, when there were no major issues of controversy or major new developments, were largely characterised by his management style of deferential co-operation with the Treasury. When Meiklejohn retired on 31 March 1939 Sir James Rae, then Treasury Establishment Officer, recommended to Sir Warren Fisher, then Head of the Civil Service, that Meiklejohn's successor should be Waterfield. Waterfield was then a principal assistant secretary in the Treasury. Rae said that there was some overhauling to be done at the Civil Service Commission, but he doubted whether the duties of the post would subsequently be sufficient 'to occupy the full time of a man of Mr Waterfield's energy' and he therefore proposed that Waterfield's spare time should be at the disposal of the Treasury. Fisher added to Rae's minute: 'This will…be an admirable appointment and I trust you will approve it.' Sir John (later Viscount) Simon, then Chancellor of the Exchequer, and Neville Chamberlain, then Prime Minister, added their initials.[41]

Waterfield had done well in the 1911 Open Competition for Class I: he came second and was assigned to the Treasury. His father had served in the Bengal Civil Service. Waterfield was educated at Westminster School, then spent four years at Christ Church, Oxford, where, in 1911, he achieved first-class honours in *Litterae Humaniores*. After graduation he received private tuition for the civil service examinations – in political science from E. (later Sir Ernest) Barker, then Fellow of St John's College, Oxford, and in Roman law from D.C. Cousins.[42]

One of Waterfield's early tasks as First Commissioner was to consider problems connected with post-Second World War recruitment, especially recruitment to the administrative class. Sir Horace Wilson, who had succeeded Fisher as Permanent Secretary to the Treasury and Head of the Civil Service, asked Waterfield to do this in April 1941.[43] The arrangements that had originated from the Leathes Committee were still in force, though there had been some changes in the 1930s as a result of discussions with Oxford and Cambridge Universities – and, of course, regular recruitment was suspended for the duration of the Second World War. The main criticism made of the administrative class recruitment scheme during the 1930s had arisen from the strain on candidates who had to be examined in one or more subjects beyond those taken in their degrees, as Waterfield had in political science and Roman law, and the consequent tendency to cramming. The changes introduced in the 1930s had reduced this problem and Waterfield wrote in May 1941 to R.S. Wood at the Board of Education:

> As far as I can see the scheme as at present constructed is sound and, with one exception, I do not expect that it will prove to require further alteration in the near future, although I propose to ask the University authorities whether they have any further suggestions to make.[44]

Waterfield nevertheless personally favoured implementing the Leathes recommendation to encourage examination in two modern languages. In fact, he wanted to go further than the Leathes Committee and restore the translation from a foreign language (other than a language chosen as an optional subject) as a compulsory subject with a *viva voce* examination in it as well as a written translation: this provision for examination in an auxiliary modern language had been dropped a few years before the war. Waterfield undertook a survey of the 115 candidates who had taken the *extra numerum* language examination in the years 1925–32. The survey results suggested that the candidates thought the experience of preparing an extra language for examination was of little usefulness and they had doubts about the value of the assessment of their additional language skills. Moreover, the survey almost assumed that educated people read books in foreign languages as part of their general reading (and this may not have been so for most educated people at that time).[45] As the evidence suggested so little potential use of additional languages, Waterfield's interest in encouraging their examination had no practical effect.

Waterfield had intended next to discuss post-war recruitment in an informal way with the university authorities, before circulating proposals, based on these discussions, to the heads of the more important departments for their consideration. What in fact happened was not at all as routine as he had expected. There had already been some informal preliminary discussion with the older universities, but what otherwise would have been a matter of conventional administration and consultation with the universities became much more sensitive and demanding. The following brief outline presents the main stages in the development of what became known as the Method II system of selection: more complete details and analysis have already been published in *Leadership in the British Civil Service*.[46] In addition, a detailed description of the reconstruction competitions was published for the Commission in 1951.[47]

Sir Malcolm Robertson was asked by Anthony Eden (later Sir Anthony and subsequently Lord Avon) to prepare suggestions for reforming the diplomatic service. Eden received Robertson's report on 12 May 1941, decided to adopt it and sought and received Cabinet authority for the principles involved.[48] Waterfield knew about this and expected to be consulted; he also expected the Treasury and the universities to be consulted. Instead, Eden asked for a detailed scheme for post-war recruitment to be prepared without delay and instructed G.M. (later Sir George) Rendel to work on the preparations within the foreign service. Rendel at the time was British Minister to the Yugoslav government in London. Waterfield felt that the Commission should have been asked to develop the scheme and noted that Rendel's appointment to the recruitment task was 'presumably on the ground that he is unemployed since I cannot imagine that he is otherwise qualified for the job'.[49] In fact, Waterfield was furious at the lack of consultation. He wrote to his colleague G.G. Mennell: 'The Foreign Office presumably call this diplomacy, but I should prefer to call it by a shorter and more unpleasant word.'[50] Mennell, in reply, wrote: 'There are times when the differentia between diplomacy and double-crossing is hard to detect.'[51] Rendel had to work in collaboration with Waterfield and Waterfield wanted to ensure that the preliminary stages of recruitment to the reformed foreign service were assimilated as closely as possible to that for the home and Indian civil services – as they were not at that time. Waterfield's hand was consequently forced, and he had to produce proposals for the home civil service without the prior consultations he had intended.

This was the background to the proposals Waterfield urgently prepared, within the Commission, and which were considerably influenced by the Commission's experience of the new, additional method of recruitment involving an interview that had been introduced in 1937 for British candidates for the Indian Civil Service. Waterfield proposed that Method I would be similar to the Class I recruitment regulations in operation since 1937. This involved three compulsory papers (essay, English and present day questions), plus a written translation from French, an improved *viva voce* test and a number of optional subjects, at university final examination level, chosen from a long list. It was envisaged that at least three-quarters of vacancies would be filled by this method. Method II would require candidates to have at least a second-class honours degree, take a written examination in the three compulsory English subjects and be interviewed for an assessment of personal qualities before a selection board. He also proposed that probation should be made more effective before any probationer became certified for permanent employment.[52] Waterfield then prepared a memorandum for consideration by the Committee of Vice-Chancellors and Principals, at their annual meeting on 25 September 1941, drawing attention to the difficulties that had emerged between his approach and the approach favoured in the report by Robertson and accepted in principle by the Foreign Secretary. The Foreign Office proposal involved abolishing the written examination, with initial recruitment by interview only. In addition, Waterfield had discussions about his proposals at a meeting on 17 September 1941 with heads of civil service departments, chaired by Wilson, Permanent Secretary to the Treasury.

As a result of these discussions and of preparing the memoranda, the purpose of the proposed changes became clearer and sharper. The proposals were to broaden the basis of recruitment: by encouraging candidates to come forward who would probably not have competed under the pre-war examination arrangements; to give greater importance to the assessment of personality, while maintaining the test of intellectual ability; and to assimilate recruitment to the foreign service with recruitment to the other civil services.

Waterfield therefore had a major political task, though largely within the context of the closed politics of Whitehall. Indeed, the files show that he had a considerable mastery of bureaucratic politics and was well endowed with determination and tenacity.[53] When he outlined the problem to Mennell he said that Robertson's:

> ideas are, I am afraid, fundamentally unsound and we must do our best to see to it that he is not allowed to publish proposals which might be difficult to overthrow subsequently.
>
> That means that we ought to have our own ideas of reform in concrete shape...[54]

As part of his campaigning task, on 29 May 1941 Waterfield consulted George S. Gordon, the Vice-Chancellor of Oxford, at Magdalen College, where he was President. Douglas Veale, Registrar of Oxford University (an ex-Ministry of Health principal) was also present. In addition, Waterfield contacted the University of Cambridge; Sir Franklin Sibley, Vice-Chancellor of Reading University (in his capacity as Chairman of the Committee of Vice-Chancellors and Principals); and London University.

H. (later Sir Henry) Wilson Smith, at the Treasury, was, in 1942 and 1943, stimulating preparations for the post-war civil service, preparations that led directly to the creation of the Civil Service Reconstruction Committee. This committee, chaired by Wilson Smith himself, had its first meeting on 25 June 1943.

Alongside this there was, on 5 July 1943, the first meeting, chaired by Sir Richard Hopkins, of Heads of Departments on Problems of the Post War Civil Service. In addition there were meetings between the Official and Staff Sides of the National Whitley Council, which analysed what had happened and what lessons could be learned from the reconstruction experience after the First World War. In the meetings of all these committees (and in numerous others, too) Waterfield displayed energy and industry in presenting papers and in drafting the reports.

From the summer of 1941 Waterfield had been serving as Chairman of the Central Interviewing Board (CIB), set up by the Treasury and the Ministry of Labour to interview candidates for temporary administrative appointments in the civil service during the war. In January 1942, recognising that the available candidates had academic and personal backgrounds different from typical pre-war entrants (in particular, many of the candidates were women), Waterfield said he wanted to add a psychologist to the Board as an experiment. He hoped this might enable him not only to improve the work of the CIB but also to assess the possible value of adding a psychologist to regular interviewing boards for administrative class selection after the war.[55] This development, it seems, was stimulated by the urgent need to find means of assessment suitable for the reconstruction period of recruitment after the war and by developments in the War Office Selection Board (WOSB) system created to select officers for the Army.

The Army had been experiencing problems because over 50 per cent of the candidates selected for officer training were failing to meet required standards. Criticisms were made that too much attention was given by interview boards to the 'old school tie' qualifications and this discouraged applications from individuals without them. The War Office therefore considered German experience, in which psychologists had been used to design selection tests; and, although German experience was unacceptable in detail, it was decided to use psychologists to develop a new system for officer selection that assessed a man's personal qualities. This new system, involving two and a half days of tests and exercises to assess personal qualities at a residential centre, was fully operational from July 1942.[56] Waterfield heard about it from Brigadier McLean, the Army Director of Selection of Personnel, and at McLean's invitation he visited the WOSB at Watford on 6 November 1941, where one of the Board Presidents he met was Col. J.R. Pinsent. He was very favourably impressed ('in comparison, our own methods...seem sadly slap-dash and amateurish')[57] and saw the potential for developing the system to assess reconstruction candidates who, like his son John, had had their university education opportunities disrupted by the war.[58]

It was the combination of these factors, Waterfield's own inclinations, pressures from the Foreign Office and the Treasury, the expected problems of recruitment in the reconstruction period and the availability of personnel who had served in a WOSB, that led to the creation of the Method II system of selection and, in particular, the Civil Service Selection Board (CSSB). In addition, Waterfield felt that if the Commission did *not* do something of this kind, and at the same time produced no convincing reasons for inertia, it would provoke a great deal of criticism.[59]

The system was at first used for reconstruction competitions but later used for normal open competitions for the administrative class. Its main elements were qualifying written examinations in general subjects (see above), three days of tests and exercises at CSSB and appearance at the Final Selection Board (FSB) under the chairmanship of the First Civil Service Commissioner.

The first Chairman of CSSB, Pinsent, was an ex-Regular Army Officer who, after his retirement, had taught for eight years at Winchester College, had served as a local authority Director of Education and during the war was President of No. 4 WOSB at Watford.[60] Preliminary to the creation of CSSB, there was a 'job analysis' of the work of assistant secretaries (the generally recognised career grade in the administrative class): this was necessary in order to determine the qualities that were to be assessed at CSSB.[61] The procedure at CSSB involved four elements. These were, first, assessing the candidate's record, references and the results of the qualifying examination; second, the results of psychological tests (to assess analysing, reasoning and drawing correct inferences; and projection tests designed to reflect attitudes, temperament and character); third, oral and written exercises based on problems analogous to work in the civil service; and, fourth, interviews by three of the directing staff – the Observer, Psychologist and Chairman of the candidate's group. The reconstruction candidates could take the qualifying examination not only in the UK but also at centres overseas such as Cairo, Caserta and Delhi.[62] Those who reached the required standard then spent three days in residence at the Manor House, Stoke D'Abernon, where, for most of the time, they were assessed in groups of seven candidates. In the reconstruction competitions, 5,969 candidates took the qualifying examination; 3,050 were reported on at CSSB and appeared before the FSB.[63]

By 1951, when Waterfield retired, the Method II system of selection, pioneered in the reconstruction competitions, was well established as a normal method of open competition for the administrative class of the home civil service, the senior branch of the foreign service and the special departmental classes in the Inland Revenue and Ministry of Labour and National Service.[64] Method I also continued. Recruitment of graduates by these methods attracted considerable criticism from time to time, and was often associated with allegations of bias in selection – these matters are considered further in chapter 11. The development of this system of selection attracted a great deal of attention both within the UK and overseas. For example, the Memorandum on it, published in 1951, specifically mentioned that the Anglo Iranian Oil Company had asked to use the CSSB arrangements for its potential recruits, on an agency basis. There were also suggestions for CSSB to undertake agency work for the Federation of British Industries, for business firms and for university entrance.[65]

The problems of conscientious objectors

At the beginning of this period the Civil Service Commission was affected in a variety of ways by the consequences of the First World War. As has been already shown, the Commission began to use the services of psychologists for developing new methods of selection; there was a large backlog of vacancies because of the suspension of most normal recruitment during the war; and there were also continuing problems of procedure and sensitivity resulting from the war. One of these areas of sensitivity after the First World War, and again after the Second World War, was the government's policy and practice relating to conscientious objectors. A case study of this experience is the subject of chapter 7: the case of Arthur Creech Jones. It shows how the issue was dealt with, concentrating on the experience of a clerk in the Commission at the beginning of the First World War. Here, the intention is to consider, briefly, some issues of administrative practice as they emerged after the wars. This provides insights into policy development and the consequences of it, in the context of the general climate of public administration practice.

In July 1919 the Treasury prepared a memorandum for the Cabinet on conscientious objectors who had failed to obtain exemption on conscientious grounds. The Treasury view was that as the Central Tribunal (set up under the Military Service Act, 1916) 'passed everyone whom they could find an excuse for passing', it could be assumed that no one who was not passed by the Tribunal was genuinely conscientious: such men should therefore not be re-employed in government departments. Absolutists were in a more serious category than most conscientious objectors because, according to the Treasury, they included men of 'the most genuinely conscientious type who object not only to military service but to all state control'. The Treasury thought that men who had absolute objections might be genuinely conscientious, but as they objected to all forms of state control they were not fit to be employed in the civil service. Conscientious objectors who passed the Central Tribunal had been recognised by the government as entitled to exemption and could therefore be re-employed.

The Cabinet's Home Affairs Committee, on 1 August 1919, felt that public opinion was not ripe for re-instating conscientious objectors, agreed with the Treasury and proposed to the Cabinet that only men who had satisfied the Central Tribunal, had worked in the non-combatant corps and were paid from Army funds, could be re-instated. Those who were re-instated, however, should only be engaged on a temporary basis and paid at their former actual rate of remuneration without increment, or at the rate which would be paid to a temporary substitute performing the duty, whichever was less, and the period of service could not count either for increment or pension in their established posts. The general principle stressed by the Treasury was that conscientious objectors had proved they were unfitted 'to form part of the Civil Service which has at least on occasion to perform duties shading off into those of the Forces of the Crown'. This was consistent with the view of Fisher, Head of the Civil Service, who regarded the civil service as the fourth service of the Crown.[66]

On 15 April 1920, W.R. Fraser, of the Treasury, wrote to L.C.H. Weekes, asking for the observations of the Civil Service Commissioners on the Treasury views on the subject. Weekes replied that the Commissioners supported the line being taken by the Treasury. On 6 December 1921 Weekes also explained to the Treasury that men who served in the non-combatant corps had served in the Army and would therefore be eligible to enter for the reconstruction examinations. He added that many of these men had served in France and he believed that at least one of them so forgot himself as to win the DCM.[67]

The Commission and the Treasury then co-operated to draft an appropriate regulation, which appeared in the *London Gazette*, 11 July 1922, making it clear that no conscientious objector who had obtained exemption from service in H.M. Forces during the war would be eligible to apply for entry into the civil service. Consequently, the Commission had to check applications to entry into its competitions to ensure that no one who had been a conscientious objector could be admitted. In the 1920s it became standard practice, in competition regulations for all situations in the civil service, to declare ineligible any person who had been exempted from military service on the ground of conscientious objection.[68] This de-barring lasted until 1929, when the Commission issued a notice to say that the regulation no longer applied.

Problems similarly arose over conscientious objectors during and after the Second World War. In connection with drafting the reconstruction regulations in January 1944, Waterfield consulted his colleague Frederic Milner, who had experience of this subject while working in the Home Office. Milner replied with a comprehensive analysis of the problem, as well as advice on the question of regulations. Two of his comments are of interest here:

> I have no soft spot for any kind of conscientious objector but it does seem a little hard that we should penalise a man because he has had to go to prison to prove the genuineness of his conscientious objections...
>
> Conscientious objection is often a characteristic of men who are out of step with their fellow men in many other ways – just awkward creatures who are incapable of the give and take which is necessary if people are to get along together. Where a Board feel that they have such a man before them they turn him down not because he has been a conscientious objector but because the characteristics which are the source of his conscientious objection would make him unsuitable for the Civil Service.[69]

A few days later, Waterfield used Milner's briefing in his letter to the Treasury. He argued that 'the profession of such principles created a strong degree of doubt whether the person concerned is fit for permanent appointment in the Service of the State'. He said it was probable they were by temperament '"difficult", pernickety and not readily adaptable; but it does not seem necessary to take one's stand on these psychological hypotheses. Their attitude to national service should be enough to settle the question.'[70]

The Commission thought of a way round the difficulties: no such person should be admitted, even to the Clerical Officer or Clerical Assistant class, without a pre-interview, as part of the test of eligibility (there was no interview as part of the competition for these classes). The Treasury, in 1944, was not only sensitive to this issue on political grounds, they regarded it, in the words of E.A. (later Dame Evelyn) Sharp, as 'highly "explosive"', especially the Commission's proposal for the clerical classes. She went on: 'So long as we could exclude such persons from the higher classes, by means of the interview, we need not bother much about the subordinate grades.' Waterfield commented 'that the Commissioners had no strong views on the point, so long as justice was done'.[71] A. (later Sir Arton) Wilson, of the Ministry of Labour and National Service, commented to Waterfield that such people were 'not likely to make the best of Government Servants, but you could take care of that, at least in all examinations above the clerical, by suitable marking for the interview'.[72] This matter then went to Wilson Smith, of the Treasury, who made it clear to Waterfield that he did not agree with Waterfield's 'desire to exclude people who have taken no active part in assisting the prosecution of the war'.[73]

When the regulations were being drafted for the foreign service reconstruction competition, Waterfield felt that instead of referring to conscientious objectors, an alternative form of wording should be used. This was in the context of the clause which required the Commissioners to be satisfied that candidates had registered for National Service.

By August 1945 the question had become less sensitive and a Treasury policy on it had developed. Dorothy C.L. Hacket wrote to W.P. Barrett that it had been agreed the Treasury would ask the Commission not to assign to any 'Service' department any successful candidate who was known to the Commissioners to be a conscientious objector. The Treasury (which had perhaps been approached by staff associations) had decided that it did not want to exclude conscientious objectors from the civil service altogether, but it did not think that the Service and Supply departments were the right place for them.[74]

A postscript to this debate occurred in 1949. D.W.G. Sawyer, who was not a pacifist, chose, instead of doing military service, to work in the mines. This was an excepted occupation and therefore he was not 'directed' to do military service. The wording of the Commission's regulation said that in qualifying in terms of age, he could deduct from his actual age time spent in compulsory National Service. Although he was just over the age limit he could not benefit from the deduction for time spent in the mines because he had worked there voluntarily and had not been 'directed' to do so. It was a shock to A.H.M. Hillis, then Secretary to the Commission, to discover that the Commission's regulations in these unusual circumstances favoured conscientious objectors against men who chose to do work of vital national importance. As soon as it could be arranged, the regulations were amended so that only men who had actually served in the armed forces could benefit from the two years' deduction from their age.[75]

At the other end of the scale, the Commission was sympathetic to helping prisoners of war. On 6 July 1944 C.J. Hayes visited the War Organisation of the British Red Cross Society, found that prisoners of war in Germany were working for civil service examinations on the pre-war syllabus and that the Red Cross had been sending out books and pamphlets for this purpose. The Commissioners therefore arranged for copies of the White Paper on reconstruction recruitment,[76] prepared by the National Whitley Council, to be sent, via the Red Cross (which had means of communication with Germany via Lisbon) to prisoners in German camps. Hayes wrote a report on this initiative and noted the failure of a similar initiative in Italy, 'owing to the ineptitude of the Italians'. Later, it also became possible to send information to libraries, but not to individuals, in Japanese camps.[77] This is further discussed in chapter 5.

The scientific civil service

In general, references to the civil service tend to relate to the large number of officials who are employed in the offices of government departments. Most of these officials were organised in classes found in all departments, and their conditions of service were, in the period from 1920 to 1951, determined by Treasury regulations. Examples of these classes are the administrative, executive and clerical; and the most junior grades, to which new entrants were recruited, were assistant principal, executive officer and clerical officer. There were also departmental classes, so-called because they were to be found only within particular departments – such as inspector of taxes or officer of customs and excise. Most of the experience referred to in this book relates to civil servants in those classes and grades that were found in all departments; they were the most numerous and recruitment to them was the responsibility of the Civil Service Commission. Indeed, in the nineteenth century the Commission was probably the most important factor for developing them into a unified and uniform civil service. A creation of comparable significance in the twentieth century was the scientific civil service; in this the Commission also played a very major role.

Although scientific work was done in various government departments in the nineteenth century, and there were departments devoted to it (the Government Geological Survey, for example, was set up in 1835), there were no service-wide classes and grades with centralised recruitment. Scientists were recruited by individual departments, often initially on a temporary basis, with the Commission becoming involved if and when certificates had to be issued for permanent appointments. There was a considerable increase in the number of government scientists during the First World War, and after the war there were attempts to regularise the recruitment and conditions of service between the departments employing them. During the Second World War there was another great expansion of scientists in government, and a committee of inquiry in 1943, chaired by Sir Alan Barlow, made recommendations which led to the creation of the scientific civil service.[78] Its creation, referred to as 'reorganisation', was announced in a 1945 White Paper,[79] which became, in effect, its charter.[80] A unified scientific civil service was thereby established: disparities in the organisation and grading of scientific work between different departments were ironed out, a unified grading system was introduced and recruitment and allocation to permanent appointments, involving competitive examination and/or interview, became centralised through the Commission, which set up a special section headed by C.P. (later Sir Charles, then Lord) Snow, who was a Fellow of Christ's College, Cambridge. Snow joined the Commission on a part-time basis in 1945 and continued until 1960.

One of Snow's most significant achievements as Commissioner was the inauguration of a scheme of selection by interview in North America. After the Second World War there was an acute shortage of scientists in the UK, especially evident in the government's service, which was the country's largest employer of scientists, and made worse by the attraction of North America to young British scientists who went there to study on research scholarships and fellowships. They were discouraged from returning to Britain for the necessary interview mainly because of the expense they would incur, so Snow stimulated publicity in North America and went there to interview on behalf of the Commission and the Atomic Energy Authority. In the beginning this was at no cost to the Treasury because Snow gave lectures at universities (e.g. Harvard, Princeton, Cornell and elsewhere) in his capacity as a literary man, and his expenses were paid for those engagements. Later some of the interviewing was undertaken by his colleague H.S. Hoff, then Assistant Commissioner in the scientific branch of the Commission. Details of potential candidates were initially supplied by the Ministry of Labour and National Service, which kept records of deferment of National Service, and by the National Research Council of Canada.[81] This became a major exercise for the Commission: in 1960, for example, 145 candidates were interviewed in North America and 70 per cent were acceptable;[82] by 1962 the number interviewed was 244.[83] The Commission also produced a booklet on the work of the scientific civil service, which was sent to Technology Colleges in the UK.[84] The Commission in the post-Second World War period was generally operating as a buyer in a seller's market, in conditions of full employment, and the difficulties it faced were at least as acute for recruiting scientists as for recruiting administrative and clerical staff. The scheme for attracting scientists back to Britain was a great achievement for the Commission: the evidence shows that it was a very professional and efficient operation, and contributed significantly to the good image of the Commission at home and abroad.[85]

Fairness and efficiency in personnel management

Whereas in the nineteenth century the great achievement of the Civil Service Commission was to get open competition accepted as the normal means of recruitment to the civil service, the Commission's achievements in the years leading up to the middle of the twentieth century were associated with its emphasis on the need for fairness in the treatment of candidates. It did this, often with help from other parts of government, mainly by making changes to its organisation and methods. The period from 1920 to 1951 was a period of considerable change. By paying attention to procedures and techniques, as well as by learning from developments elsewhere, the Civil Service Commission improved its own approaches to recruitment and was able to see its work in the wider context of civil service personnel management. Four examples of these changes concern probation procedures; the development of monitoring procedures to ensure fairness in large-scale examinations; attention to the drafting of regulations and their applications to practice; and by learning from others and comparing its work with recruitment practice elsewhere in the public sector and in business.

One of the most significant changes that occurred after the Second World War concerned probation procedures, especially for the administrative class. Before the war, as the Crookshank Report[86] recognised, probation for administrative class entrants was not a serious matter. Few, if any, cases resulted in dismissal at the end of the probationary period, though it was (and is) difficult to imagine that there were no unsuitable appointments. Although new recruits were on probation for two years, there was no genuine probationary test and confirmation had come to be regarded as a matter of routine.[87] Harry (later Lord) Crookshank, who was Financial Secretary to the Treasury, and his committee, which included Waterfield and four other senior civil servants, recommended in 1943 a less sentimental approach than hitherto, more emphasis on efficiency within departments and a system of centralised scrutiny vested in a Central Probation Board. This Board, they said, should be chaired by the First Civil Service Commissioner, sitting together with the head of department concerned and other members.

The Central Probation Board was set up on the lines recommended. The requirements were laid down in a Treasury Circular of 6 June 1946.[88] The Board was chaired by the First Commissioner and operated from 1948. The Commission took a close interest in its work because of any possible reflections on its selection procedures. The Commission acquired a copy of the Uniform Efficiency Rating System used by the US civil service: this enabled CSSB psychologists to design a special probation form that met both the probation requirements and the requirements for a CSSB follow-up review. Most cases that came before the Board were for confirmation and they were dealt with by circulation of reports; but occasionally an individual appeared because he was not a clear pass, and a re-posting involving different tasks sometimes enabled him to proceed. L.C. (later Sir Laurence, then Lord) Helsby, when he was First Commissioner, recognised that in cases of doubt departments invariably recommended extension of probation, rather than complete rejection, so the Board made it a rule to conduct a full-dress review, with an interview, whenever extension of probation was proposed. In a few cases failed probationers were offered positions as executive officer, with a transfer to another department. The Board was, in fact, an advisory body only: advice was tendered to the First Commissioner and the head of the employing department jointly, but, as it was usual for the head of department personally to be a member of the Board, difficulties rarely, if ever, occurred.[89] The evidence shows that the Central Probation Board made a significant contribution to the increasingly professional approach to personnel management in the higher civil service.

An example of the development by the Commission of techniques contributing to increasing professionalism earlier in the century was the means of ensuring fairness in large-scale examinations and of standardising examination marks between different subjects and marking by different examiners. An elaborate system of checking in the tabulation section of the examinations department sought to ensure accuracy and reliability in processing the work of candidates – all of whom were identified by index numbers only.[90] Marks were then adjusted, if necessary, so that the marks of individual examiners conformed to a standard determined by the use of statistical methods, including the Pearson curves and Bryan curves. Fairness in this system, in a competitive examination, depended on the consistency of an individual examiner in assigning marks in the correct order of merit. A great deal therefore depended on the choice, by the directors of examinations, of the examiners in particular subjects. To assist fairness and efficiency, there were rules to ensure the appropriate professional standing and seniority of the examiners; examiners were not normally invited to act for more than two examinations in succession; nor was anyone invited to be an examiner after he or she attained the age of 65 years. Frequently an examiner was asked to mark question papers in cognate subjects (e.g. Latin and Greek, or pure and applied mathematics) so that standards could be compared. This system of adjustment did, however, assume that the level of ability in each subject was constant: if there was no reliable common average and common distribution of marks, however elaborate the adjustment system was, there could be resulting unfairness.

Ensuring fairness of treatment was often mentioned when there were discussions about examination procedures and assessments. Another characteristic concern was the quasi-judicial role and nature of the Commission's work. This was most easily seen in the drafting of regulations and in difficult decisions over hard cases: there could be no concessions at the margins to rules, otherwise the whole system would become unfair. Fairness was, however, just as important in the administrative details of running large-scale examinations. Therefore after the First World War, when the Commission was expecting 1,000 candidates at the public examinations for ex-service men at Crystal Palace, the traffic superintendents of the South Eastern and Chatham Railway and the London, Brighton and South Coast Railway had to be forewarned.[91]

Much of the work of personnel selection was similar in the civil service and in business organisations. Comparisons were frequently made and standards were compared. One leading representative of business stated to the Crookshank Committee that on average as many as one-third of the recruits selected – after severe test of personality – for administrative duties in his firm were rejected as unsuitable after two years' probation.[92] When Imperial Chemical Industries (ICI) operated a selection system similar to CSSB, but which took place on one day, not two and a half days, Pinsent noted that

> it tended to favour the man who was quick and decisive and who had both social and intellectual courage; the shy man, slow starter or the

ruminator would be severely handicapped; and they are far less concerned than CSSB with intellectual standards.

J.H.T. Goldsmith commented that the ICI method was suitable where there was no need to give everybody a fair chance.[93]

There were numerous links, both formal and informal, between the Commission and other organisations engaged in comparable personnel selection. In the period between the two world wars the Commission developed an arrangement with the London County Council (LCC) whereby near-miss candidates in its administrative class competitions could, if they wished, have their names passed on to the LCC for appropriate LCC appointments.[94] The arrangement continued until 1949.[95] In 1949 there were also suggestions that the Commission could act as agents for recruiting for the BBC, by using CSSB, and a scheme along these lines worked well in 1950.[96] There was, by the end of 1947, increasing pressure for CSSB to be used on an agency basis for testing candidates other than for the civil service. The reasons were to develop and maintain goodwill to industrialists, to make use of spare capacity at CSSB during quiet periods and to recoup overhead expenses.[97] To some extent these suggestions reflected the influence on Commission work of the political environment in which it operated.

Change, development and achievement

The period from 1920 to 1951 was one of enormous change for the Civil Service Commission. Even at the purely physical level, the most obvious impact of the Second World War was the Commission's evacuation. The Commission's offices in Burlington Gardens suffered severe damage by enemy action at the end of October 1940 and the department was evacuated to Trinity College, Cambridge. This was a destination very different from the 'most secret' plans that had been developed since November 1937 by the Imperial Defence Committee for the Commission to be evacuated to hotels in Southport.[98] In 1940 the Treasury was bombed and some Treasury records relating to the Civil Service Commission were lost.[99] As part of the war economy effort, and especially because of the shortage of paper, the publication of Civil Service Commission annual reports was suspended: when it was published, the 84th Report therefore covered the period from 1939 to 1948. Most normal civil service competitions were suspended from September 1939 for the duration of the war:[100] departments therefore made temporary appointments to vacant posts. There was consequently a considerable reduction and redeployment of staff (down from 175 pre-war to 40):[101] Waterfield himself, for example, served for a time as Deputy Director-General of the Ministry of Information.[102]

The period from 1920 to 1951 was also one of considerable achievement for the Civil Service Commission. Designing and administering the reconstruction competitions were major tasks of public sector management and they were undertaken with humanity, justice and fairness. No reader of the files can doubt the magnitude of achievements after the end of the two world wars. The greatest single developments were also consequences of the wars. The inter-war examination system for the administrative class was based on the recommendations of the Leathes Committee. In particular its three part structure was a major advance in selection for the administrative class: Part A consisting of the compulsory papers of a general character (300 marks), Part B a choice from 70 optional papers in a wide variety of subjects (700 marks) and Part C the interview (300 marks). This was a significant improvement on the pre-First World War purely academic examinations. Nevertheless, by the Second World War its weaknesses were apparent. As there was no minimum mark for the interview, which was intended to assess personal qualities, it was possible for a minority of candidates to succeed who did not have the desired personal qualities. Also, the civil service was losing out to the business world because the burden of the arduous and exhausting series of written examinations in the summer, the results of which could not be known until the autumn, was a disincentive to university students. On top of this, for the reconstruction competitions the full academic examination was impracticable. Consequently, the Method II system of selection was developed. This again put the Civil Service Commission at the forefront of personnel selection procedures. Its achievements attracted wide international attention[103] and its experience was used to develop comparable selection procedures in business as well as public service.

Notes

1 *Royal Commission on the Civil Service, Fourth Report of the Commissioners* (MacDonnell Report), Cd. 7338 (London: HMSO, 1914).
2 *Civil Service – Class I Examination, Report of the Committee* (Leathes Report), Cd. 8657 (London: HMSO, 1917).
3 Minority Report, MacDonnell Report, para. 3. The authors of the Minority Report were H.W. Primrose, W. Guy Grant and A.A. Booth.
4 MacDonnell Report, Ch. 1, para. 51.
5 Ibid., Ch. 1, para. 52.
6 Ibid., Ch. 3, para. 45.
7 Ibid.
8 Ibid., QQ. 208, 271.
9 Ibid., Ch. 3, paras 38–50 and recommendations 21 and 22.
10 Ibid., Ch. 10, para 28.
11 Ibid., Ch. 9, para 91.
12 Dorothy Evans, *Women and the Civil Service* (London: Pitman, 1934); Dame Alix Meynell, *Public Servant, Private Woman: An Autobiography* (London: Gollancz, 1988).
13 Treasury Minister, dated 16 November 1916, Quoted in Leathes Report.
14 Trinity College, Cambridge, archives, Add. Ms. c. 36/24, Leathes to Jackson, 9 September 1907.
15 *Dictionary of National Biography 1901–1911* (London: Smith, Elder & Co., 1912).
16 Numa Minimus, *Vox Clamantis* (London: Macmillan, 1911).
17 *Dictionary of National Biography 1931–40* (London: Oxford University Press, 1949); *The Times*, 27 July 1938.
18 Quoted in Leathes Report, para. 8.

19 Ibid., para. 13.
20 Ibid., para. 15.
21 Ibid., para. 16.
22 Ibid., para. 28.
23 Ibid., para. 29.
24 Ibid., para. 36.
25 *The New Civilian*, 11 January 1928; see also PRO/CSC5/214.
26 PRO/CSC5/214.
27 *Report of the Committee on Recruitment for the Civil Service after the War* (Gladstone Report), Cmd. 34, 35, 36, 164 (London: HMSO, 1919).
28 PRO/CSC5/305, 'Staffing in the Civil Service in the Immediate Post-War period', Memorandum by the Treasury, November 1943; see also PRO/CSC5/340.
29 PRO/CSC5/104.
30 PRO/CSC5/397, Memorandum by Waterfield, 11 October 1944.
31 PRO/CSC5/114 contains a copy of the report.
32 PRO/CSC5/114, 37918/19, dated 2 September 1919.
33 PRO/CSC5/114.
34 PRO/CSC5/114.
35 PRO/CSC5/140.
36 PRO/CSC5/170.
37 PRO/CSC5/204.
38 PRO/CSC5/385, comments on a letter from Waterfield to Wilson Smith, 8 March 1943.
39 PRO/CSC5/195.
40 PRO/CSC5/197.
41 PRO/T162/702.
42 PRO/CSC11/260.
43 PRO/CSC5/301.
44 PRO/CSC5/300, Waterfield to Wood, 19 May 1941.
45 PRO/CSC5/300.
46 Richard A. Chapman, *Leadership in the British Civil Service* (London: Croom Helm, 1984).
47 *Memorandum by the Civil Service Commissioners on the Use of the Civil Service Selection Board in the Reconstruction Competitions* (London: HMSO, 1951); see also PRO/CSC5/338 and PRO/CSC5/437.
48 PRO/CSC5/304, Waterfield to Douglas, 14 July 1941.
49 PRO/CSC5/303, Waterfield to Wilson, 10 June 1941.
50 PRO/CSC5/303, Waterfield to Mennell, 5 June 1941.
51 PRO/CSC5/341, Mennell to Waterfield, 6 June 1941.
52 PRO/CSC5/301, Memorandum by Waterfield, 15 September 1941.
53 For example, see PRO/CSC5/341.
54 PRO/CSC5/302, Waterfield to Mennell, 12 May 1941.
55 PRO/CSC5/385.
56 PRO/CSC5/386, Note by Waterfield, 13 October 1942.
57 PRO/CSC5/385, Note by Waterfield, 10 November 1942.
58 PRO/CSC5/397, Memorandum by Waterfield, 7 October 1944.
59 PRO/CSC5/397, Memorandum by Waterfield, 7 October 1944.
60 PRO/CSC5/385, Note by Waterfield, 10 November 1942.
61 PRO/CSC5/394.
62 PRO/CSC5/323.
63 *Memorandum by the Civil Service Commissioners*, Appendix I, pp. 13 and 32; see also PRO/CSC5/437.
64 PRO/CSC5/453, Civil Service Commission: Paper B for the Select Committee on Estimates, Sub-Committee D, 9th Report (1948).

65 PRO/CSC5/388; PRO/CSC5/395; PRO/CSC5/438; PRO/CSC5/439.
66 PRO/T268/18–19, Bridges to Padmore, 24 June 1953. See also Sir H.P. Hamilton, 'Sir Warren Fisher and the Public Service', *Public Administration*, 29, 1951, 28–9 and 37; and *First and Second Reports from the Committee of Public Accounts, together with the Proceedings of the Committee, Minutes of Evidence, Appendices and Index*, HC 45, 144 (London: HMSO, 1936).
67 PRO/CSC5/85, Weekes to Craig, 6 December 1921.
68 For example, see PRO/CSC5/205, 'Regulations for the appointment of legally qualified candidates for service on the administrative staff of the Home Office', Civil Service Commission, February 1921. See also PRO/CSC5/253, Mennell to Furse, 26 January 1940.
69 PRO/CSC5/352, Milner to Waterfield, 3 January 1944.
70 PRO/CSC5/354, Waterfield to Sharp, 18 February 1944.
71 PRO/CSC5/352, Waterfield, note dated 7 February 1944.
72 PRO/CSC5/352, Wilson to Waterfield, 16 March 1944.
73 PRO/CSC5/352, Wilson Smith to Waterfield, 15 May 1944.
74 PRO/CSC5/352.
75 PRO/CSC5/531; PRO/CSC5/538.
76 *Recruitment to Established Posts in the Civil Service during the Reconstruction Period*, Cmd. 6567 (London: HMSO, 1944).
77 PRO/CSC5/364.
78 PRO/CSC5/347; see also footnote 79.
79 *The Scientific Civil Service: Reorganisation and Recruitment during the Reconstruction Period*, Cmd. 6679 (London: HMSO, 1945). This White Paper contains, as an Annex, the Report of the Barlow Committee on Scientific Staff.
80 PRO/CSC5/662, 'Scientists in the Government Service: The Scientific Officer Class'.
81 PRO/CSC5/687.
82 PRO/CSC5/817.
83 PRO/CSC5/1002.
84 PRO/CSC5/874.
85 PRO/CSC5/1002; PRO/CSC5/1062.
86 PRO/T162/931/E45491/06/2, 'Treasury Memorandum on Staffing of the Civil Service in the Immediate Post-War Period'; see also PRO/CSC5/340.
87 PRO/CSC5/420, Waterfield's Ottawa Speech, 1948.
88 PRO/CSC5/870.
89 PRO/CSC5/778, Helsby to Warne, 9 June 1959.
90 PRO/CSC5/691, 'The Preparation of Tables of Marks by the British Civil Service Commission' and 'The Adjustment of Examination Marks', papers prepared for Sir Philip Hartog, 10 February 1926. See also PRO/CSC5/287, 'Report of an Investigation into the methods of work of the Civil Service Commissioners', July 1936.
91 PRO/CSC5/128.
92 PRO/CSC5/340, 'The Home Civil Service After the War' para 23.
93 PRO/CSC5/492.
94 PRO/CSC5/265.
95 PRO/CSC5/266.
96 PRO/CSC5/316.
97 PRO/CSC5/467.
98 PRO/CSC13/1–6.
99 PRO/CSC5/450.
100 PRO/CSC5/319.
101 PRO/CSC5/420, Waterfield's Ottawa Speech, 1948; see also PRO/CSC5/453.
102 PRO/CSC5/320.
103 For example, see PRO/CSC5/521, PRO/CSC5/522 and PRO/CSC5/523.

4

THE PERIOD FROM 1952 TO 1991

By 1952 the Civil Service Commission was a long-established and significant department of government. It was responsible for most recruitment to the civil service and also ran competitions for other, usually quasi-governmental, organisations on an agency basis. It had a worldwide reputation for high standards of recruitment by merit, involving fair and open competitions. It had pioneered the use of new selection methods, not only for fast-stream graduate entrants but also for other recruits. Its prestige was enhanced by virtue of its close relationship with the Treasury, being one of what Lord Bridges termed 'the Treasury group of departments': that is, one of 'the many departments or subdepartments which are in orbit around the Treasury'.[1] This was particularly important when the Treasury was the unquestionably most important department of central government – before the Cabinet Office was established as a department and acquired its current responsibilities in matters of civil service management and personnel.

From 1952, however, the Civil Service Commission in some senses went into decline. From time to time it suffered attacks from outside, not only from individuals and interest groups but also from committees and commissions of inquiry. The Commission sometimes appeared to be behind the times, and for easily understandable reasons it was somewhat defensive. The challenges it faced in the second half of the twentieth century were different from the challenges in its earlier history, partly because there were changes in British society which included periods of more or less full employment and a decline in respect for careers in public service. Some aspects of these changes are considered in depth in later chapters; for example, changes in the education system resulted in new provisions for liaison and careers advisory work and in reviewing the Commission's relationships with schools and universities and with their representative organisations. Here, the intention is to give an overview of the most important features of the period, so that the decline in the Commission's fortune and its abolition as a department of government in 1991 may be better understood.

From 1952 to 1968

The year 1952 marks the beginning of a new phase in the history of the Commission. Sir Percival Waterfield retired on 31 January 1951 and was succeeded by A.P. (later Sir Paul) Sinker. The 'reconstruction competitions', for recruiting civil servants whose education and career opportunities had been disrupted by the Second World War, were less frequent. The new Method II scheme for recruiting graduates for fast-stream administrative positions was well into its stride. The departmental organisation had been revised after the 1949 investigation by the Treasury Organisation and Methods Division (see chapter 5). The number of staff in the Commission, which had expanded greatly in the late 1940s, was declining (from 815 on 1 April 1949 to 544 on 1 April 1952).

In terms of its actual work, most of the competitions run by the Commission were attracting enough suitably qualified candidates to fill the vacancies – this applied, in particular, to the administrative class and comparable positions, and to the executive class. As a result of virtually full employment in post-war Britain there were, however, difficulties in recruiting clerical officers, and the Commission arranged new competitions in an attempt to attract ex-National Servicemen. For clerical assistants, shorthand typists and typists, the situation was so serious that age limits were widened, competitions were opened to women and girls aged 15 to 60 and competitions were virtually continuous, involving written examinations every fortnight or so. There were also continuing difficulties in recruiting scientists (as explained in chapter 3), and competitions for them became continuous, with incentives such as temporary appointments for successful candidates while the Commission made inquiries into the health and character of individuals. The special scheme for recruiting British scientists in Canada and the United States ran until 1971, by which time the Commission was able to fill posts from well-qualified applicants in the United Kingdom. In collaboration with the Post Office the Commission was flexible and ingenious in developing new aptitude tests and other arrangements to make its assessment procedures faster and more attractive.[2]

In addition to the work of examining and recruiting, the Commission was involved in the development of new techniques to ensure the validity of assessment methods. For example, the Research Unit of the Commission had been created in 1945 and achieved significance for developing intelligence and aptitude tests for recruitment, initially through the reconstruction competitions (though research into such assessment matters had, in fact, been undertaken within the Commission as early as the post-First World War recruitment). In the later 1940s this work had been expanded for a very wide variety of competitions, to investigate the qualifications or potentialities needed for various kinds of work. The Research Unit became the basis of the Research Division – formed in 1969 after the incorporation of the Commission into the Civil Service Department. The range of research work was then extended to include follow-up and validation studies and the analysis of human factors affecting efficiency and job satisfaction. By the late 1980s it was known as the Recruitment Research Unit.

These details give no insight into the great volume of work undertaken by the Commission, and some selected details may be helpful in this context. In 1951–52 there were 160 open competitions, involving over 41,000 candidates, and 36 limited competitions involving over 20,000 candidates. In the same year there were, in addition, nearly 70,000 nominations based on previous employment in the civil service. Also in 1951–52 the Commission examined a total of 13,000 candidates on an agency basis for other organisations, including the Metropolitan Police, the armed forces, the Railway Executive Police and the Nigerian Clerical Service. The Commission had visits from representatives of 23 foreign countries and correspondence from five more.[3] There can be no doubt that the Commission was held in high regard at home and abroad in a variety of contexts; it was a significant department of government in terms of the size of its staff and the wide variety of its recruitment work. It was also a key department in maintaining a unified civil service. In 1981 Keith Reader, referring to the hundredth anniversary of the Commission in 1955, wrote that: 'The principle of open competition in recruitment to the civil service for which the Commissioners fought in the early days is now so generally acknowledged as right that one would be hard put to it to find any acceptable alternative.'[4]

Nevertheless alternatives were to be found – mostly, the alternatives were consistent with the philosophy which had motivated the Commission, but some changes may now be seen as significant markers towards its demise. An example of change consistent with the Commission's philosophy was the increasing acceptance of general educational qualifications, instead of requiring candidates to take civil service examinations in subjects already assessed by public examinations. There was considerable experience of this for recruiting specialists; indeed, in some cases professional examinations had been accepted as part of the open competitions. By the early 1950s comparable arrangements were introduced for recruiting to the much larger general classes. Here, the shortage of recruits had become so serious that, for London posts at clerical level, from 1953, the Commission accepted the General Certificate of Education (GCE) in approved subjects at Ordinary Level instead of the requirement to take its own examinations.[5] This method of recruitment became continuous for London posts from 1955, and for countrywide recruitment from 1956: the Commission already had some experience of this through its continuous recruitment arrangements at subclerical level. The traditional method of open competitive written examination was, however, still regarded as the normal procedure. For example, in 1963, when there were many more candidates for clerical officer positions than there were vacancies, the Commission decided to recruit only by the normal written examination and not use the GCE continuous entry arrangements, except in London where both methods continued.[6]

At about the same time there were discussions between the Treasury and the Commission about the possibility of extending delegation to departments. Some aspects of this had already been raised by the recent O and M study of the Commission, but the shortage of candidates for clerical officer positions and the shortage of staff in the Commission made this a more important topic. On the one hand, increased delegation from the Commission would have the advantages of speeding up recruitment processes, to the benefit of candidates and departments, and it would give some relief from the more tedious aspects of routine recruitment work so that staff could be redeployed to pressing work that was more satisfying, involving the recruitment of more senior personnel. On the other hand, there was the danger of more sub-standard recruitment (a danger which was still evident from lower quality staff recruited during the Second World War). It was recognised, for example, that 'once you have sub-standard officers you begin to need greater numbers – with corresponding increases in accommodation, establishment branch personnel and general overheads'.[7]

In 1965 a significant change was announced. Whereas there was already provision for delegation to enable departments to recruit clerical officers with GCE qualifications on a temporary basis (and not necessarily on strict Commission principles of 'fairness' and 'bestness'), for subsequent nomination to the Commission for permanent appointment, from 1966 this was to become the main method of recruitment for clerical officers.[8] Similar delegation arrangements were made to recruit postal and telegraph officers, cartographical draughtsmen and surveyors and Land Registry plans assistants.[9] By the end of 1967 the Commission had issued 10,000 certificates of qualification for clerical officers recruited through departments by delegation.[10] By 1969 the Commission referred to clerical recruitment as 'now largely delegated to departments'.[11]

Full employment, which was general from time to time but which variably affected recruitment to particular occupational groups, meant that there were more vacancies than acceptable applicants, so the element of competition to find the best was often not relevant. Instead the Commission was concerned to ensure that new recruits were of the required minimum standard (as early as 1951 it had accepted health declarations in most cases instead of medical examinations, with no significant adverse effects). Recruitment by GCE (Advanced Level) was introduced for executive officers from 1956. Also, the requirement for a good honours degree had been recognised as an acceptable qualification for candidates competing in the Method II system of selection for administrative posts. The acceptance of educational qualifications in this way, especially at the clerical level, was important, later, for enabling the delegation of recruitment to departments. An important point to note here, however, is that the annual reports of the Commissioners frequently drew attention to the shortage of candidates in many professional and specialist classes, such as accountants, lawyers and statisticians – it was not just a shortage of recruits for the generalist office classes. A general consequence of this practice of accepting educational and professional qualifications, and of delegating recruitment to departments, was that from the late 1960s the Commission virtually ceased to be an academic examining body.[12]

Difficulties arose in filling all the vacancies for assistant principals in the 1950s, and this meant that, a few years later, there was a shortage of principals. Therefore, from 1959 a new competition was introduced for direct-entry principals, recognising the need to compete in the market for experienced staff from outside capable of filling top jobs one day. The recruitment difficulties at this level were, however, further aggravated by the very significant expansion in the universities in the 1960s, which resulted in serious competition from universities themselves seeking similarly qualified candidates. From 1964 there were also occasional competitions to recruit direct-entry assistant secretaries. Both these new schemes were necessary to redress the shortfall in recruiting assistant principals in earlier years.[13] An experiment to attract more well-qualified graduates to apply for careers in the civil service was at least partially successful in 1965 when personal letters were sent to all new first-class honours graduates, drawing attention to the opportunities in the civil service and exempting them from the Method II qualifying examination. From 1966 exemption from the qualifying examination was extended to candidates with second-class honours degrees plus a higher degree.[14]

Parliament then became increasingly concerned about civil service recruitment. Partly, this was because the Civil Service Commissioners' annual reports drew attention to the difficulties they were encountering, and the annual reports were launched with appropriate press releases so that they received attention in most quality newspapers. The character of the work of the Commission was also changing as it adjusted its publicity and assessment procedures to the needs of the time. The demand for most kinds of recruit was outstripping supply and, as the 1964 annual report put it, the Commission had to enter the market and sell its goods like anyone else.[15] Some of the consequences of this are considered further in chapter 11. Partly, the press interest had been recognised as worthwhile since the debate in the House of Lords following Waterfield's speech in Oxford in 1948. That speech achieved unintended and unprecedented publicity for the new 'country house' selection system and, as an article in *The Times* put it, 'opened a useful and long overdue debate'.[16] Press interest was greatly stimulated and journalists were invited to see the system in operation. Partly, also, there had been a continuing public interest during and since the end of the Second World War in wider aspects of administrative reform and the creation of the welfare state – and there had been a number of significant publications focusing on these aspects of public administration.

Some examples of these publications illustrate this interest. During the Second World War political parties, academics and other commentators had drawn attention to the deficiencies of the civil service and made proposals for reform. One of the most significant was J.P.W. Mallalieu, whose book *Passed to You, Please*, published in 1942, contained a thought-provoking introduction by Harold J. Laski in which he proposed a reassessment of the civil service from various perspectives, including a 20 point plan for reform.[17] In 1947 the Fabian Society published a weighty report on *The Reform of the Higher Civil Service*.[18] The report was prepared by a group chaired by Bosworth Monck, a former civil servant who also wrote a book *How the Civil Service Works*, published in 1952.[19] Another Fabian publication on the administrative class followed in 1964: *The Administrators: the reform of the civil service*.[20] Academics writing about civil service reform included R.K. Kelsall,[21] Thomas (later Lord) Balogh[22] and Brian Chapman.[23] In Parliament the Select Committee on Estimates, session 1947–48, studied the Civil Service

Commission.[24] Further stimulation was added to public debate by the Priestley Royal Commission on the Civil Service, which published its report in 1955.[25] During the 1964–65 parliamentary session the Estimates Committee again studied 'Recruitment to the Civil Service'.[26] It was this last report from the Estimates Committee which made the significant recommendation that: 'A Committee… should be appointed to initiate research upon, to examine, and to report upon the structure, recruitment and management of the Civil Service.'

This recommendation may be seen as the culmination of a period of concern expressed about the civil service in general, and recruitment to it in particular. It led directly to the appointment in 1966 of the Fulton Committee on the Civil Service. Some of the effects of the Fulton Committee on the Commission are considered further in chapter 9. Here, it is sufficient to focus on the most important consequences; there were five. First, the Commission was merged into the new Civil Service Department. Although it retained its independence as far as certification was concerned, in other respects it became part of what was, in effect, a central department concerned with civil service recruitment and management. Second, there was to be a new enquiry into the Method II system of selection for what later became known as fast-stream entry into the civil service (the previous review had been in 1957, after the ten years' 'experiment' with the two methods). Third, there was to be more delegation of recruitment to departments. As noted above, delegation of recruitment was, by the late 1960s, by no means uncommon. In 1966, for example, the Commissioners reported that the majority of entrants to the scientific classes began their careers by being recruited to departments in an unestablished capacity.[27] It was a small step from such recruitment to delegation to departments of authority to make appointments to established positions. Fourth, there was to be recruitment of what were to be known as special advisers to ministers. Fifth, there was to be an inquiry by Cooper Brothers, the firm of accountants and management consultants, into ways of speeding up recruitment processes. These are considered in more detail in the next section of this chapter.

In his history of the Civil Service Commission, Reader said that the Commissioners' annual reports during the last years of the Commission's existence as a separate and independent department 'make depressing reading. So much so that *The Guardian* on one occasion commented that it detected in them a note of despair.'[28] Although it is not possible here to give an account of numerous incidents and developments that contributed to the general feelings among the Commission's staff, one example illustrates this well. It concerns the proposal to stop the use of 'nomination'.

It will be appreciated that terms like 'nomination' and 'certification' were developed as part of the everyday language within the Commission. Unkind critics may regard them as jargon, but the terms had their uses in the official context. Certification referred to the issue of a certificate to a department stating that a particular individual had been examined and had satisfied the Commissioners in relation to the requirements of a position on the grounds of age, health, character, nationality and knowledge and ability. In most cases after 1870 this related also to the success of an individual in an open competition. Without such a certificate an individual could not be accepted as an established civil servant and could not be eligible for a pension. Certification was therefore the distinctive seal of approval by the Commissioners – and the essential reason for their existence. The term 'Certificate of Qualification' made its initial and important appearance in the Order in Council of 21 May 1855. Nomination was a term used in a variety of ways but generally referred to the proposal to appoint a particular individual, normally without open competition. Occasionally, especially in the early years of the Commission, candidates could be nominated to be examined by the Commission – then, after successful examination, they could be certificated.

In 1966 the Treasury proposed dropping the use of the word nomination because of its overtones of patronage.[29] Sir Laurence (later Lord) Helsby, who had been First Civil Service Commissioner 1954–59 and was Joint Permanent Secretary to the Treasury and Head of the Home Civil Service 1963–68, had developed strong views on this. Previously the Commission had been urged not to use 'competition' and 'compete' because of their deterrent effect on prospective candidates outside the civil service, and because, for many posts, there was no longer a competition to choose the best candidate but a procedure to approve candidates who reached a required standard (there being many more vacancies than qualified candidates). This led to some ingenuity within the Commission, to find alternatives to the forbidden words for use in published documents – though the words were still widely used within the administrative system. P.J.M. Fry, one of the assistant secretaries in the Commission, exercised a flair for new terms and wrote a long memorandum about the various alternative words that might be used. Eventually it was agreed that the Commission would defer to Helsby's views, which by civil service convention could only be formally reversed by someone of the same or higher standing, but it was accepted that the Commission would be free to propose a reversion to the previous use of words when Helsby moved on – unless his successor took an equally idiosyncratic view. J.C. Seddon, then Secretary to the Commission, appreciated that this was an absurdity, but he felt the Commission could comply without disproportionate expenditure of time and effort. Meanwhile Fry exercised his talents by writing a poem, which perhaps had more significance in later years than he could have envisaged at the time:

> Is nothing sacred, nothing out of range,
> To those who float upon the winds of change?
> First, competition's an abomination:
> Now we must do away with *nomination*.
>
> On every hand our cherished terms of art,
> Like friends and colleagues, one by one depart.
> A month ago we had a prohibition
> Upon the use of 'Order of Admission'.

> What next? Methinks 'twould be no more absurd
> To brand 'certificate' a dirty word.
> How soon, I wonder, will they raise objection
> To 'candidate', 'appointment', and 'selection'?
>
> Compelled at last to delegate our powers,
> At least let's keep the jargon that is ours;
> Or else – farewell, Victorian tradition! –
> There'll be nothing left of the Commission.

From 1969 to 1991

From 1966 to 1968 there was a general feeling in the civil service that the future would be fundamentally affected by the Fulton Report:[30] decisions were deferred while everyone waited for Fulton and, like the products of many committees and commissions of inquiry, the report was somewhat later in being published than had been hoped. Once the report was available – indeed, before it was available in some respects – there was much emphasis on implementing its main recommendations as quickly as possible. As mentioned above, there were five immediate effects on the Civil Service Commission. The intention here is to outline the effects and briefly explain their consequences: some of the more controversial features of the report, and its reception within the Commission, are considered in more depth in chapter 9.

On the day the Fulton Report was published the Prime Minister announced that the government accepted the proposal to establish a new Civil Service Department (CSD) covering the Pay and Management Divisions of the Treasury, and the Civil Service Commission. The new department was established from 1 November 1968, with an assurance that the Commission would continue to have an independent and politically impartial role in selecting individuals for appointment. At about the same time, in accordance with government policy for dispersal to assist regional development and to relieve congestion in London, a substantial section of Commission staff (engaged on evidence, assignments and accounts work)[31] moved to Basingstoke.[32] The main move to Basingstoke occurred in 1970, and the Commission's headquarters in London then moved from Burlington Gardens to Savile Row. The consequence of these arrangements for the Commission was major change and reorganisation. The First Civil Service Commissioner became also the Deputy Secretary in the CSD, responsible for all recruitment matters: this ensured that recruitment, training and subsequent career development were more integrated.[33] It meant that the First Commissioner was independent when selecting staff but would also advise ministers on recruitment policy (which was previously a Treasury responsibility).

Second, there was to be a new inquiry into the Method II system of selection. In the House of Commons debate on the Fulton Report the Prime Minister announced that the chairman of this inquiry would be J.G.W. Davies, formerly

Secretary of the Cambridge University Appointments Board. Once the Davies Committee had reported that the Method II system of selection showed no evidence of bias, the Commission felt free to stop Method I recruitment: the last examinations by this method were in 1969. The ending of the Method I entry for administrative appointments was a particularly significant break. It ended a system of selection based on academic examinations that dated from 1870. Recruitment was suspended during the war but resumed in 1948 alongside Method II which involved the Civil Service Selection Board at the Manor House, Stoke D'Abernon. From the late 1950s more candidates chose Method II and in 1969 there were only five successful candidates by Method I.[34]

The main reasons for the decline in Method I applicants were that graduates were reluctant to take demanding Commission academic examinations soon after their university finals; it was difficult for papers being offered by the Commission to reflect all the new subjects being studied in universities; and it was increasingly difficult to maintain a fair and uniform standard among few candidates choosing from over 150 papers (some papers were being taken by only one or two candidates). The Commissioners said they also recognised that 'the competence of academic examinations to discriminate among candidates fairly and accurately on a fine numerical basis had been undermined by research since the 1930s'.[35] The Committee of Vice-Chancellors and Principals had been consulted, had no doubts about the fairness of Method II and favoured the abolition of Method I.

Third, there was to be more delegation of recruitment. As early as 1956 an Order in Council had prepared the way for this change. Although from 1870 the principle of open competition had been laid down, and later extended for most first appointments to permanent posts in the civil service, there were continuing opportunities for departments to make temporary appointments. This arrangement also served to emphasise the division of responsibility in personnel matters: the Treasury was responsible for recruitment policy, the Commission for the examination and selection of staff and the departments for their appointment. From the 1956 Order in Council, however, it was made clear that the Commissioners' certificate was required only in the case of permanent appointments. Consequently, the Commissioners formally ceased to have any control over recruitment by departments of temporary staff who had no security of tenure, and their powers were re-defined as approving and certifying the qualifications of all staff proposed for permanent appointment in the Home Civil Service and the Diplomatic Service.[36]

The Fulton Committee thought that departments should have a greater influence on the selection of individuals and that a higher proportion of staff should be recruited direct by departments: the practicalities of this recommendation received early attention in the Commission. In 1969, there was a marked reduction in the number of candidates applying for posts, particularly as draughtsmen, in the Post Office; recruitment to the Post Office, however, ceased to be a function of the Civil Service Commission when the Post Office became an independent public corporation on 1 October 1969. The Civil Service Commissioners'

1969 annual report also drew attention to relaxation in the rules for certification: arrangements were made for candidates who were already permanent civil servants to be appointed without formal recertification.[37] From 1970 the Commission increased departmental representation on all its selection boards, in line with another recommendation by the Fulton Committee for closer involvement of departments with centralised recruitment processes.

In 1970 the Commissioners reported that most of the certificates of qualification they were then issuing were for candidates recruited initially by departments and submitted for establishment under agreed schemes. A specifically mentioned example of this was the arrangement initiated in 1970–71 for delegating recruitment to permanent museum posts:[38] these were for museum assistants, assistant conservation officers and conservation officers.[39] This system was speeded up by the department taking responsibility for checks on a candidate's eligibility in accordance with instructions issued by the Commission. In straightforward cases this enabled the Commission to issue a certificate of qualification within two or three days of receiving a nomination.[40] In 1976 the Commission undertook a survey of delegated authority in recruitment and found it was being conducted in accordance with the principles and procedures laid down by the Commission.[41]

Fourth, the Fulton Committee made a number of recommendations for more flexible recruitment. It recommended that departments should have a greater influence on the selection of individuals, especially responsibility for recruiting specialist staff;[42] there should be more temporary appointments on short-term contracts,[43] and secondments from other employment;[44] ministers should be able to appoint specialist advisers on a temporary basis;[45] and there should be more provision for the direct appointment of late entrants.[46] All these recommendations were applied in practice, some with immediate effect: for example, the annual reports soon began to list growing numbers of senior appointments made during the year (there had always been some of these but they became much more numerous). In some respects, however, this led to difficulties and examples are given below of appointments made in accordance with these recommendations, but which later caused problems for the Commission.

Fifth, there was to be an inquiry by Cooper Brothers into ways of speeding up recruitment processes while ensuring that they remained both thorough and fair to candidates. Cooper Brothers worked closely with the Organisation and Methods staff at the CSD and their report was published in February 1969. By the end of the year the recommended changes (mainly for the greater use of computers, new procedures and restructuring the organisation of the Commission) had been implemented.[47] An example of the new procedures was that more extensive health declarations were introduced; these replaced medical examinations and recognised the improvement in the general health of the population.

Other consequences of the Fulton Report also had an impact on the work of the Commission. One of the most important of these was the decision to merge the administrative, executive and clerical classes, from the beginning of 1971, to form a single administration group. This was associated with a greatly expanded graduate entry into the civil service; the assistant principal grade was abolished; and a new grade of administration trainee (AT) created for generalist graduate recruits. The intention here was to provide some long-term strengthening of the civil service's middle management without diminishing the attraction of the service for the most able graduates.[48] The way in which this recruitment was arranged, and the personnel management details associated with it, may be seen as one of the early results of the institutional provision of having the Commission within the CSD. There were to be more than double the average number of graduates previously recruited by open competitions to positions of assistant principal; and many times more than the number of serving civil servants selected as assistant principals through limited competitions.[49] New tests for this wider graduate recruitment were developed by the department's Research Division. In the interest of a more effective and fairer open competition, a Davies Committee recommendation was also implemented at the same time, so that candidates with first-class honours or post-graduate degrees were no longer to be exempt from the qualifying examination.

Another recommendation in the Fulton Report, that had significant implications for the Commission, resulted in the new Principal Civil Service Pension Scheme, introduced on 1 June 1972. This meant that nearly all civil servants were covered by the scheme and therefore acquired pension entitlements; and the non-pensionable temporary civil servant disappeared. It will be remembered from chapter 2 that civil servants were pensionable only if they had a certificate of qualification issued by the Civil Service Commissioners. Under the previous scheme departments had recruited on non-pensionable 'temporary' terms and over a third of the civil service had, in practice, been recruited on such terms. This situation had been criticised by the Fulton Committee. The new arrangements broke the link between entitlement to a pension and certification by the Commissioners, but the Commissioners' certificate of qualification remained the hallmark of permanent recruitment. The new arrangements had significant implications: the Commission no longer needed to run limited competitions to enable temporary staff on unestablished terms to become established and eligible for a pension, although there would still be limited competitions for promotion; but new emphasis was placed on the importance of probation to ensure that staff were of the required standard before they were approved as permanent.[50]

These effects of the Fulton Report had a greater impact on the Commission than any previous inquiry into the civil service. Taken together, and seeing them in retrospect, they were the most important factors contributing to the Commission's decline. Nevertheless there were also other factors that made their mark on its work. For example, over the years from 1952 to 1991 the pattern of recruitment to the civil service was always affected by the general employment situation. When unemployment rose, the Commission was in a buyer's market, and when unemployment fell it was in a seller's market. These fluctuations became much more apparent than in the earlier years. Generally, when candidates failed to reach the required standard, vacancies were not filled: but this could not be the practice indefinitely. Where recruitment difficulties were experienced for an extended period (as with clerical assistants or clerical officers – see above) the Commission extended the age limits for candidates, adopted continuous recruitment and delegated responsibility for recruitment to departments. One year in which this was particularly noticeable was 1973, when the Commission delegated to 14 departments authority to recruit to Grades III and IV of the Professional and Technology Group and Related Grades (including architects, surveyors and draughtsmen). This added extra emphasis to the liaison work of the Commission, involving visits to departments and arrangements to monitor the recruitment procedures.

Orders in Council, which had played a major part in the constitutional basis and development of the Commission, continued to play their part in its latter days. One of the most important of these was the Civil Service Order in Council 1978 which, the Commissioners said, 'marked a significant development in the history of the prerogative powers exercised by the Civil Service Commissioners'.[51] It seems that the Commissioners received advice from the Treasury Solicitor that their control of fixed-term appointments was more limited than had previously been assumed. The purpose of the 1978 Order in Council was therefore to strengthen the Commissioners' powers. In fact it may have weakened them as far as secondments were concerned. This was because secondments were not normally seen as permanent (i.e. they were not for five years or longer and therefore not pensionable under the new Principal Civil Service Pension Scheme – see above). The implications of this became apparent in the case of Peter (now Lord) Levene.

As a result of the 1956 Order in Council (which was consolidated into the 1969 Order in Council when the CSD was set up) the Commissioners ceased to have control of temporary appointments, and temporary in this context was administratively interpreted as meaning appointments of less than five years.[52] Consequently departments were free to make all appointments of less than five years without necessarily observing the principles of open competition. In 1978, however, the arrangements were re-examined, primarily because of the appointment of special advisers, who were the personal nominees of Cabinet Ministers. From 1978 certification by the Commissioners was required for all permanent appointments and for fixed-term appointments exceeding 12 months: but the Order listed certain exceptions from this requirement, including the appointment of special advisers whose appointments would terminate 'at the end of an Administration'. In addition, under the new Civil Service Commission General Regulations, effective from 1 December 1978, departments were delegated power to appoint, following fair and open competition, specified junior staff on trial terms before certification by the Commissioners.

These arrangements remained uncontroversial and were thought to be clear and well understood until 1984 when Michael (now Lord) Heseltine, then Secretary of State for Defence, announced, with the approval of the Prime Minister, his intention to appoint Levene as Chief of Defence Procurement.[53] Levene, an industrialist, known to be a 'buccaneering entrepreneur with a flair for salesmanship'[54] had previously served as a part-time personal adviser to

Heseltine; but his new appointment involved secondment[55] from his firm to an established civil service position, because it was thought a more commercial approach to the job would result in better value for defence expenditure. He was being given a five-year contract, appointed without open competition and was to be paid a very generous salary.[56] This led to political controversy because Levene's term of appointment would exceed the life of the government elected in 1983, and he would have the status of a permanent secretary but with a salary package[57] of more than twice as much as the Head of the Civil Service. To avoid conflicts of interest, for 12 months he would not be able to take part in decisions involving the 11 companies for which he had been working before his appointment.[58]

It was said that as Levene's appointment was a secondment it did not require certification by the Commissioners. In fact, the First Commissioner was unaware of the appointment until the evening before Heseltine announced it;[59] and when the Treasury Solicitor was consulted he advised that it was an appointment that *did* require a certificate from the Commissioners. The problem was resolved, following discussion between officials in all the departments concerned, and culminated in a meeting between the Commissioners and Sir Robert (now Lord) Armstrong, then Head of the Civil Service, along with the Treasury Solicitor. The Commissioners took the matter very seriously, but Armstrong was equally anxious to do his best to see that Heseltine got his way.[60] The appointment then went ahead without the issue of a certificate and within clause 1(2)(g) of the 1982 Order in Council (it was clause 1(2)(f) of the 1978 Order) which provided for an appointment without a certificate, for a period not exceeding five years, if the Commissioners were satisfied on the desirability of the appointment 'without the issue of a certificate of qualification'.[61]

The importance of the Levene case in relation to the 1978 Order in Council has various perspectives. First, it was thought that secondments (not being 'permanent' and in practice usually for fairly short periods) did not require certificates. A five-year secondment, however, was exceptional and, without the normal recruitment procedure, could be interpreted as a political appointment. Furthermore, the appointment was made in a way that was not consistent with the intentions of the regulations for fair and open competition: David (now Lord) Owen said in the House of Commons that Levene was 'illegally appointed'.[62] In addition, the growth in the number of secondments, and ministerial involvement in them, was becoming more significant: they grew from 60 in 1977 to 150 in 1985.[63] Second, this particular appointment was made and announced without proper prior consultation with the Commissioners. The Commissioners had less than 24 hours' notice of Levene's appointment, and according to newspaper reports (e.g. *The Observer*, 31 March 1985) they were believed to have threatened collective resignation. Third, the appointment attracted considerable political and media attention because of the manner of the appointment and the salary involved. It also could not have done the Commissioners much good to have it reported in at least one press article that they had 'complied with' Levene's appointment.[64] A major and politically damaging incident was avoided – but barely so, if the newspaper coverage is taken into account. Fourth, the Levene case was the subject of a special report on secondments into the civil service, published within the Commission's 1985 annual report, and the regulations for secondments were revised (the new arrangements were introduced on 1 May 1986). The new procedure provided for the Civil Service Commissioners to dispense with tests of knowledge and ability if they had been satisfied 'that the candidate concerned should be appointed on secondment on the terms proposed'. Secondments at grade 3 level and above, or for more than five years, would in future have to involve the Commissioners.[65] In the Levene case, the original appointment was from 19 March 1985 for a period of up to five years; but it was later extended twice, taking the appointment to the end of March 1991 (with certificates of qualification issued accordingly).[66]

Levene's was not the only controversial case of an appointment to a senior civil service position of someone recruited to introduce more commercial attitudes into the civil service. Another case was that of A. Montague Alfred. In January 1982 Heseltine, then Secretary of State for the Environment, appointed Alfred, who previously had a distinguished business career, to be Second Permanent Secretary in the Department of the Environment and Chief Executive of the Property Services Agency (PSA). The appointment was for three years, apparently as a temporary appointment and therefore without the issue of a certificate from the Commissioners, and Heseltine's intention was that Alfred would reorganise the agency along more commercial lines.[67] In August 1983 Sir Geoffrey Wardale conducted an inquiry into fraud and dishonesty in the agency: the Wardale Report was then considered by the Public Accounts Committee.[68] In evidence, Wardale confirmed his findings, emphasising that, in the PSA, complacent attitudes to fraud were deep-rooted and widespread – indeed, they were the 'ethos of the organisation'.

Alfred welcomed the Wardale Report, but while he insisted that he was not complacent he also said in evidence that he could not be confident that there were no serious frauds within the organisation. He said that 99 per cent of PSA staff were doing a good job with commitment and dedication. The agency's net loss over a four-year period was £140k, which amounted to £35k a year, at a time when the agency was spending £800 million a year: the estimated loss was therefore 1/200th of 1 per cent.[69] Later, he added: 'We have a limited level of fraud and corruption in PSA...The problem is not going to go away...There is no chance, in realistic terms, that we are going to eliminate it.'[70] Robert Sheldon, chairman of the Select Committee, said that the committee found Alfred's approach complacent: it did not take into account the committee's view of corruption and 'the need to root it out and if necessary to spend more resources than might be appropriate in the private sector'.[71] When Patrick Jenkin, then Secretary of State for the Environment, learned of the line Alfred had taken before the Select Committee, Alfred's appointment was terminated 'by mutual agreement'.[72] Jenkin explained, in answer to a written Parliamentary Question, that Alfred's answers had not been consistent with the government's policy, which he had announced on 5 October 1983, on the Wardale Report.[73] It seems that the more commercial approach favoured by the government could not be easily assimilated within the civil service – at least, not until the creation of the 'Next Steps' agencies (see below).

In the late 1970s there were other changes following recommendations from official bodies. For example the 1977 Report from the Expenditure Committee recommended adding outside part-time Commissioners to the existing full-time civil servant membership of the Commission. The government accepted this recommendation and Miss M.P. Downs, Director of Personnel at F.W. Woolworth and Co. Ltd was appointed a Commissioner by an Order in Council of 24 October 1978: she was the first woman Commissioner. Her part-time appointment was followed by others in subsequent years: for example, Miss M.E. Sunderland, an independent business consultant and formerly Personnel Director of the UK Max Factor Group and Company became a part-time Commissioner in 1979.

Another consequence of the 1977 Expenditure Committee report was that the Commission investigated further allegations of bias in the selection of ATs by commissioning a re-assessment of AT selection arrangements. This review was undertaken by a committee chaired by Dr F.H. Allen, then First Civil Service Commissioner, and it was assisted by Professor F.R. Crane, Professor of Law at Queen Mary College, London, and by D. Mackenzie Davey, an industrial psychologist and consultant in selection.[74] In accordance with the Expenditure Committee's recommendations, the Commission published much fuller statistics which, they recognised, threw 'greater light on the statistical biases which the Committee identified'.[75] Two main conclusions emerged from these statistics in this and in subsequent years: first, that candidates with better degrees were more successful in the competition than those with poorer degrees; and, second, that graduates from Oxford and Cambridge were more successful than those from other universities.

The 1979 annual report began by drawing attention to a significant statistic. Although the Civil Service Commissioners continued to approve (and issue certificates for) most new appointments in the Home Civil Service and the Diplomatic Service, because of the delegation of junior grade recruitment to departments, the Commission itself carried out directly only about 8.5 per cent of the 1979 recruitment – at the level of executive officer and above and to equivalent grades of specialist and professional staff. By 1980 the staff in the Commission had been reduced to 400.

The year 1981 saw an organisational change for the Commission – but one of less significance than may at first have appeared. There had been a series of parliamentary and official reports on the Civil Service Department[76] (into which the Commission had been incorporated) then, on 12 November 1981 Margaret (later Lady) Thatcher, then Prime Minister, announced in Parliament that the Civil Service Department was to be abolished. The Commission was transferred to a new Management and Personnel Office within the Cabinet Office. There was no change in the Commission's independent responsibility for the selection by fair and open competition of civil servants to serve in government departments. The position after 1981 was therefore that the Commission came more clearly within the ambit of the Prime Minister's responsibility. Thatcher had previously been unhappy about a department (the CSD), which she found lacked credibility and power, speaking in the interests of the civil service and she had been particularly upset by civil service strikes.[77] The most significant change in 1981, however, was that the Commission's staff was reduced as a result of the new government's policy to reduce the size of the civil service. The government's policy was to reduce the civil service to 630,000 staff by 1 April 1984 (when the Conservative government was elected, in 1979, it was 732,000). To achieve this it immediately imposed a ban on recruitment from May to August 1979 – the busiest months of the year for recruiting school and university leavers. This had direct effects for some of the Commission's staff: for example, at the Civil Service Selection Board, most of the seconded resident assessors returned prematurely to their parent departments and more than half of the executive and clerical staff were redeployed to other parts of the Civil Service Department.[78] By 1 January 1982 the Commission's staff had been reduced to 315: it reported that internal reorganisation enabled the fewer staff to adjust to the new pattern of work.

A significant change from 1982 was a reversion to the exclusively 'fast-stream' entry for a smaller number of ATs: this, again, helped to reduce the staff needed for their recruitment. From 1983 a further reduction by 34 staff resulted from ending the remaining Commission responsibilities for recruitment delegated to departments.[79] For example, by the Civil Service Order in Council of 22 December 1982, departments became fully responsible for the grades listed (about 450 of them)[80] in the Schedule, and those appointments did not require a certificate of qualification from the Civil Service Commissioners. Another modest reduction in the Commission's work resulted from the disbandment, at the end of 1982, of the Commission's London Clerical Recruitment Unit, which had been set up in 1979 to recruit staff at clerical levels on behalf of some forty small departments in London.[81] By the end of 1982 the Commission's staff complement was 284.

The total number of civil servants during 1983 fell to 632,000, which was in accordance with the government's target to reduce the total number to 630,000 by 1 April 1984. In November 1983 the government announced a further reduction – to 590,000 by 1988. The Commission's own staff was reduced during 1983 to 260. In 1983 the Commission handled 108,402 applications for 6,250 vacancies. At that time there were also a number of reviews into its work, including Sir Alec Atkinson's review of Fast Steam Graduate Entrants to the Home Civil Service,[82] E.V. Adams' Review of Recruitment of Graduate Tax Inspectors and a 'scrutiny' of the Commission's work more generally.[83]

The late 1980s saw significant change for the Commission. On 1 October 1987 those functions of the Cabinet Office (Management and Personnel Office) which were concerned directly with financial management, manpower, pay and financial conditions of service were transferred to the Treasury. The Commission, responsible for selection policy and practice, remained in the Cabinet Office, within the new sub-department of the Office of the Minister for the Civil Service (OMCS) – but it should be noted that the responsibility for recruitment policy (acquired by the First Commissioner as a result of the Fulton Committee's recommendations) was transferred back to the Treasury. During 1987 the Commission produced a Recruitment Handbook, which brought together rules and guidance on civil service recruitment procedures, gave advice on how to use the Commission's services and set out recommended practices for devolved recruitment.[84] In 1988 the Commission processed 92,779 applications, which resulted in 9,859 appointments:[85] this decline in activity was the result of delegating about 85 per cent of recruitment to departments. In other respects, however, there were new demands. For example, in 1989, 21 people from outside the civil service were recruited to posts at grade 5 level and above. In the 1989 annual report there was also the first reference to the Commission working 'closely with departments which have used executive search consultants to supplement the results of open advertisement'.[86] The 1990–91 annual report reported 11 schemes where the Commissioners and departments used search consultants 'for attracting people not currently actively looking for a job'.[87]

The first executive agencies under the government's 'Next Steps' initiative were created in 1988, to carry out the executive functions of government. This policy had its immediate origins in the 1988 Report to the Prime Minister from the Efficiency Unit: *Improving Management in Government: The Next Steps*,[88] which made proposals for the government's next steps in modernising and improving the civil service. Its more general origins were, however, in the Thatcher government's determination to make government more efficient, according to an ideology which regarded business values and business methods as the most productive and preferred ideology.[89]

In 1985, following a review of executive officer recruitment, which had been failing to meet the number of vacancies, the Inland Revenue and the Department of Health and Social Security began, as an experiment, recruiting their own executive officers and equivalent grades. By the Order in Council of 1991 recruitment to all grades below grade 7 (formerly principal) was transferred to departments and executive agencies. Recruitment to the civil service was being adapted to the changed market of suitable recruits (especially graduates who had not achieved the highest honours). Instead of civil service careers many of them entered other employment, and they were not interested in having one career for life.

The demise of the Civil Service Commission[90]

It was the government's next steps programme that finally killed the Civil Service Commission. The government believed that most of the Commission's work fitted the agency approach: it was no longer a core function of government, and it was thought to be well suited to business values and business methods. The Commission was abolished and its work split between a small office serving the

Civil Service Commissioners and an executive agency. The agency, Recruitment and Assessment Services (RAS), consisting of the staff at Basingstoke and CSSB in London, offered a recruitment service on a repayment basis to departments and agencies for the grades for whose recruitment they were responsible – i.e. below civil service grade 7. The Civil Service Commissioners remained responsible for recruitment above grade 7 and for the fast-stream entrants: this amounted to less than 5 per cent of recruits. In the 1990–91 annual report, the Commissioners emphasised the clearer customer/contractor relationship that was represented by RAS, and also mentioned that the customers of RAS were to include the Commissioners.

The Commissioners continued to advise ministers on the basis of the rules for recruitment (to be applied by RAS and the departments of government) but their main executive task was to monitor the way the rules were applied. 'The Recruitment Handbook' was withdrawn and replaced by a 'Practitioners Guide'. Certification was replaced by a requirement for the Commissioners' 'written approval' before appointment. These changes were made by Orders in Council of 5 February 1991: one for the Home Civil Service and a separate one for the Diplomatic Service.

The Commissioners acquired a new legal duty to advise the Minister for the Civil Service on the rules governing departmental recruitment and to monitor their application. It was, however, decided that the monitoring function would be 'light-handed, economical and systems-based'.[91] Because the Office of the Civil Service Commissioners was so small (in 1991–92 it had 20 staff based at Basingstoke and two staff in London)[92] independent consultants were appointed to carry out audits of recruitment policies and practices to ensure that the requirements of the Recruitment Code were being observed.[93] The 1991–92 annual report recorded that delegated recruitment had extended so far – to departments and agencies, and within them to regional and local managers – that there were over 3,000 'accountable units' (which might increase with further delegation that would also require monitoring).[94] The monitoring was, in fact, arranged on a three-year cyclical programme, starting in 1992, of a sample of comparable accountable units in departments and agencies and a sample of individual recruitment schemes. The task of monitoring was more demanding than may at first have appeared because departments and agencies were free to handle the selection procedures themselves or to contract them out to selection consultants.[95] In 1994 the 1991 Orders in Council were amended to permit the Commissioners to authorise others to perform the monitoring function.[96] From 1 October 1994 the monitoring was contracted to P-E International plc. The staff of the Office of the Civil Service Commissioners was then reduced to eight and, from January 1995, relocated from Basingstoke to London.[97] By the 1995–96 annual report, with the transfer of further responsibilities to the Cabinet Office, the staff complement was reduced to five and a half.[98]

In the immediate period after the 1991 Order in Council, the Civil Service Commissioners continued to use RAS for recruitment to senior grades and posts, and for the fast-stream entries. The Commissioners noted, in their 1991–92 report, the increasing use of (and the benefits of using) executive search consultants. For a variety of other appointments, where recruitment was part of more extensive delegation to departments, they stated that as long as the Commissioners' requirements were met, departments could do the recruitment themselves, or use the services of RAS, or any other suitable agency.

Fast-stream appointments therefore at first appeared to continue as usual because CSSB was operated by RAS and the Final Selection Board continued to be chaired by a Commissioner or former Commissioner. In July 1993, however, a feasibility study of market testing was commissioned from the Human Resources Centre, Cranfield School of Management. The consultants reported in December and said that departmental ownership of the competition should be strengthened. A consortium of major departmental customers, led by the Cabinet Office, was then established as a first step to departmental ownership (rather than its being seen as belonging to the Commissioners and RAS).[99] These recommendations were implemented in a new Order in Council of 15 March 1995. From that time there were further delegations of senior recruitment to departments and agencies; departments were given responsibility for monitoring their individual recruitment units; and the Commissioners audited departmental recruitment by 'a more top–down approach'[100] (which meant they would only look at individual competitions if they decided there was a need for a spot check); the Commissioners' approval for fast-stream recruitment was no longer required; and the Commissioners issued a new Recruitment Code. This Code set out the principles and the reasons behind them to enable individuals engaged on recruitment 'to make sound decisions in every case instead of mechanistically following rules which can never be comprehensive'.[101] Although the responsibilities of the Commissioners were changed from 1995, including some modest additions (for example, the addition of responsibilities for appeals under the Civil Service Code), from 15 March 1995 the First Commissioner was no longer to be appointed from within the civil service, and the position became part-time in recognition of the removal of fast-stream responsibilities.

On 23 November 1995 it was announced that RAS would be privatised.[102] This followed a period in which the government looked at RAS in accordance with the government's 'prior options' approach. The essence of this approach was to ask (in the words of Heseltine, then Deputy Prime Minister) 'whether the services that are being provided need to be provided and if they do whether they should be provided in the public or the private sector'.[103] In making its decision the government had been advised on financial feasibility and timing by Coopers and Lybrand, the management consultants. It was believed by the government that selling RAS would free it to compete for business in a wider market; Heseltine explained to the House of Lords Select Committee on the Public Service that this sort of privatisation was 'a very exciting, wealth creating, liberating process'.[104] Roger Freeman, then Chancellor of the Duchy of Lancaster, regarded the government's prior options approach and its attitude to privatisation as a political philosophy.[105]

After RAS was privatised and purchased by Capita Group plc, the General Fast Stream Development Programme was contracted out to Capita RAS Limited. For the first three years following the privatisation of RAS the Final Selection Board was retained, though the chairman was a departmental establishment officer instead of a Civil Service Commissioner. The policy framework for the fast-stream was the responsibility of the Customer Consortium led by the Office of Public Service. In 1998, ministers in the new Labour government announced their decision to return the selection stages of fast-stream recruitment to direct civil service management. The private sector would, however, be able to tender competitively for such support services as advertising, managing applications and administering the Qualifying Test.[106] The Civil Service Selection Board returned to direct management by the Cabinet Office with the start of the 2002 recruitment schemes; it was located at 67 Tufton Street, which was specially refitted to house a purpose-built assessment centre with eight assessment suites.[107] In 2000, the Civil Service Management Board agreed that the Final Selection Board should be abolished from the 2001 recruitment scheme, for most options within the General Fast Stream, and that most of the Final Selection Board functions could be met in other ways.[108]

The period from 1952 was characterised by decline: a watershed was reached with the Fulton Report, but the end came because of the increasing emphasis on a private sector approach to management in government. The Civil Service Commission was the product of nineteenth-century concerns, primarily for greater efficiency in government, for the elimination of patronage and to develop unity in a civil service that was fragmentary. Indeed, before 1855 and after 1991 it may be argued that conditions were not conducive for the existence of a single civil service; instead there were civil or public servants within various departments (and agencies). After 1991 a case could well be argued to demonstrate that there was, from that date, a decline in efficiency, an increase in cost and the reintroduction of scope for political influence and patronage. The reasoning behind the creation and development of the Commission was very similar to the reasoning motivating its demise.

Notes

1 Lord Bridges, *The Treasury* (London: Allen & Unwin, 1964), p. 180.
2 *Report of Her Majesty's Civil Service Commissioners for the period 1st April 1949 to 31st March 1952, Being the Eighty-Fifth Report of the Commissioners* (London: HMSO, 1953).
3 Ibid.
4 K.M. Reader, *The Civil Service Commission, 1855–1975* (London: HMSO, 1981), pp. 49–50.
5 Ibid., p. 55.
6 PRO/CSC5/1226.
7 PRO/CSC5/1251, Extract from D.E.'s minute of 3 April 1964.
8 *Report of Her Majesty's Civil Service Commissioners for the period 1st January to 31st December 1965, being the Ninety-ninth Report of the Commissioners* (London: HMSO, 1966), and Civil Service Commission, *Annual Report 1981, for the period 1 January to 31 December being the*

Hundred and Fifteenth Report of the Commissioners (Basingstoke: Civil Service Commission, 1982).
9 PRO/CSC5/1201; PRO/CSC5/1231; PRO/CSC5/1251; PRO/CSC5/1252.
10 Civil Service Commission, *Annual Report 1967, for the period 1 January to 31 December, being the Hundred and First Report of the Commissioners* (London: HMSO, 1968), p. 11.
11 Civil Service Commission, *Annual Report 1969, for the period 1 January to 31 December, being the Hundred and Third Report of the Commissioners* (London: Civil Service Commission, 1970).
12 K.M. Reader, *The Civil Service Commission*, p. 55. See also *CSD Report: First Report of the Civil Service Department* (London: HMSO, 1970).
13 *Report of Her Majesty's Civil Service Commissioners for the period 1 January to 31 December 1964, being the ninety-eighth Report of the Commissioners* (London: HMSO, 1965).
14 Civil Service Commission, *Annual Report 1966 for the period 1 January to 31 December, being the Hundredth Report of the Commissioners* (London: HMSO, 1967).
15 *Annual Report 1964*.
16 *The Times*, 20 April 1948.
17 J.P.W. Mallalieu, *Passed to You, Please: Britain's Red-Tape Machine at War* (London: Victor Gollancz, 1942).
18 Fabian Society, *The Reform of the Higher Civil Service: A Report by a Special Committee for the Fabian Society* (London: Fabian Publications in conjunction with Victor Gollancz, 1947).
19 Bosworth Monck, *How the Civil Service Works* (London: Phoenix House, 1952).
20 Fabian Society (A Fabian Group), *The Administrators: The Reform of the Civil Service*, Fabian Tract 355 (London: Fabian Society, 1964).
21 R.K. Kelsall, *Higher Civil Servants in Britain, from 1870 to the Present Day* (London: Routledge & Kegan Paul, 1955).
22 Thomas Balogh, 'The Apotheosis of the Dilettante', in Hugh Thomas (ed.), *The Establishment* (London: Anthony Blond, 1959).
23 Brian Chapman, *British Government Observed* (London: Allen & Unwin, 1963).
24 *Ninth Report from the Select Committee on Estimates, Session 1947–48: The Civil Service Commission*, HC 203, 205 (London: HMSO, 1948).
25 *Royal Commission on the Civil Service, 1953–55* (Priestley Report), Cmd. 9613 (London: HMSO, 1955).
26 *Sixth Report from the Estimates Committee, Session 1964–65: Recruitment to the Civil Service*, HC 308 (London: HMSO, 1965).
27 *Annual Report 1965*.
28 K.M. Reader, *The Civil Service Commission*, p. 51.
29 PRO/CSC5/1349.
30 *The Civil, Service, Vol. 1, Report of the Committee, 1966–68* (Fulton Report), Cmnd. 3638 (London: HMSO, 1968).
31 Civil Service Commission, *Annual Report 1968, for the period 1 January to 31 December, being the Hundred and Second Report of the Commissioners* (London: Civil Service Commission, 1969).
32 *Annual Report 1969*.
33 *Fulton Report*, para. 62.
34 *Annual Report 1969*, p. 13.
35 Ibid.
36 Civil Service Commission, *Annual Report 1978, for the period 1 January to 31 December, being the Hundred and Twelfth Report of the Commissioners* (Basingstoke: Civil Service Commission, 1979).
37 *Annual Report 1969*, p. 22.
38 *CSD Report 1970–71: Second Report of the Civil Service Department* (London: HMSO, 1971).

39 Civil Service Commission, *Annual Report 1971, for the period 1 January to 31 December, being the Hundred and Fifth Report of the Commissioners* (Basingstoke: Civil Service Commission, 1972).
40 Civil Service Commission, *Annual Report 1970, for the period 1 January to 31 December, being the Hundred and Fourth Report of the Commissioners* (Basingstoke: Civil Service Commission, 1971), p. 23.
41 Civil Service Commission, *Annual Report 1976, for the period 1 January to 31 December, being the Hundred and Tenth Report of the Commissioners* (Basingstoke: Civil Service Commission, 1977).
42 *Fulton Report*, para. 73.
43 Ibid., para. 125.
44 Ibid., para. 128.
45 Ibid., para. 129.
46 Ibid., para. 124.
47 *Annual Report 1969*.
48 *CSD Report 1970–71: Second Report*, para. 78.
49 *Annual Report 1970*.
50 Civil Service Commission, *Annual Report 1972, for the period 1 January to 31 December, being the Hundred and Sixth Report of the Commissioners* (Basingstoke: Civil Service Commission, 1973), pp. 13–14.
51 *Annual Report 1978*.
52 Ibid.
53 70 HC Deb., 6s., col. 206w (19 December 1984).
54 *The Observer*, 31 March 1985.
55 73 HC Deb., 6s., col. 186w (13 February 1985).
56 75 HC Deb., 6s., col. 569w (21 March 1985). See also *Fifth Report from the Defence Committee, session 1984–85, The Appointment and Objectives of the Chief of Defence Procurement*, HC 430 (London: HMSO 1985).
57 75 HC Deb., 6s., cols. 570w and 981 (21 March 1985).
58 75 HC Deb., 6s., col. 569w (21 March 1985).
59 75 HC Deb., 6s., col. 569w (21 March 1985).
60 Interview with Nevil Johnson (Civil Service Commissioner, part-time 1982–85).
61 *The Times*, 19, 20, 21, 22, 25 March 1985; *The Observer*, 31 March 1985. See also Peter Hennessy, *Whitehall* (London: Secker & Warburg, 1989), pp. 371–3.
62 75 HC Deb., 6s., col. 981 (21 March 1985).
63 Hennessy, *Whitehall*, p. 373.
64 *The Observer*, 31 March 1985.
65 Civil Service Commission, *Annual Report 1985, for the period 1 January to 31 December, being the Hundred and Nineteenth Report of the Commissioners* (Basingstoke: Civil Service Commission, 1986), pp. 7–9 and 54.
66 Civil Service Commission, *Annual Report 1989: Report of the Civil Service Commissioners to Her Majesty the Queen for the period 1 January to 31 December 1989, being the Hundred and Twenty-Third Report* (Basingstoke: Civil Service Commission, 1990), p. 36.
67 *The Times*, 14 March 1984.
68 *Twenty-sixth Report from the Committee of Public Accounts, session 1983–84: Fraud in the Property Services Agency; The Wardale Report; System Controls in District Works Offices*, HC 295 (London: HMSO, 1984).
69 Ibid., Q. 2,241.
70 Ibid., Q. 2,342.
71 Ibid., Q. 2,307.
72 Ibid., p. v. See also *The Times*, 13 March 1984.
73 56 HC Deb., 6s., col. 75w (13 March 1984).

74 *Report of the Committee on the Selection Procedure for the Recruitment of Administration Trainees* (Basingstoke: Civil Service Commission, 1979).
75 *Annual Report 1978*, p. 12.
76 For further details, see Richard A. Chapman, 'The Rise and Fall of the CSD', *Policy and Politics*, 11(1), 1983, 41–61.
77 Margaret Thatcher, *The Downing Street Years* (London: Harper Collins, 1993), pp. 48, 139.
78 *Annual Report 1979*.
79 *Annual Report 1981*.
80 Civil Service Commission, *Annual Report 1982, for the period 1 January to 31 December, being the Hundred and Sixteenth Report of the Commissioners* (Basingstoke: Civil Service Commission, 1983).
81 Ibid.
82 Report by Sir Alec Atkinson, *Selection of Fast-Stream Graduate Entrants to the Home Civil Service, the Diplomatic Service and the Tax Inspectorate; and of Candidates from within the Service* (London: Management and Personnel Office, 1983).
83 *Annual Report 1983*.
84 Civil Service Commission, *Annual Report 1987, for the period 1 January to 31 December, being the Hundred and Twenty First Report of the Commissioners* (Basingstoke: Civil Service Commission, 1988), p. 22.
85 Civil Service Commission, *Annual Report 1988, Report of the Civil Service Commissioners to Her Majesty the Queen for the period 1 January to 31 December 1988, being the Hundred and Twenty-Second Report of the Commissioners* (Basingstoke: Civil Service Commission, 1989).
86 *Annual Report 1989*, p. 7.
87 *Civil Service Commissioners' Report 1990–91, Report of the Civil Service Commissioners to Her Majesty the Queen for the period 1 January 1990 to 31 March 1991, being the Hundred and Twenty-Fourth Report* (Basingstoke: Office of the Civil Service Commissioners, 1991), p. 9.
88 Efficiency Unit, *Improving Management in Government: The Next Steps, Report to the Prime Minister* (London: HMSO, 1988).
89 For further details see Richard A. Chapman, *The Treasury in Public Policy-Making* (London: Routledge, 1997), Ch. 4; and Barry J. O'Toole and Grant Jordan (eds.), *Next Steps: Improving Management in Government?* (Aldershot: Dartmouth, 1995).
90 The word 'demise' in this context was first used in the *Civil Service Commissioners' Report 1991–92, Report of the Civil Service Commissioners to Her Majesty the Queen for the period 1 April 1991 to 31 March 1992, being the Hundred and Twenty-Fifth Report* (Basingstoke: Office of the Civil Service Commissioners, 1992), p. 11.
91 *Annual Report, 1990–91*, p. 3.
92 *Annual Report 1991–92*.
93 *Civil Service Commissioners' Recruitment Code* (London: Office of the Civil Service Commissioners, 1995), p. 22.
94 *Annual Report 1991–92*, p. 9.
95 *Civil Service Commissioners' Report 1992–93, Report of the Civil Service Commissioners to Her Majesty the Queen for the period 1 April 1992 to 31 March 1993* (Basingstoke: Office of the Civil Service Commissioners, 1993), p. 5.
96 *Civil Service Commissioners' Report 1993–94, Report of the Civil Service Commissioners to Her Majesty the Queen for the period 1 April 1993 to 31 March 1994* (Basingstoke: Office of the Civil Service Commissioners), p. 17.
97 *Civil Service Commissioners' Report 1994–95, Report of the Civil Service Commissioners to Her Majesty the Queen for the period 1 April 1994 to 31 March 1995* (London: Office of the Civil Service Commissioners, 1995), pp. 3, 20.
98 *Civil Service Commissioners' Annual Report 1995–96, Report of the Civil Service Commissioners to Her Majesty the Queen for the period 1 April 1995 to 31 March 1996* (London: Office of the Civil Service Commissioners, 1996), p. 5.

99 *Annual Report 1993–94*, p. 15.
100 The auditing of departmental recruitment systems is explained in *Annual Report 1994–95*, p. 20.
101 *Annual Report 1994–95*, p. 5.
102 267 HC Deb., 6s., cols. 233–4w (23 November 1995).
103 *Select Committee on the Public Service, House of Lords, Session 1995–96, First Report, The Government's Proposals for the Privatisation of Recruitment and Assessment Services (RAS) with evidence*, HL 109 (London: HMSO, 1996), Q. 442.
104 Ibid., Q. 457.
105 Ibid., Q. 19.
106 *Civil Service Fast Stream Recruitment Report 1999–2000* (London: Cabinet Office, 2000).
107 *Civil Service Fast Stream Recruitment Report 2001–2002* (London: Cabinet Office, 2002).
108 *Civil Service Fast Stream Recruitment Report 1999–2000*.

Part II

COMPETITION, CONFIDENTIALITY AND COMPLACENCY

5

THE GROWTH OF WORKING RELATIONSHIPS

The Civil Service Commission had a unique role in the British system of government. It was an independent department, and for most of its life its head, the First Civil Service Commissioner, had the status of a deputy secretary. The Commissioners were appointed by Order in Council 'during the pleasure of Her Majesty' and, as far as their specific duties were concerned, they were independent of the regular civil service. This meant that no one could direct their decision-making or change their decisions on issuing certificates of qualification. The staff of the department, however, were regular civil servants, appointed as a result of normal recruitment procedures and serving in accordance with the standard terms and conditions of service for their grades, as promulgated by the Treasury, and the requirements of their department.

Whether the Commission was, in effect, a sub-department, or 'an outlying department of the Treasury' (as Professor Lawrence Lowell put it in 1908),[1] can only be determined by the context of any particular issue or sphere of responsibility. The Treasury was the government's policy-making department in matters of personnel management. In comparison, the Commission had mainly an operational role.[2] In some contexts, the Commission may be seen as the personnel recruitment department for the whole of central government (and, in practice, for much more as well). In formal terms the Commission's relations with the Treasury were originally determined in the 21 May 1855 Order in Council which created the Commission and gave it power to carry out its stated duties to examine candidates and issue certificates of qualification and, 'subject to the Approval of the Commissioners of Her Majesty's Treasury, to appoint from Time to Time such Assistant Examiners and others as may be required to assist them'. That Order in Council was followed, over the years, by numerous others. Throughout those orders there were references to the Treasury, whose consent, approval or sanction was required for certain actions or orders of the Commission.[3] In practical experience the Treasury stood above all other departments of government because it held the purse-strings; had an elite staff of selected individuals, usually transferred from other departments; and was the department of the Prime Minister in his capacity as First Lord of the Treasury. Moreover, as far as the Commission was concerned, it was normally Treasury ministers who responded in Parliament when questions were raised about its activities. On those occasions, the ministers were always briefed by Treasury officials, though they normally consulted staff in the Commission before finalising their brief.

Even if, in the above respects, the Commission might appear to have been an outlying department of the Treasury, in other respects it had distinct and separate responsibilities. The Commission's special responsibilities were for examining and allocating the staff required by individual departments of central government. This involved allocating new staff to departments after they had been declared successful in competitions for what were known as the general Treasury classes (e.g. clerical, executive or administrative staff) and also examining the numerous other staff for the specialist or departmental classes, whose qualifications related to professions or areas of work to be found only within particular departments. As a result the Commission had regular contact with all departments as well as with a considerable number of government agencies and other institutions for which it recruited.

In addition to the large number of relationships that developed with the numerous departments and agencies, the Commission was the centre of an extensive network of contacts with schools, universities, professional associations, trades unions and interest groups of various sorts. Many of the contacts in this network required the Commission's staff to exercise diplomacy, persuasion and sensitivity. Often, this was because the Commission depended on co-operation with others; it had to encourage them to help it when it had no power to direct; and it had to depend on opportunities to get good value from only very moderate expenditure of public money.

The purpose of this chapter is to demonstrate and explain how this large and varied assortment of relationships worked out in practice. Sometimes they developed in accordance with the requirements of Orders in Council or subordinate regulations, sometimes they were part of the general personnel work within government, sometimes they were simply features of the Commission's informal organisation with institutions, interests or groups whose co-operation was essential if the Commission was to be successful in its work.

Relations with the Treasury

Throughout its life the Civil Service Commission was dependent in a variety of ways on its relationship with the Treasury. As early as 20 June 1855 the Civil Service Commissioners set the tone of that relationship by writing to Sir Charles Trevelyan, then Assistant Secretary to the Treasury, that: 'the Civil Service Commissioners have made the following arrangements for carrying into effect the duties entrusted to them, subject to their Lordships approval'.[4] They went on to say that they had selected James Spedding as their Secretary and Horace Mann as their Registrar; and they made suggestions for the salaries for both men. They had been provided with an office in Manchester Buildings and were proceeding to appoint an office keeper and a messenger. Trevelyan replied on 25 June

THE GROWTH OF WORKING RELATIONSHIPS

approving the appointments, including the pay, and saying the Paymaster General had been directed to pay the salaries quarterly.

The relationship of the Commissioners with Trevelyan was primarily the result of the Treasury's responsibility for public expenditure but also reflected the personal interest of Trevelyan who had written the report which was instrumental in setting up the Commission. Consequently the Commissioners seem to have provided Trevelyan with more detail of their plans than might have been provided to any other person in Trevelyan's position.[5] This was apparently a good tactic because on 20 September 1855 they were complaining of the inadequacy of their accommodation, and also outlining their need for another clerk – and to substantiate their request they provided details of their growing workload. The Commission then asked for, and was allocated, more suitable accommodation in Gateway House, the Sanctuary, Westminster.

On 14 November 1855 the Commissioners had an interview with Trevelyan about their staffing needs, which had become more serious because Spedding had resigned. Trevelyan apparently asked to be kept informed.[6] The Commissioners then appointed J.G. Maitland to succeed Spedding, and told the Treasury. Trevelyan replied that their Lordships approved the appointment of Maitland. It seems that the early experience of relations between the Treasury and the Commission set the scene for later contacts, including many of a rather routine and detailed kind, such as the cost of coal and wood to heat the Commission's accommodation.[7] From its early years the Commission therefore assumed a subordinate role towards the Treasury, but that is not surprising in the circumstances: at the outset, the Commission was on a somewhat temporary basis, with unpaid Commissioners and was dependent on the Treasury to authorise even minor expenditure.

A few years later, when the Commission was being placed on a more permanent basis, the Treasury decided to reconstitute it. The First Commissioner was to be paid a salary, and with him there were to be associated 'one or two gentlemen of eminence whose services may be tendered gratuitously'.[8] In the early years of the Commission, the Commissioners were apparently appointed by the Prime Minister personally. Sometimes they were political appointments, but by the interwar period of the twentieth century it is clear that Sir James Rae, then head of the Treasury Establishments Divisions, took a leading role in making senior appointments, by proposing to the Head of the Civil Service names who were subsequently approved by the Prime Minister.[9]

Although in 1948 Sir Percival Waterfield said he did not know by what method he was selected to be First Commissioner,[10] he also said of the appointment of other Commissioners that it could be said, 'with some confidence', that when there was a vacancy for a Commissioner, 'the best man is proposed by the Treasury for the consideration of the First Commissioner'.[11] In fact, at that time, the senior officials in Whitehall were not numerous and they tended to know each other.[12] It is not surprising, therefore, that First Commissioners, on appointment, were often well known to, and had good working relationships with, staff in the Treasury.

Indeed, in a number of cases they had worked there themselves. This was, for example, true of R.S. (later Sir Roderick) Meiklejohn who, prior to serving as First Commissioner from 1927 to 1939, had been Deputy Controller of Supply Services in the Treasury;[13] Waterfield, First Commissioner from 1939 to 1951, who had been principal assistant secretary in the Treasury;[14] A.P. (later Sir Paul) Sinker, First Commissioner from 1951 to 1954, who served in the Treasury from 1945 to 1950; and J.J.B. (later Sir John, then Lord) Hunt, First Commissioner from 1967 to 1971, who served there from 1962 to 1967. Such backgrounds of First Commissioners may to some extent explain the flattering comments sometimes made towards the Treasury. For example, in 1944 Waterfield explained:

> the relations between us really boil down to a reliance on common-sense and an assumption that, when any question of doubt arises, we, as experienced Civil Servants, will always find it prudent to consult the Treasury, in view of their central position and their vast stores of wisdom and experience of administration.[15]

After the Second World War, Waterfield said that the Commission was kept fully informed by the Treasury. It was informed, for example, through minutes and reports, of any Treasury committee concerned with the structure of the civil service or any part of it; and if any such body was concerned with recruitment the Commission was represented on it. Waterfield said: 'the relationship between ourselves and the Treasury is very intimate and friendly and constant',[16] and 'we are kept fully informed by the Treasury and are given every opportunity to express an opinion from the standpoint of the recruiting authority'.[17] Similarly, in 1965 Sir George Abell said that communication between the Commission and the Treasury, and between the Commission and other departments was at 'many levels': 'If it is a question which seems of primary importance to us I might write myself to someone; but at all levels down to executive officer level there may be correspondence between the departments, telephone messages and so on.'[18]

The relationship between the Commission and the Treasury became particularly close when, soon after his appointment as First Commissioner, Sinker, who succeeded Waterfield in 1951, asked to receive copies of, and occasionally to contribute to, the Treasury Establishment Report (which was a sort of internal Treasury newsletter). Agreeing that this would be arranged, T. (later Sir Thomas) Padmore replied:

> we like to think that the Commission is, if not formally inside the circle, at any rate so closely linked with us that there are very few secrets which we have from them. We shall therefore be very glad to put you on the list and to receive your contributions.

There were, however, two conditions. First, that the Commission should take no offence if the report included comments about the Commission 'couched in rather less suitable language than would be usual if the author remembered that the Commission were going to receive it'. Second, that the report should only be seen by Sinker, W.H. Fisher and C.J. Hayes (then respectively Secretary and Director of Examinations at the Commission) – because the report contained 'secret matter (e.g. inside information on the progress of wage claims)'.[19] As a result of this arrangement, from time to time the report subsequently contained items of news from the Commission.

Fisher thought Sinker made this arrangement because, at the time, he felt the Commission was so very near to the Treasury that it was almost a Treasury Division. Fisher also thought that, later, Sinker's feelings changed. L.N. (later Sir Laurence, then Lord) Helsby, who succeeded Sinker, had reservations about the arrangement concerning the Establishment Report. He said that he thought it was anomalous and served no good purpose, but it could encourage in the Treasury the impression that the Commission operated 'as a sort of supernumerary Treasury Division'.[20] After discussion, however, it was decided that it was best to let the arrangement 'run quietly on'.[21]

These public statements of the close official and personal contacts between staff in the Commission and the Treasury are, nevertheless, reflections of only part of the relationships that actually existed. Two examples of the Commission attempting to assert its independence illustrate this: they relate to arrangements for medical examinations and studies of the Commission by the Treasury Organisation and Methods (O and M) division. Brief outlines of these follow.

In carrying out their responsibilities concerning the health of candidates the Commission had to be satisfied that a candidate was fit to do the particular job applied for, was likely to be available for regular service in the immediate future and was likely to retain mechanical fitness and regularity up to the normal age of retirement.[22] This assessment involved medical examination together with consideration by a case-examiner in the Commission. The case-examiner also dealt with the nationality, age and character of candidates. Before the Second World War, case-examiners required six months training before being given delegated authority, but after the war staff difficulties resulted in them receiving only two weeks training and the development of written notes which became known as the Case Examiners' Manual.

In 1950 Dr W.E. Chiesman, the Treasury Medical Adviser, who had responsibility for the health of civil servants throughout their career, said that his service suffered from the 'lack of precise knowledge of the procedure and practice of the Civil Service Commissioners at the stage of entry'.[23] He therefore proposed that a member of his staff should be associated with the Commissioners when they were assessing the health of non-industrial candidates. Waterfield did not accept the proposal because, he said, the constitutional position was for the acceptance or rejection of a candidate to be in the hands of an independent body (i.e. the Commissioners), and the Commissioners could not accept a controlling influence on their policy. He emphasised the constitutional position, and explained that the Commissioners were already co-operating by providing information (but not the medical reports) about every candidate whose medical condition might be a danger to himself or his colleagues. They did, however, agree to introduce a procedure that would in future be more helpful to the Treasury Medical Adviser, and soon afterwards a Treasury committee chaired by Padmore was set up to consider civil service medical staffs.

The Padmore Committee was impressed by the arguments put forward by the Treasury Medical Adviser in favour of closer co-operation between the Treasury and the Commission. The committee said that the arrangements for closer co-operation 'should be pressed forward as far as possible. Indeed it may be possible and desirable in time for the Treasury Medical Adviser to provide the Civil Service Commission with all the medical advice it needs'.

This stimulated a flurry of minute-writing activity in the Commission. Fisher, acting as devil's advocate, queried whether it really mattered if the Treasury Medical Adviser became also the Commission's adviser in all cases, if certain safeguards were also adopted. G.C. Heselden wrote nine pages to convey his concern. He argued that the existing system of a panel of eminent qualified doctors offering advise to the Commission, doctors examining candidates and lay officials making decisions in accordance with their 'Manual' was efficient and economical. If all the decisions on freedom from disease were to be made in the Treasury Medical Service the decisions would have to be made by doctors – and that would result in delays, a considerable expansion of staff and doctors making routine decisions and doing routine clerical work that did not require their professional expertise. Heselden referred to a 55-minute tirade he had recently endured from the Treasury Medical Adviser against the Commission. He argued that if the proposal were to be adopted the Treasury Medical Adviser would have to see candidates' files to appreciate details provided by referees and that would be unacceptable in terms of the Commission's strict rules on confidentiality. Someone in the Commission (probably Fisher) noted on Heselden's minute: 'We must be careful not to let Dr Chiesman see this minute!' R.J. Simpson agreed with Heselden and stressed that if the Treasury Medical Adviser were to make decisions on the fitness of candidates he would have to consider all the evidence in the candidate's file and he strongly believed that the file should not leave the Office of the Commissioners. He also thought that if the Commissioners gave in and delegated some of their responsibilities it would be the thin end of the wedge and there would be further requests from the Treasury Medical Adviser for more power based on his opinion that the Commissioners, as laymen, could not adjudicate efficiently on medical matters.

At a meeting in the Treasury on 25 April 1951, attended by Fisher and Sinker, the Treasury Medical Adviser argued that he doubted whether the Commission's medical examination on entry served any useful purpose and in his opinion their examinations must be expensive. Sinker recalled that his predecessor, Waterfield, had argued for their abolition and hoped the Treasury would consider the possibility carefully. This led to a compromise position whereby candidates would make a health declaration before entry and, where necessary, there would be a medical examination later. Sinker stressed the importance of the Commission retaining the right of making the final decision in all cases, 'as the ultimate safeguard against patronage in this as in other fields'.[24] This compromise position became the standard practice. The Commission retained final responsibility in all health matters, but in practice candidates would complete a simple health declaration which would be scrutinised by the Treasury Medical Service. Anyone rejected as a result of this procedure would have a right to appeal to the Commission. This meant that the Treasury Medical Service became a 'court of first instance' over a wide field; and the Commission would normally accept its decisions. As a result of these developments in the arrangements for medical examinations (and perhaps also because of staff changes in the Treasury and Commission) it seems that by the early 1950s a closer working relationship emerged between the Commission and the Treasury Medical Service.[25] Fisher noted that at one stage the Treasury Medical Adviser seemed to have thought he and his colleagues could take this work on. Indeed, Dr Roberts implied at one stage that he might be able to cope with 15 to 20 thousand cases a year:

> At the moment the total number handled annually is running at between sixty and seventy thousand, and even though the number should decline it will never come down to anything like the number which Dr Roberts and his people could cope with. Moreover I am sure that the doctors would hate having to plough through all the medical details of all the cases we handle, however straightforward they may be. Much of the work is dull, and although our own case examiners probably find it a welcome relief from the other sorts of enquiries they conduct, we could not expect doctors to do so much routine work.[26]

The other example to be considered here, of less than harmonious contacts between the Civil Service Commission and the Treasury, relates to studies by the Treasury O and M division. This division was formally created in 1941 out of the Investigating Section of the Treasury,[27] but in its early years it did little more than offer advice when asked. Nevertheless influence, through the internal, or 'closed', politics of Whitehall could sometimes result in invitations for it to offer advice. In 1947, for example, the Commission invited the Treasury O and M division to look at the work of the Commission's evidence branch; and in 1948 staff in the Treasury were internally expressing concern about the efficiency of the Commission.[28]

As a result of its 1948 enquiries into the Commission, the Select Committee on Estimates recommended that the Commission should take immediate steps to review its complement of staff, 'with the aim of making substantial reductions'.[29] Consequently, on 9 November 1948, A.H.M. Hillis, then Secretary to the Commission, wrote to J.R. (later Sir John) Simpson, then director of Organisation and Methods in the Treasury, inviting him to institute 'a full dress review of the work of the Commission'.[30]

In his reply, Simpson specifically explained that an O and M review involved an examination of the purposes and scope of the operations of the department before examining the detailed organisation and procedures; it would therefore raise some fundamental questions. Hillis drew to Waterfield's attention that this might involve reconsidering the possibility (which had been raised before) of transferring responsibility for the Commission's health cases to the Treasury Medical Adviser.[31] To Simpson, however, Hillis made it clear that the Commissioners were 'of the opinion that we ought not to transfer the responsibilities imposed on us by our Orders in Council to any outside authority'.[32]

After further discussion between the Treasury and the Commission, the terms of reference were agreed in January 1949 and the O and M review began. A draft report was available on 1 November; discussions with the Commission's officials followed, and details for the final report were agreed. There were eight main proposals, which also encompassed numerous recommendations on details: these need not be considered here – agreement on most of them was quickly reached. On 1 October 1949 the Commission had 802 staff: the report contained a conservative estimate that a saving of 70 staff could be achieved if its recommendations were fully implemented.

On 14 April 1950 Waterfield wrote to thank Simpson for the report. He acknowledged 'with gratitude and admiration the care and thought' which had been devoted to it by the O and M staff, but commented that it was 'a portentously long and detailed document'. He said he wished it had acknowledged more generously the improvements to the organisation of the Commission and economies that had already been made within the Commission. He also said he felt that many of the practical suggestions in the report had in fact originated from suggestions made to the O and M team by staff in the Commission. Nevertheless, in not a few cases the proposals put forward in the report, 'though original and ingenious, were so impracticable and so little suited to the peculiar conditions of work…that they had little value in themselves' and it was only when the Commission's staff had turned the ideas into workable schemes that a satisfactory result began to emerge. He felt sure that the Commission's share in the total was in fact much greater than the casual reader would suppose to be the case by the rather grudging statement in the report: 'The final version embodies inter alia various suggestions contributed by the Commission.' He thought, 'to be perfectly frank', that that sentence in the report was unlikely to secure the willing co-operation of the staff in implementing the recommendations. Furthermore, no-one in the Commission was hopeful of being able to reduce the staff by as many as 70, as a direct result of the O and M recommendations, 'even if we were to adopt the whole lot'.

Waterfield also wrote, on 17 April 1950, a 'Personal and Confidential' letter to Simpson. It primarily concerned the recommendation that the Commission should employ a doctor on a half-time basis. Waterfield said he had already mentioned to Simpson, over lunch, that he strongly suspected that the idea emanated from a certain quarter of the Treasury. Simpson had replied that he was pretty sure that was not so, and that the idea had emerged quite independently from the O and M review. Waterfield said that if this was so, it was a pretty curious coincidence because J.D. (later Sir John) Winnifrith, of the Treasury, had two years earlier, when the terms of the O and M review were first being considered, tried 'to include a direction to enquire into this very matter'. When this had been discussed by the Padmore Committee, Chiesman had said that the suggestion was ridiculous and impracticable and that 'no doctor worth his salt would ever be content to work under these conditions, and…if he were to attempt it he would go batty in a few years if not months'. Chiesman also 'made it perfectly clear that what he wanted was that his own people should be seconded to the Commission so as to be in a position to advise him on the reasons which lead us to accept or reject a candidate'. It was 'obvious to any far sighted person' that this 'would lead inevitably in the long run to his reporting to the Treasury that he did not agree with the action taken by the Commissioners, and hinting that it would be very much better if he did it himself'. Waterfield made it abundantly clear that he was absolutely opposed to the Treasury Medical Adviser's representative being introduced into the Commission.[33]

Simpson delayed replying until 4 May (and like Waterfield's letter his was headed 'Personal and Confidential'), in the hope that his first rather angry reaction would be dissipated, but he still felt very annoyed and said so.[34] He said he was sorry Waterfield had returned to the charge on the question of employing a doctor in the Commission because 'we here had thought we had finally allayed the suspicions which appeared to have been lurking in the breasts of the Commissioners on this topic'. Quite apart from his own discussion with Waterfield, Simpson quoted from recent correspondence between his colleague A.R. Bunker and Hillis. On 21 March, in reply to a reference made by Hillis on this subject, Bunker wrote that:

> Our recommendation about the appointment of a doctor to the staff of the Commission was made quite independently of an action by the TMA or any other Division of the Treasury. It was, indeed, put forward without the knowledge of the TMA and, for our part, we were not at the time aware of the line the TMA was taking in the wider field.[35]

Simpson also sent, on 8 May, an official reply to Waterfield's 14 April letter. It was carefully reasoned, and defended the O and M report, but also explained that: 'With one or two notable exceptions we have not had all the help and cooperation we expect and usually receive.' He concluded: 'I cannot recall being drawn into arguments of this nature on an assignment in any other Department and I am not enjoying the experience.'[36]

Hillis drafted a reply for Waterfield to send, but they decided a simpler reply would be better. As Waterfield wrote to Hillis on 19 May 1950: 'On the whole I think it better to avoid further argument and to write simply as below. I am not disposed to withdraw what I have said.' In the reply he actually sent on 18 May he said he was no less desirous than Simpson of ending their correspondence pleasantly:

> So, without seeking to argue the matter further, may I say simply that I have done my best to understand your point of view: that I am very willing to believe that an impartial judge would consider that there is much to be said for your side of the case, as I hope he would also say that there is for mine; and that I am glad to conclude by thanking you and your people again for your help, from which I hope that we shall profit considerably.[37]

These examples of the experience of the Commission's relationships with the Treasury are interesting and revealing. The Padmore Committees on civil service medical staffs (an *ad hoc* committee set up by the Government Organisation Committee and reporting on 25 May 1950) was working at the same time as the O and M review of the Commission. Some of the officials concerned participated in both enquiries. It seems highly unlikely, within such a small community, that they were not aware of the issues being considered and of the formal position taken by the Commission on its constitutional responsibilities. It was not, however, a simple matter of preparing and co-ordinating evidence: there were implications from the administrative culture as well. Simpson was, as he said on 1 June, 'feeling rather exasperated that our motives in this matter should be questioned'[38] – it was not actually said, but it was implied, that civil servants, who were expected to behave in a gentlemanly fashion, did not question each others' motives. However, to an outside observer over half a century later, the above-quoted extract from Bunker's letter appears to have been phrased so carefully that it might have been economical with the truth – or, at least, be so seen in the Commission. Whether or not it was being economical with the truth may not now matter. What does matter, however, is how the various officials were relating to each other in the context of their particular administrative, constitutional and political environment.

The examples and details presented here about the relations between the Commission and the Treasury have been selected primarily because they provide useful insights into the inter-related work of the two departments. It does not seem to matter much in which decades particular experiences occurred, because the pattern of relations was so similar right up to the late 1960s. With the implementation of the Fulton Committee's recommendations, however, there was a major change. Viewed from the perspective of the twenty-first century, the Commission was, in a number of ways, damaged by the Fulton Committee. The Commission became part of the Civil Service Department and, although it maintained its independence in the selection and allocation of staff, the familial relations it previously had with the Treasury, especially the career experience of particular senior officials, reflected fundamental change. For example, after Fulton, Hunt's successors as First Commissioner had very little, if any, previous careers in the Treasury. More important, the Fulton Report marked a watershed.

Before, there was a unified civil service; after, there were piecemeal but wide-ranging changes, often involving aspects of civil service recruitment within a wider context of personnel or human resource management. After 1991 the Commission ceased to exist, though there was an Office of the Civil Service Commissioners. The Fulton Report in this sense marked the beginning of the end, both of the Commission and of the unified civil service.

Relations with schools and universities

The administrative, constitutional and political environment conditioned all the work of the Civil Service Commission. Like any other department of government, the Commission could only do what the law empowered it to do; it had to achieve its purposes with efficiency and economy; it was constantly aware that in its activities it had to be fair and treat equally all candidates for selection; and it had to ensure there were equal opportunities for all types and categories of individual. Moreover, these qualitative expectations were not constant, they changed from time to time by acceding to pressures and being influenced by changing attitudes; and the Commission often had to carry out and advance its work by persuading individuals, organisations and interests, not only to co-operate voluntarily but also to do so for (often) no significant reward or recognition other than the feeling that they were being motivated by public service and were contributing to the public interest.

Contacts with what may be generally termed the world of education may be traced from the pre-history of the Commission. These contacts included individuals in both schools and universities, especially those from what Noel Annan called the intellectual aristocracy of the nineteenth century (see chapter 10), and the individuals so involved provided the philosophy of recruitment which was adopted at the outset by the Civil Service Commissioners and continued to be the key motivating factor for the department. That philosophy was set down in the papers relating to the Indian Civil Service, especially the 1854 Report by T.B. Macaulay, Lord Ashburton, Henry Melville, Benjamin Jowett and John G. S. Shaw Lefevre (see chapter 2).

The key features of the 1854 Report stressed, for superior positions in the civil service, the importance of a generalist education, prior to recruitment, to precede special education after admission. The best candidates would be the youths who did best what the ablest and most ambitious youths were trying to do well. No part of the kingdom, and no class of schools, should exclusively furnish the recruits: this would be consistent with democratic expectations. The philosophy stressed that superiority in educational pursuits indicated qualities which were securities against vice: 'industry, self-denial, a taste for pleasures not sensual, a laudable desire for honourable distinction...(and) to obtain the approbation of friends and relations'. The intellectual test would therefore be also a moral test.[39] The report also stressed the importance of securing the services of the ablest examiners.[40] Of particular importance in the context of this philosophy was a letter, dated

27 December 1874, from Jowett to the Marquis of Salisbury. That letter, by one of the Macaulay committee members, expanded on aspects of the report relating to examinations, the age of entry and the training of selected candidates. It reflected the continuing interest of Jowett and others in the practical details for implementing the philosophy. It is not surprising that the authors of the Macaulay report recognised that their proposals would have an effect which would 'be felt in every seat of learning throughout the realm'.

This was, indeed, what happened, both in universities and schools. In universities there was considerable interest beyond Jowett and others at Oxford and Cambridge. A good example was Dr James McCosh, of Queen's College, Belfast, who, in 1856, wrote: 'Notes on the proper mode of conducting the examinations of the Candidates for the Civil Service of India.'[41] McCosh seems to have gained experience as an examiner for the Indian Civil Service (the first examination was in July 1855) and his notes explained the purposes and advantages of written and oral examinations, offered detailed recommendations about the scheme of examinations and also made valuable comments about the advantages of using examiners from different universities to protect the equality of chances for candidates from the same or a different university from the examiners.[42] Once the Order in Council of 4 June 1870 made open competitive examinations a requirement in recruitment, the Civil Service Commissioners sent a circular to numerous people both inside and outside the civil service to seek their comments about the practical details of implementing the Order in Council. This resulted in a large number of thoughtful and constructive responses, including a particularly detailed and weighty reply from G. Johnstone Storey, Secretary to Queen's University of Ireland, Dublin, evaluating the possibilities that could result from what he called 'so mighty an agent for good or for evil as the new system of open competition'.[43]

One aspect of the examinations procedure that quickly required co-operation with schools and universities was the provision of examination centres. By the early 1880s Dublin was, after London, the largest examination centre and there was significant pressure to create more centres in Ireland. There were, for example, requests from Belfast to have a centre, especially as comparisons were made between cities; later there was pressure for a centre in Londonderry. M. Hughes of Hughes' Civil Service Academy in Londonderry was keen that there should be such a centre in the interests of his students preparing for appointments to posts in the Lower Division of the civil service, for candidates for positions as copyists or as customs officials. F.P. Barton, a junior clerk in the Commission, went to Ireland in 1881 to check on the different centres and write a report. He commented on the various halls available, their advantages and disadvantages and the charges required for them. In some places confusion led to irregularities and consequently cause for complaint, for in order to ensure fairness to candidates, conditions and procedures in the centres had to be of the same standard. Barton recommended more precise instructions to superintendents and more detailed general notices to candidates.[44] These issues were also raised about examination centres in England in the late nineteenth century[45] and in places abroad, such as

Australia.[46] Problems of ensuring fair comparison on merit, especially where oral assessments were required (as in foreign languages), were magnified when there was a number of examination centres.

In the early years of the twentieth century there was continuous pressure for additional centres throughout England,[47] Scotland[48] and Wales.[49] Wherever possible the Commission was keen to get suitable rooms, which could often be acquired without charge, with an attendant, in educational institutions.[50] Where the accommodation was not free, the Commission's officials became very successful in getting it at small or insignificant cost because there was pressure to bring examinations within easy reach of local people.[51] Most of the contacts made by the Commission with schools were of necessity with independent schools because, outside the independent sector, there was little provision for secondary education of the kind needed to prepare for the examinations. Publicly funded secondary schools only became significant in the early twentieth century, and by then the pattern of civil service examinations was already established. Consequently those examinations were significant in setting the desirable subjects to be taught in state secondary schools. An additional complication that became more apparent in the twentieth century was the difficulty of getting examiners who, while they were not indifferent to money, were not governed primarily by that consideration and were not anxious to complicate their full programme of work by serving in public examinations.[52]

On 8 December 1880 Dr James J. Hornby, Headmaster of Eton, wrote to the Secretary, Civil Service Commission, about the dangers to the moral and physical well being of boys spending two or three days in London to take the Army examinations. He proposed that a large public school, such as his, could be used as an examination centre. He was convinced that 'if this arrangement can be made, much evil may be avoided, and many candidates saved from being exposed to temptations which no parent would wish his son at such an age to be forced to encounter'.[53] The Commissioners supported this suggestion and raised it with the Director General of Military Education. Later, numerous other public schools similarly asked to be designated examination centres,[54] and in 1890 the matter was also raised by the Headmasters' Committee.[55]

Headmasters welcomed additional examination centres away from London, and suggested that any additional costs could be met by raising the entrance fee. The strongly proposed alternatives to centres in London led the Commission to consider expanding their regional arrangements for written examinations. As a result, from 1894 more than a dozen leading public schools became examination centres on certain conditions: that they guaranteed a minimum of 20 candidates (at first the minimum was ten), they provided accommodation and minor service without charge, they contributed to the superintendence costs and they admitted candidates not otherwise connected with the centre.[56]

In addition to these practical arrangements for examinations, it was also in the interest of schools to keep the Civil Service Commissioners aware of the best educational expectations. For example, they wished the civil service examinations to be run along the lines of the curriculum in schools instead of the curriculum of schools having to follow the pattern of civil service examinations. Their concern was emphasised by the fact that the curriculum for the civil service examinations affected at least ten times as many pupils as entered for the competitions. They were also anxious that there was growing experience of boys being withdrawn from schools and sent to specialist tutors or expected 'to complete' their education at evening classes designed to prepare candidates for civil service examinations. Indeed, on 6 October 1896 a deputation of 16 headmasters representing public secondary schools, attended the offices of the Commissioners to present their views in the hope that the syllabuses of the examinations would be brought 'more into touch with the educational requirements of the present day'.[57] These expressions of views had particular relevance when, in the first decade of the twentieth century, examinations were being designed for clerkships in the Exchequer and Audit Department. Views were expressed about cramming (which had advantages as well as disadvantages): Dr J. Gow, of Westminster School, wrote on 18 January 1906 that it may even be fair to expect 'the power to cram' from men 'who may sometimes have to work at very high pressure'.[58]

The relationships of the Commission with schools and their related organisations, especially the Headmasters' Conference, were continuous from the early days of the Commission. Towards the end of the nineteenth century, their effects included getting Oxford and Cambridge Schools Examination certificates accepted for granting exemptions from subjects in non-competitive examinations (such as for admission to the Army via Sandhurst and Woolwich).[59] In 1928 the Head Teacher of Chichester Secondary School for Girls suggested to the West Sussex Education Committee that it would be an advantage if the School Certificate could be accepted as a qualifying examination for the Post Office. The letter was referred to the General Post Office (GPO) and then to the Commission. The Commission took this up with the Treasury, which approved, and the suggestion was implemented in 1929 for telegraphists in London and for sorting clerks and telegraphists in the provinces; the arrangement was later extended for other posts in the GPO.[60] The acceptance of the School Certificate in this way became a valuable precedent. After the Second World War there were not sufficient successful candidates in the clerical officer competitions to satisfy the demands for new staff and, after considerable discussion, it was agreed to accept, from 1953, the General Certificate of Education as a qualifying examination – though this, in turn, led to much lobbying on whether certain subjects were acceptable for the purpose (especially religious knowledge, music, art and commerce).[61]

By 1921 the contacts with schools had expanded to include not only the associations of head teachers but also nine associations of teachers of particular subjects – such as the associations of teachers of history, classics, modern languages, science etc. – together with the Educational Reform Council and the Educational Committee of the County Councils Association.[62] Sometimes, as with the revision proposals for the Army and Air Force Examinations in the period between the two World Wars, the Commission arranged a conference with headmasters, but following the precedents of the schools generally attended by successful candidates, the schools represented tended to be public schools because they were chosen by the Headmasters' Conference.[63]

The experience of the Commission in consulting with higher education organisations, and in receiving approaches from them, was similar to its relationships with schools. The general philosophy motivating the Commission permeated contacts at both levels of education. As W.J. Courthope, then First Civil Service Commissioner, put it in 1906: 'It is not for the Civil Service Commissioners to give an educational lead; we take the conditions as we find them.'[64] Nevertheless, officials who reached, or were expected to reach, the highest levels in the civil service, were usually university graduates who competed for positions in the administrative class (or whatever term applied to the fast-stream level of entry at any particular time). Some of the special features of the relationships of the Commission with universities are covered elsewhere in this book – this applies to contacts with secretaries of university appointments boards or careers officers, and also with the creation of liaison officers (see chapter 11). There is also discussion elsewhere of the close relations maintained by particular Civil Service Commissioners (see chapters 2 and 11). In this present chapter the emphasis is on topics not covered elsewhere.

The general attitude of the Civil Service Commission towards universities was often different from the relationships of other departments with the institutions they dealt with. The Commission depended on co-operation from universities for its examiners – who sometimes examined for work other than degree level – and, as already mentioned, this co-operation could not be simply bought with fees. Universities and their staffs were also contacted by the Commission for their advice on recruitment matters at all levels, and generally their advice was expected to be given free, 'in the public interest'. A good example of this relationship in practice was revealed when, during the Second World War, reforms were being developed for recruitment to the Foreign Service. The Foreign Secretary had requested R.A. (later Lord) Butler, then Under-Secretary of State for Foreign Affairs, to take general charge of Foreign Service reform and instructed G. (later Sir George) Rendel to act as his chief assistant for the purpose. Rendel therefore had to work with Waterfield, who was keen to protect the Commission's responsibility for recruitment. Waterfield suggested that they should go together to see the Vice-Chancellor of Oxford and that he, Waterfield, should send in advance an agenda for discussion. Rendel disagreed with this procedure on the grounds that it would give the other side an opportunity for criticism, whereas if the university representatives were invited to put forward proposals, without themselves making any suggestions, they would be able to criticise the proposals to their hearts' content. Rendel subsequently said that he was, at the time, drawing on his experience of dealing with foreign diplomats and representatives of the press: he 'found it difficult to imagine himself engaged in discussion with friends'. Waterfield said he should not be anxious about his approach. He told him that: 'The universities were our friends and we could put our cards on the table and discuss our problems with them openly without anxiety.'[65]

Nevertheless such friends were generally treated with respect and sometimes with caution in a practical context. For example, when the syllabus for Class I competitions was being revised between 1908 and 1910, it seems that the universities were hardly consulted. This was because the Commissioners felt that if the universities were consulted on the question of adjusting the maximum marks to be allowed for mathematics and science they would also have to be consulted on other proposed changes. On matters of this kind the Commissioners regarded the universities 'as rival competitive bodies whose opinion is largely to be influenced by any trifling advantage or disadvantage which may accrue to their students from the proposed changes'. In these circumstances, the Commissioners preferred not 'to ask for opinions which they might not be able to accept and yet could not disregard without appearance of discourtesy'.[66] On issues such as this, the Commission developed its own working practices based on experience and an appreciation of what was practicable.

On matters of syllabus content and the acceptability of subjects offered in examinations the Commission had to liaise with the Treasury and the various government departments; but, most important, the Commission was the department that dealt directly with universities, on whose advice and co-operation it was often dependent. It is evident that this had to be so in matters of technical or professional expertise where the staff in the Commission had no personal competence: syllabuses had to be updated from time to time, as did the assessment of the relevance of particular subjects. Also, for the large-scale general civil service classes, the assessment of competence in English language or arithmetic, for example, did not require much specialist expertise beyond the well-educated staff in the Commission's directorate of examinations. More controversy, and insights into how the department actually worked, is revealed in relation to the subjects that were available in the examinations for the administrative group of appointments. These included examinations for what was known after the Second World War as the Method I system of selection.

Sometimes academics energetically pursued the cases of individual students, often as examples of ways in which the Commission appeared to be dealing unfairly with the subjects they had studied. One of the most assiduous of these was the historian J.O. Prestwich, of the Queen's College, Oxford, whose letters about apparent unfairness towards particular Oxford historians led to questions being asked that produced interesting new information about the Commission. In August 1962 Sir George Mallaby, then First Commissioner, defended the Commission in general terms which, he told Prestwich, was involved in conducting over 300 different competitions each year, examining about 90,000 people and interviewing perhaps 40,000. He stressed the importance placed by the Commission on its links with universities and how the interests of universities were cared for in practice. Prestwich replied that: 'Very few candidates would go in for the Civil Service of their own initiative: almost all have been encouraged by their tutors.'[67] Although Prestwich was regarded by W.E. Wightman, then Assistant Director of Examinations, as unreliable from a number of perspectives, his 'insinuations' about unfairness to Oxford historians and about weaknesses in the Civil Service Commission were taken very seriously. Wightman compared in detail the periods covered by Commission examination papers and the Oxford degree syllabus. R.H. Howorth, also an Assistant Director of Examinations, commented and concluded that, in fact, Oxford history candidates had an advantage over most others.[68] K.M. Reader, another Assistant Director of Examinations, accepted that the Method I syllabus was not in line with the Oxford course, but also recognised that this was not a problem confined to Oxford, nor was the problem one which affected only historians.[69] On 14 November 1962 Mallaby sent a detailed and carefully drafted reply to Prestwich – but it was a carefully drafted reply intended not to encourage further correspondence. In any case, no-one outside the Commission could at the time have appreciated how much research and thought had gone into the problems Prestwich had raised: Reader's single-spaced 12 page analysis remains a hitherto unknown great credit to the work of the Commission.

The lobbying from Oxford on behalf of history graduates was unusual and unexpected because the criticisms of the Method I examination (see chapter 11) tended to allege that Oxford historians benefited from the civil service examinations. In contrast, representatives from other universities tended to advance the causes of the social sciences. For example, Philip Reynolds, of the University of Lancaster, stressed that more scope should be given for candidates to take examinations in the social sciences. He said that in 1964 the number of students taking classics outside Oxford and Cambridge was unlikely to be more than 5 per cent of non-science students; the number taking honours in the social sciences was likely to be nearer 40 per cent of non-science students and their number was growing. The point Reynolds then made was that it was easy in the Method I civil service examinations for a student of classics to make up his maximum possible marks from the courses he had taken. It was virtually impossible for a student of the social sciences. He said: 'That 1,000 marks are available in optional subjects in classics and only 1,700 for the whole range of the social sciences seems to me ludicrous.'[70] The interests of particular social sciences were also pressed from time to time. On several occasions this was the case on behalf of sociology, administrative law and international relations. The following details concerning the London School of Economics (LSE) illustrate this.

In 1958 Sir Sydney Caine, then Director of the LSE, who had been a civil servant from 1923 to 1951, wrote to Sir Laurence Helsby about the position of LSE graduates who were not able to do themselves justice, without additional preparation. He explained that the feeling at the LSE was that the civil service examinations did not take adequate account of modern developments in the social sciences, and he enclosed suggestions for papers on anthropology, law, history and international relations and political science. Helsby, who had been a lecturer in economics at Durham 1931–45, wanted to go as far as possible to meet

Caine's position and they had lunch together on 21 July 1958 at the Oxford and Cambridge Club. W. Deakin and Reader prepared a detailed brief, approved by H.A. Needham, then Director of Examinations, for Helsby's lunch appointment. The brief accepted that the examinations neglected developments in the social sciences, but argued 'it is not up to us to encourage new subjects at the behest of small pressure groups'.[71] As a result of the lunchtime discussion it was agreed that staff at the Commission might have informal talks with K.B. Smellie and M.J. Oakeshott, whose names were suggested by the Commission, and who were regarded by Caine as among the most sensible people at the LSE – they were both professors of political science. Reader wrote to Smellie and Oakeshott about this on 3 October 1958. There was no early reply but Reader noted that he was 'in no hurry to introduce more opportunities for the jargon jugglers'.[72] Oakeshott replied on 3 December that he and Smellie did not think they were in fact too badly served by the papers offered by the Civil Service Commission, but he made some suggestions. The suggestions were examined in the Commission. Reader commented that he did not much like the proposal for a paper on the Social Structure of Modern Britain and said he would prefer some general papers on theories and methods. O.M.C. Buchan, an Assistant Director of Examinations, noted that the B.Sc. (Econ) Part I standard did not match the civil service Method I standard. He also commented that: 'Everyone has to "waste" part of his degree and do a little fresh work for Method I.' Early in 1959 Reader and Deakin met Oakeshott and Smellie. Oakeshott thought the sociology students could take the Moral Philosophy paper II (which had been designed from the Oxford syllabus), but both he and Smellie favoured papers on the Social Structure of Modern Britain and on theories and methods of sociology. Deakin checked on the numbers of students taking these subjects in University Grants Committee statistics (relating to 1955–56 and 1956–57); he also contacted a few university registrars for additional information, though surprisingly not Leicester or Liverpool, which both had large departments of sociology. He later wrote draft syllabuses for the sociology papers and sent them to seven sociology professors for comments. Deakin's approach to seven university registrars seems to have resulted in misunderstanding. He asked for information about the numbers of students graduating in sociology in the most recent three academic years, and it seems that the responses did not relate to the number of students taking individual degree courses in the subject (but registered for combined or joint honours degrees) but to the number of students who had graduated in sociology as a single honours degree; nor did the figures include Leicester, Liverpool or London (external) students. Nevertheless, the information received showed that there were likely to be sufficient students reading sociology to justify including it in the list of optional examination subjects:[73] the criteria were that the subject was fairly generally taught and there was the prospect of a reasonable number of candidates.[74]

This example of contacts with the LSE, mainly concerning the recognition of sociology in the Method I examinations, shows how seriously suggestions and criticisms from universities were received. Other subjects considered similarly were psychology,[75] international relations[76] and administrative law.[77] Such matters received attention in the Commission with care and integrity, though sometimes the evidence was collected from sources that were hardly the most up to date; and wherever possible contacts for consultation were chosen because they were regarded as safe and, if possible, had a record of civil service inside knowledge and experience. The usual view adopted, in line with the generalist approach to education and the already quoted report by Macaulay and others, was expressed by R.N. Burton in connection with international relations: 'Method I was not designed to cater for first degree students who specialised so completely in various branches of one main field of study.'[78] It was also expressed by Deakin in connection with administrative law: 'We are not concerned with a subject's direct value to civil service work.'[79]

Relations with other government departments

The 1855 Order in Council, which created the Civil Service Commission, recognised the independence of the departments of central government. The requirements for granting certificates (i.e. certification), in terms of age, health, character and knowledge and ability, had to be settled, with the assistance of the Commissioners, according to the discretion of the chief authorities of the departments. This meant that, from its inception, the Commission had to consult and, where necessary for uniformity[80] and efficiency, persuade departments to agree to the standards which the Commissioners would apply.

One of the first actions of the Commissioners was to consult all the departments of state, to find out what their requirements were. The Commissioners recognised that some qualifications for certain positions would be the same everywhere: for example, junior clerks had to be able 'to write a good hand', to be able to spell correctly, to be able to write a simple letter grammatically and to be conversant with elementary arithmetic.[81] Other positions specific to a particular department required the department to inform the Commissioners what additional qualifications or expertise they would need to examine.

Some of the correspondence between the Commissioners and the heads of different departments was published by the Commissioners in their annual reports. The Commission was very sensitive about its position in this context, perhaps even to the point of minimising the role it played. For example, the report published in 1868 said:

> we have scrupulously avoided interfering with the discretion vested in the chief authorities of the several departments, rarely even suggesting modifications of such rules as they have proposed; and the regulations under which the candidates are examined have in fact been prescribed in every case by those authorities.[82]

An example of how this worked out, with open competition, was reported in the annual report published in 1872.[83] It concerned appointments for the

Commissioners of Works to the position of Assistant to the Clerk of the Furniture. The Office of Works stated the required qualifications:

> Candidates must be competent practically to superintend the supply and repairs of all articles of furniture and fittings, &c, which may possibly be required in public buildings and royal palaces; they must be able to frame estimates of the probable cost of such supply and repairs, and to prepare working drawings and sketches showing the design and construction of all articles of furniture, of book-cases, presses, cupboards and other fittings.

The Civil Service Commissioners obtained the consent of the Treasury, then issued notices in the London Gazette and several professional newspapers inviting applicants between 25 and 35 years of age who could produce satisfactory evidence of their training and occupations to show that they met the requirements. The Commission received 37 applications. Of these nine subsequently withdrew; eight did not appear to have the qualifications and were excluded; and 12 failed a preliminary examination in handwriting, spelling and arithmetic. The remaining eight were competitively examined, under Civil Service Commission directions, by a leading member of one of the most eminent firms concerned in the manufacture and sale of furniture. The examiner assessed the comparative merits of the candidates and on the strength of his report two persons were selected who were deemed to be 'in every respect admirably qualified for the peculiar and difficult duties which they have to discharge'.[84]

The general pattern of departments co-operating in this way worked well and in 1857 the Civil Service Commissioners were asked by the East India Company to conduct examinations for the home service of the Company. The Commissioners sought the consent of the government before undertaking the additional duties beyond the provisions of the 1855 Order in Council, and permission was granted. Details in the Commissioners' annual reports show that this was very successful. Later the Commission acquired recruitment and assessment responsibilities for other public service organisations. As explained in chapter 2, the responsibilities of the Commissioners rapidly extended from testing nominated candidates to testing candidates by open competitive examinations, and such competitive examinations were required for recruitment to most positions after 1870.

Over time, certification, the next stage in the recruitment process, became a more complex procedure. On initial appointment, the requirement for an individual candidate was clear: a certificate was issued to a department (not to the individual) certifying that the individual had met the requirements that had been applied by the Civil Service Commissioners. The procedure became more complex with the promotion and transfer of staff. Over the years, the Commission developed an effective working procedure. The Commissioners applied a rule, in co-operation with departments and with the approval of the Treasury, that meant recertification would be waived when an individual was advanced in accordance with 'the customary course of promotion' – this still involved discretionary decisions, often in consultation with departments, but it worked well in most cases. In areas of doubt the recertification requirement was preserved, thus respecting the key role of the Commissioners.[85]

There were always periods of more intense discussion with departments when it was difficult to recruit good candidates. For example, just before the Second World War there were complaints, especially from the Admiralty, Royal Ordnance Factories and Health, about the poor executive staff they were being allocated from the open competitions. Various suggestions were made. One of these from the Admiralty was for an interview to be added to the executive competitions, because it was thought this would be a check on personality: personality was thought to be an increasingly evident weakness in terms of the work required of executive officers in the Admiralty. It would have been difficult, however, to add interviews to the general recruitment tests at executive level because the task was so large and there were so many examination centres. Eventually it was agreed in 1937 that the Admiralty would interview candidates offered to them for service in their supply departments, and any candidate who failed the interview would revert to the list of successful candidates available for allocation elsewhere.[86]

Part of the challenges facing the Commission in recruiting civil servants was that the market for candidates was constantly changing. Many of the type of candidates who in the period before the 1930s would have been successfully certificated and allocated, in the period afterwards were going to university instead. This difficulty became more acute with the considerable expansion of university-level education. Indeed, it caused special difficulties even in earlier years for recruiting directing staffs for supply departments in the Admiralty and elsewhere. These staff had, in 1891, been described as 'a type of officer of very much the same original material as that from which the First Division was formed, but of less complete educational finish'.[87] The difficulty in continuing to recruit such staff was part of a wider problem that has never been resolved in British civil service recruitment. If recruitment qualifications and practices depend on and follow the system of education, when there are changes in education provision and output, civil service recruitment cannot easily anticipate or quickly adjust to the consequences. The civil service is consequently always limited to trying to resolve the difficulties after they have become evident. It is therefore especially important that the recruiting department (i.e. the Civil Service Commission) monitors the education system and develops plans to resolve problems. In practice, this was done by working in close collaboration with the departments involved. In the Commission, the Commissioners themselves, and their support staff, played an important part in this, but much also depended on good inter-departmental relations and courtesy in the context of a service-wide administrative culture.

Nevertheless there were, from time to time, occasions when inter-departmental relations were less harmonious. One of these, which illustrates the role of the

Commission in this context, occurred in 1904. Difficulties arose from the application of the Order in Council of 26 February 1897 that said that in making regulations (about the examinations for admission to the Royal Military Academy, Sandhurst, and the Royal Military College, Woolwich) the Secretary of State for War 'shall have the advice and assistance of the Civil Service Commissioners in matters relating to the educational tests and examinations'. In 1904 the War Office drafted new regulations and sent copies to the Commission, where it was noticed that the new regulations for the competitive examination included a change of great importance that had not been discussed with them. This change meant that candidates would not be able to offer Greek *and* Latin, but Greek *or* Latin. This change had not been specifically drawn to the attention of the Commissioners, and there had been no request for their observations on it.

The Commissioners argued that the change would 'produce the most mischievous consequences'. In the past it had been found that many of the more-able candidates had come from 'the Classical Side of the Public Schools'; with the change such boys would be deprived of the advantage of their skill in Greek. Boys wishing to enter the Army competitions would have to be withdrawn from classics and put into Army classes and modern studies. The consequence would be to debar able candidates and give an undue advantage to the less able. 'Classical students' were already handicapped by 'the inclusion of History and of a Modern Language as equivalents for Greek and Latin, since it cannot be contended that these subjects are of equal difficulty'.[88] The Commissioners asked that the change be deferred for consultation; the War Office refused and issued the regulations. The Commissioners therefore noted that the advice of the Civil Service Commission appeared to be no longer required by the War Office and requested that the Order in Council of 26 February 1897 be rescinded. The Order in Council was therefore repealed by an Order in Council of 10 May 1905.[89] The effect was to return to the arrangement laid down in the Order in Council of 18 August 1892, for the Commission to test candidates for first commissions in the Army 'in conformity with regulations...issued by Her Majesty's principal Secretary of State for War'. Consequently the Civil Service Commission no longer had an obligation to give 'advice and assistance on matters relating to the educational tests and examinations' for the Army.[90]

Most contacts between the Commission and the various government departments were, on a much more harmonious basis. Indeed, relations with some departments not strictly within the civil service, such as the departments of the Clerk of the House of Commons and the Clerk of the Parliaments, had the characteristics of an old-world courtesy. The Commission ran limited competitions among nominated candidates for these departments, though they were not part of the civil service and therefore not subject to the Orders in Council relating to civil service recruitment. W. J. Courthope, First Civil Service Commissioner from 1892 was, however, able to persuade the two departments to move towards a common examination syllabus and this later led to them being part of the fast stream recruitment arrangements. As with the departments of the Clerk of the House of

Commons and the Clerk of the Parliaments, many of the day-to-day contacts between the Commission and other government departments were what are sometimes called 'semi-official'. They were courteous, often informal and depended on consultation and persuasion.[91]

The relationships between government departments, and between their most senior officials, have often been of special interest to students of public administration. Rarely, however, is there evidence of how they work out in practice. The evidence in the Civil Service Commission files provides material in which these relationships can be seen and understood. The Commission's relationships were probably more extensive than most other departments because of its crucial responsibility for recruiting staff. In some ways the relationships that developed were similar to those that have developed in consequence of new public management reforms in the late twentieth century. As Waterfield put it in 1941, in connection with his intended consultation with departments, the Civil Service Commission stood to departments in the relation of purveyor to customer.[92]

Contacts outside the civil service

The category of most numerous contacts outside the civil service was with candidates. They enquired about competitions and vacancies; they sat examinations and were sent results; and details of their health and character had to be enquired into. Sometimes the interests of certain candidates or potential candidates were represented by professional organisations and some of these will be considered next. The Civil Service Commission took considerable care in dealing with individuals or groups that experienced problems of a humanitarian nature: two examples outlined in this chapter are prisoners of war and disabled candidates. Towards the end of the chapter a case involving copyright issues provides unusual insights into the responsibilities of an examining body and the attitudes of some of the Commission's staff.

From its early life in the mid-nineteenth century until its demise in 1991 the Commission had relationships with a very large number of professional bodies and interest groups. These included the Association of Certified and Corporate Accountants,[93] the Institute of Cost and Works Accountants,[94] the Institute of Quantity Surveyors,[95] the Incorporated Society of Auctioneers,[96] the Psychologists Committee,[97] and organisations representing the interests of various subjects of study (such as geography[98] and sociology).[99] Most of the contacts initiated by these bodies were to influence the acceptability of their qualifications in civil service examinations and to enhance their standing. Two examples illustrate this.

In 1904 the Royal Geographical Society wrote to the India Office suggesting that geography be included in the Indian Civil Service examinations. J. Brodrick, India Office, noted that geography was a 'promising aspirant which had not yet attained the dignity of a sister science to those in our group of Natural Sciences'. The Commissioners were uneasy about a subject, which appeared to cross other subjects and could become 'loved as a soft option open to all comers'.

S.M. (later Sir Stanley) Leathes therefore replied, explaining that: 'In such a matter the Commissioners cannot act as pioneers. When a subject has taken a definite place in the higher educational system of the country they will be prepared to consider its inclusion.' He pointed out that, although at Cambridge a Board of Geographical Studies was being established, and there was a school of geography at Oxford, no final honours school had yet been established. The civil service examination was not an examination for specialists but an examination to test general ability.[100]

J. Scott Keltie, Secretary to the Royal Geographical Society, was instructed by the Council of his society to tell the Commission that it had underestimated the position of geography in university examinations, and that its value in education was widely admitted: 'and if the Civil Service Commission would give expression to this admission in the examinations which they conduct, it would give an impetus to geography in schools and Universities which is not likely to be given by any other course'.[101]

It seems that this correspondence from the Royal Geographical Society was part of a general effort to get geography accepted more widely as a subject of study. It was taken up in *The Times* in 1906 by which time there were schools of geography in Oxford and Cambridge, there were comparable developments in other universities and a variety of other indicators (such as an association of geography teachers with a journal) that geography was well established as a subject of study.[102] W.J. Courthope, the First Civil Service Commissioner, in a published letter replied with a well-argued defence of the Commission and its philosophy as outlined by Macaulay in 1854. He said that the Commissioners aimed 'in framing large schemes of examination, which directly influence the course of education...to make these conform...to the lines of general education actually established'.[103] An equally well-argued reply from H.J. Mackinder, of the LSE, said that the Commissioners should not 'shirk their growing duty of co-operating with the Universities in the matter of educational progress' and 'the Civil Service Commissioners are, whether they like it or not...trustees for the public as regards education no less than as regards the Civil and Diplomatic Services'.[104] In 1907, the Hebdomadal Council of the University of Oxford agreed a formal request to the Commission that geography should be included in the list of subjects examined for the civil service. In 1907 it was decided to include geography in the list of optional natural science subjects, and to use, as a guide for framing the civil service syllabus in geography, the syllabuses prescribed for the diplomas in geography at Oxford and Cambridge. Considerable further negotiation occurred between the Treasury, the India Office and the Commission before agreement was reached on the maximum number of marks allowable for geography.[105]

Numerous other examples could be cited of professional institutes and societies seeking to gain recognition for their members by having their qualifications accepted for various competitions. Examples include the Incorporated Society of Auctioneers and Landed Property Agents and the National Association of Auctioneers, House Agents, Rating Surveyors and Valuers. Despite their persistence during the years 1935–54, neither of these organisations succeeded in getting their qualifications accepted.[106] An example of an association that was, however, successful in this way was the Association of Certified and Corporate Accountants (ACCA). The ACCA was an amalgamation of the London Association of Certified Accountants Ltd and the Corporation of Accountants Ltd. The ACCA wished its qualification to be accepted as equivalent to that of the Institute of Municipal Treasurers and Accountants, the Institute of Chartered Accountants and the Society of Accountants and Auditors. In this case the burden of a full investigation by the Commission was short-circuited because on 26 September 1945 the Treasury issued an Establishment Officers' Circular, which proposed the creation of a general service class of Professional Accountants and recognised the qualifications of all the main accounting bodies, including the ACCA, which enabled the ACCA to get all the recognition it had been seeking.[107]

Whilst considerable time and trouble was devoted to the interests of professional societies and their representatives, no less attention was given to the interests of individuals. Two examples from within the Commission illustrate the great care taken to assist hard personal cases, either of groups or of individuals. The first example relates to helping a category of potential applicants; the second relates more specifically to individuals.

The first example focuses on organisations assisting prisoners of war during the Second World War. In 1940 the Educational Books Scheme of the Prisoners of War Department of the War Organisation of the British Red Cross Society and the Order of St John of Jerusalem, received a request from a prisoner of war in Germany for information and help with regard to the civil service examination for Preventive Officer in the Customs Service. The first request forwarded to the Commission, dated 18 September 1940, came from E. Hardman. This was followed in November by requests from eight more men, and in January 1941 with a further list seeking assistance. Others followed – sometimes two or three a week. Sometimes there were bulk requests (e.g. 21 July 1942, for 100 copies of the regulations for the Male Sorters examination) or lists indicating the details of prisoners and what they wanted.

Some responses from the Commission were returned undelivered. The Red Cross could only send 'acceptable' books and Miss E. Herdman of the Red Cross, operating from the New Bodleian in Oxford, became very knowledgeable about Commission regulations and what was 'acceptable', and acted as an intermediary between the prisoners of war and the Commission. A typical difficulty is illustrated by the request from Sgt J. Buckfield RAF, and Sgt T Michie RAF, in Stalag Luft 1, who requested information about competitions for GPO Engineers. The regulations sent by the Commission on 12 November 1941 were returned because the German censor did not allow any books to be sent relating to wireless or the transmission of messages. The Red Cross had to explain this to the prisoners and to the Commission. Occasionally similar arrangements worked successfully for prisoners in Italy, but the Italians were not as well organised as the Germans for this purpose. Large quantities of the White Paper on the reconstruction competitions were sent from the Commission to individual prisoners as well as in bulk through the Red Cross.[108]

The second example is of finding employment for blind persons in the administrative and executive classes. From 1920 a number of cases of blind persons were considered by the Commission but in 1945 the case of D.G. Church, in particular, was referred to Waterfield, then First Civil Service Commissioner, who noted that the Secretary General of the National Institute for the Blind was confident that such persons could be employed. Waterfield asked him to come and tell the Commission what he had in mind, and invited the Treasury to join the meeting.[109] This led to what was noted in the Commission as 'alarm and despondency in the Treasury'.[110] E.A. (later Dame Evelyn, then Baroness) Sharp, in the Treasury, regarded this as a matter of policy and therefore a Treasury matter. For the Commission, it was pointed out that, whatever view the Treasury had, the Commissioners must, in the last resort, be the judges of whether a physical disability was severe enough to disqualify, 'and in this connection the Treasury had no comparable standing whatever'. In March 1945 the Commission heard informally that Sir Ian (later Lord) Fraser, of St Dunstan's, had made so impressive a case that the Treasury felt obliged, in the words of Waterfield, 'to modify their former obscurantist attitude, and look closely into the possibilities'.[111] Later, the Treasury acquired some of the functions of an employment agency for finding specialist posts that blind people could do in the civil service. Perhaps this would not have been achieved without the sensitivity and motivation of staff in the Commission.

Another category of relationships, revealing the actual working of the Civil Service Commission, was with authors. In the 1920s the Commission acted as a valuable channel of communication and assistance between the India Office and authors of books on Indian languages. The authors were facing difficulties with publishers because the small demand meant the books were not commercially viable. From the viewpoint of the Indian Civil Service, however, these books were important for teaching Indian languages, and consequently material in the languages was important for examinations run by the Commission. In several cases grants were obtained towards publication costs: print runs tended to be for 1,000 copies and the authors received no royalties.[112]

A quite different type of experience developed from the use, for examination purposes, by the Commission of copyright material. Holloway Horn wrote to the Civil Service Commissioners on 31 August 1937 because his short story 'The Old Man' (the complete story, not an extract), originally published in a book entitled *Great Short Stories of Detection, Mystery and Horror: Second Series*,[113] had been used in the Navy, Army and Air Force entrance Examinations in November 1933, and subsequently the story had been published in a set of examination papers. He thought it extraordinary that a government department should use a copyright work without communicating with the author, and he asked what fee the Commissioners proposed to pay. G.G. Mennell, then Secretary to the Commission, accompanied by a colleague (possibly L. Blaikie, Assistant Director of Examinations), saw Sir William Codling, Controller of the Stationery Office on 10 September to discuss the question of copyright. Codling advised apologising, regretting the oversight of not asking Horn's permission, explaining that the secrecy that had to be observed before the paper was set to candidates meant that the Commission had not been in a position to ask permission, and expressing the hope that the author would not object to the Commission's use of his work. If he asked for a fee Codling said it would have to be paid, but 'we might think it desirable not to use any of his works again'. He also recommended telling Horn that the period laid down in the Copyright Act for taking action had elapsed, and the Commissioners had no authority to pay a fee.

This development was a shock in the Commission which had not appreciated the copyright implications of setting examination questions, and staff in the Commission had no recollection of the Stationery Office's official advice on preparing copy for printing. Blaikie said that carrying out the Stationery Office's advice on copyright would be very burdensome and would almost certainly cause delay. He added:

> We have hitherto, in making question papers, disregarded the question of copyright, presumably on the ground that the amount of matter we take is small and that most authors would probably regard it as a compliment for a piece of their work to be chosen for this purpose...
>
> I think it would hamper us considerably if it were decided that in future no copyright matter should be used, or that such matter should not be used without the consent of the holders of the copyright...So far as I can recollect, Mr Horn is the first person to complain. Incidentally he has now no legal right to redress, as under the Copyright Act 1911, action must be brought within 3 years of the date of publication.

The Commissioners next sought the advice of the Treasury Solicitor's Department. R.N. Hanscombe advised that Horn might, indeed, have a legal claim, in view of the published booklet of past examination papers, and advised reconsideration of paying him. The Commissioners asked Codling's advice on the amount that might be paid. Codling thought two guineas would not be excessive, so Treasury approval was sought for payment 'providing it does not exceed two guineas'.[114] P.G. Inch, of the Treasury, replied that although Horn had raised the question of a fee, 'one might reasonably assume that he will not press the point'. Inch recommended that the Commissioners' letter to Horn should assure him that the oversight would not be repeated and that 'in all the circumstances you will accept this apology as settling the matter'. If pressed, Inch suggested that a fee of one guinea might be offered.

Horn did not react as hoped. He pointed out that 'the copyright in a story is as much the author's property as his watch'. He said he accepted the apology but that it did not settle the matter. His fee was five guineas. He also complained about the hardly courteous delay between his letter of 30 August and the

Commissioners' reply of 20 October. He said that unless the matter was treated in a less cavalier manner he would bring it before the Society of Authors. The Commissioners sought further advice from the Treasury Solicitor who recommended paying the fee asked. The fee was then approved for payment by the Treasury and the Commission reconsidered its policy of publishing sets of examination papers.

During the Second World War there was a further attempt to resolve the matter. One reason for this was that the Commissioners had been avoiding the use of copyright material: 'good, modern interesting matter'. Instead they relied upon 'either heavy material from government publications or the antiquated verbosity of the early Victorians'.[115] In 1944 Waterfield wrote to Sir Thomas Barnes, the Treasury Solicitor:

> A possible solution would be to ask authors for permission in each case, offering a standard (and very small) fee, but there are objections to this since it would entail a great deal of work and correspondence, besides imperilling the secrecy of examination papers, and you might feel that the offer would prejudice our case if a greedy author should demand a larger fee.

Later, a compromise was developed by the Commission, the Treasury, the Stationery Office, the Treasury Solicitor and the Publishers' Association. The Treasury was to pay fees up to £5 and new procedures were introduced to safeguard the Commission against infringing copyright. These included ceasing to publish sets of examination papers containing copyright material. The position was later complicated by the 1956 Copyright Act; but by 1958 the Commission had developed new office procedures involving standard letters for all regular purposes and the matter had become a clerical level responsibility.[116]

The account in the files of Horn's experience in the 1930s is a revealing illustration of how certain civil servants regarded their relationship to authors. It is also somewhat surprising how unaware they were of the copyright requirements and how easily decisions about such matters could be made within a confident but misguided context of Crown privilege (i.e. that the Crown was absolved from the general requirements of the Copyright Act). The officials may have had a clear conception of the public interest, but it was not necessarily a view shared by authors – or by others.

This chapter has shown how the Civil Service Commission was part of a significant network of contacts and relationships, both inside and outside the civil service. Like all departments of government and, indeed, many business organisations, the Commission dealt with individuals and groups within its sphere of activities. The purpose here has not been to use this experience to develop sophisticated theories about policy communities and networks (on which there is already a large academic literature), but to present the facts about the wide range of types of relationship which existed. Other writers may wish to use these empirical details, often not as easily available for their purposes as here, to illustrate their theories. Perhaps the most important lesson to learn from these details is that the Civil Service Commission, throughout its life, was involved in a much more complex spread of operations than might previously have been appreciated in the public administration literature.

Furthermore, this network and spread of operations demonstrates a particular understanding of the mission of the Commission. There was a strong belief in high standards of conduct and standards of operations, and a clear view of the public interest. This was based in the philosophy and structures laid down in the mid-nineteenth century. Indeed, these aspects of its work did not change much throughout the life of the Commission and they provided its main motivation. The motivation of the Commission was not a matter of self-aggrandisement, in the sense that is sometimes stated or implied by students of bureaucracy, but dedication to a view of the public interest that required the staff to work towards its implementation within an almost quasi-judicial pattern of proceeding. Nevertheless beneath this mission and attitudes towards public service it was sometimes possible to see evidence of complacent and questionable assumptions. This is nowhere more evident than in the circular line of reasoning which accepted that students of classics (as nineteenth-century pupils in independent schools were) rose to senior positions in the army or civil service, and, therefore, the 'best' form of education for public service was one based on classical studies.

Notes

1. A. Lawrence Lowell, *The Government of England*, vol. I (New York: Macmillan, 1908). See also Lord Bridges, *The Treasury* (London: Allen & Unwin, 1964)), Ch. 18.
2. *Ninth Report from the Select Committee on Estimates, Session 1947–48, The Civil Service Commission*, HC 203, 205 (London: HMSO, 1948), Q. 1,802.
3. *Royal Commission on the Civil Service Minutes of Evidence* (MacDonnell Commission), Cd. 6210 (London: HMSO, 1912), Q. 20.
4. PRO/CSC2/33.
5. PRO/CSC2/33, Civil Service Commissioners to Sir C. Trevelyan, 12 July 1855.
6. PRO/CSC2/33, Civil Service Commissioners to the Treasury, 14 November 1855.
7. PRO/CSC2/35.
8. PRO/CSC2/41.
9. See *Top Jobs in Whitehall and Promotions in the Senior Civil Service*, Report of an RIPA Working Group (London: Royal Institute of Public Administration, 1987), Ch. 1; and Lord Bridges, *The Treasury*, p. 112.
10. *Select Committee on Estimates, Minutes of Evidence taken before Sub-Committee D*, HC 203, 205, Q. 1,919.
11. Ibid., Q. 1,922.
12. H.E. Dale, *The Higher Civil Service of Great Britain* (London: Oxford University Press, 1941), Ch. 6.
13. PRO/T162/702.
14. PRO/CSC11/260.
15. PRO/CSC5/520, A.P. Waterfield to H. Wilson Smith, 20 January 1944.
16. *Select Committee on Estimates, Minutes of Evidence taken before Sub-Committee D*, HC 203, 205, Q. 1,931.

17 Ibid., Q. 1,928.
18 *Sixth Report from the Select Committee on Estimates, Session 1964–65, Recruitment to the Civil Service*, HC 308 (London: HMSO, 1965), Q. 124.
19 PRO/CSC5/539, T. Padmore to A.P. Sinker, 8 March 1951.
20 PRO/CSC5/539, Minute by L.N. Helsby, 21 December 1954.
21 PRO/CSC5/539, Minute by L.N. Helsby, 4 January 1955.
22 PRO/CSC5/482, Minute dated 30 July 1951.
23 PRO/CSC5/467, Note of a meeting at the Civil Service Commission, 23 February 1950.
24 PRO/CSC5/482, Minute by W.H. Fisher, 26 April 1951.
25 PRO/CSC5/482, Minute dated 31 January 1952.
26 Ibid.
27 Richard A. Chapman and J.R. Greenaway, *The Dynamics of Administrative Reform* (London: Croom Helm, 1980), Ch. 3.
28 PRO/T214/72, Dorothy Johnstone to T. Padmore, 22 August 1948. See also Richard A. Chapman, *Leadership in the British Civil Service* (London: Croom Helm, 1984), p. 111.
29 PRO/CSC5/471.
30 PRO/CSC5/471, A.H.M. Hillis to J.R. Simpson, 9 November 1948.
31 PRO/CSC5/471, A.H.M. Hillis to A.P. Waterfield, 9 December 1948.
32 PRO/CSC5/471, A.H.M. Hillis to J.R. Simpson, 14 December 1948.
33 PRO/CSC5/471.
34 PRO/CSC5/507.
35 Ibid.
36 PRO/CSC5/471.
37 Ibid.
38 PRO/CSC5/507.
39 PRO/CSC2/12, *Report on the Indian Civil Service*, November 1884.
40 Ibid.
41 PRO/CSC2/14.
42 Ibid.
43 PRO/CSC2/63.
44 PRO/CSC3/69. This file contains numerous requests for additional examination centres and reports on the operation of local centres 1881–1907.
45 PRO/CSC3/78.
46 PRO/CSC3/77.
47 PRO/CSC3/313.
48 PRO/CSC5/194.
49 PRO/CSC3/314.
50 PRO/CSC3/313.
51 PRO/CSC3/314.
52 PRO/CSC5/194.
53 PRO/CSC3/71.
54 PRO/CSC3/72; PRO/CSC3/73.
55 PRO/CSC3/217.
56 Ibid.
57 PRO/CSC3/234.
58 PRO/CSC3/350.
59 PRO/CSC3/58.
60 PRO/CSC3/232.
61 PRO/CSC5/1175. See also PRO/CSC5/342 and PRO/CSC5/343.
62 PRO/CSC5/144.
63 PRO/CSC5/190.
64 PRO/CSC5/355.

65 PRO/CSC5/302.
66 PRO/CSC5/8, Civil Service Commission to Permanent Under-Secretary of State, India Office, 9 February 1910.
67 PRO/CSC5/1080, J.O. Prestwich to G. Mallaby, 29 August 1962.
68 PRO/CSC5/1080, R.H. Howorth to K.M. Reader, 12 October 1962.
69 PRO/CSC5/1080, K.M. Reader to Director of Examinations, 6 November 1962.
70 PRO/CSC5/1102, P.A. Reynolds to R.N. Burton, 27 October 1964.
71 PRO/CSC5/977, K.M. Reader to Director of Examinations, 11 July 1958.
72 PRO/CSC5/977.
73 Ibid.
74 PRO/CSC5/729, K.M. Reader to Director of Examinations, 16 June 1958.
75 PRO/CSC5/730.
76 PRO/CSC5/1102.
77 PRO/CSC5/729.
78 PRO/CSC5/1102.
79 PRO/CSC5/729.
80 PRO/CSC3/316.
81 *First Report of Her Majesty's Civil Service Commissioners, together with Appendices* (London: HMSO, 1856), PP. 1856, vol. XXII, p. 361.
82 *Thirteenth Report of Her Majesty's Civil Service Commissioners, together with Appendices* (London: HMSO, 1868), PP. 1867–68, vol. XXII, pp. i–xx + 569.
83 *Seventeenth Report of Her Majesty's Civil Service Commissioners, together with Appendices* C. 672 (London: HMSO, 1872), PP. 1872, vol. XIX.
84 Ibid.
85 PRO/CSC5/241.
86 PRO/CSC5/279.
87 PRO/CSC5/279, Admiralty Memorandum, 'Recruitment of Directing Staff for the Admiralty Supply Departments'.
88 PRO/CSC3/320, Stanley Leathes to the Secretary, War Office, 4 November 1904.
89 PRO/CSC3/320.
90 Ibid.
91 Lord Bridges, *The Treasury*, pp. 177–9.
92 PRO/CSC5/301, draft letter to Sir Thomas Phillips.
93 PRO/CSC5/485.
94 PRO/CSC5/1267.
95 PRO/CSC5/1274, PRO/CSC5/1275 and PRO/CSC5/1277.
96 PRO/CSC5/500.
97 PRO/CSC5/344 and PRO/CSC5/1223.
98 PRO/CSC5/337 and PRO/CSC5/1223.
99 PRO/CSC5/977.
100 PRO/CSC3/337, Stanley Leathes to Secretary, Royal Geographical Society, 19 July 1904.
101 PRO/CSC3/337, J. Scott Keltie to Secretary, Civil Service Commission, 25 November 1904.
102 *The Times*, 3 December 1906.
103 *The Times*, 6 December 1906.
104 *The Times*, 10 December 1906.
105 PRO/CSC3/359.
106 PRO/CSC5/500.
107 PRO/CSC5/485.
108 PRO/CSC5/489.
109 PRO/CSC5/498, A.P. Waterfield to Miss W. Hunt, Board of Trade, 24 January 1945.
110 PRO/CSC5/498, L.B. to First Commissioner, 3 February 1945.

111 PRO/CSC5/498, Note on file by A.P. Waterfield, 19 March 1945.
112 PRO/CSC5/189.
113 Dorothy L. Sayers (ed.) *Great Short Stories of Detection, Mystery and Horror: Second Series* (London: Gollancz, 1931).
114 PRO/CSC5/291, G.G. Mennell to the Secretary, Treasury, 7 October 1937.
115 PRO/CSC5/291, C.J. Hayes to First Commissioner, 6 May 1944.
116 PRO/CSC5/291.

6

SETTING STANDARDS IN THE CIVIL SERVICE

Building upon the authority it derived from Orders in Council, the Civil Service Commission quickly established itself because it was energetic, pioneering and efficient in its work. It had a reputation for high standards of propriety through its adoption of publicly known and widely respected rules and procedures; and it made a major contribution to the development of an administrative culture. In particular, it was dedicated to the practice of personal integrity in the public interest. It is therefore appropriate to consider in more detail how the Commission acquired its reputation for such high standards.

The first point to note is that from the beginning the Commissioners were determined to be independent and to be seen to be independent. They emphasised this in their First Report, by recording the 'entire absence of interference, and a tacit but complete recognition of the judicial nature of our functions, on the part of Your Majesty's government'.[1] This was why they wanted to appoint their own Secretary and Registrar (the two chief officers of the department). They wanted the Commission to be like other independent departments rather than being regarded as a sub-department of the Treasury. As explained in chapter 2, the first Commissioners were successful in this, though they accepted Lord Palmerston's requirement for informal consultation. By 1859, when J.G. Maitland succeeded James Spedding as Secretary, the practice for making senior appointments had been established: on 14 November the Commissioners notified the Treasury of their intention to appoint Maitland, explained how well fitted he was for the position, and the appointment went ahead. The Treasury response was to approve the intended appointment.[2]

In the matter of their internal work, especially the setting and marking of examinations, they faced different challenges, mainly because of the political environment in which they were working. Public interest in and apprehension about their work was evident in 1855 and in some respects continued throughout the life of the Commission. An early example of this is revealed in questions raised by Palmerston, then Prime Minister, and the reactions in the Commission to them.

On 6 July 1857 C.G. Barrington wrote from Downing Street to say that Palmerston had asked to see the examination papers for 'the gentlemen who lately competed for the Clerkship in the Treasury'. In his reply, of 8 July, Maitland recalled that in May 1856 a similar request had been made. On that occasion the Commissioners had complied with Palmerston's wish and the papers were sent accompanied by a note, which stated

> that they had deemed it right in order to protect the independence of their judgment to decline acceding to the formal demand of a public department for the production of answers of a candidate but that they were willing to place the documents in question confidentially in his Lordship's hands.

The letter continued by saying that experience had confirmed the Commissioners in the belief that the maintenance of the principle of not revealing the details requested was 'essential to the success of their examinations'. With his letter Maitland sent a copy of the Table of Marks but refused to release the scripts. Barrington, on 21 July, wrote that Palmerston's intention was not to engage in controversy over the Commissioners' decision, but 'as Head of the government Lord Palmerston deems it his duty to inform himself as to any matter connected with the Administration of the affairs of the country' and 'he again requests to see...the examination papers'. This resulted in a reply direct to Palmerston from J.G. Shaw Lefevre, one of the Commissioners, explaining that the Commissioners were convinced of the essential importance of maintaining the independence of the authority of the Commission and that the efficiency of the Commission would be 'totally destroyed' if 'any interference on the part of the Government were to take place with respect to our judgment in individual cases'. As Barrington had also said, however, that Palmerston wished to disclaim any intention of querying the cases of individual candidates, and had specified that his request was so as to be informed 'as to the manner in which our system of examination is carried on' (and had also drawn attention to the controversy associated with the nature of the questions being asked in the examinations), then the Commissioners transmitted for Palmerston's 'own information' the examination papers, 'including the questions proposed, the answers given, and the reports of the examiners'. The point was nevertheless made, and a precedent was established that ministers, including the Prime Minister and First Lord of the Treasury, could not interfere in the judgments of the Commissioners.[3] This was further emphasised in the Commissioners' Second Report where a general outline of the experience was given and it was stated that the Commissioners' judgment on the performances of individual candidates must be exercised without the review of any external authority – otherwise it would be quite impossible for the Commissioners' duties to be justly and effectively executed.[4]

A second point to note is that the Commission wished to be regarded as an example of good practice, following the philosophy laid down in the Macaulay and Northcote–Trevelyan Reports. Recruitment of staff to the Commission was, from its outset, by competition, and in their first Report the Commissioners remarked that their experience of competitions in their own and other offices (compared with nomination and examination elsewhere) was that the successful candidates were much better qualified.[5] The first competitions for recruiting to the Commission were not, in fact, 'open': details were communicated to certain schools and colleges and mentioned casually to other persons by the Commissioners. In 1857 they reported on this experience for four clerkships in the Commission. There were 46 candidates and 44 of them were examined; 28 of the 46 were the sons of professional men and independent gentlemen, 14 were either at school or college; 25 out of the 46 had finished their education at one or other of the universities (five Oxford, six Cambridge, 13 London, one at Trinity College, Dublin); of the remaining 21, who did not proceed to universities, 16 were educated at large public schools or well-known grammar schools and five were educated at private schools.[6]

Another example of this practice was the competition in February 1866 for Supplementary Clerkships in the Office of the Commissioners. Candidates were required to compete in tests lasting two days. These tests consisted of exercises to test handwriting and orthography; copying and indexing; arithmetic, including vulgar and decimal fractions; and English composition. The candidates were to be from 16 to 20 years of age, evidence of date of birth was required and character references and a medical examination were also required. There were 54 candidates, 16 passed in all the subjects prescribed.

The records show that the Commission had developed an advanced recruitment procedure that was a credit to it and also compares well with anything comparable in more modern times.[7] When C.S. West (a supplementary clerk) resigned on 30 December 1865 there were 79 applications for the post he vacated; when R.J. Collins (another supplementary clerk) resigned on 24 December 1867 there were 138 applications for his post; and when T.A. Wilson resigned in 1869 there were 235 applications for his post.[8] This seems to indicate that open competitions, at least for posts in the Commission, had become well established. As the Commissioners said as early as 1857, the evidence showed that if opportunities for competitions were more easily and generally available, 'a highly-instructed class of industrious young men would present themselves as candidates'.[9]

Third, the Commission developed, generally in consultation with the departments of government, practices for the examination of candidates who had been nominated. This was done soon after the Commissioners were appointed, as their letter of 12 July 1855 to Sir Charles Trevelyan explained:

> As soon as a nomination has been made, the department to which it belongs will report it to the Commissioners; at the same time directing the candidate to attend at their office at a certain time, with his certificates of age, health and character. These will be inspected and the candidate questioned, and if his answers prove satisfactory a day will be fixed for his examination. If the situation to which he is nominated be of the lowest class, the qualifications for which in respect of knowledge and

ability admit of a very simple test, he will be examined at once by one of the officers of the establishment. But if it be one requiring an examination of a higher order, the Commissioners will call in the aid of assistant examiners, as contemplated by the Order in Council. They do not foresee any difficulty in procuring such assistance, which has already been offered to them by persons of acknowledged merit and scientific and literary distinction. At present however they do not think it expedient to conclude any arrangement by which this duty shall be entrusted always to the same persons; but they intend to engage, pro rata, the services of those whom they believe to be competent, at such rate of remuneration as may be considered fair and reasonable. For the assistance thus to be rendered they have reason to believe that 3 guineas per diem will be accepted as a sufficient remuneration and if the Lords Commissioners of Her Majesty's Treasury should be willing to sanction such expenditure the Civil Service Commissioners propose to adopt it as their ordinary scale of payment.[10]

This was approved by a Treasury letter of 18 July 1855.

Because there was no unified civil service in the mid-nineteenth century, the Commissioners had first to agree, with the authorities of each department individually, the details of the rules applicable to the various posts for which they were to examine. The formal authority of the Commissioners came from the Orders in Council but their powers were essentially dependent on the requirement for their certificates, which were issued not to individuals but to the employing departments. Therefore the process of consulting departments became important from the outset of the Commission's work. The Commissioners wrote to the departments in June 1855 to ask for details of the subjects which they wished to prescribe for examinations.[11] It was not a difficult exercise because the departments were largely agreed that, for junior appointments, the basic requirements should be good handwriting, correct spelling, arithmetic, an abstract or précis of correspondence or official papers and English composition. Some departments required additional examinations for particular positions.

For recruitment to the less junior positions the guide adopted was always the philosophy expounded in the Macaulay and Northcote–Trevelyan Reports.[12] For posts in the Indian Civil Service, Macaulay specifically said that the examinations should be 'confined to those branches of knowledge to which it is desirable that English gentlemen who mean to remain at home should pay some attention'. Macaulay had also emphasised the importance of literary examinations as a guide to other qualities. His report said: 'the youth who does best what all the ablest and most ambitious youths about him are trying to do will generally prove a superior man'.[13] It also said:

> it is not among young men superior to their fellows in science and literature that scandalous immorality is generally found to prevail... Indeed

early superiority in science and literature generally indicates the existence of some qualities which are securities against vice – industry, self-denial, a taste for pleasures not sensual, a laudable desire of honourable distinction, a still more laudable desire to obtain the approbation of friends and relations. We therefore believe that the intellectual test which is about to be established will be found in practice to be also the best moral test that can be devised.[14]

In practice, however, not everyone was agreed that these qualities were enough. For example, on 20 August 1861 Sir George Couper, Secretary to the Government of the North Western Provinces, wrote to the Secretary of the Government of India:

there is no guarantee that the best of scholars will be even a mediocre administrator; a highly cultivated intellect is not always accompanied by common sense and good judgment; studious habits give no assurance of a determined will, or of energy in enforcing the execution of it…there is in this competitive system no security that the services of men more honourable, more conscientious, more devoted to their duty, or better qualified to influence the Native mind and uphold, in their own persons and bearing, the dignity of the British Government, will ever be obtained. In the quality of physical activity, hardly less needed in most branches of the Indian Service than sound sense and steady judgment, the men of the competitive system are far inferior to the sons of Haileybury.[15]

Similar comments were sent by F.B. Gubbins, Commissioner of the Benares Division, in a letter dated 7 August 1861:

I object to the gentlemen whom we now receive into the service – *First*, because they are, generally speaking, wanting in the tone and manners of gentlemen – a point which is, in my opinion, of great importance among quick-sighted people like the Natives of India, and which imperatively requires to be attended to in 'a governing class'; *secondly* because they are, generally speaking, wanting in that energy and bodily activity which is so essential in a District Officer; *thirdly* because they are, generally speaking, narrow viewed; and *fourthly*, because I have among their whole number met with but two who could learn to ride, and as it appears very probable that the future duties of the members of the service will be limited to mere district work, I look upon this defect as almost a fatal one.[16]

These comments have wider significance than may at first appear because in a variety of forms they occur again and again in comments about the recruitment of graduates to administrative posts in the civil service. The Macaulay and Northcote–Trevelyan Reports contained the basic philosophy for the Commission; but there were modifications and concerns expressed from time to time about their sufficiency for assessing candidates. An example illustrating this is in a letter of 25 June 1855 from E. Hammond (Foreign Office) to Horace Mann. He wrote:

> if a rule as to age at the time of admission is to be laid down, it will be necessary to take into consideration the circumstances whether the family of the candidate resides in Town or not: for it is not desirable that a young man under twenty years of age should be appointed to a Clerkship in the Foreign Office without his Family having a house in the Metropolis.[17]

The important lesson emerges that the Commission kept in mind the philosophy embodied in its basic documents (its Orders in Council, and the Macaulay and Northcote–Trevelyan Reports) but at the same time was sensitive and astute in developing assessment procedures in consultation with departments. The creation of the Commission and the system of examining nominated candidates was a compromise because open competitions for recruitment were not at that time generally acceptable; but the Commission's good track record from 1855 to 1870 created the conditions in which open competitions could become a requirement.

Fourth, the Commission had a strong policy for dealing with candidates and its own staff who deviated from the high standards of conduct it expected. It became known, often from the lessons to be learned from particular cases, that high standards would always be demanded and applied. These standards were encouraged by the social and political environment within which the Commission worked, which encouraged the highest possible standards in the administration of literary examinations.

An example which drew the Commissioners' attention to this expectation was a memorandum, sent on 14 April 1859 from the British Consulate in Shanghai to the Foreign Office in London, and forwarded to the Secretary of the Civil Service Commission on the direction of the Foreign Secretary, the Earl of Malmesbury. The memorandum, dated 13 April 1859, was written by Thomas T. Meadows. It was about the Imperial Edict reported in the *Peking Gazette* on 18 March, and illustrated the importance attached in China to the integrity of public service examinations as the basis of its system of public administration. The Commissioners exemplified this high expectation by publishing, in their Fifth Report, Meadows' memorandum, including the following extract:

> Pih-tseum, one of the four principal ministers of state, officers similar to our prime minister, with the secretaries of the foreign, colonial and home affairs, having been found guilty of conniving of the substitution of a set of essays for the degree of Ken-jin (the second counting from below), he was condemned to decapitation by a specially constituted

court, composed of Imperial princes, ranking next to the Emperor himself, of members of the Cabinet, of high officers of the Imperial household, and of presidents of the boards. The Emperor having summoned into his presence the members of his court, confirmed this sentence, and though 'unable to restrain his tears', ordered the minister to be immediately decapitated, appointing the president of the criminal board with another officer to witness the execution.

The edict speaks of three other officers being condemned to death, in connection with the case, and common report says that 12 in all have been executed, and that many others who were convicted of negligence, though not of connivance, have been cashiered.[18]

Of course, in Victorian Britain the expectations for high standards, and the sentences on individuals who themselves slipped from the highest standards, were not as extreme as in Imperial China. Nevertheless, expectations were high, as was concern about inefficiencies and corruption in the public services, and penalties were sometimes severe. An example from consultations with the Foreign Office illustrates this. When the Commissioners were considering the requirements of departments and setting standards for the examinations, the Foreign Office explained their requirements: 'The Foreign Office requires of its Clerks great sacrifices of time, of comfort and of amusement, and that they should take such an interest in the Office as to consider its credit and reputation as their own.'[19]

An example of an individual case comparable in terms of the severity that could be expected in Britain to the Chinese example mentioned above, and which contributed to the internal precedents developed by the Commissioners into rules of practice akin to case law, occurred in 1887. Arthur Mowbray Berkeley, the second son of Colonel, later Major-General, F.G. Berkeley, was 16 when convicted, on his own confession, of copying from his neighbour during the Preliminary Sandhurst Examination. Representations were made by his headmaster, the Rev J.M. Eustace of the Oxford Military College, and by Douglas Jones who wrote on behalf of the Field Marshall Commanding in Chief, the Duke of Cambridge, to ask whether Berkeley could be 'put back twelve months, as a sufficient punishment' instead of being barred from being a candidate at *any* future public examination. The matter was considered at a meeting of the three Commissioners: the Earl of Strafford, Sir George Dasent and Theodore Walrond, but they felt they could not abandon 'the principle that candidates guilty of such offences should be held ineligible for admission to any future examination'. A carefully worded but very firm letter was sent to the Army pointing out how serious would be any deviation from their rule. The consequences would, in their opinion, have to include a publicly announced modification to rules approved by His Royal Highness the Field Marshall Commanding in Chief; it would create a difference between the rules for entrance into the Army and the rules for entrance to the civil service; and 'the Army Examinations conducted by the Commissioners are just as broadly distinguished by their public character from examinations held at Educational Institutions as the examinations held by the Commissioners for Civil appointments'.[20] In the event, no relaxation of the rule was allowed. When it came to the needs of the Army during the First World War, however, recruitment conditions inevitably changed. Berkeley, who had joined the staff of the Assam Bengal Railway in 1893, and was its Chief Engineer from 1906 to 1914, served in the First World War in France and Mesopotamia, rising to the rank of Lieutenant Colonel in the Royal Engineers; he was mentioned in despatches and became a Companion of the Order of the Indian Empire.[21]

Such attitudes and standards were also expected of examiners, and great emphasis was put on them serving the public interest. As far as the Indian Office was concerned, it made clear that the pensions of professors at Haileybury were granted with the proviso that they would 'engage, if called upon to give their assistance, in the Examination of candidates for the Civil Service of India without remuneration',[22] though travelling and other incidental expenses were later authorised if the professors were not resident in London or its immediate vicinity. Even into the twentieth century, the expectations of public service were reflected in the arrangements for paying fees and expenses to interviewers. C.M. McDowell commented in 1949: 'The majority of our interviewers do tend to claim less rather than more of what is their legal right. This, it seems to me, is the quality of character we are entitled to expect from interviewers.'[23]

Especially in its early years, the Commission also sought to disseminate its expectation of high standards from candidates. To do this it dealt severely with and publicised cases of attempted bribery and cheating connected with its examinations. Cases of fraudulently altering birth and baptismal certificates so that an otherwise ineligible candidate could compete were, it seems, not uncommon.[24] There was occasional cheating in examinations, including personation;[25] there was even a case in Liverpool of a candidate for a position as clerk in the Stationery Office, Frederick William Partington, fraudulently attempting to arrange a reference for himself from someone who had not employed him.[26] What is remarkable about many of these cases is that some of the individuals were extraordinarily naïve and/or desperate to get jobs in the civil service. Sometimes they did not appear to appreciate that their behaviour was improper.[27] People generally had therefore to be educated in the standards to be expected by the Commission. The Commissioners contributed to this by issuing notices with examination timetables, outlining the rules for behaviour in examinations, with an explanation that disqualification would follow detection of impropriety. They fully explained their decisions to individuals concerned; wherever possible they prosecuted or encouraged departments to prosecute for fraud;[28] they publicised details of incidents in their annual reports and, above all, they adopted a rule that anyone caught cheating would be prevented, on grounds of character, from ever again becoming a candidate in a Civil Service Commission public examination.[29] Their generally severe approach was well reflected in the case, in 1862, of a dockyard apprentice whose date of birth on his birth certificate had been altered. The Admiralty was prepared to accept a punishment more lenient than the Commissioners.

Maitland, writing for the Commissioners, argued that it was an offence 'of only too frequent occurrence and, therefore, one which, for the sake of example, cannot be lightly passed over'.[30]

Nowhere were standards more rigorously expected than among the Commission's own staff or others engaged on work for the Commission. Mrs Champion, in an attempt to get examination papers in advance for her son who was a candidate for the Royal Military College, Sandhurst, tried to bribe someone on the staff of Messrs Harrison and Sons, the printers. This led to the Civil Service Commissioners persuading the Treasury to insert a clause into the bill that became the Official Secrets Act 1889, to prevent the disclosure of such information from firms engaged on work for government departments.[31] An Acting Sergeant in the Royal Irish Constabulary was found, by a Court of Inquiry, to have tampered with official examination marks and he was dismissed: he claimed to be innocent, but his case attracted considerable publicity in the *Irish Daily Independent*.[32]

The Commissioners were, however, not simply applying rigid rules to individual cases without taking their discretionary powers seriously. For example, in 1878 they considered the case of F.E. Richardson. Richardson, a clerk of the lower division in the Commission office had for some time, with the assistance of his wife, been carrying on a business as a tobacconist. Circumstances later compelled him to compound with his creditors. The Commissioners considered the matter in the light of a recent Treasury Minute and decided that while Richardson ought, on his appointment as a permanent Clerk, to have taken steps to sever his connection with the tobacconist's business, because his difficulties were not the result of extravagance or culpable improvidence, he could be retained in his post at the Commission.[33]

An example of the Commissioners displaying their use of discretion in a less sensitive way, which may have contributed to the loss of an otherwise satisfactory member of staff, occurred in 1861. On Friday 5 July, Reginald H. Paynter, a senior clerk in the Record Department of the Civil Service Commission, left the office at 8.30 to go home, but he had a cold and fell asleep on the train, missing his station, Weybridge, so that he continued to Southampton, where he arrived at 1.30 a.m. He immediately sent a telegram to Mann, then Registrar and Chief Clerk, in the hope that someone else in the office could take his place on duty for Saturday. He took the earliest train back to Weybridge, but did not arrive until 4.00 a.m., too tired to go to work that day. At about 1.30 p.m. on the Saturday, however, T. Walrond, who was then in charge of examinations at the Commission, saw Paynter in Regent Street. Paynter said he had to go to London on private business, and when asked for further information declined to give details because he reckoned he would in any case be losing a day's leave because of his absence on Saturday. The Commissioners, at their meeting on 12 July, recorded their disapprobation, found Paynter's explanation unsatisfactory and recorded that Paynter's attitude showed 'a want of courtesy towards the Registrar who was acting under the express directions of the Commissioners'.

They directed that a copy of their minute be not only given to Paynter but also circulated in the office. On 31 December 1861 the Commissioners accepted Paynter's resignation from his position at the Commission.[34]

Fifth, the Commission paid particular attention to ensuring that its examinations were as fair as possible; that candidates experienced equality of treatment; and that appointments were made on merit, assessed preferably through open competition.[35] Efforts were continuously made to ensure that potential problems of unfairness in examinations were avoided. The Northcote–Trevelyan Report had drawn attention to the difficulty of holding all examinations for the lower class of appointments in one place: 'If the scheme of examinations were more favourable to one locality than another...it would be set aside as unjust.'[36]

An example of this arose from the accommodation and supervision of examinations from the early 1880s. Fred Barton, a junior clerk in the Commission, went to Ireland to inspect and report on examination centres there.[37] Later, there were requests for more centres. Fred H. Houston wrote in 1886 asking for Belfast to be used as a centre (mainly on the ground that 'Aberdeen, a smaller place, is already made a Centre'); the Town Clerk of Londonderry also asked for his town to be recognised in this way. Barton's report stressed the confusion he observed at some centres, which led to irregularities and complaints. He found that dictation was 'an unknown art in Ireland, except at Civil Service Examinations, and the superintendent must therefore construe his paper of printed instructions without any extraneous assistance whatever'. In Dublin, the superintendent employed a 'repeater'. He dictated himself from one corner of the room, but before commencing the critical part of the dictation, i.e. the second reading, in which the candidates took down the passage sentence by sentence, he stationed an assistant precisely in the centre of the room, who repeated each sentence after him. A similar procedure was used by the superintendent in Cork. This procedure was not used in London or, apparently, elsewhere in England or Scotland. Although Barton noted that complaints from Dublin and Cork were rare, he added his criticism that 'the repeater would be better heard and could make more use of his eyes if he had no candidates behind him'. In Belfast, Limerick and Galway, no repeater was employed but as the superintendent stood among the candidates instead of facing them, he 'is unable to watch and is indistinctly heard by those seated behind him'. At Belfast, when a candidate complained that he had not caught a sentence, the superintendent left his place and repeated it to him *sotto voce*: the absurdity was that there was no time to give a private repetition to each candidate so that favours were, in effect, bestowed on some candidates but not on others. In Belfast the hall in the Queen's College was used for examinations. It was capable of accommodating 150 candidates comfortably, but owing to its great height the acoustics were bad and the echo made it difficult to distinguish words during dictation.

The report by Barton provides ample evidence of the difficulties of ensuring equal opportunities for candidates taking examinations at different provincial centres. In the Commission the difficulties were well understood and considerable effort was spent on ensuring that candidates had equal opportunities to compete at local centres in conditions that were comparable and well suited to the purpose, otherwise the work of the Commission would be seriously undermined. As K.M. Reader put it in 1968: 'In our recruitment…we have tried not only to avoid unfairness but the appearance of unfairness, or procedures where unfairness could be seen as a possibility.'[38]

Sixth, the Commission took very seriously its responsibilities in assessing the age, health and character of candidates. Within the department a branch specialised in checking such evidence and as a result it acquired skill in collecting and processing the information, and experience in detecting potential problems. The Commission took similarly seriously its responsibility for probation. Probation was specifically mentioned by Northcote and Trevelyan in their report, where they made it clear that they envisaged candidates successful in the examinations as being selected only as probationers. In their Third Report the Commissioners elaborated on aspects of the Northcote–Trevelyan approach by saying that superiority in science and literature implied:

> to some extent at least, the like superiority in some moral qualities, such as self-denial, regularity, perseverance and energy. We admit nevertheless, that there are other moral qualities, such as 'judgment', 'discretion', 'moral courage', 'stability of purpose', 'fidelity', respecting which a certain conclusion cannot be drawn.[39]

They went on to argue that although these qualities were not measurable or comparable between candidates in intellectual examinations they could be assessed during probation and during promotion by merit. In the twentieth century some of these comments were taken further and had an important part to play in the development of what became the Method II system of selection for the administrative class.

In 1862 the Commissioners considered the principles that should guide their decisions on these matters (i.e. the second and third heads mentioned in the Order in Council of 21 May 1855). On 18 November they minuted that

> by this provision the duty of satisfying them as to his eligibility is thrown upon the candidate and…unless he can satisfy them they cannot grant their certificate. The benefit of any reasonable doubt which may exist must, they conceive, be given not to him, but to the public. As long as there is such doubt it is impossible for them to say that they are satisfied. The question should not be looked at as if the candidate had a vested right to an appointment, liable only to be divested on his being proved unfit. It is, in reality, whether he can gain a title by proving himself fit, and the difference is so considerable that the Commissioners are anxious to keep it present to the minds of those to whom they apply for advice.[40]

Later, on 7 October 1902, the Commissioners considered the matter again, with a view to regulating the disallowance of increments at the end of the probationary year of clerks in the Second Division. They decided that each case should be considered on its merits, but having regard to the causes of failure in cases occurring during the previous five years, they laid down for their own guidance a scheme for disallowance. There were to be two categories. The first category related to cases involving moral default, and this consisted of four classes. For carelessness, inaccuracy, unpunctuality etc. there would be a loss of increments for two years. For insubordination, stubbornness, unreliability and calculated attempts to obtain discharge from departments etc. there would be a loss of increments for four years. For character and conduct reported unsatisfactory in a minor degree, absence without leave etc. there would be a loss of increments for six years. For character and conduct unsatisfactory in serious matters there would be removal from the list. For cases in the second category, simple failure not involving moral default, service was to be allowed.[41] Although the Commissioners developed these rules early in the twentieth century the entries in the Minute Book of Board Meetings from 1855 show how conscientiously they considered the probation requirements for each individual member of staff – and they did not hesitate to extend probation in cases of doubt.[42] When, in 1904, there was a serious malfunction in the Commission as a result of the negligence of a superior officer the Commissioners impressed on each member of staff 'the necessity of maintaining the high character of the Commission by exercising thought and public spirit in the discharge of his own duties'.[43]

Not only did the Commissioners set a high standard in applying the probation requirements in their own department, they also used the experience of other departments as a check on their own efficiency. After they published their First Report in 1856, they sent a letter to departments drawing attention to an extract from the report (which was enclosed). They said that:

> if, notwithstanding the Examination by the Commission, any incompetent person should find his way into the Public Service, the period of six monthly probation, which the Order in Council provides, will afford an opportunity to the department to dispense with his services. We expect to derive advantage from watching the results of this probation, and accordingly we propose to request the several Departments to inform us of any case in which Candidates who have received our certificates shall have been found insufficient, so as not to justify the confirmation of their Appointment. We think that this information may enable us to ascertain and to remedy defects which may exist either in the principle or the practice of our examinations.[44]

The letter then asked for details, in confidence, of such information for appointments to junior situations between 21 May 1855 and 21 May 1856, with causes in specific instances leading to dismissals.

The probation requirements were formally strengthened by the Order in Council of 4 June 1870. One consequence was that the Commissioners were to be informed by departments of the result of probation before the Commissioners' certificate was issued. This ensured that whatever might be the ability of the persons selected by examination, there was evidence of their practical efficiency. The process of appointment was, in effect, formally extended until after a candidate had been tried in the actual discharge of his duties. As the Commissioners said in their Seventeenth Report:

> The record of this decision was to be transmitted to us, not...with any intention that we should review such decision, but in order that, according to its tenor, we might issue or withhold the definitive certificate of qualification without which the candidate would not be finally appointed to the public service.

When the Order in Council of 19 August 1871 weakened this arrangement the Commissioners expressed their regret.[45]

This chapter has outlined six ways in which the Commission set high standards in its work and promulgated them. Much of its experience was reflected in its annual reports. Indeed, most of the annual reports published in the nineteenth century were major documents of several hundred pages: for example, the First Report was 361 pages[46] and the Sixth Report was 570 pages.[47] It is not surprising that by 1862 Treasury officials and ministers, including W.E. Gladstone who was Chancellor of the Exchequer, recognised that the experiment of creating the Civil Service Commission had been 'eminently successful' and the time had arrived to treat it as a permanent institution.

The important and widely respected role quickly achieved by the Commissioners was to a large extent the result of the industry and high standards set and publicised within the civil service by the Commissioners themselves. Their rules were applied with judicial precision and authority. Where their experiences and decisions on particular cases might be used as lessons for others they were publicised – in annual reports and correspondence. In particular, corruption and fraud was, whenever possible prosecuted and reported in the press: general standards were to be improved by lessons of bad examples made public. All this activity contributed to setting high standards and educating people about them, and also to enhancing those standards. It was not long before the Civil Service Commission acquired other functions normally associated with a central department of personnel administration. The Commission quickly became the guardian of the rules for admission to the civil service, while the Treasury was increasingly representing what it saw as the general interests of the service. Rarely did the Commissioners lose an opportunity to assert their role as they saw it, of promoting the efficiency of the civil service in the public interest. In addition, administrative provisions were made which, in effect, strengthened their position. The Commission was told when clerks were surplus to requirements: they could then be re-allocated to another department. Sometimes staff did not satisfy probation requirements but could successfully be re-allocated by the Commission. Provision was made for successful candidates to choose the departments in which they would prefer to work, with preference being given according to their place in the examination list. The Commission also became increasingly consulted for advice when criteria were being considered for filling vacant positions. All these developments buttressed the position of the Commission as a unifying authority within the civil service. The standards set by the Commission, especially those relating to recruitment by fair and open means, probation and promotion on merit, made a major contribution to the values generally referred to as the administrative culture.

Notes

1 *First Report of Her Majesty's Civil Service Commissioners, together with Appendices*, PP. 1856, vol. XXII.
2 PRO/CSC2/33.
3 PRO/CSC2/35.
4 *Second Report of Her Majesty's Civil Service Commissioners, together with Appendices*, PP. 1857, Session I, vol. III.
5 *First Report*.
6 *Second Report*.
7 PRO/CSC2/49.
8 PRO/CSC8/4.
9 *Second Report*.
10 PRO/CSC2/33.
11 *First Report*. See also PRO/CSC2/24.
12 PRO/CSC3/249.
13 *The Indian Civil Service, Report to the Right Hon. Sir Charles Wood*, by T.B. Macaulay and others (London: W. Thacker and Co, 1855), reprinted in *The Civil Service, vol. I, Report of the Committee 1966–68*, Cmnd. 3638 (London: HMSO, 1968), Appendix B. See also PRO/CSC2/12 and PRO/CSC2/13.
14 Ibid.
15 PRO/CSC2/16.
16 Ibid.
17 PRO/CSC2/5.
18 *Fifth Report of Her Majesty's Civil Service Commissioners, together with Appendices*, PP. 1860, vol. XXIV.
19 PRO/CSC2/5, Hammond to Mann, 25 June 1855.
20 PRO/CSC3/155.
21 *The Times*, 24 March 1937 and 27 March 1937.
22 PRO/CSC2/8, enclosure to a letter dated 12 May 1855.
23 PRO/CSC3/354, comments by C.M., dated 11 August 1949.
24 PRO/CSC2/20, PRO/CSC2/45, PRO/CSC3/269, *Eighth Report of Her Majesty's Civil Service Commissioners, together with Appendices*, PP. 1863, vol. XX, *Ninth Report of Her Majesty's Civil Service Commissioners, together with Appendices*, PP. 1864, vol. XXX.
25 PRO/CSC3/138, PRO/CSC3/149, PRO/CSC3/213, *Forty-first Report of Her Majesty's Civil Service Commissioners, with Appendix*, C. 8569 (London: HMSO, 1897), PP. 1897, vol. XXIV.
26 PRO/CSC3/351.

27 PRO/CSC3/87.
28 PRO/CSC2/45, PRO/CSC3/351.
29 PRO/CSC3/70, PRO/CSC3/87, PRO/CSC3/144.
30 *Eighth Report*.
31 PRO/CSC3/207.
32 PRO/CSC3/334.
33 PRO/CSC8/6.
34 PRO/CSC8/3.
35 *Seventeenth Report of Her Majesty's Civil Service Commissioners, together with Appendices*, C. 672 (London: HMSO, 1872), PP. 1872, vol. XIX.
36 *Report on the Organisation of the Permanent Civil Service* (Northcote–Trevelyan Report) (London: HMSO, 1854), PP. 1854, vol. XXVII, reprinted in *The Civil Service, vol. I, Report of the Committee 1966–68*, Cmnd. 3638, Appendix B.
37 PRO/CSC3/67–9.
38 PRO/CSC5/1638.
39 *Third Report of Her Majesty's Civil Service Commissioners, together with Appendices*, PP. 1857–58, vol. XXV.
40 PRO/CSC8/4.
41 PRO/CSC8/7.
42 PRO/CSC8/1.
43 PRO/CSC8/7.
44 PRO/CSC2/15.
45 *Seventeenth Report*.
46 *First Report*.
47 *Sixth Report of Her Majesty's Civil Service Commissioners, together with Appendices*, PP. 1861, vol. XIX.

7

THE CASE OF ARTHUR CREECH JONES

Clerk in the Civil Service Commission

As a consequence of the Military Service Act, 1916, the civil service had to decide how to deal with civil servants who refused military service on conscientious grounds. The importance of the Military Service Act was that it introduced conscription – i.e. compulsory military service: previously the army relied on volunteers. The Act, however, also conferred the right on conscientious objectors to apply for exemption from combatant service to tribunals empowered to grant such exemptions, which could be absolute or conditional. During the First World War there were about 300 conscientious objectors throughout the civil service, including some 40 or 50 who were not prepared to accept the conditional exemption they were given – usually on condition that they served in the non-combatant corps, which they generally regarded as the equivalent of rejection by the tribunal.[1] Among those who did so was A.C. Jones, a Second Division clerk in the Civil Service Commission. Creech Jones (as he was later publicly known) became Colonial Secretary in the post-1945 Labour government. His experience during and after the First World War provides insights into the attitudes of certain officials in the Commission and the Treasury, and into relationships between the Treasury and other departments.

Some cases of civil servants who were conscientious objectors came to the notice of the Treasury in 1916, only a few months after the Military Service Act was passed. It should be remembered that at that time civil servants held their posts, legally, at the pleasure of the Crown (i.e. the government), and they could therefore be dismissed at any time without notice: the right to dismiss was absolutely unqualified[2] and, as R.G. (later Sir Ralph) Hawtrey, then in the Treasury, minuted on 17 March 1917:

> the power of dismissing an officer resides in the head of his Department and...the Treasury is not prepared to interfere with the latter's discretion. It is not the case that civil servants can only be removed for grave dereliction of duty or conviction of felony.[3]

Although they had no formal contracts, an implied contract meant that established civil servants could reasonably expect to continue in service until retirement age and receive a pension, and their remuneration was said to take account of this benefit.[4] There was, however, no legal provision for pensions except on grounds of age or the incapacity of officials to discharge their duties. Heads of departments had considerable discretion not only on who was employed in their departments but also, in war-time, on deciding what work should be deemed to satisfy exemption on grounds of its being of national importance, though the Treasury, as the central department for policy on staff matters, issued guidance and developed rules that were in practice applied throughout the civil service. The Treasury first developed rules to be applied to its own staff and in departments within the ambit of the Treasury, and these included the Civil Service Commission. In these matters the Treasury acted not on its own initiative but in reaction to the law.[5] It was therefore implementing government policy and its circulars were issued on the government's authority.[6]

Nevertheless, the evidence suggests that Treasury officials individually and as a group may have influenced the rigour with which the rules were applied. Moreover, the Treasury was concerned not only with implementing the law, but also with the prestige and reputation of the civil service. For example, Treasury files refer in 1916 to the popular and parliamentary fulminations against 'lurkers', 'shirkers' and '*embusqués*'[7] – these were references to civil servants of military age, retained in departments on work categorised as of national importance, but whose work should, according to critics, have been given to unfit men, men over military age or women. In the Treasury it was observed that during the House of Commons debate on 15 May 1916[8] member after member suggested that there were many civil servants hiding behind such exemptions given by heads of departments. Subsequently, a Treasury minute of 19 May 1916 noted that:

> the fact that this belief is widely prevalent in the House of Commons is proof that it is widely held outside. Most civil servants have probably had this suggestion conveyed to them more or less politely; and that it should be made as frequently as it is not only privately, but in the Press and now in Parliament, is not only exceedingly unpleasant and humiliating for the individual, who has been anxious to join the Army ever since the outbreak of war, but is likely to have a bad effect on the prestige and reputation of the Service as a whole.[9]

The civil service at this time was therefore facing considerable criticism and had to be sensitive to public opinion, especially when expressed in Parliament. Also, since they could not publicly defend themselves against criticisms they felt were unjust, some officials were particularly anxious not to appear lenient in the treatment of their colleagues.

These preliminary remarks are intended to indicate the background to the case of A.C. Jones.[10] It should be remembered that Jones was one of about 300 conscientious objectors whose cases were at the time being considered in some seventeen departments: the Report of the House of Commons Select Committee on the Civil Service (Employment of Conscientious Objectors) 1922, provides an important record of some of them, though not of Jones. Arthur Creech Jones was born in Bristol on 15 May 1891. His father, Joseph Jones, was a journeyman lithographic printer. From 1898 until 1905 he was educated at Whitehall Boys' School, Easton, Bristol, where he won a scholarship which enabled him to study French, mathematics and commercial subjects for an additional year. At school he was held in high regard. For example, his class master, Gilbert E. Lear, wrote in 1904: 'It is impossible to speak too highly of his abilities or character. The latter is absolutely above suspicion. He was ever truthful, honest and straightforward.'[11] From 15 May 1905 until January 1907 he worked as a junior clerk for 7/- a week in the office of J.L. and E.T. Daniell, Solicitors, 44 Baldwin Street, Bristol.[12]

Having taken evening classes as a preparation, in September 1906 he competed in the Civil Service Commission examinations for the position of boy clerk. His success in the examinations resulted in his assignment to the Exchequer and Audit Department (E and AD) and he moved to London, finding lodgings at 68 Crystal Palace Road, East Dulwich. For the E and AD he worked from 31 January 1907 in the War Office in London. On 7 July 1910 he successfully competed in the assistant clerks competition, being examined in five subjects: English composition, arithmetic, digesting returns, précis and indexing and bookkeeping, and came seventh in order of merit among 342 candidates.[13] As a result he worked as an Abstractor in the Estate Duty Office, Inland Revenue, from 26 September 1910 until 12 October 1910; as an Assistant Clerk in the Crown Agents from 13 October 1910 until 16 January 1912; then, from 17 January until 24 March 1912, in the Central Office for Labour Exchanges and Unemployment Insurance within the Board of Trade. On 21 March 1912 he was selected for temporary service as a Second Division clerk in the Civil Service Commission, and on 8 July 1912 his appointment was made permanent.[14] In his early years as a civil servant he was called plain Arthur Jones, but later he made greater use of his second name and became known to all but his closest friends as Creech.[15]

In 1906, when he first competed in examinations for the civil service, his referees were Lear and George F. Russell, YMCA Secretary; in addition the Commission contacted his employers, J.L. and E.T. Daniell. All three character references were strongly supportive, saying that Jones was good, very satisfactory and undoubtedly honest. In 1910, when Jones was a candidate in the examination for Second Division clerks, the reference from the Chief Clerk, Crown Agents, said that his character had been in all respects satisfactory and his health had been good.[16]

He read widely and in a letter dated 5 November 1912 he wrote that he had:

> a strange sympathy toward both the realist and the idealist, as witness my admiration for Galsworthy and my delight in Rosetti...We live in a time when, if we are to be true to ourselves, we must look facts in the face – see life as it is – and not attempt to throw over them an idle glamour.[17]

The evidence suggests he was an earnest young man. His obituary in *The Times* (24 October 1964) said he was a modest and unassuming man, whose sincerity won him many friends. He was a vegetarian; and a non-denominational 'Free Church' Christian. He was a member of the Methodist Church until 1912, but from 1910, when he began to question Church dogma, he became active in the Liberal Christian League. He was interested in socialism at an early age and fulfilled his membership pledge to personal social service, made to the Liberal Christian League, by becoming a founder-member and honorary secretary to the Camberwell Trades Council and Borough Labour Party (1913–22) and also, from 1913, honorary secretary of the Dulwich branch of the Independent Labour Party (ILP). He became a humanist and was actively against militarism and for the international socialist movement.[18] As early as 1913 he was active in the ILP anti-conscription campaign; he also joined the South London Federal Council against Conscription and the No Conscription Fellowship.

On 6 March 1916 he appeared before the Local Advisory Committee. Each army recruiting district had an Advisory Committee, appointed by the War Office to scrutinise applications to the Local Tribunal and to instruct the Military Representative to the tribunal much as a solicitor instructs counsel.[19] Jones stated to the Advisory Committee that he was not prepared to do any military service. It seems that the Advisory Committee accepted that he was a genuine conscientious objector but was not prepared for him to be given absolute exemption from military service. He then appealed to the Local Tribunal at Camberwell Town Hall, which heard his case on 17 March. The Tribunal upheld the Advisory Committee decision, recognised him as a conscientious objector and decided that he should be passed for non-combatant service. He next appealed to the County of London Appeal Tribunal, which considered his case on 5 May, decided that there was not sufficient evidence to reverse the decision of the local tribunal, consequently dismissed the appeal and refused leave to appeal to the Central Tribunal. The decision of the Appeal Tribunal, against Jones' case for absolute exemption, was on the ground that as no previous complete exemption on conscientious grounds had been granted by the Tribunal, it would be unfair to others to grant it to Jones.[20] Jones then went back to the Local Tribunal and, on 9 June, asked it to reconsider its certificate of exemption and to change it from conditional to absolute. Jones heard on 5 July from the Advisory Committee of the Local Tribunal requesting him to appear before them to support his application for revision.[21]

Meanwhile, in the Civil Service Commission, Jones' position was no secret: indeed, he seems to have had very good relations with his colleagues – if his letter of 14 September 1916 to his immediate superior, S. J. Guppy, a Second Division clerk, higher grade, is any guide. The letter began 'My greetings to everyone...'.[22] However, at the highest level in the Commission there was uneasiness about Jones' position and on 5 June 1916 L.C.H. Weekes, then Secretary and Registrar, wrote on behalf of the Commissioners, and with their approval, to the War Office Chief Recruiting Officer, Central London Recruiting Depot.

Weekes provided full details of Jones, who was then living with the Tidman family at 46 Keston Road, Goose Green, London. He also gave an outline of Jones' case up to the decision of the Appeal Tribunal to refuse leave to appeal to the Central Tribunal. He continued:

> Thereafter he received a summons to report himself for service, but states that he returned it saying that he intended to exercise his right of appeal back to the Local Tribunal. He maintains that he has the right and has been so advised.
>
> No further action appears to have been taken by the military authorities, and Mr Jones continues to hold his position in this office.
>
> As the case stands the Commissioners probably have no right to suspend Mr Jones from service and they are anxious not to give him occasion to raise a grievance.
>
> On the other hand they have no desire to shield Mr Jones or make any undue concession to him; and they desire me to lay the case before you in order to make their position clear.[23]

This had quick effect. On 10 June 1916 Jones wrote to the Secretary, Civil Service Commission, reporting that he had, the previous night, received a notice dated that day, instructing him to present himself for military service that morning (10 June). However, he had, before receiving the notice, lodged with the local tribunal a notice for revision of the conditional certificate he had been granted, and an application for an absolute certificate of exemption because of his religious and moral convictions, and he had attended the office that morning because Clause 3, paragraph 5, of the Military Service Act, 1916, seemed to allow him exemption until his application had been finally disposed of. A note on Jones' file recorded that Jones had been instructed to report for military service at 9.00 a.m. on 6 September, but he had not complied with the summons, and was, in fact, still attending the office, and expected to be arrested 'tonight or shortly'. Instructions were requested as to Jones' position at the office 'pending his being fetched by the military authorities'.[24]

As there were no further developments the Commissioners decided on 8 September 1916 that Weekes should write again to the Chief Recruiting Officer:

> the Commissioners think it well that they should again make it clear that they have no desire to shield Mr Jones... They apprehend that the further action by which his attendance at this Office will presumably be discontinued will be taken by the military authorities, and that no direct action is called for on their part.[25]

The Chief Recruiting Officer replied the same day: 'the action to be taken in the case of Mr Arthur Creech Jones has the attention of the Military authorities. The necessary steps to enforce his compliance with their requirements are now in course'.[26]

Jones wrote from 'somewhere in Kent' to Guppy on 10 September 1916:

> I am scribbling this note sat on a grassy bank in the damp on a Sabbath evening. I have heard that the police called for me on Saturday afternoon, so I may conclude that this is my last day of freedom. They will probably call for me on Monday. In any case I shall present myself at the police station and shall probably be charged at Lambeth Police Court on Tuesday morning. In the circumstances it seems useless to turn up at the office on Monday (tomorrow) because I shall be arrested there. I shall be glad therefore if tomorrow may be counted as ordinary leave. I had intended to present myself to the military, but as I appealed to the Central Tribunal on Friday last in order that the military should take no action against the friends with whom I live for harbouring a 'deserter' I cannot follow that course without admitting that such appeal was not valid…
>
> I shall, when before the magistrate, argue that pending the decision regarding appeal to go to the Central Tribunal, my case is not yet clear, but I do not anticipate that I shall get a remand. If my case were clear I should probably not bother with the Police Court business but go direct to the Recruiting Office. I had already informed the military that I would write them as soon as I heard about the Central Tribunal. Actually my immediate arrest is out of order! but the magistrate will determine differently. To him, C.O.s are a 'peculiar' people. If I get a remand I will call up…My appeal to Central secures the office from risk for continuing to employ me since Tuesday.[27]

He appeared at Lambeth Police Court on Tuesday 12 September, was fined 40/- for being an absentee under the Reserve Forces Act 1882, was handed over to an escort and was taken first to the Recruiting Office at Camberwell Baths, where he refused to sign his documents or to be medically examined, then taken to Hounslow Barracks that evening.[28] He was attached to the Royal Fusiliers. The next morning he refused to obey the order of a Sergeant to stand to attention. He stated: 'I refuse to do anything for the Military as I am a conscientious objector' and was taken to the guard detention room where he remained until his Court Martial on 29 September. While in detention he wrote to the Secretary, Civil Service Commission, on 23 September, explaining that he was awaiting Court Martial for disobedience to military orders:

> For religious and moral reasons I have been unable to sign any papers, to accept any pay, to consent to medical examination or to obey any military orders.
>
> I was granted a non-combatant certificate by the Tribunals. Both the Local and Appeal Tribunals admitted the genuineness of my conscientious objection to all forms of military service and admitted their satisfaction; indeed they refused to hear testimonials and evidence because

of their satisfaction. I therefore submit that as each man should be faithful to the inner light, the responsibility of my present position is due to the failure of the Tribunals to administer the Military Service Acts – a failure which the Government has admitted by subjecting objectors to a fresh examination by the Central Tribunal some time after their arrival in prison.

...I have received no military summons that was in order. The police called at my home in my absence and, on my own responsibility I attended the police station where I was placed under arrest and charged as an absentee. At the Police Court the magistrate accepted the statement of Lieut Lucy that the Appeal Tribunal had given me written notice of their decision and had refused me the right of appeal to the Central Tribunal. This was absolutely untrue as I tried to explain to the magistrate, and it was only on the evening of the 20th instant (eight days after I was charged) that my case was disposed of and notice to that effect received at my home address (notice was dated the 19th instant). Consequently, under the regulations I was not liable for three clear days after the receipt of written notice and I was covered by Section 3, Subsection 5 of the principal Military Service Act. Indeed, it was my intention on the disposal of my case and on receipt of the military summons to report to you and to report myself to the military authorities.

...Although in military detention I am not a prisoner until the court martial has delivered its judgment. I therefore submit that I should be treated as other men passed for military service and receive my salary (less deductions) until that judgment is announced.

...I will report to you the decision of the court martial.[29]

Weekes replied on 27 September that the Commissioners has caused Jones' salary up to and including the 10th to be paid to his nominee (Mrs E. Tidman); payment of his salary since that date was suspended. He added:

in the event of your refusing to perform duty in a Non-Combatant Corps and being subsequently committed to a civil prison by order of a Court Martial the Commissioners would have to consider the termination of your appointment as Second Division Clerk in their Department.[30]

Following his sentence of six months' hard labour at the Court Martial on Friday 29 September 1916[31] Jones was removed to Wormwood Scrubs prison. There, he spent the first month in solitary confinement and was not allowed writing materials (the usual procedure for a hard labour prisoner); he then worked under supervision as a laundryman and maker of mailbags. He wrote: 'As a worthy civil servant I scrubbed shirts and pillowslips morning and afternoon. It was a funny picture – beard, clogs, leather apron, scrubbing brush!'[32] Conditions were harsh, prisoners were worked ten hours a day; they were allowed to write and receive one letter a month, plus one personal visit.[33]

Despite the constraints on writing materials he managed to write to the Secretary, Civil Service Commission, on 2 October 1916 to tell him that the court martial sentence was six months' hard labour. He urged further consideration to the fact that the military authorities claimed him eight or nine days before he was liable to service, claimed his salary for those days and also for the war bonus from July and pointed out that military service was never a condition of his employment and that he was therefore not guilty of a breach on that account:

> Further, conscientious objectors are definitely recognised and provided for by Act of Parliament and the failure of Tribunals to administer the Act, while recognising me to be a genuine objector, and to grant me that form of exemption consistent with the faith I hold is not an offence by myself. The only honourable thing for me to do is suffer the sentence imposed on me.[34]

While at Wormwood Scrubs the Central Tribunal interviewed him and again offered him exemption from military service, but on conditions he could not accept. On 1 January 1917 he was transferred back to Hounslow Barracks, disobeyed another order on 13 January, was therefore court martialled again on Saturday 13 January, this time sentenced to two years' hard labour, and on 20 January sent to Wandsworth Prison. At the end of his sentence he was returned to Hounslow Barracks, on 20 February 1919 refused to put on a suit of Service Dress, was court martialled again on 27 February and on 4 March 1919 was sent to Pentonville Prison with another two year sentence. During his prison sentences he attended the prison Chapel and Quaker meetings, which he found very helpful.

Recognising what was likely to happen to him, Jones had asked for special leave without pay, but this was refused by the Civil Service Commissioners on 11 July 1916, and Jones was informed of their decision, apparently by Weekes, on 12 July 1916.[35] After Jones' arrest, Weekes wrote, on 16 September 1916 to L.J. Newby, Principal Clerk, HM Treasury, asking whether the Treasury had laid down uniform rules for the treatment of conscientious objectors, adding: 'We have one, now I believe awaiting a Court Martial, and a very proper case for a year's hard labour. We don't know whether we exercise our discretion in dealing with him, or ought to ask you for a ruling.'[36]

In fact, as early as 31 July 1916 R.S. (later Sir Roderick) Meiklejohn, then in the Treasury, wrote to his colleague G.L. Barstow, outlining his views on conscientious objectors and, presumably, the Treasury attitude. He wrote:

> For the honour of the Civil Service it is to be hoped that there are not many conscientious objectors in its ranks...Whether a man is a soldier or a Civil Servant, he is equally in the King's Service, and a man who has so gravely misconducted himself in one capacity as to merit a sentence of hard labour is...not a suitable person to continue in the King's service in another.[37]

Barstow added his comment on 1 August 1916: 'the offence is that of a bad citizen; and I agree that dismissal from employment under the Crown is not too severe a penalty'. On another occasion, towards the end of 1916, Meiklejohn commented to Sir Thomas Heath on the case of Ernest Robinson, an official in Customs and Excise:

> I do not think that when a man has been called up...he has any right to fail to attend...His subsequent conduct...makes it to my mind abundantly clear that this man was designedly intent to be as contumacious and disobedient as possible and I feel that the Civil Service is well rid of him.

About this time officials in the Treasury decided to give a lead to other departments and made a decision that a conscientious objector who failed to obtain total exemption and refused to obey his superior should be dismissed from his civil department. Although this was noted as merely the view of the Treasury 'as to what its action would be in the case of its own subordinate Departments', it was also noted that in other cases the decision rests primarily with 'the Head of the Department and would have to be defended by its own Parliamentary Representative if necessary'.[38]

As Weekes apparently did not receive a reply from the Treasury to his letter of 16 September 1916, he wrote again on 4 October.[39] He enquired, on behalf of the Commissioners, whether the Treasury had laid down rules to deal with conscientious objectors. He explained that in the case of Jones, the Commissioners had suspended payment of his salary on the ground that he had been performing neither civil nor military duty and the Commissioners were

> of the opinion that his refusal to perform duty in military service to which he is subject under the terms of the Military Service Act 1916, taken together with his sentence of imprisonment for that refusal should entail the termination of his civil appointment and dismissal from the Civil Service.[40]

A.P. (later Sir Percival) Waterfield, then a second class clerk in the Treasury, had noted to his colleague F. Phillips, on 6 October 1916: 'If this man deliberately refused to obey a military order it would seem that as in the case of Everitt of Customs and Excise, he should be dismissed from the Civil Service.' Heath, confirming the Treasury view on this matter, in a letter of 11 October 1916 to Sir Sydney Olivier, Board of Agriculture and Fisheries, had similarly written:

> The Treasury view...is that the State in its capacity as an Employer must be regarded as one, and that it is impossible for one branch to shut its eyes to deliberate breaches of the law committed by an employee while assigned for service in another branch. A breach of the law involving a sentence of hard labour is in our opinion an absolute bar to retention in Government employment.[41]

Meanwhile, the Commanding Officer, Royal Fusiliers Depot, Hounslow, wrote to Weekes on 3 October 1916, confirming that No G/43668 Private A.C. Jones

> of the Depot Royal Fusiliers, was tried by District Court Martial on 29th ultimo, and sentenced to undergo 6 months imprisonment with Hard Labour. This sentence was confirmed by the Officer Commanding Troops, at Hounslow on 1st October 1916. Private A. C. Jones will be removed to HM's Prison at Wormwood Scrubbs (sic) on 5th October 1916.[42]

Weekes replied on 5 October, asking to know the offence for which the punishment was awarded, as this information was of material importance in regard to Jones' civil service appointment. Major T.W. Thomas replied on 7 October 1916, on behalf of the Colonel Commanding the Royal Fusiliers that the offence was 'When on active service disobeying a lawful command given by his superior officer.' In fact, Jones had on this occasion refused to go on parade when ordered to do so. In replying on 12 October, with a letter of thanks for this information, Weekes added that he found it 'strange' to have been addressing his enquiries 'to the Royal Fusiliers as the regiment has not won a reputation, at Namur in distant days or anywhere at any time since, for non-combatant service'. The reference would not have been lost on the Commanding Officer or any other officer of the Royal Fusiliers: the Battle of Namur in 1695 was one of the costliest sieges in history for an attacking army – William III had besieged the French at a cost of 18,000 casualties.[43]

In reply to Weekes' letter to the Treasury of 4 October, Sir Robert Chalmers wrote on 12 October:

> My Lords have laid down a rule for general application in the subordinate Departments of the Treasury that, in cases where a civil servant, when in the Army (including non-combatant corps) deliberately refuses on so-called conscientious grounds to obey his superior officer, he should be dismissed from his civil Department. They concur therefore in the proposed dismissal of the man now in question with forfeiture of pay from the date of his arrest.[44]

Pencilled in the margin of the CSC file was a query: '? arrest on refusal to obey orders or arrest as absentee'. It seems that S.M. (later Sir Stanley) Leathes, then First Civil Service Commissioner, decided on the earlier date (i.e. 10 September).[45]

On 13 October, with the approval of the First Commissioner, Weekes wrote to Jones:

> The Commissioners have decided that you can be paid civil salary only up to the 10th ultimo and that, in view of the sentence passed upon you and the nature of your offence, viz – when on active service

(non combatant) disobeying a lawful command given by your superior officer, your appointment as Second Division Clerk is terminated.

I am to add that the Lords of the Treasury concur in these decisions.[46]

At the Board meeting of the Civil Service Commissioners on 6 November 1916 the Commissioners confirmed the decision to terminate Jones' appointment in their department.[47]

Jones found imprisonment hard to bear, especially as rambling and sketching had been his chief relaxation. When he died, Vera Brittain wrote that his experience in prison never embittered him; and in his subsequent career he was able to do much to mitigate the hardships of conscientious objectors in the Second World War.[48]

Jones was finally discharged from the Army on 8 April 1919. He had to write to the Secretary, Civil Service Commission on 21 April for another copy of the letter (13 October 1916) telling him his appointment had been terminated because the original had not survived his prison experiences.[49] This was sent with a covering letter dated 23 April 1919 which added, in case there should be any lack of clarity, that 'On the termination of your appointment as Second Division Clerk you ceased to be a member of the Civil Service.'[50]

The Treasury rules in these matters in practice extended beyond the civil service. For example, James Bird, the Clerk to the London County Council, wrote on 28 November 1917 for information about what steps HM Government had taken in relation to conscientious objectors. Heath replied that:

> If a man's appeal to a tribunal fails and he accepts military service as and when required, he receives the usual benefits of the Treasury Circulars of August 1914 and subsequent dates...(but) A man who, having failed to obtain total exemption deliberately refuses on so-called conscientious grounds to obey his superior officer should, in our opinion, be dismissed from his civil Department on the ground that he has thereby proved himself unfit to hold a position of trust in the public service.[51]

After the war Jones resumed work in the trade union movement. On release from prison he became Secretary of the National Union of Docks, Wharves and Shipping Staffs and editor of its journal, *Quayside and Office*. When his union amalgamated with the Transport and General Workers in 1922 he was promoted national secretary of the administrative, clerical and supervisory group.[52] In 1920 he married Violet Tidman (of the family with whom he was living when he was arrested). He was Organising Secretary of the Workers' Travel Association 1929–39. He later had a distinguished political career. He unsuccessfully contested the Heywood and Radcliffe Division of Lancashire in the 1929 general election, was elected Member of Parliament (Labour) for the Shipley Division of Yorkshire 1935–50 and for Wakefield, which he won in a bye-election, 1954–64. He was Parliamentary Private Secretary to Ernest Bevin (Minister of Labour and

National Service, 1940–45); Parliamentary Under Secretary of State, Colonial Office 1945–46; and Secretary of State for the Colonies 1946–50. He was keenly interested in adult education and believed it was a necessary preliminary to self government. Among his numerous other appointments he was Vice-President of the Workers' Education Association; Governor of both Ruskin College, Oxford and Queen Elizabeth House, Oxford; Vice-President of the Anti Slavery Society; UK delegate to the United Nations 1946 and 1947–48; and Treasurer of the Pit Ponies Protection Society. He resigned from Parliament for health reasons in August 1964 and died in London on 23 October 1964. At his funeral Harold Blackman, Hon Director of the British Humanist Association was in charge of the ceremony and gave a tribute, as did Margery (later Dame Margery) Perham, the distinguished scholar of colonial history.[53]

Jones' experience during the First World War was not untypical of what happened to conscientious objectors. Tribunals set their own rules of procedure, which varied from place to place; but there was a general reluctance to grant absolute exemption. At the Middlesex Appeal Tribunal, for example, it was resolved on 29 May 1916 that 'the maximum exemption to be granted to conscientious objectors was exemption from combatant service'.[54] It has been estimated that of 16,000 conscientious objectors who went before tribunals, no more than 200 received absolute exemption.[55] Sydney Palmer, for example, served in the Post Office on work deemed to be of national importance but he declared himself to be a conscientious objector as a matter of principle, to give support to others. Although he was exempt from military service his strong views were, he said, notorious, and he deliberately went before a tribunal to have himself given the status of conscientious objector to set a good example.[56] Palmer was granted special leave, without pay, then re-employed in a temporary capacity at about half the pay he was previously receiving. His position was consistent with the Treasury instruction to departments of 10 February 1917, that conscientious objectors remaining at work in departments would not have their service counted for pension or increment and their remuneration would be either their former actual rate of remuneration (without increments) or the rate which would be paid to a temporary substitute performing the duties, whichever was less.[57] The Treasury also decided that conscientious objectors should not be promoted over the heads of ex-soldiers and that any application to join the civil service from a conscientious objector should be rejected:[58] this resulted in extra checks by the Civil Service Commission to ascertain how applicants had spent their time during the war. The restrictions remained in force until 1929.[59] In addition, under the Representation of the People Act 1918, conscientious objectors were disfranchised for five years after the war.

The Treasury was the key department for advising departments in all aspects of policy concerning conscientious objectors as, indeed, it was in all aspects of conditions of service. Nevertheless personal views of officials were frequently expressed. One example related to the proposed employment of conscientious objectors in the National Health Commission. Meiklejohn had a telephone call in October 1916 from Sir Matthew Nathan, Secretary to the Ministry of Pensions, asking for the Treasury view on the proposal. Meiklejohn recorded the conversation:

> I gathered that C.O.s would be segregated in a workhouse and that only a few Civil Servants, who would give them orders, would have to see them. I told him that speaking entirely for myself I did not think there would be as much objection to this proposal as the previous one for their working at Somerset House where large bodies of Civil Servants would have to undergo contagion from their presence.[60]

The Treasury lead and advice was not, however, always received without question. Some officials in other departments felt that the Treasury on occasions wanted to have the benefit of distancing itself from difficulties whilst keeping departments under control. For example, Sir L. Guillemand, Chairman of the Board of Customs and Excise, wrote to Meiklejohn on 7 March 1917 about H.S. Britton, one of his assistant clerks, and commented:

> the Treasury decided that disobedience to a lawful military authority is to be punished by dismissal...
>
> The Treasury papers speak as if the decision to dismiss him was a decision of this Board, but it was nothing of the kind. It was a decision of the Treasury on the facts reported by us.[61]

Guillemand did not dissent from the decision to dismiss, but it seems that he did not wish the decision to be seen as his when the Treasury was taking such a leading role. To some extent the Treasury attitude is very understandable; it wished to ensure that Treasury ministers, who had to answer questions in Parliament relating to the departments within its ambit, had the least trouble and were as well covered as possible from criticism or attack.

Jones' case nevertheless provides insights into the way the Civil Service Commission actually worked in the second decade of the twentieth century. It had to work within the framework of the law, and like any other employer it was affected by the Military Service Act, 1916 – an act which was a serious constraint on normal employment conditions. Like all departments of government, the Commission had to work according to the instructions and advice it received from the Treasury because the Treasury was the key department for co-ordinating and enunciating civil service practice.[62] The Commission was also one of a group of largely operational (rather than policy-making) departments for which Treasury ministers were accountable to Parliament. While it was true to say that individual civil servants could be dismissed only by their head of department, the discretion, as in Jones' case, was not narrow in scope: the scope by the end of the twentieth century was much narrowed by employment legislation and the activities of trade unions.

Jones himself was in a particularly difficult position. He was doing work of national importance in the Civil Service Commission (though not certified as such for the purposes of the Military Service Act), and it was work which, in normal circumstances, caused no problems for someone with pacifist inclinations. As he pointed out in letters to the Secretary of the Commission, military service was never a condition of his employment, so he was not guilty of any breach on that account. It may therefore seem particularly hard that the line taken in 1914 was that employment in the service of the Crown could have made an individual liable to transfer to any form of other work in the service of the Crown. Indeed, one of the consequences of a case like this could mean that no civil servants should have a sensitive conscience and they should all accept the need to work with unquestioning obedience. One wonders whether the implications of this were appreciated at the time.

Some of the harshness associated with Jones' case must be seen as a reflection of the attitudes of society at the time. To adopt words written by Lord Cross, then a second class clerk in the Treasury, conscientious objectors were 'branded as criminals by sentences of hard labour for cold blooded disobedience while in the Army'.[63] On the other hand, the Military Service Act made provision for conscientious objectors, and Jones convinced four tribunals that he was genuine, sincere and consistent in his beliefs. It may now seem far from right that in these circumstances tribunals should (apparently) normally accede to the influence of the Military Representative, and also should impose a self-denying limitation on granting absolute exemption from military service. There were no criticisms of Jones as a civil servant, except that he acquired a criminal record on a matter of conscience.[64] This was because, as he argued at tribunals,[65] he could not accept conditional exemption to non-combatant service because it would make him part of the machinery of militarism by releasing other men for actual fighting and would consequently involve him in killing by proxy.

Notes

1 John W. Graham, *Conscription and Conscience: A History 1916–1919* (London: George Allen & Unwin, 1922), p. 70.
2 *Report from the Select Committee on the Civil Service (Employment of Conscientious Objectors), together with Minutes of Evidence and Appendices*, HC 69, (London: HMSO, 1922), Q. 142.
3 PRO/T1/12039/8860; see also PRO/T1/12004/34163.
4 'Statement of Treasury on Treatment of Conscientious Objectors' in *Report from the Select Committee on the Civil Service*, 1922, p. x.
5 *Report from the Select Committee on the Civil Service*, 1922, Q. 85.
6 *Report from the Select Committee on the Civil Service*, 1922, Q. 83.
7 PRO/T1/11986/30227; *The Times*, 23 May 1916, letter from Reginald J. N. Neville.
8 HC Deb. 5s., vol. 82, col. 1294 (15 May 1916).
9 PRO/T1/11986/30227, author unknown.
10 See also the authoritative study by John Rae, *Conscience and Politics: The British Government and the Conscientious Objector to Military Service 1916–1919* (London: Oxford University Press, 1970). The book contains a useful bibliography.
11 Oxford: Rhodes House Library, Creech Jones Papers, Mss. Brit. Emp. s. 332, Box 1, file 1.
12 PRO/CSC11/148.

13 PRO/CSC10/3216.
14 PRO/CSC11/148.
15 *Dictionary of National Biography, 1961–70* (Oxford: Oxford University Press, 1981).
16 PRO/CSC11/148.
17 Creech Jones Papers, Box 1, file 1.
18 Creech Jones Papers, Box 1, file 2.
19 Rae, *Conscience and Politics*, p.17.
20 Creech Jones Papers, Box 1, file 2; HC Deb. 5s., vol. 347, cols. 1689–90 (18 May 1939).
21 PRO/CSC11/148, Jones to the Secretary, CSC, 10 June 1916; Jones to the Secretary, CSC, 5 July 1916.
22 PRO/CSC11/148, Jones to Guppy, 14 September 1916.
23 PRO/CSC11/148, Weekes to Chief Recruiting Officer, 5 June 1916.
24 PRO/CSC11/148, Note dated 6 September 1916.
25 PRO/CSC11/148, Weekes to Central Recruiting Officer, 8 September 1916.
26 PRO/CSC11/148, Central Recruiting Officer to the Secretary, CSC, 8 September 1916.
27 PRO/CSC11/148.
28 *Peckham Mail and Gazette*, 12 September 1916.
29 PRO/CSC11/148.
30 PRO/CSC11/148, Weekes to Jones, 27 September 1917.
31 PRO/WO86/71, entry for 9 October 1916.
32 Creech Jones Papers, Box 1, file 2.
33 David Boulton, *Objection Overruled* (London: McGibbon & Kee, 1967), pp. 222–3.
34 PRO/CSC11/148, Jones to the Secretary, CSC, 23 September 1916.
35 PRO/CSC11/148.
36 PRO/T1/12006/34272.
37 PRO/T1/12006/34272.
38 PRO/T1/12039/8860.
39 PRO/CSC11/148; PRO/T1/12006/34272, Weekes to the Secretary, Treasury, 4 October 1916.
40 PRO/CSC11/148; PRO/T1/12006/34272.
41 PRO/T1/12006/34272; see also PRO/T1/12142/9411.
42 PRO/CSC11/148.
43 John Laffin, *Brassey's Battles: 3,500 Years of Conflict, Campaigns and Wars from A–Z* (London: Brassey's Defence Publishers, 1986); Michael Foss, *The Royal Fusiliers* (London: Hamish Hamilton, 1967).
44 PRO/CSC11/148; PRO/T1/12006/34272.
45 PRO/CSC11/148.
46 PRO/CSC11/148, Weekes to Jones, 13 October 1916.
47 PRO/CSC8/7.
48 *The Times*, 27 October 1964.
49 PRO/CSC11/148, Jones to the Secretary, CSC, 21 April 1919.
50 PRO/CSC11/148 Brackenberry to Jones, 23 April 1919.
51 LMA/LCC/CL Estab/3/45, Heath to Bird, 12 December 1917.
52 *Dictionary of National Biography, 1961–70*.
53 *The Times*, 24 October 1964.
54 PRO/MH47/5; see also Boulton, *Objection Overruled*, Ch. 5.
55 Boulton, *Objection Overruled*, p. 139.
56 *Report from the Select Committee on the Civil Service*, 1922, QQ. 194–313.
57 *Report from the Select Committee on the Civil Service*, 1922, Appendix B; PRO/T1/12039/8860.
58 Rae, *Conscience and Politics*, p. 236.

59 Rae, *Conscience and Politics*, p. 236.
60 PRO/T1/12012/34809.
61 PRO/T1/12006/34272.
62 See PRO/T1/12006/34272, Meikeljohn to Barstow, 31 July 1916.
63 PRO/T1/12006/34272.
64 Note on file, apparently by Weekes, PRO/CSC11/148.
65 Creech Jones Papers, Box 1, file 1.

8
CENTENARY CELEBRATIONS

Chapter 2 explained that the Northcote–Trevelyan Report was signed in 1853 and published in 1854. As a consequence of its publication the Civil Service Commission was created in 1855. In the mid-twentieth century, politicians, scholars and public servants were all aware of the significance of these developments. On 21 February 1952 Herbert (later Lord) Morrison wrote to R.A. (later Lord) Butler, then Chancellor of the Exchequer, to remind him of the centenary of the civil service.[1] Butler queried the historical accounts which emphasised one or other as the most significant of the dates and replied emphasising 1855, as the centenary of the Civil Service Commission, rather than 1853 or 1854. In November 1953 *The Times* published four articles celebrating 100 years of the civil service.[2] Around the same time, the Treasury was being pressured by A.J.T. (later Sir Albert) Day, of the National Staff Side, to celebrate the centenary of 1854 by publicly recognising the virtues of the civil service.[3] In May 1955 K.M. Reader, then Assistant Director of Examinations, wrote an article on the Civil Service Commissioners, published in *The Times Educational Supplement*.[4] These and other events[5] and publications[6] had related themes but focused on different events of the 1850s.

As early as 1950 senior staff in the Commission were increasingly aware that it would not be long before the hundredth anniversary of the creation of their department. In addition, there were numerous requests from other countries asking about the Commission's experience. Requests of this nature came from Burma and China in 1947, Pakistan, India and Ceylon in 1948, Peru in 1949, the Gold Coast and Burma in 1951 and Germany and Japan in 1952.[7] In 1948 Sir Percival Waterfield, then First Civil Service Commissioner, toured North America, received the honorary degree of LL.D. from Ohio Wesleyan University, and attended a conference in Ottawa where he gave a major speech about recruitment to the British civil service and the work of the Commission. He also visited Germany in 1948 and, on 3 August, gave a major speech to the German Universities Commission in Hamburg (the speech was printed by the Oxford Society in *Oxford 1949*,[8] and later reprinted by the Civil Service Commission, with the permission of Oxford University Press). Such activities reflected not only a general interest in the Commission's long experience but also special interest in modern methods of selection, especially what had become increasingly widely known as the House Party experience of CSSB. Parliamentary interest was reflected in the work of the 1946 Select Committee on Estimates, the 1948 Public Accounts Committee, and the debate in the House of Lords in 1948. There was also interest from scholars and journalists. One example was the request in 1946 from D.N. Chester, editor of *Public Administration*, for an article on the Commission for publication in the journal. Waterfield was not keen on this but asked Frederic Milner, Secretary of the Commission, to write it. There was a delay, and when Milner contacted the Treasury about it, T. (later Sir Thomas) Padmore discussed it with Sir Edward (later Lord) Bridges, then Head of the Home Civil Service. Bridges urged caution because the Chancellor did not want civil service selection brought into the limelight and said he hoped Milner would use a 'relatively light touch'. Milner's draft was approved by the Treasury in February 1947 and it was published soon afterwards.[9] Requests were also received from Bosworth Monck[10] and T.A. Critchley.[11] J.E. Whitehead in the Commission was appointed as liaison officer to deal with Monck's request for information. Liaison for Critchley was a less straightforward matter than for Monck because the former was an assistant principal in the Home Office. Critchley had set himself the task of writing a descriptive account of the civil service and he already had approval from the Home Office and was aware that the typescript would have to be officially approved before publication. Whitehead was again appointed as liaison officer and A.H.M. Hillis (then Secretary and Establishment Officer in the Commission) minuted to him 'we shall have to vet his material, of course'. Critchley asked if he might be permitted to visit CSSB – because, as a limited competition entrant to the administrative class, he had not been required to compete at CSSB. The request was referred to the First Commissioner. Waterfield minuted on 15 August 1948 that Critchley:

> is not, I gather a person of much weight. It is to his credit that he has decided to write his book: but I see no reason why we should give him the special privilege of a visit to CSSB...If he had been a writer of acknowledged reputation, whose book was likely to be widely read, and whose opinions might have considerable influence, I should take a different view. As it is, say that we regret to be unable to give him the privilege...but add that we shall be publishing during this autumn a White Paper containing a full description of the procedure at CSSB, which he will find useful for his purpose (Mr Padmore and Mr H.A. Strutt agree).[12]

In October 1948 Critchley sent a draft chapter to the Commission, which was read by several members of staff. Hillis wrote to Whitehead on 21 October:

> I am afraid that I dislike Mr Critchley's draft *in toto* and see little possibility of our being able to knock it into tolerable shape. We cannot write his book for him. But I suppose...we had better try to prune some of the more glaring misconceptions...

Critchley's book was published on 29 January 1951. Lord Beveridge wrote an Introduction in which he referred to it as dealing with its subject 'objectively and picturesquely' and praised Critchley for helping 'the public outside to share his intimate knowledge'.[13] The Commission bought a copy for its library.

In 1949, while Critchley was writing his book, Padmore sent a letter from the Treasury to Establishment Officers about a proposal to produce a Civil Servant's Guide. The idea was for a purely historical and factual compilation, 'anything argumentative or controversial being avoided'. It was not intended to deal with the functions of the major departments, because it was hoped that they would be covered in 'the series of booklets on Government Departments which, with the approval of the Government Organisation Committee, the IPA is proposing to publish'. It was, however, proposed to include information about 'common service' departments (i.e. departments providing services for other departments in central government).[14] The proposal was not developed further at that time.

Some aspects of the idea were, however, taken up enthusiastically in the Civil Service Commission, where it was decided to print a revised note on the history and duties of the Commission. There was a suggestion that it should include a specially commissioned picture 'by the pen or brush of a first class artist', as an illustration. It was argued that Burlington Gardens, where the Commission's offices were, was one of the finest structures in London and the best example of middle Victorian architecture: 'our facade would be famous'. An estimate of the cost for the picture was 50 guineas, but it was doubted whether the Treasury would sanction such expenditure from public funds. Waterfield thought 'they might perhaps be willing to contribute half, if we could raise the rest from among ourselves: and I have been thinking that we might ask Sir Roderick Meiklejohn and Mr Mennell if they would contribute. Both are bachelors, and I would think fairly well off.' He asked the Secretary: 'What do you think of the prospects of raising 25 guineas between us?' It seems, however, that Meiklejohn and Mennell were not asked for contributions, but after enormous effort the text of the pamphlet was finalised in 1951 and printed (375 copies) by HMSO in 1952, with an attractive picture of Burlington Gardens on the front.[15] The picture used was not, in fact, specially commissioned but given free, with acknowledgement to *Illustrated London News*.

These examples of publications and requests for information indicate the considerable interest around the middle of the twentieth century in the work of the Commission. It was regarded with some pride and reverence in the United Kingdom, and there was a demand from many other countries for information about it. It was therefore not surprising that official minds became increasingly aware of the approaching centenary of the Commission and, in a modest way, A.P. (later Sir Paul) Sinker, the First Commissioner, who succeeded Waterfield in 1951, began imagining an appropriate 'Jamboree' – a small conference of Chairmen of Commonwealth Public Service Commissions. Sinker floated the idea with Treasury officials but Alec (later Sir Alexander) Johnston replied from the Treasury that:

> On balance…we should prefer to cut out the proposed hospitality for the Chairmen of Commonwealth Civil Service Commissions…If, of course, you get some of them together in the ordinary way, on the basis that they would have been coming to this country at the cost of their own Governments, no doubt something could be laid on by way of a meal by Government Hospitality.[16]

It was, however, pointed out that special regulations laid down the previous year precluded officials being offered government hospitality: such hospitality was for ministers, not officials, and, unfortunately, in order to maintain their independence from political influence, Chairmen of Civil Service Commissions had no ministerial heads. Johnston wondered whether Sinker had consulted the Commonwealth Relations Office (CRO) about it and whether they might wish to put forward a plea that the Chairmen ought to be brought together.

Sinker wrote to W.A.B. Hamilton at the CRO, outlining his ideas and the response he had received from the Treasury. Hamilton replied that the CRO would support Sinker's request to the Treasury for, for example, a dinner in honour of the guests attending the conference. Sinker wrote again to Johnston, explaining that the plan was now 'for a conference for one week without offering Government Hospitality except for a dinner towards the end of the conference and perhaps a reception at the beginning'.

Sinker was then encouraged by Johnston to take informal soundings among the eight Chairmen of the Civil Service Commissions in Canada, Australia, New Zealand, South Africa, India, Pakistan, Ceylon and the Federation of Rhodesia and Nyasaland, and he wrote to them on 29 January 1954. They responded with considerable interest, but after further delay it appeared by 26 June 1954 that only four of the eight would in fact be able to attend. Late in 1954 W.E. Dunk, Chairman of the Public Service Board of Australia, wrote to Bridges. He said he hoped that the idea had not been dropped because he felt there was a good deal to be gained from such occasional meetings. Bridges replied:

> I still hope that we may be able to have such a conference but I am bound to say that at the moment there seems little enthusiasm for it on the part of our colleagues in most of the Commonwealth countries.[17]

Progress on the suggestion was discussed at the Civil Service Commission Board meeting on 9 July 1954, when it was clear that only four of the eight Chairmen had been able to accept the invitation, and the First Commissioner, by now L.N. (later Sir Laurence) Helsby, said that as he doubted whether it would be in the public interest to hold the conference it would be better to drop the idea. At the same meeting there was a discussion about the history of the Commission that Reader was preparing. At an earlier meeting on 8 April 1954 Reader had reported making good progress, and it was agreed in July that Reader's history should be published, together with an account by Hayes of other public service commissions, in one volume. Helsby asked that the first draft should be ready for consideration at the Civil Service Commission Board meeting in October 1954. Helsby then wrote to all the Commonwealth Public Service Commissions telling them that the idea for a conference was off.

As the centenary was approaching, another project, by C.J. (later Sir Claude) Hayes, then Director of Examinations, was making good progress. The project began with Hayes applying for a Nuffield Foundation Home Civil Service Fellowship.[18] His application had the support of the CRO and the Colonial Office as well as the Commission. He explained that the Commission ran examinations for India, Pakistan, Nigeria and the Gold Coast. Many foreign countries (France, Belgium, Sweden, Germany, Greece, Japan, Indonesia and others) sent missions to study the British Civil Service Commission, and 'we feel the lack of a history and description of Public Service Commissions'. He therefore proposed to study the growth of Public Service Commissions, to see how their functions and purpose developed from the original one in the United Kingdom, and to consider the application of the principle of a politically independent civil service selected and promoted on merit. He wished to publish, in connection with an account of the Civil Service Commission for its centenary in 1955, a brief account of other Public Service Commissions and their work. He added that there was only a casual interchange of experience and information among the Commonwealth Public Service Commissions; and a brief but comprehensive survey at the present time of rapid change might be of value and interest to the Commonwealth as a whole, as well as to students.

Sinker strongly supported the application. He wrote:

> The United Kingdom Civil Service Commission has its centenary in 1955. It is the *fons et origo* of all the existing Commonwealth Civil and Public Service Commissions, and we know that some of them are looking to us in that year for a suitable gesture as head of the family. A survey of the Commonwealth Public Service Commissions is peculiarly appropriate in 1953/54 if it results in some publication for the centenary, and also because the present time of political and constitutional changes calls for a re-examination of the principles on which the commissions are based. A complementary study of the Civil Service Commission in the United States of America was made by Mr A.H.M. Hillis in 1951 under the Commonwealth Fund, and this might form part of the publication.
>
> Apart from the collection of material which may be useful to us here, I believe that the proposed discussions would provide an indirect and therefore acceptable method of making better known our ideas on Civil Service recruitment to the benefit of certain other Commonwealth countries. The extent to which India and Pakistan, for instance, have

consulted us recently on Civil Service matters is gratifying, and the proposed tour would help to strengthen such links. We receive fairly frequent visits from our opposite numbers in other Commonwealth countries also: a return visit of the kind proposed will help to show that we are not too proud to learn. Amongst the present Civil Service Commissioners, Mr Hayes has had the longest experience of the work of the Commission. On all counts I can recommend him without reserve for a Nuffield Fellowship.

Hayes heard in a letter dated 24 February 1953 from Leslie Farrer-Brown, Secretary to the Nuffield Foundation, that he had been awarded up to £15,000 to visit Sudan, Pakistan, India, Ceylon, Malaya, Australia, New Zealand, South Africa, Central Africa, West Africa, the West Indies and Canada. Later the Commission added, from its own vote, and with Treasury permission, an extra £350 to enable him to extend his tour in Canada, and also (later) an extra £46.17.00 for the additional expenses incurred in visiting Fiji, San Francisco and New York. He left the UK on 24 September 1953 and returned in June 1954. The CRO contacted the eight high commissioners in London to facilitate Hayes' contacts with the various governments. His approach was to prepare a list of 82 questions to which he sought answers (Sinker suggested another three when he saw the list). In his letters to the Commissioners he was to meet he stressed that anything he was told would be as confidential as his contacts wished:

> While I am naturally going to the Public Service Commissions, I regard it as my job to find out how they are regarded by the public and by the Government; but I have no intention of publishing anything controversial on this question.[19]

Hayes contacted Hillis, who had by then been transferred to the Treasury, and Hillis replied on 10 August 1953 that it would be 'a good idea to get the history of ourselves and our derivative Commissions between two covers, and…I will be glad to take on the United States side'.

It is clear that Sinker was very supportive, not only in the reference he wrote, but also in keeping in touch with Hayes and encouraging him. While he was abroad, Hayes heard that Sinker was moving on from the Commission to become Director-General of the British Council. On 19 March 1954 Hayes wrote to him: 'I am, for myself, very sorry that you are leaving; you have given me a sense of direction and firmness of purpose which Percival, with all his merits, could not give.'

On his return to the UK in June 1954, Hayes confirmed the Civil Service Commission's intention to mark the centenary with the publication of a short account of the British Commission and of those of the Commonwealth. In October 1954 the Commission's Establishment Officer received confirmation that the Stationery Office would regard the book as a 'prestige case', and would print the book using the 'litho' method. Proofs would be for checking typing errors only. HMSO would deliver 100 copies within a month or six weeks of the copy being lodged with them.

The book that emerged was a straightforward factual account of nearly 200 pages. It covered Australia (together with the details of the arrangements in its six states), New Zealand, South Africa, Canada (together with details of its eight provinces), Northern Ireland, Southern Rhodesia, India, Pakistan (together with details of Punjab and North-West Frontier Province, Sind and West Bengal) and Ceylon. There was no comparative analysis, evaluation or conclusions, though as far as possible a common framework was adopted, based on the 85 questions Hayes set himself. The book looked like an official report in typescript, with all the paragraphs numbered.

It was not an impressive production. To Raymond Nottage, Director of the Royal Institute of Public Administration (RIPA), Hayes wrote: 'It lacks excitement. Perhaps I ought to say that this report is not in commerce and should not be mentioned in print.'[20] To G.M. Young, the historian, he referred to it as in 'the ditchwater class'.[21] To Sinker he wrote: 'It is pretty dull stuff and you won't want to read more than an odd paragraph...I enclose with it four confidential insets; would you please destroy, return or otherwise keep these out of harm's way?' To R.C. Griffiths, at the Treasury, Hayes wrote: 'practically all criticism has been squeezed out...I can't recommend it as light reading'. He also added that he hoped 'to publish most of it soon, together with a brief historical account of the Commission and Hillis's USA report. Would you please let me know if there is anything in this report which ought not to be published?'[22]

Griffiths did, indeed, find an unacceptable sentence in the chapter on Australia. The sentence read: 'The Board, not being dominated by financial considerations, can consider [pay] claims from associations on their merits, while the associations have learned from arbitration to base their cases on firm grounds.' Griffiths wrote to Hayes on 1 June 1955 that this could well be interpreted as a direct suggestion that in the UK wage claims from Civil Service Staff Associations are not considered on their merits – which would be completely false. Hayes replied on 2 June 1955 that his sentence was in a report about nine Commonwealth countries and there was nothing in the context to suggest it applied to the United Kingdom. Griffiths wrote again, arguing that:

> it can undoubtedly be read as indicating that the author feels that a body with financial responsibilities cannot consider Civil Service wage claims on their merits...you must, I think, recognise that the sentence coming in a publication written by a UK Civil Servant, is potentially embarrassing to UK ministers.

Hayes agreed to reconsider Griffiths' comments if the report was ever published. In fact, neither the report nor Hillis' report on the USA were published. Reader's history of the Civil Service Commission was not published at the time but continued up to 1975, appeared in 1981, as number 5 in the 'Civil Service Studies' series (HMSO) sponsored by the Civil Service Department.[23] In it, Reader explained that it had grown out of a request by Hayes, when the Commission was coming up to its hundredth anniversary, to write a history of the department.

In addition to the plans initiated from within the Civil Service Commission for celebrating the Commission's centenary, there were also proposals from outside the Commission and these were more successful. In 1954 the RIPA journal *Public Administration* reprinted the Northcote–Trevelyan Report in honour of the centenary: a gesture which was welcomed by its readers and which could not be criticised on grounds of embarrassment or sensitivity because it was accompanied by no comments at all. There was also another initiative, perhaps more revealing of administrative behaviour than the saga of Hayes' Report. This initiative originated from Professor W.A. Robson, and it may be helpful to outline some of the main details of Robson's career before recalling what happened in connection with what became the 1954 special issue of *The Political Quarterly*.

William Alexander Robson was born in 1895 and educated at the London School of Economics and Political Science (LSE), graduating with the degree of B.Sc. (Econ) in 1922 with first-class honours. He was awarded the degrees of Ph.D. in 1924 and LL.M. in 1928, was a Lieutenant in the Royal Flying Corps and RAF during the First World War, was called to the Bar (Lincoln's Inn) in 1922, and became a Lecturer at the LSE in 1926. He was promoted to Reader in Administrative Law in 1933 and was Professor of Public Administration 1947–62 (he was then the only Professor of Public Administration in the United Kingdom). During the Second World War he was a principal in the Mines Department 1940–42, then at the Ministry of Fuel and Power 1942–43. He was promoted to assistant secretary in the Air Ministry 1943–45, and also served in the Ministry of Civil Aviation before demobilisation. Among his numerous positions of professional and public service he was Vice-President of the RIPA. He had an international reputation as a leading scholar of public administration, and an impressive list of publications, beginning with a very substantial (48 pages) Fabian Pamphlet published in 1922: *From Patronage to Proficiency, An Inquiry into Professional Qualifications and Methods of Recruitment in the Civil Service and the Municipal Service*. By the time he died in 1980 he had eight honorary doctorates from universities at home and abroad.

For this present purpose it is important to recall that Robson was the founder in 1930, and for 45 years the joint editor, with his friend Leonard Woolf, of *The Political Quarterly*. The journal was founded with money Robson begged from George Bernard Shaw and with the support of John Maynard (later Lord) Keynes, and its purpose was to bridge the gap between theory and practice. Robson's obituary in *The Times* (1980) stressed that he was 'the last of the great generation of Fabian scholars, the foremost teacher of public administration of his day...who, however disappointed he was with the politics of the 1960s and 1970s, never lost faith in reason and progress'.[24] Professor G.W. Jones later wrote:

> He was an idealist who sought to use his talents to serve society, and to improve the quality of life, not only materially but also morally. His great ability was to assemble a huge mass of data, to analyse order out of complexity, and to argue a coherent case for change...He was as if impelled by a sense of public duty to put his learning and scholarship to the service of society.[25]

On 23 June 1954 Robson wrote to Helsby to say that *The Political Quarterly* was proposing to devote a special issue to the civil service. It would mark the centenary of the Northcote–Trevelyan reforms, but its purpose:

> would not merely be commemorative. It will be partly retrospective but it will look forward to the future and its problems...
>
> Sir Edward Bridges has agreed to do an article on 'The reforms of 1854 in Retrospect' and we should very much like you to do the article on 'Recruitment and Training'...
>
> We have been partly motivated in planning this issue by the fact that little of importance has so far been published in the press on the Civil Service this year, and I might say in this connection that the special numbers of *The Political Quarterly* devoted to one subject attract a very wide audience and are used extensively by serious students and teachers.[26]

Helsby wrote a note to Hayes, Director of Examinations: 'May we have a word together about this?' Someone in the Commission added in pencil on the letter, alongside Robson's signature, 'Eco Prof'.

Later, Hayes wrote to the First Commissioner:

> Robson...knows that the control of training is a Treasury function, but would like you to consider it in your article in its relationship with recruitment (which, in my opinion it has)...
>
> The Political Quarterly is intended for the educated but not the expert public; its readers are mainly academic (University) but include MPs and Ministers. It has a Socialist bias (to judge from the editorial board, which includes G.D.H. Cole, R.H.S. Crossman, Lord Simon of Wythenshawe, and some of its articles)...
>
> I will try to produce a draft in a week or so. If you will return the file after writing to Robson I will ask Dr Snow and Major Sumner for a brief contribution on their side.[27]

Helsby added:

> I notice...that Professor Robson himself wrote a book some years ago entitled 'From Patronage to Proficiency in the Public Service'. I have

never come across it, but it struck me that it might be tactful to avoid controverting any of his pet ideas too fiercely if we can!'

On 9 July 1954 Helsby commented to Reader: 'Can we get this?' Reader added to Miss Dell 'Is not this the book you tried to get for me? (And no one at the LSE had ever heard of it!)'

Helsby then sent a formal letter to Robson on 9 July 1954 saying he would write the article, though he was doubtful whether the word training should appear in the title. Robson acknowledged this letter on 13 July and added: 'May I add that I trust you will feel able to deal with some of the problems of today and tomorrow concerning recruitment and training, even if you cannot solve them all!' Staff in the Commission quickly set to work to prepare Helsby's article. Major A.T. Sumner, then Additional Commissioner, contributed three paragraphs. C.P. Snow (later Lord) Snow, then part-time Temporary Commissioner, offered to comment on Hayes' draft. Reader made extensive comments and suggestions. J.H.T. Goldsmith, then Chairman of CSSB, also offered comments on Hayes' draft. On 16 July 1954 the draft was then passed by Hayes to Helsby as 'a skeleton'. Hayes added: 'I have read Robson's 1922 booklet "From Patronage to Proficiency". It is a young work and relates to conditions now changed; I don't think we are now offending any strongly held convictions.'

On 19 July Helsby read the draft prepared for him by Hayes and made extensive comments for revision. Hayes re-contacted Sumner and Snow. On 24 July Hayes submitted a revised draft to Helsby. Helsby made further comments, both in discussion and by minute dated 24 July.

On 31 July Helsby wrote to A.J.D. (later Sir John) Winnifrith in the Treasury, explaining that he had been pressed by Robson to say something in his article about training:

> I have therefore included a paragraph or two referring in broad terms to some of the general issues arising over training. I hope that what I have said is quite harmless: and in any event I am insisting that the title of my article should refer to recruitment only.
>
> ...I do not think that the text includes anything likely to upset anybody, but I should be grateful if you would let me know if it contains anything which you might find embarrassing.

Helsby enclosed a copy of the manuscript and added that he was pretty sure 'that we can safely rely on being able to make minor amendments at the proof stage'.

From the Treasury, on 7 August 1954, Griffiths replied on behalf of Winnifrith, who had just gone on leave. Griffiths had shown the article to P.S. Milner Barry and enclosed for Helsby a foolscap page of comments. On 30 August Helsby asked Hayes for advice on the Treasury's comments; the same day Hayes replied with notes on all the points made by the Treasury.

When Robson received the manuscript he wrote to Helsby and said the proofs would soon arrive. He also enclosed a proof copy of the article by R.K. Kelsall, for Helsby to compare the figures in the two articles. The figures were checked by Hayes, the proofs were corrected by Miss Dell on 9 September, and Helsby sent the proofs back to Robson the same day, with a letter in which he thanked Robson for the opportunity to read Kelsall's article in proof. Helsby added:

> Kelsall appears to have it in mind that graduates of Oxford and Cambridge tend to come from different social strata from graduates of other universities. You may wish to consider whether he would like to be warned that I have used some figures (quite unaware of what he was writing of course) which go to show that the recruits whom we draw from Oxford and Cambridge are now much more broadly representative in the social sense than of old...

When the special issue of *The Political Quarterly* was published, and he was sent his author's copy, Helsby was shocked and irritated to discover that Robson had written a nine page editorial in which he did as he had asked his contributors, to 'look around and to look forward': it was an exercise in thinking aloud about the problems of the contemporary civil service as he and others saw it. Helsby was even more shocked to discover that in Robson's own contribution to the special issue, 'Recent Tends in Public Administration' he had, on page 343, made some critical comments on recruitment to the civil service. He wrote to Goldsmith:

> Professor Robson gave me no warning of his intention to say anything of this kind and apart from anything else, I am irritated by his lack of courtesy. The invitation to me to provide an article came from him as Editor; and he ought in decency to have said that he contemplated some comments of his own in my field...[28]

Helsby asked Goldsmith to tell him whether Robson had any first-hand information about CSSB.

Goldsmith replied on 14 October. Robson had visited CSSB in 1953 and was, in fact, attached to Goldsmith's group. After two years, none of the directing staff of that group could remember a great deal about Robson, except that Goldsmith had been warned by the First Commissioner that they might find him in some ways a hostile critic and a rather tactless and difficult visitor. Goldsmith was therefore very much on his guard, but in the event he and Mrs McArthur, the psychologist, were surprised to find him a much more friendly and appreciative visitor than they had expected. Goldsmith continued:

> Having explained the circumstances of Professor Robson's visit, I can only say that his criticism of the 'failure of the Civil Service Commission to analyse the qualities of mind temperament required for different types of administrative work' and 'those responsible for conducting the CSSB tests

have not a clear conception of the type of man or woman they are seeking beyond the vague notion of "a balanced type"' has no foundation in fact. When we started CSSB for the Reconstruction Competition, we went to a great deal of pains to analyse the work of the administrative officer in all different kinds of Departments. We have two voluminous files about this subject but our work is summarised in paragraphs on 'The Nature of the Task', which appear on pages 8, 9 and 10 of the Memorandum by the Civil Service Commissioners on the use of the Civil Service Selection Board in the Reconstruction Competitions...

We naturally regard it as an ordinary courtesy that, before any criticism of CSSB is made by a visitor, he should at least discuss the object of his criticism with the Chairman of CSSB. It is quite clear that this could not have happened, because the reply to his criticism is so readily available in the White Paper. It seems clear, therefore, that Professor Robson is merely airing a preconceived notion and that the warning by Paul Sinker was only too justified.

Helsby then wrote to Bridges on 15 October, drawing attention to Robson's criticism on page 343, and saying that Bridges might be interested to know that he was taking the point up with Robson – he enclosed a copy of his letter to Robson. Helsby asked Robson if he could spare the time to lunch with him one day soon, and went on to defend CSSB against Robson's criticism and to enclose for him a copy of the White Paper (officially it was the Memorandum, mentioned above), drawing attention to pages 8 to 10.

Bridges replied to Helsby on 19 October. He had been so annoyed by Robson's editorial 'Notes and Comments' that he had not really read anything in the issue properly. He had, however, shown Padmore the offending editorial and he enclosed with his letter a copy of Padmore's reactions. Bridges continued:

It seems to me that it was rather obtuse and insensitive – if not bad manners – on Robson's part not to tell me when he had asked me to write an article, that the whole number was to be prefixed by some critical notes and comments. If I had known that there were to be these Notes and Comments, I am not sure that I would have written an article for this number. Although it may not be very logical, people are bound to some extent to associate me with the points in these Notes and Comments.

A second point is that a lot of these points in the Notes and Comments are bosh and it is really rather stupid of Robson if he wants to produce a decent number, not to take the trouble of getting the material checked by people who know the facts: and all the more so, since the names of his contributors show that he is in touch with people who can put him right about the facts. But when you ask me what I am going to do about it, the answer is that I am going to sulk in my tent unless I meet

Robson in my Club. And if I do I shall not be able to resist saying that I think it is a pity that a number of the points in the Notes and Comments are factually inaccurate and misleading.

If Robson accepts your invitation to lunch, then I don't suggest that you should make yourself the vehicle for passing on any of my ill temper. But if the occasion arises, and it would suit your book to give him some indication of what I am feeling, it is open to you to do so.

The minute of 18 October to Bridges from Padmore offered both advice and comments. He told Bridges that:

> on the whole I think I have come to the conclusion that you cannot very well do anything about it. It was certainly impolite, to say the least of it, not to warn you that you were going to be published within the same covers as this editorial rubbish, and the fact that you are so published might in some people's eyes in some degree associate you with the stuff. But if you complain, it can only be, as it were, for the sake of complaining and cannot, I think, do any good.
>
> I cannot resist making some comments on some of the points made. Thus:
>
> (1) 'Much remains to be done before equality of opportunity will have been achieved.' Those possessing privileges of family background and of education have special advantages – as apparently do those who are members of one sex or the other, though I am not sure which. This is rubbish. And was rubbish before the war. I can say this the more firmly because I personally had no privileges of family background and none of education except so far as it may be regarded as a privilege to find one's way to Cambridge on scholarships in competition with everyone else who cared to put himself forward. My civil service career has not been specially unsatisfactory so far, and I am quite certain that it has not been affected in any way by my lack of privilege. And in this respect I am quite sure that there is nothing at all unusual about my personal history.
> (2) 'The central need is for a Civil Service Training College.' This at the very least is a highly arguable proposition. The French have gone in for one in a big way since the war, and many Frenchmen are far from being convinced that it has been a really good thing....
> (8) 'The dead hand of the Whitley Council's preference for seniority still lies heavily on the lower grades.' This again I believe to be rubbish. 'Seniority' is of course a pejorative word; if one talks about 'experience', the thing assumes a different complexion.

Helsby was grateful for Bridges' letter and replied on 25 October saying how much he shared Bridges' irritation. He then said:

> One sentence in particular made me see red. 'The domination of Oxford and Cambridge graduates still continues in the Administrative Class. Is this possibly due to most of the examiners being appointed from those universities?' Even the Beaverbrook press would blench at this kind of smear by innuendo: and the facts are straightforward – examiners know the candidates by code numbers only and anyhow London provides more examiners than any other university.

Helsby's letter continued by saying that Robson had accepted his invitation to lunch, and he was grateful to be able to refer to Bridges' views if the talk went that way,

> but I feel that in the long run it may prove more useful if I concentrate in the main on trying to get down to the origins of the feelings of resentment against the Service which undoubtedly exists in this quarter. I believe that it arises from a sense of inferiority, or possibly a genuine sense of injustice, which has allowed Robson and others to persuade themselves that it is only our snobbishness or clannishness which leads to such a predominance of Oxford and Cambridge graduates in the Service. Linked with this there is, I fancy, some resentment of our lack of appreciation of the possibilities of vocational training outside the Service – which London University in general and Robson in particular, would be better able than Oxford and Cambridge to supply. Indeed, I fancy that it is partly because they feel qualified to teach us something about our jobs that they especially resent our preference for Oxford and Cambridge, who make no such claim.

Bridges replied the next day, 26 October, agreeing to Helsby's approach and offering further suggestions about the line to be taken depending on Robson's. In his letter there was, however, a hint that perhaps they were making too much of this matter:

> if, for example, he takes the view that he is surprised at your worrying about what was said in the 'Notes and Comments' inasmuch as none of the other contributors to the special number have taken this attitude. In that case, you might say that you happened to run into me and you know that I feel a little unhappy about one or two things.

In preparation for his lunch, Helsby sought further advice from Hayes. Hayes was not sure that Padmore's comments were as objective as other people's would be, though he agreed in general with Padmore's reactions and provided more factual details. Hayes added (27 October 1954): 'Should we ask Nottage if we can speak to any reviewer the RIPA may ask to handle this for the journal?'

Helsby and Robson had lunch together on 28 October 1954 and the next day Helsby sent Bridges an account of what had been said. They had a very long talk but Helsby did not find Robson altogether receptive, 'for he is not a man who very easily sees the other point of view'. Moreover, Helsby discovered that Robson had:

> a curious and rather insensitive insistence that it would be quite inappropriate for an editor to consult anybody, about what he proposed to write...(and) while he was understandably distressed that he should have incurred your displeasure in any way and said that he must write to say as much, he clung stoutly to the view that, even so, he could not see that he was in any way at fault.
>
> On the whole I made perhaps best progress over the general suggestion that we tend to favour Oxford and Cambridge graduates too much. My own 'red brick' background may have helped a little but I think he did accept that we do not pick people because they have gone to some particular university and that indeed the assumption that Oxford and Cambridge are the home of 'privilege' is in many respects out of date now.

Robson may well have been surprised by Helsby's comments. According to Helsby, he defended what he had written 'perhaps with more zeal than discrimination', and accepted that his article 'did us rather less than justice'. Robson said he thought the special issue of *The Political Quarterly* was the best tribute that had been paid to the civil service in its centenary year. If there was criticism as well as praise, he said it should carry all the more weight with people of judgment. He said the review of the special issue in *The Manchester Guardian* had aroused some interest and there was a proposal to republish it in book form; but in that event the 'Notes and Comments' would be omitted and he would gladly make some adjustment to the reference to CSSB in his own article. Robson offered to publish a letter in the next issue if Helsby would care to reply to what he had written about CSSB and examiners from Oxford and Cambridge. The talk was friendly and cordial throughout but Helsby was left with the feeling that Robson felt a little hurt

> that we had not expressed more gratitude for this special number of *The Political Quarterly* and had shown more interest in the criticisms of the Service which it contained than in its praise; but I thought that the slightly plaintive note came partly from a slight feeling of guilt and later in our talk it disappeared.

After the lunch, on 29 October, Helsby sent Robson some figures about the provenance of examiners. Robson replied on 1 November asking for more information. Helsby wrote again on 5 November with more details using figures supplied by Hayes, and explaining that

> We do not normally employ any examiner more than two years running; and when the time comes to find a new man our policy is first and

foremost to select a good examiner independently of his university. We do watch the general distribution of examiners between the universities and like to see a good broad spread.

In preparing the details for Helsby to send, Hayes stressed to Helsby (3 November) that the point was 'we always try to get the best man, whatever his university... The university distribution is therefore fortuitous.'

Robson discussed the figures with one of his colleagues who specialised in statistical analysis, and wrote to Helsby pointing out that it was important to know how many candidates were being examined by examiners in various universities. More details were collected in the Commission. Reader offered thoughtful comments in a minute dated 8 December 1954, which ended with: 'I think Robson has got some kind of *idée fixe* and no facts or figures are likely to convince him we do not go out of our way to make things easier for the products of the older universities.' Hayes stressed (6 January 1955) that the first consideration was to get the best examiner available, though they tried in a general way to have universities widely represented. He thought, however, that all the details collected should not be sent on to Robson. Hayes drafted a reply for Helsby to send to Robson, and they discussed it. Hayes did not want to encourage Robson into further statistical analysis but Helsby was for giving him more information: 'To withhold all figures would undoubtedly arouse his suspicion, especially in view of the inevitable delay in replying to him; and I do not want to refuse information now which I might feel obliged to give later on if he returns to the attack.' In any case, Helsby recalled that when he met Robson he was at pains to emphasise that, in his view, it was the setting of papers by an examiner from a particular university which gave an advantage to graduates of that university; and that he did not at all intend to imply that the marking of scripts would be biased. The redrafted letter from Helsby was sent to Robson on 10 January 1955.

There was almost daily exchange of correspondence in January 1955, because by then Robson was preparing the material from the special issue and commissioning other material for the book. Helsby discussed this with Bridges and Padmore on 10 January, by which time Bridges had also seen Robson. Padmore had agreed to contribute a chapter on Treasury control of establishment affairs. On 11 January Helsby reminded Robson that he had previously agreed that the 'Notes and Comments' would not be included in the book and also that Helsby would see Robson's revised contribution because of the feelings in the Commission that Robson's reference to CSSB did not do it justice, especially in regard to the comprehensive job analysis that was undertaken. Bridges also wrote on 12 January to ensure that if anything from the 'Notes and Comments' was reproduced, Robson would first consult Bridges and Padmore.

Robson's letter to Helsby of 17 July gave him the assurance he sought: the editorial from the special issue would not be included in the book, and Robson agreed to redraft his own chapter to take account of the points made by the Commission.

Throughout these discussions and correspondence Robson continued to emphasise the importance of the question: *who* set the questions and where were those examiners located? Helsby and the Commission staff continued to reply with facts about the locations of the Assistant Examiners who marked the papers. Robson maintained that these were different questions, and whilst he was 'extremely anxious not to make any unfounded insinuations about this or anything else connected with the Civil Service',[29] and stressed that he was anxious not to be unjust in any way, he must be free to express his opinion.[30] Hayes interpreted Robson's position as: 'Because you cannot draw valid conclusions, I am entitled to allege what I like, and as you can't prove the contrary you mustn't object.'[31]

When Robson sent his revised passage on CSSB to Helsby on 6 June 1955, McArthur and Hayes offered their comments. Helsby wrote to Robson on 10 June, along the lines of the comments provided, though Hayes felt there was no point in trying to argue with Robson: 'I think that the nearer we bring his comments to common-sense the more damaging they will be.'[32]

Robson then invited Helsby for lunch at the Athenaeum on 11 July 1955 (for which Helsby was briefed by Goldsmith and his other colleagues) and the next day Helsby wrote a record of their discussion which was seen by Hayes; Goldsmith; H.A. Needham, Senior Assistant Director of Examinations; Reader; and Miss Diplock. Goldsmith's confidential minute of 5 July is among the last papers in the file. He concluded that 'if a man does not intend to be convinced very little can be done about it; indeed an unprejudiced reader of this file could scarcely come to any other conclusion than that we are dealing with an "unbalanced personality" '.[33]

The special number of *The Political Quarterly* quickly sold out and a second printing was required. Most of the essays in the subsequent book were revised or expanded from the journal, though it had a rather different focus, and six more essays were commissioned. The additional material included a chapter on 'The Colonial Service' by A. Creech Jones (Secretary of State for the Colonies 1946–50 – see chapter 7). The book, however, did not attract the attention and acclaim Robson may have hoped. Various reviews referred to 'the book's dullness',[34] said that it was 'rather on the defensive about recruitment to the Administrative Class',[35] noted that the civil service contributors were 'reticent',[36] and commented that 'the officials...sometimes give the impression that they are wondering what dreadful "repercussions" may arise among the staff associations from anything they might say'.[37]

The experience of the Civil Service Commission in relation to its centenary is particularly revealing about the attitudes of officials. They wanted to recognise, in an appropriate way, the achievements that were so widely recognised by others, but at the same time they were constrained by the administrative culture which was against them saying or writing anything about their work. Perhaps the suggestion for a conference of heads of public service commissions would have been suitable in a different context or at a different time, but it was clearly not thought appropriate in the United Kingdom in the mid 1950s. Instead, there was official backing for Hayes' project which now looks amateur in its approach. The list of 85 questions was hardly how a social scientist would have approached a comparative study even at that time, and may have revealed more about Hayes' background and the official approval he received, than it contributed to lessons from the experience of public service commissions. A social scientist at the beginning of the twenty-first century might feel that Hayes was exceedingly fortunate in getting a Nuffield Fellowship and in being so generously funded for findings which could have been written by a post-graduate student using published information and writing a few letters to overseas public service commissions.

Whilst none of the suggestions or plans from officials was successfully achieved there was considerable embarrassment that Robson managed to bring his much more modest projects to apparently successful conclusions in the journal and the book. Nevertheless it now appears surprising how ignorant civil servants were of Robson and his work. The officials in the Commission seemed to think he was a Professor of Economics and did not appreciate that he was not only an academic specialist in public administration but also a leading figure in the social sciences, both nationally and internationally. Helsby appears to have found out about Robson's Fabian pamphlet only by seeing it mentioned in Robson's *Who's Who* entry. Robson was trying to advance the study of public administration by raising questions, making evaluations and offering criticisms. It is noteworthy how many officials contributed to writing Helsby's article, and how much official time was spent on it. It is also enlightening that Helsby and Bridges thought they would be compromised by having their essays published in close proximity to Robson's rather restrained editorial (which raised the sort of questions he had asked Helsby and Bridges to consider). Perhaps official ignorance is explained by their being out of touch with academic journals in the social sciences. Special issues generally contain editorials and Robson may well have thought it would be obvious to others that he would be intending to write one. It is also rather odd that Helsby should refer to his own 'red brick' background when he was educated at Sedbergh School and Keble College, Oxford – which is, indeed built of red bricks (though before joining the civil service he had lectured at the University College of the South West, now Exeter University, and at the University of Durham). Comments from officials that, in dealing with Robson they were dealing with an 'unbalanced personality' and that it was rather stupid of Robson not to get his editorial checked with them, suggest that the officials were out of touch with academic approaches to their own work and unappreciative of the well-motivated and constructive intentions of specialists in public administration. The most senior officials may have felt hurt by their experience but today must appear somewhat ignorant, and certainly rather loftily superior.

Notes

1 PRO/CSC5/1381, Morrison to Butler.
2 *The Times*, 23, 24, 25, 26 November 1953.

3 PRO/CSC5/1381, minute by Sinker, 8 September 1953.
4 *The Times Educational Supplement*, 20 May 1955.
5 For example, a lecture by Professor K.C. Wheare, by arrangement with the Treasury and the University of London – see K.C. Wheare, *The Civil Service in the Constitution* (London: Athlone Press, 1954).
6 For example, Edward Hughes, 'Civil Service Reform: The Trevelyan Report', *Manchester Guardian*, 23 November 1953; Wyn Griffith, *The British Civil Service 1854–1954* (London: HMSO, 1954).
7 PRO/CSC5/521; PRO/CSC5/522; PRO/CSC5/523.
8 Oxford Society, *Oxford*, Special Number, 1949, pp. 36–55.
9 PRO/CSC5/520; Frederic Milner, 'Recent Developments in the work of the Civil Service Commission', *Public Administration*, 25, 1947, 61–70.
10 Bosworth Monck, *How the Civil Service Works* (London: Phoenix House, 1952).
11 T.A. Critchley, *The Civil Service Today* (London: Victor Gollancz, 1951).
12 PRO/CSC5/522.
13 Critchley, *The Civil Service Today*, p. 12.
14 PRO/CSC5/524.
15 *Her Majesty's Civil Service Commissioners, A Note on their Duties and History* (London: HMSO, 1952).
16 PRO/CSC5/554, Johnston to Sinker, 3 December 1953.
17 PRO/CSC5/554, 29 January 1954.
18 PRO/CSC5/989.
19 PRO/CSC5/989, Hayes to H.E. Sir Girja Shamber Bagpa, 6 August 1953.
20 PRO/CSC5/989, Hayes to Nottage, 2 May 1955.
21 PRO/CSC5/1381, Hayes to Young, 8 October 1955.
22 PRO/CSC5/989, Hayes to Griffiths, 2 May 1955.
23 K.M. Reader, *The Civil Service Commission, 1855–1975* (London: HMSO, 1981).
24 *The Times*, 15 May 1980.
25 *A Bibliography of the Writings of W.A. Robson*, Compiled by C.E. Hill with a Preface by G.W. Jones, Greater London Papers No. 17 (London: London School of Economics and Political Science, 1986).
26 PRO/CSC5/579.
27 PRO/CSC5/579, Hayes to First Commissioner, 7 July 1954.
28 PRO/CSC5/579, Helsby to Goldsmith, 13 October 1954.
29 PRO/CSC5/579, Robson to Helsby, 12 January 1955.
30 PRO/CSC5/579, Robson to Helsby, 6 June 1955.
31 PRO/CSC5/579, Hayes to First Commissioner, 18 January 1955.
32 PRO/CSC5/579, Hayes to First Commissioner, 9 June 1955.
33 PRO/CSC5/579, Goldsmith to First Commissioner, 5 July 1955.
34 London: Archives of the London School of Economics and Political Science, Robson Papers, D10. ALH in *The Yorkshire Evening Post*, no date.
35 Robson Papers, D10. W. McLaine, *Red Tape*, 1956.
36 Robson Papers, D10. J.H. Warrender, *Political Studies*, February 1957.
37 Robson Papers, D10. *The Times Literary Supplement*, no date.

9

THE EFFECTS OF FULTON

The purpose of this chapter is to give some account, first, of the setting up of the Fulton Committee on the Civil Service[1] and the contribution of the Civil Service Commission to its work and, second, of one of the consequences of its recommendations, the review by the Davies Committee[2] of the processes of selection for the administrative class of the home civil service. There is no space here to consider all the details of the recommendations of the Fulton Committee – some of which are mentioned elsewhere in this book, but on which there is already a voluminous literature.[3] Though some details of the reports will be provided to enable the effects to be considered in an appropriate context, the focus is not on the reports but on some of the effects of these inquiries on the Civil Service Commission.

The Fulton Committee was appointed in 1966 against a general attitude in Britain critical of British institutions and calling for modernisation. Publications indicative of this attitude include the stimulating essay by Thomas (later Lord) Balogh, entitled 'The Apotheosis of the Dilettante' (1959),[4] the book *British Government Observed* by Professor Brian Chapman (1963)[5] and the Fabian Tract *The Administrators* (1964).[6] The recommendations in the Fabian Tract called for wider recruitment, better training and more movement in and out of the civil service. The main pre-cursor to the Fulton Committee was, however, the *Recruitment to the Civil Service* Report of the Select Committee on Estimates, published in 1965. That report included the proposal that: 'A committee...should be appointed to initiate research upon, to examine, and to report upon the structure, recruitment and management of the Civil Service.'[7] It is therefore not surprising that the Fulton Committee acknowledged the report of the Estimates Committee as laying the foundations for its work.[8] The recommendation was accepted by the government and on 8 February 1966 Harold (later Lord) Wilson, then Prime Minister, announced in the House of Commons the appointment of the Fulton Committee 'to examine the structure, recruitment and management, including training, of the Home Civil Service, and to make recommendations'.[9]

The Fulton inquiry had more resemblance to a royal commission than to an enquiry on the lines of the Plowden Committee[10] as envisaged by the Estimates Committee. It was a departmental committee; it met in Treasury buildings and received support from Treasury staff. It was hoped that this status would enable it to work quickly. It was decided that, unlike the previous royal commissions on the civil service, its minutes of oral evidence would not be published, in the hope that individuals giving evidence would speak more freely.[11] Furthermore, the committee included civil servants, as envisaged by the Estimates Committee, and it was hoped that this would result in its recommendations being more acceptable within the civil service.

Although the members of the committee were chosen by the prime minister, it is unlikely he would not have received advice from Sir Laurence (later Lord) Helsby, then Head of the Civil Service, a former First Civil Service Commissioner. Such advice is likely to have particularly applied to the choice of the civil servant members, whom *The Economist* referred to as 'four very able top civil servants (at least three of them rather unconventional)'.[12] The first person to be appointed Secretary to the committee was Mary Loughnane, a principal in the Treasury, who had previously served as Secretary to the Priestley Royal Commission on the Civil Service 1953–55, but she soon withdrew on grounds of health and was replaced by R.W.L. Wilding, also a principal in the Treasury. Michael Simons, from the Ministry of Labour, served as Assistant Secretary. Neither the Secretary nor the Assistant Secretary, who were significantly involved in advising on research projects and co-ordinating them, was a graduate in a social science discipline, though they had knowledge and experience of the working of the civil service. Instead of formally appointing a director of research, as was becoming increasingly common for commissions of inquiry, Norman Hunt (later Lord Crowther-Hunt), a member of the committee, became in practice its unofficial director of research as he had been given leave of absence from Exeter College, Oxford.

The first effect of the Fulton Committee on the Civil Service Commission, in fact pre-dating its creation, was to stimulate a large amount of work, all of it urgent, in preparing evidence. Sir George Abell, then First Civil Service Commissioner, attended the Heads of Departments conference, the 'Sunningdale Conference', in October 1965 and the next week sent a minute to his senior colleagues telling them that it looked as though there would be a committee on the civil service (though probably not a royal commission). He told them about the preliminary talks there had been.[13] K.A.G. Murray, then Chairman of the Civil Service Selection Board (CSSB), responded on 16 January 1966, with some general views on behalf of CSSB staff.

As early as 13 January 1966 C.J. Hancock, in the Treasury, wrote to J. Seddon, then Secretary, Civil Service Commission, asking for information for the Treasury Memorandum being prepared for the expected committee. At that stage the Commission was simply asked to provide tables of figures.[14] Immediately after the Fulton Committee had been set up, however, Hancock wrote again to Seddon and said the deadline for the Treasury's Introductory Memorandum was 25 February.[15] Some of the evidence from the Commission did not require much special effort, such as a description of how it currently worked, but more work was required to produce later evidence, for example, to prepare a suggested method of selection for a wider graduate entry. When the Commissioners' 100th Annual Report was published, in May 1967, they recorded in relation to the Fulton Committee: 'We have presented oral and written evidence to it on various aspects of our work.'[16] Some of the memoranda prepared for the Fulton Committee were, in fact, the direct consequences of specific recommendations from the Estimates Committee – such as the Executive Class Follow-up Survey.[17] The supporting volumes of evidence to the Fulton Committee show how significant the papers from the Commission were: they included ten memoranda from the Commission.[18] Some of these were major pieces of work containing very sophisticated analysis, such as Edgar Anstey's 'Administrative Class Follow-up 1966'.[19] They also included a number of Treasury Memoranda to which the Commission had contributed: for example, 'The Introductory Factual Memorandum on the Civil Service'.[20]

Helsby, as Head of the Home Civil Service, wrote a memorandum for the Fulton Committee on 'Central Management of the Civil Service'.[21] Its main purpose was to outline the machinery at that time and give balanced comments for and against the proposal for a Civil Service Department. The paper had been circulated to all permanent secretaries, took account of their views and was submitted in November 1966 (before Abell's second appearance to give oral evidence on 6 December). Abell commented to K.M. Reader, then Director of Examinations, that the memorandum was a strong and effective argument for leaving management with the Treasury. He continued:

> Since it would, if accepted, probably leave the Commission in its present relationship to the Treasury and to departments my first reaction is not to oppose it tooth and nail. There are clearly great practical difficulties in the notion of a separate ministerial department, and I have never liked a management-cum-selection type of enlarged Commission.[22]

Reader made some thoughtful observations about the relationship of the Treasury and the Commission and included the rather resigned comment that 'Wade and Phillips, a standard textbook on Constitutional Law, says that the Civil Service Commission is a subordinate department of the Treasury. I now feel that whatever happens we have nothing to lose!'[23]

In May 1966 the Treasury presented a paper to the Fulton Committee on 'The Future Structure of the Civil Service'.[24] In June, Wilding wrote to Murray asking for a great deal of information about the background of the members of the Examinations Directorate and an analysis of the examiners. As a consequence, Murray drafted a long paper on 'The Nature and Functions of the Civil Service Selection Board'. This was later revised and shortened for inclusion in the Commission's paper for the Fulton Committee, on selection procedures.

The revised version was circulated to all senior staff in the Commission, for comment. Seddon at that stage (16 September) queried whether the Treasury should have 'a (courtesy) sight of our stuff'. Reader's reply ended:

> Do we really need to bring in Treasury? To heck with courtesy when this will mean not only delay but niggling criticisms from Ross designed to produce a document which will put the most unfavourable light possible on the Commission's activities. On too many occasions we have later regretted having paid heed to Ross's amendments. It is time the Commissioners made it plain that you and I are not always willing to dance to Ross's tunes! Selection procedures are entirely our province.[25]

In the event, Seddon sent 25 copies of the final version on 'Selection Procedures for Civil Service Appointments'[26] to Wilding on 10 October and at the same time sent three to P.S. Ross, at the Treasury.

The Fulton Report's comments on the civil service in general and on recruitment in particular were highly controversial. The report began with a challenging and provocative first chapter which asserted that the home civil service was:

> still fundamentally the product of the nineteenth century philosophy of the Northcote–Trevelyan Report. The tasks it faces are those of the second half of the twentieth century. This is what we have found; it is what we seek to remedy.[27]

This first chapter called for fundamental change to rectify the inadequacies the committee found. These were: the philosophy of the amateur; the system of classes; the separate hierarchies of scientists, engineers and other specialist classes; the inadequacy of management training; the isolation of the civil service from the rest of the community; and weaknesses of personnel management. Subsequent chapters considered these issues in some depth.

The Civil Service Commission was affected by all the comments and recommendations of the committee on matters of recruitment, but it was also involved in other major topics which had implications for recruitment, such as the system of classes. The Fulton Committee criticised the Commission for being separate and remote from other departments and recommended that it should cease to be a separate and independent organisation. It recommended that it should become part of the new Civil Service Department. It also criticised the methods of recruitment for being slow, and recommended that departments should play a larger part in the recruitment process and that more staff should be recruited directly by departments. From the viewpoint of the Commission a particularly important recommendation said that 'a review of the processes of recruitment should be put in hand'. Besides seeking to reduce the time they take, it should examine the problems of methods of selection for non-specialist graduates and their equivalents.[28]

Although the Fulton Report was published on 26 June 1968, drafts of the final version of the report were available within the civil service well before that, and the parts specifically affecting the Commission were known to senior staff there for two months before publication. Indeed, on 2 May, Wilding sent Seddon a copy, marked 'Personal and in Confidence', of the sections dealing with recruitment. Although this was for the purpose of correcting any factual errors, it also enabled staff in the Commission to suggest some minor amendments. When they read the sections Wilding sent they were shocked by the severity of the criticisms about their selection procedures, which they felt were totally unjustified. John (later Lord) Hunt, Abell's successor as First Commissioner, saw Sir Philip (later Lord) Allen, then Permanent Under-Secretary of State, Home Office, and a member of the Fulton Committee, privately on 9 May to see if he could get the detailed proposals on selection couched more in terms of suggestions rather than firm recommendations.[29] In his talk with Allen, John Hunt made three main points. First, there was no selection bias for graduates in Greats. Second, more thought should be given to the effects on staff morale from comments about remoteness and tired members of selection committees. These criticisms were regarded as unjustified on the facts and calculated to hurt. Third, many of the suggestions about CSSB and the Final Selection Board (FSB) 'were plainly silly' and ought to be omitted or toned down to tentative suggestions. Allen was sympathetic and promised to do his best, but, not surprisingly, he said he could make no promises.[30]

On 27 May Hunt wrote to Murray and Reader, drawing attention to the Fulton recommendation that there should be a further enquiry into the Method II system of selection. Hunt said that this enquiry would have to be accepted and, indeed, should be welcomed by the Commission 'in order to redress some of the half (or less than half) truths'. Hunt said the details would not be settled for a while, but he asked for reactions from Murray and Reader. He recognised that they would have to be clear on whether to go for one man or a committee. He also wondered how, when the Commission was in the lead in this field, they could reconcile objectivity and impartiality in committee members with sufficient knowledge of what was involved.[31]

Murray gave his immediate reactions the next day, 28 May. He was particularly concerned with Appendix E, 'Recruitment Procedure', in the report. He wrote:

> I am not going to accept this as in any conceivable way an intellectually worthwhile analysis of a procedure which in many respects leads the country. If not dishonest it is slatternly and journalistic and ignorant, and the Committee should be ashamed of lending their names to it... When people read 'We have serious doubts about the staffing and methods of the Civil Service Selection Board' they will take this for Civil Service language that the Committee feel the methods are bloody awful... it is a travesty of twenty years' work and research and results... that this should be allowed to be given the authority of what should like to appear as a great reforming Committee...[32]

The next day, Murray followed this up with a more substantial paper, for discussion at the Commissioners' meeting on 4 June. He said that he agreed wholeheartedly with much in the report, but he took strong exception to Appendix E. He referred to this as a 'hurried and partial document', which contained 'factual errors even in these few paragraphs', and which stated a philosophy of selection which showed ignorance of how people are assessed or of how the act of judgment must be made. He said: 'to make baldly the statement "We have serious doubts about the staffing and methods of the CSSB" is not good enough'. He recalled that Norman Hunt was the only one of the 12 committee members to visit CSSB (and it took great efforts to get him there, and, after twice altering dates, the third time he just did not appear, although he did appear on the fourth). Hunt, however, saw less than the ordinary visitor to CSSB; his hurried visit enabled him to see only an over-age intake (i.e. not undergraduates), without a psychologist in the assessing team; he did not allow time to discuss his impressions with the staff; and he paid no attention to his own promise to return for a talk on what he had seen.

Murray emphasised that this was an attack on one particular institution, with the morale of whose members he was very much concerned. His worry was not only a personal one: he felt that in making his comments he was representing a Board which had 'a reputation throughout the country and in a sense throughout the world as an exponent of up to date and thorough methods of assessing people, and equally of assessing its own assessments'.[33] He gave a detailed list of what had been apparently ignored about the work of CSSB including its recognised eminence, the valuable 'Follow up' studies of its work, the organisations that had adopted CSSB methods (including the Coal Board, Atomic Energy Authority, Post Office, Police, University Grants Committee, a number of Commonwealth countries and West Germany), the high quality and high productivity of CSSB staff and the important research work it was undertaking.

Murray felt the Commission should welcome the proposed enquiry into the basis of the Fulton Committee's allegations as well as into CSSB's methods. He agreed with the First Commissioner, however, that it would be difficult to find suitable people to undertake it. He suggested someone like Jack Davies (who for many years had been Secretary to the Cambridge University Appointments Board), someone from Management Selection, perhaps a bright assistant secretary with relevant experience and himself.[34]

The Commissioners met on 4 June and afterwards John Hunt wrote to Sir William (later Lord) Armstrong, the new Head of the Civil Service. He said that the Commission could not take amiss most of the Fulton comments and recommendations on selection, but that Appendix E was a different matter. Some comments appeared to be based on a misunderstanding of the facts, and the 'serious doubts' expressed in paragraph 18 about the staffing and methods of work of CSSB were 'a cause for much greater concern, since...they conclude by saying that the way the final assessment is made is "disturbing"'. The remark was bound to be damaging to morale in the Commission, particularly as it was made without any proper examination by the committee of the facts. If endorsed by the government, 'it could be harmful to our recruitment image besides being...most unfair to the staff concerned'. He said that he had been told by Allen that Appendix E had originally been designed by Norman Hunt for the body of the report but was relegated to an appendix because the committee as a whole did not feel they knew enough about the subject. John Hunt hoped, for both practical and morale reasons, that some way could be found to minimise its effect, and as a minimum he hoped it would be made clear that the Government did not accept the criticisms in the appendix pending further enquiry. He also asked for a meeting with Armstrong.[35]

The request to see Armstrong was quickly met. Armstrong then spoke to Norman Hunt on 6 June, and A.M. (later Sir Alan) Bailey (Helsby's private secretary) noted the next day that Norman Hunt had said it was too late to change the wording of the report, in particular the adjective 'disturbing' about the way the final assessment was made, which had given particular offence. He was, however, conscious that he had not spent as long as he would have liked at CSSB and he would like to have a talk with Murray when it could be arranged. Armstrong then spoke about this to John Hunt and it was agreed they would have another talk about it before the report was published. At the meeting between John Hunt and Armstrong, Hunt made suggestions about the membership of the committee of inquiry, suggesting Mr Goff of ICI, someone from a management selection firm with a background in psychology, a representative of the universities and a representative of the civil service. During his talk with Armstrong on 6 June, Norman Hunt had explained that Appendix E was only intended to point to ways in which the selection procedure might be improved ('he himself thought very highly of it and recognised its leadership in the field').[36] He also made it clear that he would like to be a member of the committee of enquiry. Armstrong did not commit himself on this request but it was noted by Bailey that, if Norman Hunt was to be included, it should be as an ex-member of the Fulton Committee, and there should be a separate representative of the universities nominated by the Vice-Chancellors. Armstrong told John Hunt that he would aim to see that the government did not accept the criticisms in the appendix.

At a lunch meeting on 18 June of Armstrong and his colleagues involved in the Fulton work, John Hunt argued that Norman Hunt should not be invited to take part in the inquiry: he had already lost the confidence of the civil service, he was known to be *parti pris* on the particular issue and he had acquired the reputation of being unwilling to change his mind. There was some support for these arguments in the discussion and Armstrong took note in case he was approached.[37] John Hunt later explained to Murray that he had heard Armstrong was spending the weekend in Oxford and might see Norman Hunt, and he thought it wise to get his position firmly on the record. He hoped he had heard the last of the suggestion that Norman Hunt might be a member of the inquiry. Murray commented that he did not suppose now that Norman Hunt would be anxious to come and see him, 'but if so the invitation is strong, if not in the usual sense warm'.[38]

After the Fulton Report was published, John Hunt spoke to the staff on 27 June. He gave an optimistic, morale-boosting talk, commenting on all the main recommendations in the report. When he came to the enquiry into the processes of selection at CSSB and FSB, he said he particularly welcomed the enquiry because the committee's comments on these matters were very much open to challenge, and the government was not committed to its recommendations about CSSB. He indicated the limitations of the Fulton Committee's knowledge on these matters and welcomed this opportunity to get the full facts of what CSSB did and how it operated on the record. He made the same points when he earlier met the Departmental Whitley Council on 25 June.[39]

Shortly before the Fulton Report was published, Murray wrote a personal memorandum to assessing staff, in his capacity as Chairman of CSSB. Like the First Commissioner's talk, it was a personal approach to the situation they found themselves in, and intended to boost morale. It was drafted on 19 June and sent to John Hunt who said it was excellent, made a few comments and added that he was quite content for it to be sent. In fact, after amendments it was sent on 17 July, marked 'Very Strictly Confidential', together with a copy of the transcript of John Hunt's talk to Commission staff.[40]

On 17 July Murray sent to John Hunt a 'Very Strictly Personal' minute about a number of possible members of the inquiry. J.G.W. Davies was high on the list, as also was Elizabeth Sidney. On 30 July Edgar Anstey sent a minute with personal particulars of five suggested names for the inquiry, including Davies and A.T.M. Wilson. On 1 August Hunt wrote to Bailey, who had become Armstrong's private secretary, about the proposed committee. He hoped the committee's report would be published in due course. He recognised the need to choose the members carefully, to avoid any grounds for thinking that the Commission was attempting to be judge in their own cause. He therefore thought the inquiry should be predominantly an outside one (and he did not think it necessary that it should include a Commission representative). For Chairman, John Hunt recommended Davies. Davies was just leaving the post of Secretary of the Cambridge University Appointments Board after 22 years and was about to join the Bank of England as its Director (Personnel). He was born in 1911; educated at Tonbridge School and St John's College, Cambridge, where he took a first in classics; worked for the National Institute of Industrial Psychology before the war; was Chief Psychologist at the Army Directorate for Selection of Personnel during the war, where he played a leading part in the development of the War Office Selection Board (WOSB); and had been awarded the OBE for war service. Davies already had a good relationship with staff at the Commission. For example, Abell had had a long and useful talk with Davies on 21 March 1966. Davies thought the best candidates would be discouraged from applying if there was a wider graduate intake and emphasised that it would not be possible not to have an elite, however unfashionable it might be.[41] Davies had kept in touch with the progress of the Fulton Committee: for example, he had called on John Hunt on 9 April 1968 to enquire about the expected date of the report and offered strong comments in favour of starring some of the graduate entry – i.e. to indicate recruits assessed as having the potential to rise to the highest grades.[42]

For the member from industry, John Hunt felt the best man might be A.T.M. Wilson, the Adviser in the use of Social Sciences at Unilever. He was aged 62, took a BSc and MD at Glasgow, and during the war he served as a psychiatrist at WOSB. For the member from the academic world he thought the Vice-Chancellors' Committee should be asked for a nomination. For the member from the civil service, by way of example he suggested Desmond Keeling or John Moore. For a member with experience of working with CSSB the best person would be Elizabeth Sidney. She was aged 43, had graduated in English at Oxford and in Psychology at London and, after serving for a time at the National Institute of Industrial Psychology, became a writer and freelance consultant on personnel matters. She knew CSSB procedures intimately but was very independently minded and was in no sense in the Commissioners' pocket. None of these individuals had been 'sounded'. He recommended the committee's terms of reference and suggested its secretary should be R.N. Burton, of the Commission, who would also be associated with the 'speeding up selection processes' enquiry which Fulton had recommended. Armstrong endorsed the minute, adding his own comments, and sent it to Lord Shackleton, then Paymaster General.

Wilding, who had received a copy of the minute to Armstrong, responded to Hunt the next day. He reminded him that paragraph 22 of Appendix E said that the inquiry should take account of the analysis by A.H. Halsey (one of the Fulton Committee's commissioned research projects: Halsey, a sociologist, was a Professorial Fellow, Nuffield College, Oxford). Appendix E said: 'In our view, the inquiry we have proposed should include a thorough examination of this evidence and of the inferences that should be drawn from it for future methods of selection of all kinds.' Wilding added that he thought it highly desirable that the new committee should consider and comment on Halsey's chapter on the administrative class, otherwise 'the implied imputations of bias in that chapter will survive and do damage'. Unfortunately the Halsey memorandum had not yet been published. Wilding therefore thought he should contact both Norman Hunt and Halsey and ask them to agree that the members of the new committee should see and examine the latest draft of chapter 3 before the Halsey Report was published. John Hunt did not agree. He wanted the membership of the committee to be first approved by ministers, otherwise earlier contact with Norman Hunt 'might put back into Dr Hunt's head the thought that he should be a member!' John Hunt agreed, however, that Wilding's suggestion be adopted after the composition of the inquiry had been definitely settled.[43]

Armstrong had a letter drafted for him by John Hunt, asking the Governor of the Bank of England to release Davies to chair the committee. The letter was sent on 9 August 1968. The Governor, Sir Leslie (later Lord) O' Brien telephoned John Hunt on 13 August about the commitment that would be involved. John Hunt estimated one day per week. O' Brien though this 'a little optimistic' and suggested not more than two days per week. Hunt saw Elizabeth Sidney on 13 August and she agreed to serve on the committee. A.T.M. Wilson also accepted the invitation on 20 August. After considerable discussion with senior civil servants in other departments it was agreed that the civil servant on the committee would be Johnny Moore, then Principal Establishments Officer, Ministry of Transport (who was the Commission's first choice). This took considerable effort. John Hunt persuaded Armstrong to approve the choice of Moore. Moore said he would like to accept, although he was overworked. John Hunt therefore wrote, both officially and privately, to Sir Thomas Padmore, Moore's Permanent Secretary at the Ministry of Transport. He mentioned the support he had received from Armstrong and said that he had some reason to think that Moore would himself like to take on the job. Padmore replied on 18 September: 'your two letters...do not leave me with much option...But owing to my negligence in going on holiday the horse has said that he passionately wants to run over this additional course'. Moore was educated at Whitgift Middle School and graduated in history from Selwyn College, Cambridge. As a result of war service he was awarded the DFC. The fifth member of the committee, Professor Bryan (later Sir Bryan) Thwaites, was nominated by Professor D.G. (later Sir Derman) Christopherson, then Vice-Chancellor of the University of Durham and Chairman of the Committee of Vice-Chancellors and Principals. Christopherson told Armstrong and Armstrong told John Hunt. John Hunt thanked Christopherson on 20 September and said he would like to meet him in October when he would stay in Durham on his way to holiday in Scotland. Thwaites was educated at Dulwich College, Winchester College, and Clare College, Cambridge. He had been an assistant master at Winchester College and Professor of Theoretical Mechanics at Southampton University before his appointment as Principal of Westfield College, University of London, in 1966. As this was a departmental inquiry all the invitations to serve were sent by John Hunt (though with the approval of Armstrong and Shackleton). The terms of reference were:

> To examine the selection arrangements under Method II in the light of the Fulton Report and such further evidence as the Committee of Inquiry obtains, and to make recommendations on the staffing and methods of work at CSSB, and on the role, composition, and methods of work of the Final Selection Board.[44]

John Hunt wrote to Davies on 12 September outlining a number of documents he would provide for the committee. He also said there were a number of points he would like to discuss with Davies soon. He then had lunch with Davies at the Royal Automobile Club, where Davies was a member, on 17 September. He explained that Davies would be told that CSSB already tried to pick 'the relevant men' and he would be asked to examine the various tests and exercises against that background. Davies was also told that the immediate requirement was 'a fairly quick report on the objectivity and efficiency of CSSB as it is and in the light of Fulton's comments'.[45]

Burton, the Secretary, was by then already working on a paper for the committee, giving a general summary of the complete procedure at CSSB. John Hunt approved Burton's approach but said he wanted to see the paper in draft. He also kept himself closely informed of the committee's progress by asking Burton to see him from time to time. Burton, however, felt it necessary to mention to John Hunt on 24 February 1969: 'the Chairman is peculiarly sensitive about any interference with the independence of the Committee and tends to look upon me as the voice of the Commission'.[46] In addition to his contacts with Burton, from time to time John Hunt discussed with Davies 'the sort of people who ought to give evidence'.[47]

The committee quickly began work. At its first meeting, on 7 October 1968, John Hunt outlined the position on issues raised by the Fulton Committee. At the meeting on 22 November Wilding gave background information about the Fulton Committee's attention to the Method II system of selection, explaining that the Committee had been affected by two main influences. One was Norman Hunt who, apparently on the basis of what he had seen at CSSB and FSB, thought the system of selection was too subjective and not scientific enough. He was supported by other committee members who had been favourably impressed by the French system. Five members, with the Assistant Secretary, had visited France from 7 to 10 November 1966.[48] They were impressed by the quality of the staff and their confidence. They found that the French system produced highly professional, well-trained elites; and the French view was that the British method of selection was intellectually dishonest and favoured the glib and the articulate. The other influence was early drafts of the Halsey Report which pointed to the preponderance of entrants to the administrative class from middle-class backgrounds in the south of the country, who had been to school in the private sector and to the older universities, where they had taken degrees in the arts and humanities. The Halsey survey suggested that since 1948 the trend had been to strengthen this predominance and it was also coupled with a decline in the number of first-class honours candidates among those successful. As the Fulton Committee had been unable to decide whether these influences were valid, they had proposed the Method II inquiry. The other evidence on these matters, such as that from the Commission, did not have much effect on the Fulton Committee and they did not take oral evidence from the Commission on the question.

The Davies Committee received strongly argued evidence supporting the work of CSSB. It also received from its secretary comments on the draft of the chapter on the administrative class in the Halsey Report. In addition, the committee became aware of the strong feeling in the Commission regretting that its 'Follow-up Survey' of the administrative class had not been succeeded by a request for oral evidence and because the 'Follow-up Survey' had not been mentioned in the Fulton Report. The general feeling about these matters in the Commission was not helped by the delays in producing the final version of the Halsey Report. When it was commissioned the target date for delivery was the end of February 1967, but as late as June 1968 the Commission learned that the Fulton

Committee had decided the Halsey Report would have to be re-written because it was unsatisfactory in its method of preparation and its content.[49] Meanwhile, the staff in the Commission were devoting many hours to commenting on drafts of various chapters of the Halsey Report.

The Davies Committee had 34 formal meetings, including seven meetings devoted to drafting its report. John Hunt gave oral evidence on five occasions; Murray attended nine meetings; Seddon and Reader each attended on one occasion.[50] Burton kept in close touch with John Hunt, as he was asked to. Burton wrote a detailed minute to John Hunt on 16 April 1969 because on the evening of the next day John Hunt was to see Davies. Members of the Davies Committee had taken responsibility for drafting chapters of the report. John Hunt used Burton's minute as a checklist for his discussion with Davies.[51] On 18 April Davies produced a draft statement, intended to be helpful to John Hunt, on the implications of the report for Method I. Although Method I was outside the committee's terms of reference, he said that, if the Commission wished to abolish Method I, it should not be inhibited from doing so by reason of any doubt about the fairness of Method II. He warned John Hunt, however, that drafting was taking longer than the committee had expected and the final version would not be ready before the middle or end of May.[52] In addition to its formal and informal meetings, all the committee members had followed a group of candidates through the entire Method II selection procedure; they had also all sat on the Final Selection Board. Altogether 38 witnesses were seen and 161 documents were received in evidence. Of the 62 individuals and organisations who gave evidence (oral and written) only 15 were serving civil servants, and of these seven were members of the Civil Service Department.

The committee concluded that Method II was a system of selection 'to which the Public Service can point with pride'.[53] They found 'no evidence of bias... either in the procedures or on the part of the assessors'.[54] The most powerful determinant of the makeup of the entry into the administrative class was probably 'the "streaming" influence of social and educational forces which predispose young people to opt for certain careers'.[55] They endorsed the CSSB philosophy, which was to attempt to assess as many characteristics as possible so as to achieve a picture of a candidate's total qualities.[56] The report contained a number of detailed suggestions and recommendations and at the end of the report the committee included a short but very bland 'Note on Future Developments'. The government issued a statement on 24 September 1969 saying that it accepted the committee's detailed recommendations in whole or in part.[57]

In the Civil Service Department the report was regarded as 'a welcome one'.[58] *The Times* said of the Davies inquiry: 'Seldom has a piece of public administration come so well out of an expert and searching inquiry.'[59] *The Guardian*, however, found the committee's comments about self-selection 'sinister'.[60] On the BBC 'Ten o'clock' programme Ivor Crewe (Halsey's colleague on the Halsey project) referred to the Davies Report as 'a very complacent, white-washing report'. John Hunt was particularly concerned about Crewe's comments and obtained a copy of the transcript but proposed to take no action, though he said 'we will watch carefully for anything Crewe may say in print'.[61]

Two interesting developments were associated with publication of the report. The first related to Davies' 'Note on Future Developments', which he was proposing to include as an annex to the report. The essence of the proposed short note – it was only four paragraphs – was that if there was to be a much larger entry into the service by Method II, one result would be to lose its function of picking a small elite. This would raise questions about the refined and costly nature of Method II. Davies warned that if, in these circumstances, the Commission was tempted to abridge the selection system there might then be doubts about its validity. Alternatively, if the CSSB stage was to continue with manageable numbers of candidates the soundness and validity of the qualifying examination, which would have to be used to reduce the field, would have to be all the more convincingly demonstrable. He therefore indicated that significant attention would have to be given to the system of appraisal and advancement within the service. The Davies Committee's inquiries had shown that Method II had a function of enabling representatives of the public interest to see the process of selection. He concluded that to provide the public with the same reassuring evidence about in-service arrangements would be a far more subtle and challenging task, but one which should not be overlooked.

When John Hunt saw Davies on 22 July he must have been very upset by Davies' proposed annex. Hunt's view was that the wider graduate entry was not within the committee's terms of reference and the committee had taken no evidence on the matter. He felt that Davies' text would give the impression, to the universities and to the National Staff Side, that the Commission was going for a large undifferentiated entry and that the committee had reservations about it. This could be embarrassing. As Davies was reluctant to make any change to the draft John Hunt told him that if he did not agree he (John Hunt) would advise ministers not to publish the annex. An expurgated report always led to speculation and he hoped that would be avoided. If Davies attached importance to making 'these rather speculative points he should do so in a separate letter to Lord Shackleton'. John Hunt said he was not in the least concerned to suppress Davies' views but merely to avoid publication of them. On 23 July John Hunt wrote to Burton saying that Davies had promised to reflect on the matter, but he thought that Davies would agree. He added that before the report went to the printer he would like to see what had happened about the 'Note', so as to make quite sure there was nothing he felt it necessary to exclude from the published version.

On 1 August John Hunt spoke to the private secretary to Shackleton, Lord Privy Seal, telling him that the report had gone for printing and enclosing a copy. He gave an outline of the findings and said the report would be published on the same day as the Halsey Report. He also explained about the 'Note' – on which he said he had remonstrated with the committee and 'rather reluctantly' the committee had agreed to do as he had asked. The comments in the 'Note' would therefore be incorporated in a letter to the Lord Privy Seal. John Hunt added that he thought he ought to explain the background to the letter Shackleton would probably be receiving from Davies. In fact, Davies wrote to Shackleton on 4 August incorporating the comments he had originally drafted for the annex, but which had been deleted when John Hunt intervened. This seemed to allay the expressed anxiety. Some months later John Hunt sent Davies a copy of the report from the Working Party he chaired on selection arrangements for the wider graduate entry. He did this because, given Davies' warning that Method II was not 'infinitely versatile', he felt the Civil Service Department would have been worse placed if Davies had not been given an opportunity to comment and he had subsequently complained.[62] Davies replied on 1 April that he would like to discuss some queries and comments he had. John Hunt therefore called on Davies at the Bank of England on 7 April 1970. Before doing so he refreshed his memory on the details of the original 'Note on Future Developments'.

The second interesting development from the Davies Report concerns the arrangements for its publication. The Davies and Halsey Reports were both published on 24 September 1969. John Hunt recognised the need for 'a public relations job to secure that Halsey does not scoop the headlines at the expense of Davies'.[63] Shackleton was also anxious about the public relations implications. He thought that there was a risk that it might be regarded as a whitewashing operation aimed largely at the Halsey Report. He said the press release should be carefully drafted to emphasise the independence of the members of the committee and the reality of the move towards a less restrictive pattern of successes in recent years (i.e. that since 1964 there had been greater representation in administrative class recruits of people from less privileged backgrounds).[64]

It was Burton's responsibility to prepare for a possible House of Lords debate in early November 1969.[65] He felt it important to stress the independence of the Davies Committee: 'If the main criticism is going to be that the committee was an "establishment body" the only...answer...is to give the biographical details of the members...and to indicate how they performed their task.' He also noted that the Davies arguments were pretty strong by themselves and had been accepted widely in the university world and with little public dissent generally.

The first effect of the Fulton Committee on the Civil Service Commission was an enormous increase of work for staff, especially at the highest levels. Numerous papers had to be prepared, questions answered, and meetings attended – all without any increase in resources for the Commission. This activity related not only to those aspects of the work of the two committees which have been the focus of this chapter, it also related to other aspects of the reports not covered in depth here, such as the creation of the Civil Service Department and the 'speeding up' review of the work of the Commission. The increase in work for the Commission was to be expected, for extra work in the departments concerned is always created when there is a major commission or committee of inquiry. Much less expected is the scant attention that seems to have been paid to the Commission by the Fulton Committee. The files make this abundantly obvious. It was thought to have happened by certain academics, commissioned to undertake research projects for the committee, who felt that their own work was inadequately appreciated – but the proof has only recently been released. The evidence that some of the Fulton Committee's comments and recommendations resulted from inadequate and scanty considerations now appears shocking when the committee itself was so critical of amateurism and made serious criticisms about the work of the Commission.

It is tempting to speculate why so little attention was paid to the evidence presented to the Fulton Committee from the Commission but it is unlikely that firm conclusions will be reached. Perhaps it was because the secretariat were ill-informed about these aspects of public administration. Perhaps the Commission was regarded as only a subordinate department of the Treasury and therefore was not given as much care and attention as other interested parties making representations to the Fulton Committee. Perhaps the work of the Commission was simply regarded as operational by people to whom policy making was more important. Perhaps for these or some other reasons civil service recruitment issues simply did not attract the right sort of scholarly attention from the committee or from its *de facto* director of research, Norman Hunt.

The second effect on the Commission related to the role of Norman Hunt. Geoffrey Fry, in his major study of the Fulton Committee, gives an amusing account of how Norman Hunt was so little known to Treasury officials that the wrong Norman Hunt was nearly appointed to serve on the committee – there was, at the time, another, and much more widely known Professor Norman Hunt in the University of Edinburgh. Fry's story becomes even more amusing given that *The Times*' item on the publication of the Fulton Report was accompanied by pictures of its members, including the professor from Edinburgh.[66] When the committee was appointed in 1966 the Oxford Norman Hunt was not in *Who's Who*, and his most significant publication was *Two Early Political Associations: The Quakers and the Dissenting Deputies in the Age of Sir Robert Walpole* (apparently his Ph.D. thesis, revised). Norman Hunt was not only not an academic authority on the civil service, he was also virtually unknown to the academic community of specialists in public administration. As Fry has recorded, he owed his position on the Fulton Committee to the friendship he had formed with Wilson, the Prime Minister, and to the generosity of Exeter College which gave him a year's sabbatical leave to devote himself to the work of the committee.[67]

An indication of the esteem in which Norman Hunt was held after the report was published is given in a report to Murray by Sir Arthur Benson. Benson, formerly of the Colonial Service was, in 1968, a CSSB Chairman and Hon Fellow of Exeter College. Soon after the Fulton Report was published Benson met Norman Hunt at dinner in the College. His account of the occasion is revealing.

> I started on the allegedly classless structure and asked how he thought recruitment for it should be arranged. He floundered a bit and the others took over while I kept quiet until I was able gently to point out that what he was suggesting was quite different from the report's suggestions.

One of the younger dons then said 'Not your night, Hunt: you did better on television when the only man you had to contend with was Fulton'. It was an amuzing evening. But he is a very second-class brain. He would honestly make a first-class executive officer; but I would not take him for A.C. [administrative class]. He is very ambitious, personally, and he is lacking in intellectual integrity as well as perception.[68]

Other comments were offered to Armstrong by Sir Louis Petch, who was Second Permanent Secretary, Civil Service Department, from 1968. Norman Hunt had applied for the principalship of the Civil Service College, but if he did not get it he hoped to be associated with the new Civil Service Department in some advisory capacity. Wilson had seen Hunt during the Labour Party conference in Blackpool in 1968 and thought it might be useful for Hunt to be involved in the follow-through work on the Fulton Report.[69] Petch wrote:

> we would all prefer to see him excluded...not for spiteful reasons but because of the nature of the man. We feel that his mind is closed on many of the subjects dealt with in the Fulton Report, and that from now on he will be more concerned to vindicate his own attitude than to find the right solutions to outstanding problems.[70]

Norman Hunt was not, however, insensitive; he could be good company, was very friendly and well meaning, and he was regarded in Oxford as an outstanding teacher.[71] The reactions he received from others were probably hurtful and that may explain why, when he gave evidence to the Davies Committee, he asked for a copy of the minutes of the committee's session in which he gave oral evidence so that, he said, he could be sure that he did not in any way inadvertently mislead them in some of his answers.[72] Burton sent the notes asked for by Hunt, but in doing so he 'avoided reflecting the hard line suggested by some committee members for example, the feeling expressed that we should emphasise the finality of the record and its confidentiality'.[73] It seems likely that Hunt had acquired, from his Fulton Committee experience, knowledge of how the practice of government committees worked and he wished to safeguard his position.

The relationship of the Davies Committee to the Civil Service Commission was of a different order from the Fulton Committee. Whereas the Fulton Committee was a Treasury departmental committee, the Davies Committee was a departmental committee of the Civil Service Commission. Consequently its Secretary came from that department. This clearly had advantages, especially as Burton was also associated with the 'speeding up' inquiry. Questions may be raised about the provenance of secretaries to such committees: the established practice, as with the Fulton Committee, has advantages as well as disadvantages, but any disadvantages might be modified if an appropriately independent outsider is appointed, for example as a director of research or specialist adviser. It should always be remembered that however able and industrious, and however well imbued with integrity a committee may be, the secretary cannot be separated from the administrative culture which is so important in conditioning official behaviour, nor can such a secretary easily escape from seeming to have allegiance to the department.

No where is this more evident than in Burton's belief that any criticism levelled at the independence of the Davies Committee could be rebutted by drawing attention to the committee members themselves. There is, it must be emphasised, no evidence that Davies and his colleagues were not independent and persons of integrity. Nevertheless it does look a little odd that such a committee of inquiry into alleged bias in favour of recruiting graduates from Oxford and Cambridge Universities should consist of five persons, three of whom were graduates from Cambridge, and one of whom was a graduate from Oxford. Committees of inquiry should not simply be fair and independent; they should also be seen as fair and independent.

Among the other effects of the Davies Committee on the Commission, two points stand out from the papers. First, John Hunt seemed, understandably, very anxious that the committee came to what he thought were the right conclusions, but it may be that the regular and frequent attendance of Commission staff, in advising as well as giving evidence to the committee, indicates that they were a little too enthusiastic. Had this been publicly known at the time it may have cast a shadow on the reception of the committee's report. Second, there is the suggestion of special interference by John Hunt on the question of Davies' 'Note on Future Developments'. It does seem unfortunate that committees or individuals who undertake inquiries should be precluded from using their expertise to offer comments or suggest conclusions on the significance of what they have found, whether or not such comments and conclusions are strictly within their terms of reference. It also seems unfortunate that non-social scientists should so often insist on associating more objectivity with the work of social scientists than the social scientists themselves would claim. John Hunt, it seems, wanted the Davies Committee to find the Method II system of selection to be fair and objective. Selection is, however, as Murray made clear, essentially a matter of judgment and it seems that was the position also taken by Davies and his colleagues. It may even be that they chose their words with more care than others appreciated and that their report raised more questions than they were permitted to formulate.

Notes

1 *The Civil Service, Vol. I, Report of the Committee 1966–68, (Fulton Report)*, Cmnd. 3638 (London: HMSO, 1968).
2 *The Method II System of Selection (for the Administrative Class of the Home Civil Service), Report of the Committee of Inquiry 1969, (Davies Report)*, Cmnd. 4156 (London: HMSO, 1969).
3 See, for example, Geoffrey K. Fry, *Reforming the Civil Service: the Fulton Committee on the British Home Civil Service 1966–1968* (Edinburgh: Edinburgh University Press, 1993), which also contains an extensive bibliography.
4 Thomas Balogh, 'The Apotheosis of the Dilettante', in Hugh Thomas (ed.), *The Establishment* (London: Anthony Blond, 1959).

5 Brian Chapman, *British Government Observed* (London: Allen & Unwin, 1963).
6 Fabian Society (A Fabian Group), *The Administrators, the Reform of the Civil Service*, Fabian Tract 355 (London: The Fabian Society, 1964).
7 *Sixth Report from the Estimates Committee, Session 1964–65, Recruitment to the Civil Service, together with the Minutes of Evidence taken before Sub-Committee E*, HC 308 (London: HMSO, 1965), para. 5(1).
8 *Fulton Report*, Appendix L, para. 14.
9 HC Deb. 5s., vol. 724, cols. 209–14 (8 February 1966).
10 *Control of Public Expenditure (Plowden Report)*, Cmnd 1432 (London: HMSO, 1962). See also Richard A. Chapman and J.R. Greenaway, *The Dynamics of Administrative Reform* (London: Croom Helm, 1980) and Richard A. Chapman, *The Treasury in Public Policy-Making* (London: Routledge, 1997).
11 PRO/BA1/2, Minutes of the first meeting, 10 March 1966.
12 *The Economist*, 12 February 1966.
13 PRO/CSC5/1254, minute by Abell, 18 October 1965.
14 PRO/CSC5/1194.
15 PRO/CSC5/1254, Hancock to Seddon, 10 February 1966.
16 PRO/CSC5/1209; Civil Service Commission, *Annual Report 1966* (London: HMSO, 1967).
17 PRO/CSC5/1210; Memorandum No. 5, *Fulton Report*, vol. 3(2).
18 See volumes 3(2), 4 and 5(1).
19 *Fulton Report*, vol. 3(2), Memorandum No. 4, pp. 106–53.
20 For example, 'The Introductory Factual Memorandum on the Civil Service', *Fulton Report*, vol. 4, pp. 9–191.
21 'Memorandum No. 14, submitted by the Head of the Home Civil Service, November, 1966, Central Management of the Civil Service', *Fulton Report*, vol. 5(1), pp. 94–103.
22 PRO/CSC5/1256, Abell to Director of Examinations, 27 September 1966.
23 PRO/CSC5/1256, Reader to First Commissioner, 27 September 1966.
24 *Fulton Report*, vol. 5(1), Memorandum No. 1, pp. 1–7.
25 PRO/CSC5/1257, Reader to Seddon, 17 September 1966.
26 *Fulton Report*, vol. 4, Memorandum No. 9, pp. 297–331.
27 *Fulton Report*, vol. 1, para. 1.
28 *Fulton Report*, vol. 1, para. 70; recommendation 28.
29 PRO/CSC5/1445.
30 PRO/CSC5/1445.
31 PRO/CSC5/1350.
32 PRO/CSC5/1350, Murray to First Commissioner, 28 May 1968.
33 PRO/CSC5/1350.
34 PRO/CSC5/1350, Murray to First Commissioner, 29 May 1968.
35 PRO/CSC5/1350, Hunt to Armstrong, 4 June 1968.
36 PRO/CSC5/1350, Armstrong to Hunt, 7 June 1968.
37 PRO/CSC5/1350, note by A.W. Wyatt.
38 PRO/CSC5/1350, Murray to Hunt, 20 June 1968.
39 PRO/CSC5/1800.
40 PRO/CSC5/1350.
41 PRO/CSC5/1453, First Commissioner to Secretary, 21 March 1966.
42 PRO/CSC5/1453, Hunt to Pratley, 9 April 1968.
43 PRO/CSC5/1350, Hunt to Burton, 5 August 1968.
44 *Davies Report*, p. iv.
45 PRO/CSC5/1350, Hunt to Burton, 19 September 1968.
46 PRO/CSC5/1520.
47 PRO/CSC5/1522, Hunt to Chairman of CSSB, 2 January 1969.

48 *Fulton Report*, Appendix C.
49 PRO/CSC5/1449, Secretary to First Commissioner, 7 June 1968.
50 PRO/CSC5/1525.
51 PRO/CSC5/1520.
52 PRO/CSC5/1520.
53 *Davies Report*, para. 9.2(i).
54 *Davies Report*, para. 9.2(ii).
55 *Davies Report*, para. 9.2(iii).
56 *Davies Report*, para. 9.2(v).
57 PRO/CSC5/1683.
58 PRO/CSC5/1639.
59 *The Times*, 25 September 1969.
60 *The Guardian*, 25 September 1969.
61 PRO/CSC5/1683, Hunt to Moore, 1 October 1969.
62 PRO/CSC5/1683, Hunt to Fells, 7 April 1970.
63 PRO/CSC5/1521 and PRO/CSC5/1639.
64 PRO/CSC5/1521.
65 PRO/CSC5/1527.
66 *The Times*, 27 June 1968 (corrected in *The Times*, 28 June 1968).
67 Fry, p. 18.
68 PRO/CSC5/1513, Benson to Murray, 6 July 1968.
69 PRO/CSC5/1644, minute dated 23 October 1968 (apparently by someone in the Prime Minister's Private Office).
70 PRO/CSC5/1644, Petch to Armstrong, 6 November 1968.
71 *The Times*, 18 February 1987.
72 PRO/CSC5/1446, Hunt to Burton, 3 January 1969.
73 PRO/CSC5/1446, Burton to Davies, 9 January 1969.

10
ADMINISTRATIVE CULTURE

The Civil Service Commission had its own administrative culture. Its most tangible elements were procedures, patterns and guidelines for behaviour that were, in some respects, distinctive from, but which in many aspects reflected the more general culture of the British civil service. Its less tangible, but to some extent more important, elements were the attitudes and standards, values, beliefs and assumptions of individual civil servants. This administrative culture had a variety of sources: some aspects were the result of pressures from the social and political environment, some had familial and educational origins, some developed from the work experiences and procedures in the department; some came from precedents and evolved into traditions and working philosophies of administration. Because of these origins and the flexible nature of the administrative culture, it changed over time and was affected by various pressures and influences.

Towards the end of its life, as mission statements and straplines became fashionable, the Commission published the key words which represented this culture on the cover of its annual reports. In this, as in many other aspects of its work, the Commission was not out of line with the civil service in general, nor was it out of line with practices and attitudes in other organisations. The Commission's key words were: selection on merit, fair and open competition, and equal opportunity.[1] The origins of these three principles do not require much explanation: it will be obvious from chapters 2, 3 and 4 of this book how they arose. They were nurtured and passed on primarily as a result of socialisation, for there were no training programmes or codes of conduct to guide their development or aid their implementation. Nevertheless they were of great importance to the staff of the Commission as well as to the applicants for posts in the civil service. It should not be forgotten that they were also of major importance to the system of government, especially to other departments, and to citizens. The guardians of this culture were the Commissioners themselves. They ensured that the culture was continuously borne in mind in the day-to-day work of the office and they also represented this culture in their annual reports, in evidence to official bodies and in publications, talks and lectures.

The intention in this chapter is not to give a comprehensive and authoritative account of the Civil Service Commission's administrative culture, but to present some examples of how it was manifested and/or tested in practice. These examples should be seen as further insights into how the department actually worked, for they suggest that there is plenty of scope for a wider-ranging study of administrative culture in British government. In a democracy, this aspect of government should be known; perhaps is should also, from time to time, be reviewed as a matter for possible change or reform, so that it is kept in line with the standards and expectations of society. In this chapter three main themes will be considered: they are the employment of women and the civil service, the publications of officials and the attitudes and practices of officials towards the work of scholars attempting to understand the administrative work of government. One reason why these three themes have been chosen is that they are well documented in the files that are available. From a more theoretical perspective, they illustrate the attitudes of officials in the Commission and in other government departments towards people with whom they were involved, and towards ideas and approaches which were alien to their view of the world.

Women and the civil service

The Playfair Commission, 1874–75, recognised that women were already successfully employed for clerical work in the Post Office and felt that their employment could be extended to other departments if they could 'be placed in separate rooms, under proper female supervision'. The Ridley Commission, 1886–90, repeated the recommendation of the Playfair Commission, again stressing the need to keep women separate from men and under proper female supervision. The employment of women was later extended to the offices of the Registrar General, the Public Trustee, Labour Exchange offices and the Board of Education.[2] The MacDonnell Royal Commission, in 1914, reviewed and supported the earlier recommendations but added that, whilst women should be eligible for administrative situations where it was in the public interest to employ them, they should not be admitted to the Class I examination. It recommended continuing the rule requiring termination of established service on marriage, and said the Treasury should set up an inquiry to ascertain which posts should be filled by women and the salaries they should receive. It also recommended that there should be one or more women of experience on the staff of the Civil Service Commission to advise the Commissioners.[3]

In the early years of the employment of women in the civil service they were recruited by nomination to the clerical level, or joined the service by open competition to posts in lower grades and rose to the clerical level by promotion: it should be remembered that the provision of secondary education for girls lagged behind that for boys. During the First World War there was an expansion of temporary posts to which some women were appointed and, from 1916, the Treasury approved a scheme for the temporary appointment of women junior administrative assistants. After the war, in 1919, the Gladstone Committee recommended the wider employment of women in the civil service.[4] Perhaps the Haldane

Report on *The Machinery of Government*, published in 1918, expressed these sentiments, most significantly when it recommended the extension of the range and duties entrusted to women. In particular, it said:

> The practical question whether women can be found suitable to perform duties comparable with those assigned to men in Class I has to a large extent found an answer in the experience of the last four years, which has gone far to resolve any doubts upon the point. We understand that in certain Departments women have undertaken duties of the Class I standard during the greater part of the War period, and have been found to have performed these duties to the satisfaction of the Heads of the Departments in which they are employed.
>
> We, therefore, think that it is no longer expedient in the public interest to exclude women on the ground of sex from situations usually entered by Class I examination, or from other situations usually entered by competition.[5]

Three examples from the files, of experiences in the Civil Service Commission relating to women and the civil service reveal aspects of the administrative culture on this matter. The examples are: attempts in the immediate post-First World War period to get a woman appointed as a Commissioner; the medical examination of women applicants, particularly in the 1920s; and attitudes towards wives of applicants for posts in the foreign service in the 1920s.

First, the possibility of appointing a woman Commissioner. In July 1921 questions were asked in Parliament about implementing the recommendation of the MacDonnell Royal Commission on the Civil Service that there should be one or more women on the administrative staff of the Commission.[6] Stanley Baldwin, then Financial Secretary to the Treasury, said that the matter was 'engaging consideration'.[7] During a parliamentary debate on 5 August 1921 questions were more specifically asked about the possibility of appointing a woman Commissioner. In asking the questions, Lord Robert Cecil specifically said that he did not 'suspect the Civil Service Commissioners of any unfairness at all', but of course it was possible that, 'unintentionally and unconsciously' they could be 'biased against...women candidates' and he made it clear that the appointment of a woman Commissioner would help to allay suspicions about methods of appointment in the civil service. Sir Robert (later Viscount) Horne, then Chancellor of the Exchequer, undertook 'to consider' Cecil's request.[8]

W.R. (later Sir Robert) Fraser, in the Treasury, wrote to his colleague J.H.M. (later Sir John) Craig that the proposal to appoint a woman Commissioner either meant a redundancy or the pitch-forking of a woman into a higher post over the heads of men who had rights of promotion to that post.[9] Craig sent a note about this to L.C.H. Weekes, Secretary to the Commission. Weekes consulted Sir Stanley Leathes, the First Commissioner, who himself replied to Craig that the Commissioners had no objection to the appointment of a woman Commissioner or Assistant Commissioner, but the Board was not overworked and did not need another Commissioner, who would be superfluous and expensive; the existing three Commissioners were quite capable of carrying out all the necessary duties; and there should be no unnecessary new appointment when economy was imperative.[10]

On 22 September 1921 Miss D. Smyth, Hon Secretary of the Federation of Women Civil Servants, pursuing the issue, wrote on behalf of her Executive Committee, to R.R. (later Sir Russell) Scott, Treasury Controller of Establishments, outlining the case for a woman Civil Service Commissioner. On the same day, Elizabeth Abbott (Hon Secretary for the Letter) wrote to the Prime Minister enclosing a Memorandum about Miss Alice Smith and a petition signed by over 40 representative women urging favourable consideration to the appointment of Alice Smith as a woman Commissioner. The Memorandum said that Smith had taken no part in controversial movements of any kind and she was not a member of any feminist association other than the Federation of University Women. She was educated at Girton College, Cambridge (first-class honours in history) and had been awarded the Gilchrist Fellowship. In May 1915 she was appointed by the First Civil Service Commissioner, apparently on a temporary basis,[11] to fill a vacancy on the Higher Division staff, and continued until the end of June 1921 to render services which were described by the First Commissioner as 'invaluable'.[12]

Fraser wrote to Craig:

> No doubt the petition from various busybodies for the appointment of Miss Smith will be referred to Sir Stanley Leathes.
>
> It seems monstrous that outside persons should endeavour to corrupt the public service by actually submitting a name for a Commissioner's post. Appointments to such posts cannot depend on support of influential persons.
>
> ...the petitioners seem misinformed if they think that the appointment of Miss Alice Smith would meet with the Commissioners' approval; though it is understood that they would have welcomed her appointment to their ordinary executive staff...
>
> I hope Miss Smith herself has nothing to do with this petition!

Craig responded: 'The memorial, to which Miss A. Smith must have consented, should be regarded as disqualifying her for appointment now or hereafter; after answering the Federation it should be referred to Civil Service Commissioners.'[13]

Around this time the Treasury received other letters on behalf of the Council of Women Civil Servants, the Edinburgh Women Citizens Association, the Women's Political and Industrial League and the National Union of Societies for Equal Citizenship. They all reported resolutions to give effect to the Chancellor's promise to consider Cecil's request. It is clear that the Treasury kept the Commission informed of these developments; indeed, Leathes saw the Treasury file on the matter.[14] The correspondence was followed up on 8 November 1921 when a deputation to support the correspondence called at the Treasury. On 17 February 1922 Fraser noted that not only had the memorials pressed for the appointment of a woman Commissioner, but for the appointment of Miss Alice Smith in particular. He added: 'It should be made clear at some stage that this sort of "patronage" cannot be allowed.'

The second example arises from the medical examination of women. It will be remembered that, from the beginning of the Commission, Orders in Council gave the Commissioners responsibility for ensuring that the health of potential established civil servants met the required standards. In the early years of the Commission this meant that a doctor appointed by the Commission medically examined candidates (after the Second World War, as an economy measure, a less burdensome system of self-declaration was introduced).[15] Revealing correspondence relating to the 1920s shows insights into general attitudes at the time towards the medical examination of women and the response of the Commission.

On 22 March 1923 Mrs R.A. Lucking wrote to the Secretary, Civil Service Commission, about what appeared to her to be a scandalous state of affairs:

> Unless my information is incorrect, young women before entering the Civil Service are required to undergo medical examination, in the course of which they are required to appear under pain of not receiving an appointment, before a doctor and *strip* without the alternative of examination by a doctor of their own sex.
>
> That decent girls should be required to strip, as if they were girls of the streets, before a doctor, a man, is a disgrace to them and to the country, degrading and immoral. That it should be part of the regulations of a Government Department is astounding...(and) a scandal. Women candidates of the Civil Service, should be given the alternative of medical examination by a woman doctor and should be informed of this alternative. It is surprising that this should not now be the case. The whole matter wants ventilating in the press and in Parliament, if necessary...

This sort of experience had already been a matter of concern to other interested women and their organisations. For example, Miss M.A. (later Dame Maude) Lawrence, then Director of Women's Establishments at the Treasury, was approached about this in 1922 or 1923; and Miss Dorothy Spece Allan wrote in August 1922 to Miss Ritson, of the Scottish Board of Health:

> ...It happened in my own case but as I had only 24 hours notice and did not know to whom to protest I acquiesced. It happened again here when my clerk Miss Young was sent to a young doctor in Dundee (he is married!). Miss Young's mother is dead and she has no near woman relative...

In fact, the practice at that time was already to send women candidates to women doctors wherever possible, and where not immediately practicable any request from a woman for examination by a woman was acceded to, if possible; and if not they were told they could take their mother or some responsible woman friend with them who might be present during the examination. In 1923, the Commission had a list of women doctors in London and 16 other towns, whom they used for this purpose. Candidates residing within about ten miles of central London were usually sent to women doctors. In the Commission it was noted:

> We try to avoid putting candidates to the expense of travelling long distances, a matter I think in which candidates take a greater interest than in the doctor's sex... as far as this Department is aware the demand by women candidates for examination by their own sex does not exist, or we should have taken steps to meet it, and... generally speaking women have more faith in men than women in times of sickness.

On 3 May 1923 a letter giving details of the Commissioners' procedures was sent to Lucking, who replied on 5 May:

> You will, I think, agree, as any gentleman would, that it is neither decent, nor moral, nor right that young girls, many aged 18 or thereabouts, should be forced to strip themselves nude to the waist or completely nude according to a male doctor's discretion, while they undergo examination. To think these young girls, presumably properly brought up, should be compelled... so to strip themselves, should be enough to bring the blush of shame to the faces of those responsible for the regulations...
>
> These girls are not prostitutes and nothing can excuse their being treated as such, and their being subjected to every conceivable form of indignity and insult...

The correspondence shows the care taken in the Commission to arrange for the medical examination of women by women doctors and it kept a much longer list of such doctors than might be expected for the 1920s. The experience of the Commission was, however, that there was in rural districts and largely, but not universally, in urban areas a very strong public prejudice in favour of male doctors. Indeed, occasionally the Commission was asked by female candidates for the arrangements for them to be seen by women doctors to be changed. The Civil Service Commission also explained, where appropriate, that medical examination was required before admission to the pensionable civil service and that candidates and their parents were presumed to be aware that examination could not be carried out without some removal of clothing.[16]

At the end of the Second World War E.A. (later Dame Evelyn) Sharp, then in the Treasury, asked Sir Percival Waterfield, the First Civil Service Commissioner, whether the Commission still insisted on what she called the 'old fashioned' practice of sending women candidates to women doctors. She remembered that, when a candidate herself, she was given no option: she thought this quite unnecessary nowadays, and saw no reason why women should not be medically examined by male doctors. In fact, the Commission had a clear procedure that had been approved by the Commissioners in 1932 and F.L. Howard, at the Commission, was immediately able to present the details to Waterfield. In London the Commission sent to a woman doctor all women candidates within a radius of about 18 miles. For the provinces, women were sent to a woman doctor if they lived within a radius of ten miles of one of the towns where the Commission had a woman doctor. Women outside this radius but within a radius of 18 miles were given the option of examination by a woman doctor or by the local Post Office man. Outside the 18 mile radius examination was in all cases by the local Post Office man. In all cases, if the candidate raised objection to examination by a woman, the Commission arranged examination by the Post Office doctor.[17]

Whereas the Commission internal procedure for the medical examination of women developed piecemeal, from experience, the Commission was sometimes contacted for advice before a procedure was instituted elsewhere. An example of this arose in 1945 in connection with the foreign service problem of foreign wives, and this provides the third example of attitudes of senior civil servants towards women.

Candidates for entrance to the foreign service before the Second World War had to be unmarried. In the reconstruction competitions, however, when candidates were older, this presented difficulties and it was recognised that the unmarried requirement might not be as acceptable as before the war. The Foreign Office therefore issued a circular to all members of the service which, while not forbidding the marriage of members with 'ladies of foreign birth', pointed out that such marriage might diminish the officer's utility as a British representative abroad and limit the number of posts in which he could be employed. It also stated that the Secretary of State reserved the right to inform an officer who proposed to marry a foreigner that, if he did so, he would have to resign.

Difficulties were envisaged in the Foreign Office because it was thought that some of the reconstruction candidates might have become engaged or married to foreigners, and it was thought conceivable that in those cases marriage would have made or would make the candidate unsuitable for employment in the foreign service or reduce his utility to the service. E.A. Chapman-Andrews, of the Foreign Office, wrote to Waterfield about this on 28 June 1945, pointing out that the Foreign Office thought the Final Selection Board (FSB) should know whether a candidate was married and, if so, whether his wife was of foreign birth.[18] Waterfield agreed that this information should be available to the FSB.[19] J.R. Pinsent, Chairman of the Civil Service Selection Board, said it would not be difficult to get the information about marriage and it could also be arranged to find out at interview about engagement.

Later, Waterfield raised the matter with FSB members and wrote to Sir David Scott, of the Foreign Office, about it. He said:

> ...One thing...is clear: if any action at all is to be taken it must be by the Foreign Service, not the Civil Service Commissioners...
>
> For what it is worth, here is my suggestion. I feel pretty sure that if the wife is a white woman of British birth, there can be no question of rejecting a candidate because the authorities think he has married the wrong type of woman. The only possible course is to persuade him to withdraw voluntarily. If this is right, then I should like to suggest the following procedure for your consideration. As soon as the list of successful and reserve candidates is ready, we will send it to you in advance, indicating which of them are married and whether there appears to be any particular need for enquiry into the personality of any particular wife. Then, if you think fit, you might ask all or some of the candidates in question to call at the Foreign Office, bringing their wives with them, for a friendly talk. I think you would then be able, without much difficulty, to judge whether or not the wife would be likely to be a positive handicap to her husband in the Foreign Service or not. If you think she would be, and that the case is so serious as to call for action, it would be open to you to advise the candidate, in his own interest and that of his wife, to withdraw his candidature. This would be an extreme step to take, and I hope that it would rarely, if ever, happen. But I can conceive cases in which you would feel quite sure that for one reason or another the wife that the candidate has chosen would be so great a handicap to him as to make life in the Foreign Service difficult for both of them: they would both be unhappy, and his prospects and his usefulness in the Service would both be impaired. In such a case it would surely be no more than a kindness to the man himself and his wife to advise him to seek another career...
>
> If I thought that any of these candidates were *prima facie* suitable for the Home Civil Service I would tell you so, in sending you the list; if then you should feel obliged to warn anyone against entering the Foreign Service you might at the same time advise him to try the Home Civil Service, adding that you have reason to think that he would have a fair chance of success, because success in any examination necessarily depends upon the quality of the competitors. You could assure him that in the Home Civil Service no question would be asked about his wife, and you would no doubt explain why the Foreign Secretary must take a stricter line. Some such encouragement to the candidates to try elsewhere might make your task a good deal easier.
>
> If the candidate should indicate that he accepts your suggestion, then I would recommend that he should be advised to write to the Commissioners saying that, after giving further consideration to the matter, he has decided to withdraw his application. We can then publish the list

of successful candidates with his name included (he is entitled to that amount of public credit), but with a footnote saying that: 'This candidate subsequently withdrew his application.'

I attach a good deal of importance to our receiving such a letter of withdrawal from the candidate himself, giving us an answer to any accusation of bias. You will appreciate how necessary it is for us to retain our reputation for complete impartiality by selecting candidates in strict accordance with the regulations.

If... a man should refuse to accept this advice (perhaps because he believes his wife has qualities not immediately apparent to the observer, which would enable her to surmount these obstacles), then I am sure you can do no more than say: 'you have been warned', and admit him, with the knowledge that he may subsequently prove a failure and have to be got rid of.

It may be that you will only think it necessary to apply this procedure to cases where there seems to be some *prima facie* doubt. For instance, in the first CSSB intake I notice one candidate whose wife is described as 'Somewhat exotic looking'; and one aged 25 with a wife of 40 (who, however, is spoken of as being 'a charming woman'). Needless to say I do not regard either of these qualifications as necessarily imposing a handicap upon the husband in his career. I only mention them as indicating the kind of evidence which we are likely to have at this stage.

So far I have dealt only with candidates whose wives are white women of British birth. I realise, however, that a marriage or engagement to a foreigner or a coloured woman is a different matter, and that in such a case it may be necessary for you to advise the Secretary of State that a candidate is positively unsuitable for appointment. We have already been warned of this in Chapman-Andrews' letter to me of the 28th June... Chapman-Andrews writes as if the responsibility for taking an adverse decision in such a case should rest with the Final Selection Board, but I am clear this cannot be, and that the Foreign Secretary must himself take the responsibility.

As the Regulations stand, however, there is no power even for the Foreign Secretary to reject a candidate on this or any other ground; he could only appoint him and then immediately dismiss him. I expect you would rather not do this, and would prefer to come out into the open, even at the cost of some publicity... After all, it is only the logical application of your present policy in regard to candidates who enter at the normal age. I suggest therefore that we should make, with your approval and that of the Treasury, an amendment to Regulation 3 (the nationality rule)...[20]

When the Treasury was consulted, it agreed to the proposed revised regulation, but on condition that if a question was raised in Parliament the Chancellor of the

Exchequer might ask the Foreign Secretary to answer. The Home Office was also consulted and agreed – on the understanding that, if challenged, it would be for the Foreign Secretary to defend it. There was a considerable discussion between the interested departments about the exact wording of the amended regulation. Waterfield's suggestion was that special permission of the Secretary of State for Foreign Affairs would have to be obtained by a successful candidate:

> who is married to a woman who is not both a natural-born British subject and born within the United Kingdom or one of the self governing Dominions of parents both of whom were also born within the United Kingdom or one of the self governing Dominions...

Sir John Stephenson, of the Dominions Office, pointed out that the proposed wording might not cover Southern Rhodesia; and if India, Burma and Ceylon achieved Dominion Status their citizens might be quite unintentionally covered. Stephenson suggested an alternative wording, avoiding the place of birth requirement, and simply say 'a woman who is not a natural born British subject of European descent'[21] – the phrase was, he said, well established as covering people of European origin in the Dominions as much as in the United Kingdom. Scott, however, felt that this could lead to other difficulties: 'it does rather seem to make a racial discrimination not altogether dissimilar from e.g. "of Aryan descent" '. The revised regulation worked as intended and otherwise successful candidates were turned down because they were married to, for example, Bengali or Polish wives.[22] There were later relaxations in this approach and, in March 1946, Ernest Bevin, Foreign Secretary, announced in the House of Commons that women would be eligible for admission to the foreign service – though, like women elsewhere in government service, they would normally have to resign their appointments on marriage.[23]

Publications by officials

The second theme of administrative culture being considered arises from attitudes towards the publications of officials. This is a significant matter because it has potential importance in the wider field of the British system of government. As far as the Civil Service Commission is concerned this was of importance from the beginning of the Commission in the mid nineteenth century. Throughout its life the Commission had close connections with the universities; and a number of Commissioners maintained their academic links, especially through continuing to write books and articles after their appointment to the Commission. Some of these links are mentioned here, to provide an appropriate context for the examples that follow.

Lord (Noel) Annan, in *The Dons*, explained how in the nineteenth century there were certain dons and key families that formed what he called an 'intellectual aristocracy'. These 'worked for the creation of a public service open to talent';

their 'Bill of Rights' was the Northcote–Trevelyan Report; and their 'Glorious Revolution' was achieved in 1870–71, 'when entry to the public service by privilege, purchase of army commissions and the religious tests were abolished'.[24] Among the 'intellectual aristocracy', in the early years of the nineteenth century it was thought safer to train the mind on the writings of Greek and Latin authors. Modern studies, it was thought, encouraged speculation and political controversy, so the classics took priority.[25] As a result of the university reforms of the 1870s and 1880s, dons at Oxford and Cambridge could, since 1882, marry; in addition, they were no longer required to take holy orders.[26]

Nevertheless, dons after that time often were bachelors,[27] and they followed what Anthony Sampson referred to as 'a semi-celibate way of life'.[28] They lived in college and this was conducive to a lifestyle of scholarship and writing. These characteristics of life in the universities are relevant for understanding the interests and activities of some of the Commissioners, especially in the period before the First World War. This literary environment is, however, hardly surprising when it is remembered that on a number of occasions it was made clear that, when considering the appointment of Commissioners, scholastic experience was a quality that should be represented on the Commission. Indeed, the MacDonnell Royal Commission specifically recommended criteria for appointing Commissioners, which included the need 'to secure men possessing wide experience both of school and university education to work under the chairmanship of a man of affairs possessing official experience as well as sympathy with academic studies';[29] and Sir Stanley Leathes wrote in 1921 that until a recent date, Commissioners were selected partly on the ground of academic distinction.[30]

It is hardly surprising that writing for publication was regarded as normal to men of this intellectual aristocracy. Furthermore, writing for publication was facilitated by the celibate collegial way of life in universities at that time. H.W. Paul, who was a Commissioner 1909–18, published 13 books, including *Life of William Ewart Gladstone* (1901); *History of Modern England*, 5 vols (1904–06); and *Lord Acton* (1904). W.J. Courthope, who was a Commissioner 1887–1907, published 11 books including *Ludibria Lunae* (1869); *Life of Addison* (1882); and *History of English Poetry*, 6 vols (1895–1909). Leathes, who was a Commissioner 1907–27, and who never married, was one of the editors of the *Cambridge Modern History*, to which he also contributed; his seven other books included *The People of England*, 3 vols (1915–23); *Rhythm in English Poetry* (1935) and his pseudonymous *Vox Clamantis* (1911). Fergus H. Allen, who was a Commissioner 1969–81, is a poet of considerable acclaim whose published work includes *The Brown Parrots of Providencia* (1993); *Who Goes There?* (1996) and *Mrs Power Looks over the Bay* (1999). Lord Macaulay, the historian and author of the famous report on the Indian Civil Service, who never married, was not a Civil Service Commissioner, but he was certainly part of the 'intellectual aristocracy' and was probably the most influential man in the creation of the civil service (and especially the Commission). He was a prolific writer, whose books included *History of England*, 5 vols (1849–61). It should also be remembered that James Spedding, who was the first Secretary to the Civil Service Commission, resigned in November 1855 to devote himself to editing the works of Francis Bacon, 14 vols (1857–74).

For nearly all these publications the authors wrote in their own names; and in their writings they did not draw upon their experience as officials. However, sometimes officials did write about matters which, either directly or indirectly, related to their work as civil servants. One example of this was Leathes' *Vox Clamantis*,[31] his pseudonymous book, where the author is given as Numa Minimus because he recognised that some of the opinions in it might displease some Members of Parliament, 'and if one Member of Parliament has an edge against the Head of a Department he can make it very uncomfortable for him'.[32] It may be laudable that he had such sensitivity, though the book, containing his general comments on public affairs, was by no means a significant contribution to the literature. In much the same way, perhaps, W.P. Barrett, Secretary to the Commission, who wrote a short factual contribution on the Civil Service Commission, but containing no analysis or comments, for the *O and M Bulletin* in 1945, used the pseudonym 'Scrutator'.[33]

The main reason for this care and sensitivity was the political context of civil service work. This means that the convention was maintained that politicians made policy and civil servants carried it out. It was ministers who were expected to answer in Parliament and in public for the activities of their departments and their civil servants (though their answers were usually drafted by the civil servants whose actions the ministers were defending). It consequently became the rule that civil servants should avoid publicity and, above all, avoid anything that could attract publicity or that could cause embarrassment for their ministers.

An example of this in practice was the personnel work of Dr N.A.B. Wilson. In 1947 the Treasury had imposed (as A.H.M. Hillis, of the Commission, put it in a minute of 4 February) 'a ban on publicity for CISSB', but on 10 February Waterfield wrote to T. (later Sir Thomas) Padmore in the Treasury, asking that 'notwithstanding the general ban on publicity, Norman Wilson might be allowed to give a talk on CISSB procedure at the Easter conference of the NIIP' (National Institute of Industrial Psychology). In fact, Wilson had been asked to join a symposium on selection of high-grade trainees, and to describe CISSB's procedure, or if that was not possible, to talk more generally about psychological principles and practice in high-grade selection work. Waterfield argued that he should be allowed to participate on the ground that:

> this would be an expert speaking to other experts on a subject of general interest to them all as scientists; and that if necessary we could probably see to it that no report appeared in the press. You felt however that you ought to mention the matter to Bridges; and you said it would help if I could give you an assurance that in fact no reporters would be present.
>
> I have now received from Dr Wilson a minute...which shows that reporters may be present, and that the NIIP could not guarantee that no

report would appear in the Press, though Wilson thinks it unlikely that it would be in any but the most colourless terms.

I am afraid that, knowing the way in which the Press have reacted to CISSB in the past, he takes too optimistic (or modest) a view of the publicity which a talk by him on CISSB procedure is likely to receive. It would be more prudent to assume that such a talk will in fact attract a good deal of attention.

If this is right, I must ask for a ruling by the Treasury whether he may speak on CISSB procedure or not.

My own view, with due respect, is that to refuse permission would be to carry the ban on publicity to an absurd length. As things stand, the Press get hold of the wrong ideas (e.g. a recent article by Cummings in the *News Chronicle*, and some ill-informed, if not malicious, remarks on the wireless): to which the best answer is an honest statement of the facts. This we shall of course give in our Annual Report, which it is high time we started to publish again.

Do you not think that in the circumstances a talk by Wilson might be allowed?[34]

Wilson's request was approved by the Treasury, and the decision was conveyed by Padmore to Waterfield on 1 March 1947.[35] Wilson then took part in the symposium which attracted no press coverage. The next year, in July 1948, Wilson read a paper at the Twelfth International Congress of Psychology. His paper, which was a useful but essentially factual description of the work of the Civil Service Selection Board, was subsequently published.[36]

An article which, soon afterwards, caused a degree of sensitivity for the Commission appeared in *Occupational Psychology*, April 1950.[37] It was the result of a statistical analysis and conclusions of a study by Professor P.E. Vernon, who had been Psychological Research Adviser to the Admiralty and War Office 1942–45, and Consulting Psychologist to the Commission, and was Professor of (Educational) Psychology in the University of London 1949–68. Vernon, who wrote his article with the approval of the First Commissioner, produced a summary which Waterfield intended to include in an appendix to the *Memorandum by the Civil Service Commissioners on the use of the Civil Service Selection Board in the Reconstruction Competitions*.[38] Unfortunately approval for this was delayed, then prevented by the Treasury. Waterfield explained this to Vernon in a letter of 23 January 1951:

> we were involved in quite considerable argument with the Treasury over the inclusion of certain passages which, in view of the past history and particularly the debate in the House of Lords in May 1948, they considered too provocative of criticism. I am very sorry to say that the Summary of your paper was one of the items which we had to agree to omit. And I am quite genuine in saying I am very sorry as I looked upon your paper as important outside support and indeed a feather in our cap.

I am glad to say, however, that we have at least managed to retain the references to your paper in the body of the Memorandum.[39]

Vernon replied that he was 'naturally surprised at the Treasury's decision to suppress the only scientifically sound evidence you possess of the value of CISSB methods of selection'. He asked which points were regarded as objectionable, as it might be possible to modify them whilst retaining the gist of the objectively determined facts. He added: 'If, however, there seems to you to be no disposition to compromise, I hope I may be allowed to submit this correspondence to the Council of the British Psychological Society.'[40]

Waterfield replied immediately:

> I think I had better explain, for your very private and confidential information, what lies behind the Treasury request that we should omit the summary of your paper from our published Memorandum. The fact appears to be that there is still a great deal of scepticism in certain political quarters about the value of the CISSB experiment in general, and the psychological element in the system in particular. What the Treasury feared was that, if the Memorandum should appear to lay stress on this element, these sceptics would immediately be provoked into re-opening the whole question, thereby not only endangering the success of the experiment, but perhaps making things very uncomfortable for the Government itself (for the sceptics are not to be found in the Opposition ranks only). It mattered not a whit, said the Treasury, that Professor Vernon's scientific appreciation has nothing to do with the psychological tests which form part of the CISSB examination: the mere fact that he is himself a psychologist, that his paper is couched in the technical language of psychology, and that his professional judgment is relied upon by the Commissioners as evidence of the value of the system, will be as a red rag to a bull in the eyes of these critics. Nor does it matter that the critics are mostly very stupid and prejudiced people (as indeed is obvious from their attitude); the point is that they have power, and the opportunity to use it. It is the duty of civil servants to foresee and guard against the political consequences of their actions, and to protect their political masters from trouble arising therefrom. I therefore had no doubt where my duty lay. Whether or not I myself shared the Treasury's fears, I knew that they were in a much better position than I to judge how the political wind was likely to blow; and it was clearly incumbent on me to follow their advice, however much it went against my own inclination.
>
> I have thought it best to be quite frank with you in this matter, but so that you may see not only that there is no room for a compromise such as you suggest (I had tried that already, without success), but that I cannot possibly agree to your request that you should disclose this correspondence to the Council of the British Psychological Society, or indeed any other person at all. On the contrary, I must ask you to treat it as *strictly confidential*.[41]

Vernon replied:

> I am sorry to learn of the extent to which expediency is preferred to truth in the Civil Service; but I will respect your wishes regarding the confidential nature of the correspondence.
>
> It is somewhat embarrassing for a University Professor to be regarded as 'a red rag to a bull' and my natural inclination was to resign from the Commission's Technical Committee. However...I will continue to attend the meetings whenever I am free.[42]

A rather different experience resulted from the publication, in 1965, of Sir George Mallaby's *From My Level: Unwritten Minutes*.[43] Mallaby was First Commissioner from 1959 to 1965. He was born in 1902; educated at Radley College and Merton College, Oxford (Classics); was a schoolmaster from 1923–38 in various posts, culminating in Headmaster of St Bees School, Cumberland; and from 1942 to 1945 worked in the Military Secretariat of the War Cabinet. He became Secretary to the National Trust; worked again in the Cabinet Office in 1946; became assistant secretary in the Ministry of Defence; was Secretary-General of the Brussels Treaty Defence Organisation, became under secretary in the Cabinet Office 1950–54; then High Commissioner for the UK in New Zealand 1957–59.[44]

As background to the discussion on Mallaby's book, some of the general guidelines issued to civil servants should be recalled. For example, following the report on the Francs case in 1928 (which was the result of an inquiry into improper conduct by civil servants), Scott, of the Treasury, sent a copy of the report, together with a circular requesting that the principles outlined in it should be incorporated in departmental rules, and saying that it should be brought to the notice of each new entrant to the department. In particular, these rules mentioned the civil service's unwritten code of ethics and conduct; that a civil servant should not put himself in a position where his duty and his interests conflict; and that he should not make use of his official position to further his interests.[45] The Treasury circular and related papers became known – at least to W.B. Thomas, of the Ministry of Health – as the literature on the 'jealous honour of our calling'.[46] These principles were re-emphasised by R.V. (later Sir Richard) Hopkins in 1940. He said that it was highly important that no one holding a government appointment should 'be placed in a position where his official duties conflict, or appear to conflict, with his private interests, or where information acquired in his official capacity might be utilised for the benefit of such interests'.[47]

Mallaby's book, *From My Level*, was not based on documents or the diaries of famous people; instead it was an account of the 'lasting impressions and sensitive memories' Mallaby had of some 'of the great characters of our age'.[48] It was therefore somewhat autobiographical and demonstrated the author's keen talent for observation. Mallaby's reflections were intended to provide new details about some of the people he saw at work in his official capacity. There must have been a file on the book, because it was formally approved for publication, but the file does not appear to have survived.

What have survived, however, are the consequences of its publication, and certain comments about Mallaby's career. When he was being considered by the Central Probation Board (CPB) in 1950 it was said that he was 'quite an expert on Wordsworth and has just had a book published on him...He is not perhaps the typical Civil Servant but...he is...a valuable member of the Service'.[49] Waterfield, who chaired the CPB, had already met Mallaby privately because he was a friend of his son, asked for more details about Mallaby being not typical. H. Parker, of the Ministry of Defence, therefore explained that 'there was a rather more cosmopolitan or even bohemian atmosphere about Mallaby than one would normally find in Civil Servants... He is, I think, rather more a man of the world than is perhaps always the case with civil servants.'[50]

It was probably these personal characteristics that resulted in Mallaby writing his book and publishing it soon after his retirement in 1965. Extracts from the book were published in *The Sunday Times* on 28 February, 7 and 14 March 1965. Sir Alexander Johnston, Chairman of the Board of Inland Revenue, was very unhappy about Mallaby's disclosures and wrote to Sir Laurence Helsby, then Head of the Home Civil Service:

> To take one illustration, the rather unflattering account of Attlee's role as chairman of the Cabinet and Cabinet Committees is reasonably accurate, as far as my recollection goes, but it does not seem right that an official should take part in official business of a confidential character and then publish his impressions a few years later. This is the sort of stuff that should await the expiration of fifty years. His account of Churchill's rejection of Padmore seems to me a plain breach of the confidentiality rule.
>
> I do not believe that in the end one can allow this and maintain the approved line on serving civil servants. If a civil servant is to be allowed on retirement to pontificate on the qualities of Ministers, on the basis of secret information, the public may be thought to be entitled to know what kind of person this civil servant is, so as to judge whether his opinion is worth anything. That would mean free comment while he is serving. What seems difficult to defend is that a civil servant should claim anonymity and freedom from criticism, while serving, and then on retirement should be able to air his views on ministers and affairs on the basis of highly confidential information, not available to the public.[51]

In the House of Lords, Attlee went up to Bridges and said, 'I don't like Mallaby's book. Quite wrong. I hope you did not pass it.' Bridges, who had been Head of the Civil Service until 1956, assured Attlee that he had known nothing about it until he saw extracts in *The Sunday Times*, but he shared Attlee's view.[52] Sir Laurence Helsby, then Joint Permanent Secretary to the Treasury and Head of the Home Civil Service, told I.P. (later Sir Ian, then Lord) Bancroft, then private secretary to the Chancellor of the Exchequer, that neither he nor anyone in the Treasury knew that Mallaby had produced the book and the extracts in *The Sunday Times* were a most unpleasant surprise to him.[53] Bancroft wrote to the Chancellor that clearance was given to the text by the Secretary to the Cabinet, then Sir Burke (later Lord) Trend; the Treasury was not consulted. Bancroft also understood that Mallaby left clearance until very late in the day – until, indeed, he was already committed to publication.[54] Helsby explained to an informal meeting, with several permanent secretaries, on 15 March, that the Cabinet Office had not been approached until after Mallaby had signed a contract with the publisher and the serial rights had been sold.

At the meeting on 15 March it was pointed out that there were no effective sanctions against the writers of memoirs if they did not refer to matters of policy which would be covered by the Official Secrets Acts: 'The description of personal relationships between ministers and officials was not the kind of matter for which the Official Secrets Acts could in practice be invoked; while stoppage of pension rights might seem too drastic a remedy in many cases.'[55] It was also pointed out that:

> the publication of memoirs of this kind must tend to imperil the basis on which business between ministers and officials was conducted. It would be a great pity if there was a reversion to the earlier practice of excluding officials from meetings simply because ministers felt that officials might be storing up recollections for subsequent publication. Moreover, such reminiscences must be based on events which the officials concerned could only have attended in their official capacity, for which they were paid at the time. It was wrong in principle that they should try to derive an extra profit from their official activities in this kind of way.[56]

Reviews of the book were far from complimentary. The most favourable was by C.P. Snow, who said that 'it is by far the best short memoir of official life in our time'.[57] Kenneth Rose said the book 'erodes the standards of civil service discretion without making a contribution to serious knowledge'.[58] Woodrow Wyatt referred to it as 'ghastly pot-boiling…we learn nothing of interest'.[59] Robert Rhodes James wrote: 'Those officials who…write their reminiscences have to walk a very delicate tightrope between dull conventionality and unintended indiscretion. I am not sure that Sir George Mallaby has managed this delicate feat with complete success.'[60]

As a result of Helsby's meeting on 15 March, he concluded that he should issue general guidelines on the publication of memoirs. In his covering letter he referred to memoirs in the style of Mallaby's, published 'in spite of official disapproval', that were not within the scope of 'official secrets'. In his guidance he referred to the established rule requiring scrutiny before permission could be given for publications based on official information. Working relations between ministers and their advisers, and the official secretariat, would be seriously affected if ministers were unable to speak their minds plainly in front of their advisers and he said these advisers were in a position of special trust and it was 'quite wrong that that trust should be abused for personal profit or acclaim'. He said that private records in diaries or otherwise should not be made or retained. He emphasised that texts for publication should be submitted in advance for clearance – and this did 'not apply only to documents that reflected on matters of policy. It applies to all documents based on information which the writer obtained by virtue of his official position'.[61]

The experiences related here give insights into the publications records and associated behaviour of civil servants. Many of the Civil Service Commission's senior officials had strong academic backgrounds and moved in circles where writing for publication was the norm. There were, however, official expectations for how this should be done and, in particular, a culture developed on how people should behave when the substance of their writing touched on their work. In this, as in other matters, civil servants were expected to avoid embarrassment, for themselves, for their departmental colleagues and, above all, for their ministers. Much of this culture was fashioned by the constraints of the political environment, but as the civil service grew it was necessary to develop formal rules and procedures to enshrine what was previously achieved by understandings communicated by informal contacts. An example of this is to be found in *A Handbook for the New Civil Servant*, issued by the Treasury:

> if you have made use of official time, official papers, or official experience – and it is probably impossible to write or otherwise create anything that relates to your job without using the last of these, consciously or sub-consciously – you should tell your department about it and ask permission before going ahead with it...[62]

The work of scholars

The attitudes of officials towards writing for publication were not always straightforward. There were rules (often unwritten); there was a sense of approval towards writing for publication, especially when the publications were historical, literary or practical; but for reasons of constitutional propriety, whenever publications related to official duties, there was a desire and expectation to cloak authorship in anonymity. Attitudes towards academic research, especially by people who studied the social sciences, were of a different order but in retrospect revealing. Two examples are considered here, arising from the work of Edwin A. Bock and Peta Rickerd.

Edwin A. Bock was an American postgraduate student at the London School of Economics (LSE). His research was into the backgrounds of civil servants and the effects of such factors on decision making in the administrative class of the civil service. In 1951 he wrote to the Civil Service Commission asking for information on candidates to supplement published details. For example, he was interested in a candidate's position in a family (eldest son, etc.) and whether candidates came from a rural or urban background. A.P. (later Sir Paul) Sinker, then First Civil Service Commissioner, wrote a minute to the Secretary outlining his own attitude:

> we must exercise the utmost care to ensure that no unsuitable person has access to confidential material. On the other hand we must not...be accused of being obscurantist about those sides of our work which may be of interest to the social historian. This is particularly the case with questions which have sometimes in the past aroused political controversy, e.g. the question of the social and educational backgrounds of members of the Civil Service and Foreign Service.
>
> ...Sir Percival Waterfield...sees no objection in principle to allowing access to confidential material to responsible academic persons who wish to pursue research into questions of this kind. He himself is...proposing to make a study of a subject allied to that of Mr Bock.
>
> In taking this line I do not propose to open the door to a large number of academic research workers. If we allow access to Mr Bock this will in my view be a reason for declining to give access to anyone else who might apply for similar reasons. We should then be able to say that the ground has already been recently covered and we do not think that the usefulness of the purpose to be served is sufficient to justify making another exception about access to confidential material...[63]

On the same day, Sinker wrote to Sir Alexander Carr-Saunders, then Director of the LSE, asking for his opinion of Bock.[64] Carr-Saunders replied on 6 December, pointing out that Bock was a graduate student, not a member of staff (and, presumably, unlike an Oxford or Cambridge college, the Director could not be expected to personally know all the students in the School). He did, however, enquire of H.R.G. Greaves, Bock's supervisor, and wrote again on 13 December to tell Sinker that Greaves would recommend Bock 'on the score of reliability and discretion', adding that, 'It would seem...that we have reason to have confidence in Mr Bock.'[65]

Within the Commission there was a distinct lack of enthusiasm to help Bock. H.C.H. Norman, in the Records Branch of the Commission, explained to his senior executive officer what would be involved and added, 'We have had a year with Mr Kelsall.'[66] W.H. Fisher thought that:

> If this sort of work is to be done at all I think it is certainly preferable that it should be done by someone from the academic world in his own time and at his own expense, rather than by us.[67]

J.H.T. Goldsmith, then Deputy Chairman of CSSB, said he was not happy about it, and asked how a man could pledge to forget things? The Commission's finance officer was then asked to suggest a charge for the extraction of the information.

He estimated that the total cost, including accommodation, lighting, telephone and stationery, could not be less than 40 guineas, added that any payment received would have to be brought to account as Exchequer Extra Receipts and would also appear on the Appropriation Account, so it would be as well if the Treasury were consulted beforehand. Also, Bock ought to be required to sign the usual documents – by which he meant awareness of the provisions of the Official Secrets Acts. Eventually Fisher proposed that the First Commissioner should frighten Bock away 'by saying that we should have to charge him for all services rendered and that this is likely to cost him at least 40 guineas'. Sinker saw Bock on 12 January 1952. He told Bock that the material he had asked for 'would take months rather than weeks to obtain and for...some items which would need reference to Departments he might need as much as a year'. He also said that the Commission would have to charge him for services rendered. Bock, he added, went away to think things over. Bock subsequently had a very distinguished academic career and is now Emeritus Professor of Political Science, Syracuse University.

The second example of academic research on Civil Service Commission information was the work of another LSE student, Peta Rickerd, a Canadian. In 1966 she was engaged on research for her doctoral thesis in sociology, on mobility into and out of the civil service. In particular, she wanted information about direct entry recruitment at the principal and assistant secretary level in 1964, 1965 and 1966. Rickerd initially wrote to Edgar Anstey, then Chief Psychologist at the Commission, for help. Anstey passed her request to K.A.G. Murray, then Chairman of CSSB, who passed it on to J.C. Seddon, Secretary to the Commission, to reply.

Much of the information Rickerd wanted was already available from other sources, though it would have required much labour to assemble it. She also contacted the Treasury. The Commission provided some, but not all, of the information requested. Rickerd also asked to interview 50 direct entry principals, but the Commission was anxious that, if she did, she might be able to link up some of the names with the detailed background information already supplied to her. Therefore A.S. Pratley sought advice about this from P.S. Ross, at the Treasury.

Ross was clearly apprehensive, as his letter to Pratley of 12 June 1967 shows:

> As I told you, when we spoke about this, I was very worried to see that so much time has been spent on helping this young lady to get her Ph.D. (or whatever it is she is working for) and it is even more worrying that she is going to take up at least another 50 hours of official time – if she has the perseverance to carry her plans through.
>
> But now that she has got so far I feel we can hardly put impediments in her way especially as it would not be at all difficult for her to circumnavigate them. I do, however, want to satisfy myself, so far as I can, that the end product of her work will not be embarrassing to us as employers and

I am, therefore, grateful to you for agreeing that we should see her jointly at 11.30 a.m. on Thursday morning. I hope we shall have no trouble in persuading her that she should show us her thesis in draft. We must have the right, which we should certainly not use capriciously, to ask for modifications of any material that would be embarrassing to us.[68]

Pratley and Ross then saw Rickerd on 15 June 1967. Ross said he was not happy about the official time spent on helping with this project and was reluctant to agree that she would take up another 50 hours of time with interviews. A condition of giving permission to interview was that Rickerd should show them her thesis in draft:

> so that we might correct any inaccuracies and ask for modification of any material that might be embarrassing to the Service. Ross said that she would probably hear complaints from people who had come in before 1965 about the lack of any adequate induction course and she should bear in mind that this had been put right to a large extent. He also said that the direct entry Principals were not by and large in the fast stream of the Administrative Class and she should not therefore expect to be confronted by intellectual giants.[69]

Pratley (this time accompanied by David Holmes, of the Treasury) again saw Rickerd on 9 May and wrote to the Secretary of the Commission about it on 20 May. In the interview, Pratley concentrated on three points. First, he offered further explanation of using over-age recruitment to meet the resettlement obligations of the government. Rickerd agreed to change her emphasis on this and to make more of the resettlement factor. Second, he queried a particular sentence which he felt needed more precision. Rickerd agreed to add a footnote to cover this. Third, Pratley was concerned about the accuracy of remarks of civil servants who were not identifiable – he felt this should be considered further before the Commission and the Treasury were asked for formal permission before submission of the thesis. Pratley followed up the interview by writing to Rickerd on 21 May, detailing the points he had made. He re-emphasised the point about checking statements by interviewees (though their statements would be anonymised to preserve their identity). In her reply of 5 June 1968 Rickerd agreed to the record of the points raised during the interview and dealt with them. In particular, she was patient and tactful, but also firm in commenting about the use of unattributed quotations:

> as I mentioned to you, this is standard research procedure and one of the advantages of carrying out this type of interview rather than using a closed questionnaire. Provided that individuals cannot be identified with any particular comment – and I have tried to take great care so that this is not possible – I don't see why the respondents should have any objection. The theory behind the practice is, of course, that provided that the

anonymity of respondents is respected, it is only the individual who is in any position to identify himself with any particular quotation – assuming, of course, that he can and that he does not lay claim to a similar opinion that has been expressed by another respondent. In this sense, confidentiality is ensured through anonymity, and the group is big enough to ensure that this should not cause any problems. To take Mr Holmes' point, I cannot agree that the questions do not add to the text which, on the contrary, would read very strangely without them.[70]

Within the Commission, comments were made on the correspondence. In particular, W.E. Wightman wrote, 'for the record':

> When she reaches the pre-publication stage and submits the drafts of the book to us, we must be very careful indeed on this one, not so much from the point of view of protecting members of the Service, but from interfering in an academic field that is not strictly our province. Miss Rickerd is right in saying that 'on the subject of direct quotes from interviews… this is standard research procedure'. But it is standard research procedure only amongst third-rate sociologists, and one that is tending to bring the discipline into disrepute in the academic world generally. If we insist, successfully, that she alters the technique of presentation, we shall be improving its standard and value quite considerably, and much more kudos will accrue to her than she would otherwise deserve. The way in which she has used these quotations is so appallingly naïve that only the similarly lunatic journalistic fringe of the sociological world will even try to take it seriously, despite the ultimately sensible nature of many of her conclusions.[71]

Wightman was expressing his personal feelings towards sociologists but his comments reveal a view on social scientists similar to those reported elsewhere in this book (on Centenary Celebrations and on matters associated with the Fulton Committee). Such attitudes were quite freely expressed within official circles but never openly revealed outside. Peta Tancred (previously Rickerd) is now a full Professor of Sociology at McGill University, Canada. After completing her Ph.D., amongst other appointments, she was engaged on research at the Civil Service College.[72] Tancred is an eminent scholar who pioneered the study of gender in organisations, and whose work has been very influential in the field.

The administrative culture

This chapter has presented insights into particular events which have significantly revealed the attitudes and behaviour of particular individuals. The intention has been to demonstrate the existence of the administrative culture in the Civil Service Commission and to indicate how it was manifested in practice. Numerous other examples, of similar types, could have been chosen, but the general culture, the 'departmental view' (as Edward Bridges used to refer to it)[73] must not be lost in the examples.

From its beginning, the staff of the Commission were motivated by their terms of reference, as primarily given in Orders in Council and legislation, and by the associated qualitative aspirations: selection on merit, fair and open competition, and equal opportunity. Nevertheless, there were occasions when what was fair and open at one time seemed quite different from what was fair and open at another time. This is, perhaps, well illustrated by expectations of concepts like 'public interest' and 'public service'. Values and standards change over time. It is said that many years ago Sir Henry Campbell-Bannerman, the Liberal Prime Minister, enlivened a dinner party with the story of a Scottish Judge, sentencing a man to death for stabbing a soldier: 'You have hurried a human soul', he said, 'into eternity; and worse than that, you have – for which God may forgive you! – protruded a lethal weapon through your victim's trousers, which were the property of His Majesty.'[74]

Some of the details that have been presented in this chapter about the employment of women in the civil service are both revealing and worrying. Clearly, in the early years of the twentieth century, there was a feeling that there should be more opportunities for women. This was expressed in debates in Parliament, in such legislation as the Sex Disqualification (Removal) Act, 1919, and in the recommendations of numerous committees and commissions of inquiry. When it came to implementation, however, it was hard going for interested persons. Women may not have appreciated how best to further their cause, and unsympathetic attitudes may have been too entrenched for change to have been easy, but it now seems somewhat surprising that by proposing a particular person to become a Civil Service Commissioner, well-meaning individuals disqualified her 'for appointment now or hereafter'. If this approach applied to women in the 1920s, for a Civil Service Commissionership (a post that had never been filled by open competition), it may be wondered how similar tactics, perhaps in later years, may have had similar adverse effects on the prospects for other particular individuals.

It is also surprising to read details of the selection of married staff to posts in the foreign service. It seemed quite acceptable, to certain staff in the Commission, to find out details of the marriage intentions of candidates during CSSB interviews and then, if thought necessary, to exclude particular individuals. It is not easy, many decades later, to find out all the implications in practice, but it may be questioned whether the outcomes were always acceptable in terms of, say, security vetting, inappropriate discrimination, or even the public interest.

Considerable controversy and sensitivity arose over publications by civil servants and by academics, and it is easy to feel sympathy for Vernon, whose work, for reasons of political sensitivity as interpreted by officials, seems not to have received the attention it deserved (not only in his own personal and professional interest, but also in the interest of the work of CSSB). Nevertheless, all work in the public sector, as distinct from business work, has to be done in the context of its political environment. The Commission was part of the civil service and had to accede to political constraints. It is surprising, however, to read that Waterfield felt it would be possible for him to ensure no press coverage of the conference presentation by Wilson. This may stimulate questions about the freedom of the press in British society and the influence, if not power, of the First Civil Service Commissioner. Similar questions might be asked about the contents of Mallaby's book. His comments about Padmore's posting (Churchill's personal decision) now seem innocuous, especially when compared with the comments on Padmore by Barbara Castle,[75] but it is easy to appreciate how unhappy Attlee was about Mallaby's comments on him. These, and other events recalled in this chapter, relate to sensitive and complex issues, but it seems particularly surprising that Mallaby, as First Commissioner, should have acted in the way he did, for in publishing his book so soon after his retirement it is likely that negotiations with his publisher were completed in one form or another while he was still in office.

The examples of Bock and Rickerd, which reveal attitudes and values within the Commission, contribute to knowledge about official attitudes to social science research in the 1960s. Of course officials have to be accountable for public resources being used in the public interest, but it seems that staff in the Commission were sometimes unaware and perhaps even prejudiced about such academic work. It was almost a response of self-righteous defence when, in fact, the public resources involved were probably much less than the quoted figures. Later research experience[76] has shown that, even in the 1960s, many individual civil servants were much more willing to co-operate in such research, even using their own time; but this was quite different from the official attitudes in the Treasury and the Civil Service Commission.

In practice, much of the day-to-day work and experience in the Civil Service Commission had to depend on common sense in making judgements and agreeing to co-operate with others. Where a common sense approach is deemed insufficient, rules and codes of conduct may be introduced – as happened with the instructions issued after the publication of Mallaby's book. The consequence is that, as time goes by, incidents and cases help to build up a body of experience and practice; these in turn lead to more and more statements of practice, codes and rules. Such increased regulation does not eliminate opportunities for judgements and common sense in everyday official life. It does, however, result in changes in focus, in a more rule-bound administrative system and, ultimately, it may result in consequences not only unintended but contrary to the intentions of those formulating the rules.

Notes

1 For example, the *Civil Service Commissioners' Report 1990–91* (London: Civil Service Commission, 1991).
2 Dorothy Evans, *Women and the Civil Service* (London: Pitman, 1934), p. 4.
3 *Royal Commission on the Civil Service, Fourth Report of the Commissioners* (MacDonnell Report), Cd. 7338 (London: HMSO, 1914), Majority Report, recommendation 73.

4 *Civil Service: Recruitment after War*, Final Report (dated 22 April 1919) of the Committee appointed by the Lords Commissioners of His Majesty's Treasury, Cmd. 164 (London: HMSO, 1919).
5 Ministry of Reconstruction, *Report of the Machinery of Government Committee* (Haldane Report), Cd. 9230 (London: HMSO, 1918), Part I, paras 42–3.
6 MacDonnell (Majority) Report, recommendation 73. See also Evans, *Women and the Civil Service*, p.50.
7 HC Deb., 5s., vol. 132, cols. 236–7 and 430.
8 HC Deb., 5s., vol. 145, col. 133.
9 PRO/T162/375, Fraser to Craig, 10 August 1921.
10 PRO/T162/375, Leathes to Craig, 7 September 1921.
11 No evidence for this has been found; files to clarify this seem not to have survived.
12 PRO/T162/375, Smith to Scott, 22 September 1921.
13 PRO/T162/375.
14 PRO/T162/375.
15 PRO/CSC5/469, Leathes' minute, 4 November 1921.
16 PRO/CSC3/304.
17 PRO/CSC5/321.
18 PRO/CSC5/325.
19 PRO/CSC5/325, Waterfield to Pinsent, 8 August 1945.
20 PRO/CSC5/325, Waterfield to Scott, 27 August 1945.
21 PRO/CSC5/325, Stephenson to Waterfield, 14 January 1946.
22 PRO/CSC5/325, Barclay to Boys Smith, 28 February 1947.
23 PRO/CSC5/325.
24 Noel Annan, *The Dons: Mentors, Eccentrics and Geniuses* (London: Harper Collins, 1999), p. 15.
25 Ibid., p. 24.
26 Noel Annan, *Our Age: Portrait of a Generation* (London: Weidenfeld & Nicolson, 1990), p. 23.
27 Ibid., p. 102.
28 Anthony Sampson, *Anatomy of Britain* (London: Hodder & Stoughton, 1962), p. 204.
29 MacDonnell (Majority) Report, Ch. 9, para. 91.
30 PRO/T162/375, Leathes to Craig, 7 September 1921.
31 Numa Minimus, *Vox Clamantis* (London: Macmillan, 1911).
32 Trinity College, Cambridge, archives, Add. Ms. c. 36/27.
33 Scrutator, 'The Civil Service Commission', *O and M Bulletin*, December 1945, pp. 3–7. See also PRO/CSC5/391.
34 PRO/CSC5/388, Waterfield to Padmore, 10 February 1947.
35 PRO/CSC5/388, Padmore to Waterfield, 1 March 1947.
36 N.A.B. Wilson, 'The Work of the Civil Service Selection Board', *Occupational Psychology*, 1948, vol. 22, pp. 204–12.
37 P. E. Vernon, 'The Validation of Civil Service Selection Board Procedures', *Occupational Psychology* (1950) vol. 24, pp. 75–95.
38 PRO/CSC5/437.
39 PRO/CSC5/437, Waterfield to Vernon, 23 January 1951.
40 PRO/CSC5/437, Vernon to Waterfield, 24 January 1951.
41 PRO/CSC5/437, Waterfield to Vernon, 26 January 1951.
42 PRO/CSC5/437, Vernon to Waterfield, 30 January 1951.
43 George Mallaby, *From My Level: Unwritten Minutes* (London: Hutchinson, 1965).
44 PRO/CSC11/175.
45 PRO/CSC5/200, Treasury Establishment Circular E. 19377, 13 March 1928.
46 PRO/CSC5/200, Thomas to Lloyd, 7 May 1931.
47 PRO/CSC5/200, Treasury Establishment Circular E. 39856, 24 February 1940.
48 Mallaby, *From My Level*, Preface.
49 PRO/CSC5/621, Parker to Waterfield, 23 May 1950.

50 PRO/CSC5/621, Parker to Waterfield, 9 June 1950.
51 PRO/BA19/58, Johnston to Helsby, 1 March 1965.
52 PRO/BA19/58, Bridges to Helsby, 19 March 1965.
53 PRO/BA19/58, Helsby to Bancroft, 8 March 1965.
54 PRO/BA19/58, Bancroft to Chancellor of the Exchequer, 9 March 1965.
55 PRO/BA19/58, Note by J. Anson, of a meeting 15 March 1965.
56 Ibid.
57 *The Sunday Times*, 21 March 1965.
58 *The Sunday Telegraph*, 21 March 1965.
59 *The Standard*, 23 March 1965.
60 *The Yorkshire Post*, 25 March 1965.
61 PRO/T199/1030, 'Publication of Personal Memoirs', 3 May 1965.
62 *A Handbook for the New Civil Servant, Issued by H.M. Treasury*, Fifth Edition (1952), p. 34.
63 PRO/CSC5/846, Sinker to Secretary, 30 November 1951.
64 PRO/CSC5/846, Sinker to Sir Alexander Carr-Saunders, 30 November 1951.
65 PRO/CSC5/846, Carr-Saunders to Sinker, 13 December 1951.
66 PRO/CSC5/846, Norman to Wares, 5 December 1951.
67 PRO/CSC5/846, Fisher to Chairman of CISSB, 17 December 1951.
68 PRO/CSC5/1604, Ross to Pratley, 12 June 1967.
69 PRO/CSC5/1604, Pratley's 'Note: Miss Peta Rickerd', 15 June 1967.
70 PRO/CSC5/1604, Rickerd to Pratley, 5 June 1968.
71 PRO/CSC5/1604, W.E.W., 'For the record: Miss Peta Rickerd', 1 July 1968.
72 Peta Sheriff, *Career Patterns in the Higher Civil Service* (London: HMSO, 1976).
73 Sir Edward Bridges, *Portrait of a Profession: The Civil Service Tradition* (Cambridge: Cambridge University Press, 1950).
74 Horace G. Hutchinson (ed.), *Private Diaries of the Rt Hon Sir Algernon West GCB* (London: John Murray, 1922), p. 6.
75 Barbara Castle, *The Castle Diaries 1964–70* (London: Weidenfeld & Nicholson, 1984).
76 For example, Richard A. Chapman, 'Profile of a Profession: The Administrative Class of the Civil Service', Memorandum No. 2 in *The Civil Service, Vol. 3(2), Surveys and Investigations, Evidence Submitted to the Committee under the Chairmanship of Lord Fulton 1966–1968* (Fulton Report) (London: HMSO, 1968), pp. 1–29.

11

'BIAS' IN SELECTION

The dictionary definitions of 'bias' include inclination (towards), prejudice and influence. The word can be used in a scientific or statistical sense – and it was in this sense that in 1977 Sir Douglas Allen, later Lord Croham, said he would not quarrel with its use to refer to aspects of recruitment in the civil service. In the context of selection in the British civil service the word has, however, become associated with considerable controversy. The controversy arises because allegations of bias in recruitment imply that there is intentional preference where such preference is inappropriate or irrelevant and amounts to partiality or unfairness in selection. Allen made it quite clear that he did not accept that there was such prejudice in civil service recruitment.[1] It is not the intention in this chapter to consider in detail the statistical approaches that have been adopted by some writers (and apparently accepted by Allen to be valid): such details are accessible in the literature[2] and in the reports of the Civil Service Commissioners. Instead, in this chapter, the main considerations will be qualitative material found in the files and in evidence to official bodies.

Allegations of bias in recruitment to the most senior levels in the British civil service have been most frequently associated with the educational system. There were other allegations (such as prejudice against women or against non-white candidates), and there were refinements of the general allegations, but it is not possible to consider them all here. The general allegations, primarily associated with the direct entry recruitment of graduates to the old Class I or administrative class, or more recently the recruitment of administration trainees, were that it was easier for a candidate to get in if he went to a public school rather than a state school; it was easier to get in if a candidate went to Oxford University or Cambridge University rather than to another university; and it was easier to get in if a candidate was an arts graduate rather than a science graduate.[3] Sometimes the allegations were directed at the selectors and their social attitudes; sometimes the allegations were directed at the educational system; sometimes the allegations were directed at the nature and content of the selection system or procedures in it; sometimes the allegations were directed at the publicity and liaison arrangements intended to attract applicants.

Public interest and the interest of commentators, both academics and journalists, has focused in particular on the recruitment of graduates into administrative positions. This is mainly because of the important role in the British system of government that graduate recruits to administrative positions potentially have; but it is also because the information about successful candidates published by the Civil Service Commission was apparently chosen because of its (political) importance in terms of the social or class characteristics of British society. It was this information about candidates that the Commissioners must have decided was of public interest. As with the reforms of the nineteenth century, interest was motivated by concern for efficiency in executive government. It was also motivated by concern for representativeness as reflected in the belief that in a democracy those who are engaged in policy making and its execution should be in touch with and appreciate the concerns of ordinary citizens.

The selectors and their social attitudes

There is a sense in which the selectors, in their published statements or in oral evidence to official commissions and committees, have provoked criticism and allegations of bias because they have given the impression that they were unaware of the education system or social conditions beyond their personal experience. This may be seen on numerous occasions during the twentieth century and is illustrated by the following examples.

Evidence to the MacDonnell Royal Commission, which reported in 1914, is illuminating because it revealed both the attitudes of the selectors and the views of those outside the establishment about the selection process. It showed that in the years 1906–10 there were 473 candidates for the examination for the Home Civil Service Class I, India Civil Service, and the Eastern Cadetships. Of these, 247 came from Oxford, 142 from Cambridge, 75 from other universities and nine belonged to no university.[4] It should, however, be remembered that what are now regarded as the large civic universities were then very new and the subjects they taught were somewhat specialised. Birmingham University began in 1900;[5] Leeds University received its charter in 1904;[6] and Liverpool's charter was granted in 1903.[7] At Durham, which dates from 1832, it was reported that practically all the students, except the women, were reading theology; they intended to 'take orders', and were unlikely to be deflected from their intended course;[8] and theology was not included in the list of subjects for the administrative examinations.[9] Sir Henry Reichel, Vice-Chancellor of the University of Wales, told the MacDonnell Commission that he did not think there had been a single candidate from Bangor University College, where he was principal; Reichel also said that the civil service examinations had no effect whatever on the teaching in the University of Wales, and most of the students were poor men who could not afford the special preparation (as by crammers).[10] Professor Dudley J. Medley, representing the University of Glasgow, specifically drew attention to the cost of competing in the Class I examination which, he said, involved 'a whole month's residence in London'.[11] He also explained that many students at Glasgow were not looking out for a career: their intended career was already settled. Indeed, only about 10 per cent of Glasgow men went to the university with their careers unsettled. When they went to university in Scotland, the vast number of men already knew what they were going to do.[12]

The First Civil Service Commissioner, S.M. (later Sir Stanley) Leathes, in his statements to the MacDonnell Commission, revealed his ignorance of some of the factors presented in such evidence. His evidence showed that he knew little of university education outside Oxford and Cambridge. He told the MacDonnell Commission that the 'ladder of education' was such 'that people, wherever they come from, if they want to do so and have sufficient ability, can get to one of the old universities',[13] where the education was superior, where the final school was 'the widest and completest school that exists in any university'[14] and where the Oxford Greats examination was 'the best preparation for an administrative life'.[15] When Philip Snowden pointed out that the poverty of the parents was the main reason why boys left secondary school at 15 or 16 instead of continuing their education, Leathes replied that there were now a good many scholarships. While he was not 'fully *au fait* with the curricula of the new Universities', he thought to a very large extent they gave a professional education.[16] He also said that although he knew very little about the newer universities, he imagined that they were largely concerned with training people for particular professions (he believed Birmingham had a professor of brewing, for instance).[17] He thought that people did not go to the new universities 'in order to get a considerable all-round education'[18] – and that, of course, was what the Civil Service Commissioners were looking for. Sir John Anderson, later Viscount Waverley, then Permanent Under Secretary of State for the Colonies,[19] held opinions similar to Leathes. He told the MacDonnell Commission: 'There are numerous scholarships now, and you get boys passing from elementary schools to the universities as a matter of everyday occurrence.'[20]

The MacDonnell Commission also heard that in Scotland there was no family tradition of government service and 'these things are very largely a matter of tradition'. It was not an established tradition to go in for the civil service examination: indeed, according to Professor Richard Lodge, of the University of Edinburgh, there was a prejudice or assumption 'that the examination is specially designed to suit Oxford and Cambridge'.[21] Nor did Scottish universities, unlike Oxford and Cambridge, 'have a large number of open scholarships which drew from the best secondary schools the best products of those schools'.[22]

Before the Second World War, when there was only one method of selecting graduates for the administrative class, much depended on the interview, which lasted about 15 minutes. Sir Roderick Meiklejohn, First Civil Service Commissioner, told the Tomlin Royal Commission on the Civil Service in 1929 that a candidate's personality could be estimated in a quarter of an hour's interview;[23] and, indeed, in his opinion anything could be tested by a process of interview.[24] He explained his approach in the interview:

> There are five of us, and directly the young man comes in I try to put him at his ease, by looking at his record, and saying: 'You were at Rugby; you went on from there to Corpus; you got a scholarship there'. Then I should say 'What schools did you read?' He says 'Greats and Mods'. I ask: 'Have you any preference for history or philosophy?' and he says which he has a preference for. I do not want to take all the questioning myself, so one of the others says: 'Have you been abroad much?' He may say: 'I have been to Germany'. Then he is asked: 'Did you notice any difference between Bavaria and Saxony, and the people and the customs?' The other people ask him, has he done any social work in the East End, or has he been interested in the Boy Scouts. Then we might try to find out whether he has any interest in natural history. Has he read much German or Italian literature, or any other languages. You may ask him almost anything which occurs to you, to find out what his interests are, and how he reacts to other people and things. It is as wide as we can make it. Of course, you ask him about his games and his sports; everything under the sun really.[25]

Notwithstanding the introduction of the Method II system of selection, with its much more penetrating programme of interviews and tests, this view of the interview for Method I candidates was still held within the Civil Service Commission in the late 1940s. A.P. (later Sir Percival) Waterfield explained to a sub-committee of the House of Commons Estimates Committee in 1948 the sort of favourable impression that a candidate could make at the Final Interview Board. He said it was a more thorough approach than the pre-war interview:

> We take very great account...of references in the referee's reports on candidates to their home origin, the fact that their family have brought them up well and the fact that they have been persons well respected in their community, whether high or low in the social scale, and references to achievements of relatives in the Services, and that kind of thing, are all taken into account...Obviously it is a point in the candidate's favour if he can show that he has good stuff in him, or that his family have served the State well and have shown themselves to be possessed of the qualities that we are looking for...[26]

As long ago as 1912 Medley had suggested that in the interview students from Glasgow University, who were 'not English public school boys', would not get a fair chance unless there was someone on the selection committee who knew 'our kind of men', who 'have not the same outward polish and outside manner'.[27] One of the lessons from this sort of evidence is the effect statements made by the Commissioners and others had on students who were potential candidates.

Professor W.J. Ashley, of the University of Birmingham, said in 1912 that when he was a history student he realised what a very inferior class the history students were supposed to be compared with Greats students. He admitted that many of them were inferior but he said they were made to feel their inferiority too acutely 'and it required years of mixing up with men of different kinds to diminish the awe I felt for your typical Greats man'.[28] Much the same consequence can arise from the confidence and feelings of superiority from persons educated at public schools.

The concern of critics observing this sort of evidence is that students educated in state schools and the newer universities may not have entered the civil service competitions because they felt they were inferior or would have little chance of success in examinations modelled on Oxford and Cambridge syllabuses, and those who did enter might, through lack of confidence, be less motivated to give of their best. It will, however, be remembered from chapters 2 and 3, that the MacDonnell Commission came to no firm conclusion on this matter, instead it was the medium for presenting the evidence and it recommended a full investigation into the facts.[29] This became the task of the Leathes Committee, which reported in 1917.

What emerges from these examples is that from the early years of the twentieth century there was concern about the educational backgrounds of candidates for the administrative examinations. Political patronage may have been removed by the introduction of open competitive examinations, but there was a growing awareness that openness and fairness in examinations should be considered from other perspectives. The wealth and social backgrounds of candidates were by no means irrelevant. Though persons in influential positions may have thought it was easy to acquire education and other relevant experience to make unprivileged people eligible for the competitions, in practice it was by no means easy. Moreover, influential persons often had little insight into the actual educational plans or alternative career opportunities available to people with backgrounds quite different from their own.

When criticisms became more widely publicised in the mid-twentieth century, staff in the Civil Service Selection Board became more self-aware. The background to this may have been not only the evidence to official enquiries from staff in the Commission but also the publications of commentators. One of the most significant critics was R.K. Kelsall, whose book *Higher Civil Servants in Britain* was published in 1955 (though some of the questions it raised about social class arose from an earlier research project at the London School of Economics).[30] In his book, Kelsall referred to evidence to royal commissions on the civil service, and made an analysis of the published and unpublished recruitment statistics. In particular he examined evidence to the MacDonnell Commission, as considered above, and focused on the expense of competing for the administrative class. For example, candidates would have to pay for a week's residence in London to attend the examination, and cramming for the examination was more of a necessity than a luxury: in 1910, of 33 successful Cambridge candidates, 21 received tuition at Wren's College for six months or more and three attended Wren's for seven weeks.[31]

Kelsall paid particular attention to the interview. He referred to Meiklejohn's evidence to the Tomlin Commission (see above) and commented:

> Little perspicacity is required to see how this kind of approach would prejudice the chances of a candidate from the lower social strata, where no point of contact, in his educational career or elsewhere, existed between him and the Chairman. Such a candidate, far from being put at his ease, might well tend to become more and more uncomfortable as the interview proceeded.[32]

Kelsall also commented on the change in 1937 whereby the weight of the interview was substantially increased: instead of a maximum mark of 300 out of an aggregate of 1,800 marks, the interview was given a maximum of 300 out of 1,300 marks.[33] Nevertheless, the Commissioners found it unacceptable[34] that occasionally a candidate succeeded despite a very poor mark for his personal qualities,[35] and Meiklejohn had expressed to the Tomlin Commission in 1929 his personal view that the interview should, as in recruitment for the foreign service, be a qualifying one that weeded out bad interviewees altogether.[36]

It seems likely that Kelsall's published work and the writings of others in the mid 1950s[37] had an effect not known outside the Civil Service Commission at that time. In particular, it drew attention to facets of the education system and the civil service selection procedures that had not previously received attention. This is illustrated by a memorandum to the First Commissioner and others dated 18 October 1955 (author unknown) which said

> I have had a list made of the more regular members of the CSSB Directing Staff since the Open Competitions began to see how representative the list looks...On the psychological side we are beyond reproach but otherwise, except for John Swindale, we are all public school boys... Do you think that we ought to consider this angle in future?

The list showed that eight of the nine Group Chairmen had been educated at Oxford or Cambridge Universities and one at the London School of Economics; of the 12 Observers, 11 had been educated at Oxford or Cambridge and one at Aberdeen; but the five Psychologists had all attended universities other than Oxford or Cambridge.[38] About ten years later there was another analysis which showed that, in 1964, 14 of the 17 CSSB Observers were from Oxford or Cambridge. K.A.G. Murray, then Director of CSSB, who was educated at Aberdeen University, commented that this was because Observers were drawn mainly from the 'best people': he advised getting a better balance to meet increasing criticism.[39]

Perhaps it should be mentioned that this was not the first time questions had been raised about the educational background of selection staff. As early as 1932 H.A. Roberts, Secretary to the University of Cambridge Appointments Board, wrote to Meiklejohn pointing out that the interviewing board for the Colonial Service consisted almost entirely of Oxford people, and though he did not wish to challenge the impartiality of the board he asked whether Meiklejohn thought it was, as a matter of public policy, wise to have the board consisting almost entirely of Oxford names. He mentioned that, the previous August, the result of the selection for the administrative services was 12 Oxford men and five Cambridge men, and he wondered whether 'the type of the typical Oxford and Cambridge candidate might be somewhat different and that it is not unnatural that the Oxford type would appeal to the Oxford man even without his knowing it'.[40] Meiklejohn's reply said that until recently he had 'never noticed the fact, as in the selection of members we had not taken into account their University origin but rather what was thought to be their fitness for the duties of the post'. Nevertheless he agreed 'that it would be desirable to consider whether the Cambridge element should not be strengthened so as to avoid any ideas of partial treatment of candidates from the two Universities'.[41] In some quarters, it seems, there was sensitivity about possible allegations relating to preference for Oxford candidates over Cambridge candidates, but not necessarily much concern about other possible preference.

The educational system

The MacDonnell Commission addressed the question of equality of opportunity as an important factor in civil service recruitment. Its majority report stressed the importance of university education for ripening natural ability and developing administrative capacity, and it urged more facilities for promising boys to get to the universities. It said:

> We cannot too earnestly repeat that it is not by lowering the educational standards of the highest ranks of the Civil Service, but only by enabling the clever sons of poor parents to benefit by University training, and thereby enter the Civil Service, that the interests of democracy and of the public service can and ought to be reconciled.[42]

Throughout the life of the Civil Service Commission there was tension, or at least co-operation tempered with sensitivity, between the educational system and the structure of the civil service. In broad terms, during the twentieth century the structure of the civil service, and recruitment to it, reflected the school leaving ages. Pupils who left school at 16 competed for clerical class positions, pupils who left at 18 competed for executive class positions and university graduates competed for administrative class positions. It was not impossible to be promoted from one class to the next, but the opportunities were limited. Equality of opportunity in recruitment therefore depended to a considerable degree on the prior opportunities for education; and opportunities for education depended to a considerable degree on wealth. When the Northcote–Trevelyan Report was published there were some free places at the preparatory and public schools but there was hardly any provision for the poorer people. The state assumed responsibility for primary education in 1870 and by 1895 most of the elementary schools were free or nearly so.[43]

The degree of tension between the educational system and recruitment to the civil service, mentioned earlier, arose because representatives of the education system were often looking to the Commission for guidance on what was required for recruitment, while the Commission was pursuing its practice (since the time of Macaulay, Northcote and Trevelyan) of examining educational achievements on the basis of what the schools and universities were providing. Consequently there was a philosophical question of which should be the determining interest. The question was raised from time to time, and this is illustrated by two examples. First, as early as 1906, W.J. Courthope, then First Commissioner, stated very clearly to a conference of university representatives who were lobbying for examinations in Irish, Welsh and Scotch Gaelic Languages that it was not for the Commissioners to give an educational lead; 'we take the conditions as we find them'.[44] Second, E.H. Ritson, of the Treasury, wrote to Waterfield in 1942: 'the true order of things is for the educational authorities to say what scheme of education they want, and for us to fit our programme into it'.[45] The question was raised in this way in 1942 because at that time the Norwood Committee was considering, for the Ministry of Education, the curriculum of examinations: this was the Committee that recommended abolishing the School Certificate and replacing it with the General Certificate of Education.

The Committee was chaired by Sir Cyril Norwood, then President of St John's College, Oxford, and Waterfield called on him on 31 May 1943. Waterfield at that time was thinking about the proposed new scheme (Method II) for recruiting graduates for administrative positions. The Norwood Committee, Waterfield found, shared his concern about 'the increasing tendency to attract young people of the "clever little swot" type'; both the School Certificate and the Higher School Certificate were thought to be cramping and lead to an undesirable degree of cramming.[46] In Waterfield's opinion such students had 'very little to offer their country in return for the time and money spent on their education'. He was pleased to learn that the Norwood Committee was proposing to recommend that a certain number of scholarships and entry places in the universities should be reserved 'for candidates who are taking their stand on their record and their personality as judged by an interview'. Waterfield said that he heartily welcomed this, but wished Norwood could 'go further and introduce the interview test for all scholarships and entrances with power to the interviewing board to exclude a candidate who seemed to them unsatisfactory'. It is clear that as early as 1941 Waterfield had been developing his ideas of post-war recruitment, probation and training for the administrative class, and he took advantage of every opportunity to raise questions about it when he met such senior figures in the world of education as Norwood and G.M. Trevelyan, then Master of Trinity College, Cambridge.[47]

Throughout its life the Commission was involved with examining the best products of the educational system, and those involved in deciding what this meant did not doubt what was best in this context, at both school and university level. Meiklejohn explained to the Tomlin Commission in 1929 that the written examination for the administrative group was 'based on the five great schools of classics, mathematics, history, natural science and modern languages'[48] and it was so wide that it embraced every subject, other than theology, that was studied in the universities.[49] At that time the scheme required candidates to take five subjects: essay, English, present day knowledge, every day science and an auxiliary language. Candidates also selected academic subjects up to a maximum of 1,000 marks; and up to 300 marks could be awarded for the interview. During the 1930s proposals for reform were considered, and after 1937 the maximum marks for the compulsory and optional written subjects was reduced to 1,000. Brief details of how this came about provide valuable insights into processes which may be helpful for understanding how allegations of bias might arise.

Sir Warren Fisher, then Head of the Civil Service, visited Cambridge in 1933 and said he was not satisfied with recruitment to the higher civil service.[50] This was discussed by the Executive Committee of the Appointments Board in the University, and they produced a memorandum for discussion. The memorandum said that the position since the early years of the civil service examination had changed: 'it is now possible for any really clever boy to secure adequate assistance to enable him to go to a University'. This meant that a wholly independent examination appeared unnecessary, though complete reliance could not be placed on an academic record because of the difficulty of equating standards at different universities. The memorandum made a number of suggestions (not necessary for consideration in detail here) and within the Civil Service Commission G.G. Mennell wrote an outline of a method of recruitment based on the Cambridge proposals. This was discussed in detail at a meeting in the Treasury on 20 October 1933. Fisher said that the proposals, 'though good in themselves, were impracticable on political grounds'. Suggestions for re-timing the examination were considered, but this would involve careful arrangements to avoid clashes with Oxford vivas. The Commission then contacted 17 universities for details of their examination dates, and there was another meeting on 14 May 1934 to discuss the information acquired. Fisher pointed out that, while the courses of all universities must be considered, the great bulk of candidates came from Oxford and Cambridge, and it would be sufficient in practice to base the rules on the courses of these two universities, with any necessary adjustments to avoid hardship to candidates from other universities.

Representations were received that some candidates (e.g. reading English Language and Literature, and modern languages) were badly off for subjects in the examinations and such comments were considered.[51] A new draft was prepared in the Commission. W. (later Sir Will) Spens, Master of Corpus Christi College, Cambridge, suggested a conference involving Oxford and Cambridge, plus someone from the Scottish universities and someone from London University.[52] This was discussed with Fisher, who thought that in the first instance consultation had better be limited to Oxford and Cambridge. Spens was told by Sir James Rae, of the Treasury, that it was thought the other universities might be left until later.⁵³ The draft proposals were then sent to Oxford and Cambridge. A covering letter, dated 4 October 1934, explained the objectives of the proposals, said it was recognised that at some stage it would be necessary to ask the views of the other universities, and added that: 'The Commissioners think it desirable that such invitation should be deferred until a substantial measure of agreement has been reached between the Commissioners and the two older universities.'⁵⁴

Mrs Mair, of the London School of Economics (LSE), heard about these consultations from the Master of Balliol College. She said London would not like to be left out, and that the LSE wanted to make representations: indeed, she was anxious to make representations before the matter was settled.⁵⁵ She also said that the civil service needed people trained in modern subjects (L. Blaikie noted 'presumably such as the product of the School of Economics').⁵⁶ Blaikie raised this at the Commissioners' Board meeting but was told that the intention was to say nothing to other universities until recommendations had been received from Oxford and Cambridge. It would expedite matters considerably for the Commissioners to have fairly definite proposals before contacting the other universities. Blaikie telephoned, and then wrote to Mair on these lines. In June 1935 there was a conference with representatives of Oxford, Cambridge and London, to discuss questions relating to economics and politics. On 16 July 1935 one of the London representatives, Sir William Beveridge, sent Meiklejohn details of a proposal on sociology that had been drafted by T.H. Marshall.⁵⁷

Meanwhile, in Oxford, Douglas Veale, of the University Registry, was somewhat embarrassed to receive a letter from the LSE which made it clear they knew what was happening, having heard details from Cambridge. Veale's embarrassment was because the correspondence from the Commission laid stress on the confidential character of their communication. He told Rae, on 1 November, that he had said he would keep the LSE informed when Oxford had its own proposals in shape.⁵⁸ He added: 'I suppose there is no harm in this, and if so, when we do meet them that we need not keep up the solemn farce of pretending that they know nothing about what the Civil Service Commissioners have in mind.' On 16 November Veale wrote again to Mennell about the scope of the proposed coverage in economics. Mennell replied that it was intended that it would include some other subjects such as politics and modern history.⁵⁹

Both Oxford and Cambridge prepared major responses to the proposals from the Commission. Rae thought Blaikie and Mennell should attend the Treasury to discuss the documents. W.R. (later Sir Robert) Fraser, at the Treasury, therefore asked them to visit. He also gave his first impressions:

> On the main point the Cambridge document seems to us to win. The argument in their penultimate paragraph is very convincing. On the other hand, on certain details Oxford makes strong points, and we feel that Oxford – and particularly the Greats man – do seem to be unfairly treated, both in the existing scheme and under the new scheme. It does seem to us that it should be possible to get an arrangement which suits both Universities.⁶⁰

There were further discussions on 18 January 1935 between the Treasury and Commission representatives. Rae said he wanted a statement on details that he could put before Fisher. A report was therefore prepared and sent as a letter to the Secretary, Treasury, for the Lords Commissioners. The reply, from the Treasury, sent on 19 February 1935, said that the Treasury was in favour of the compromise proposals agreed with the two universities. The Treasury wished, however, to be kept informed of the progress of the discussions with Oxford and Cambridge, and then with the other universities. Letters were sent to both Oxford and Cambridge on 27 February 1935. Detailed replies were received from Oxford (16 March 1935) and Cambridge (2 May 1935). The Treasury then approved the proposed changes and details were sent to all universities and colleges.[61] In a parliamentary question (16 December 1935), Lieut-Colonel Sir Arnold Wilson asked whether educational and scientific interests had been consulted about the new arrangements.[62] He followed this up with a letter to W.S. Morrison, then Financial Secretary to the Treasury. The reply, drafted by J.I.C. Crombie, of the Treasury, was referred to the Civil Service Commissioners: it was commented on by Blaikie and Mennell and seen by Meiklejohn. It included the information that the Commissioners 'obtained the concurrence of the Universities of Oxford and Cambridge, whose considered advice may be taken as representative of general well-informed opinion'.[63]

This much abbreviated example of consultation is valuable for three important reasons. First, it is not otherwise known how the process of consultation proceeded on the matter of changing the examination regulations for the administrative group competitions in the 1930s. What was apparently chosen as a procedure of convenience and efficiency – that is, consultation first with Oxford and Cambridge – may have been economical and convenient but it gave almost no opportunities for consultation with other universities and colleges. Second, the procedure set a precedent, and in a bureaucracy like the Civil Service Commission such a precedent became the procedure to be followed in future. For example, Waterfield, writing to C.G. Nelson on 18 July 1941 about administrative class and foreign service recruitment reform, said: 'My recollection is that our usual practice is to see Oxford and Cambridge first, and then to bring in the provincials.'[64] Third, Fisher's suggestion to contact Oxford and Cambridge first (because most recruits came from those universities) may not have been a suggestion based on all the facts fully considered. To Fisher, it may well have been a matter of minor administrative convenience – but it was a suggestion from the Head of the Civil Service, and in the culture of British central government administration, for perhaps a variety of reasons, any suggestion from the top tends, it seems, to be received uncritically by such subordinate officials as may happen to be involved.

The nature and content of the selection system

Before the First World War, recruitment to the administrative group of positions was by open competitive academic examinations. After the First World War an interview was added to the written examinations. After the Second World War two methods were used for recruitment to these posts. Method I consisted of academic written papers and an interview. Method II, introduced to deal with reconstruction candidates after the war, was developed for open competition purposes: it consisted of Qualifying Tests (QTs), the three days of tests and interviews at the Civil Service Selection Board (CSSB) and the Final Selection Board (FSB).

From time to time there were representations about the fairness of the subjects available for examination in Method I. For reasons that have already been mentioned, the subjects and syllabuses were modelled on what was taught at Oxford and Cambridge. Sometimes it was alleged that the examinations were more suited to candidates from one university or the other. Occasionally there were requests for the inclusion of new subjects – so that students reading those subjects at other universities as well as students at Oxford and Cambridge would have better opportunities to compete. This happened, for example, with law, geography and sociology – but the Civil Service Commission was always cautious about this sort of expansion, partly because they had to be confident that the new subjects merited inclusion (was the subject academically respectable? how many candidates might there be who wished to offer it?), and partly because there was already a long list of papers from which candidates could choose. Consequently, it often took years from the time of the first suggestion until a new subject was included in the list. For example, there were requests to include sociology in the late 1930s, but the first sociology paper, on the social structure of modern Britain, was not included until 1961.

Whatever modest changes were made, evidence from the reports of the Civil Service Commissioners showed that candidates from Oxford and Cambridge still emerged with better rates of success than candidates from elsewhere. There is no opportunity here to cover all the avenues for criticising the selection system, but the files show that staff within the civil service, especially in the Commission, were often anxious about allegations of bias in this context. The files also draw attention to little-known features of the stages of assessment. This is illustrated by the following comments about these stages in the selection process.

Before the First World War the written examination covered a wide selection of subjects studied at the universities. As Meiklejohn told the Tomlin Commission, it was framed to preclude cramming[65] and to measure the intellect,[66] but candidates who took it often devoted a year to cramming,[67] and many more spent shorter periods of time with one of the colleges that offered specialised tuition for civil service examinations. Fisher, for example, spent four years at Oxford, graduated in 1902, had a futile shot at the Indian Civil Service examinations, spent six weeks at 'Wrens', plus reading at home for the examination, then (successfully) sat the civil service examinations again in 1903, when he was nearly 24.[68] Waterfield left school late, after he was 19 years of age, spent four years at Oxford, then received private tuition for six weeks from Ernest Barker and two months in Roman law from D.C. Cousins,[69] in preparation for the civil service examinations in August 1911.[70] It is clear that a number of Oxford and Cambridge dons were coaching or teaching for the civil service examinations and of course this could give rise to ethical implications where the teacher was also a civil service examiner because the teaching could so easily be closely related to the questions he had set for the examination.[71] There were advantages for a candidate who was able to pay for specialised tuition, and extra advantages if the tutor was setting the examination questions.

The feelings of a student at a provincial university about the 'bias' that could arise because of the selection systems were well expressed in a letter from Raymund Fitzpatrick to *The Times*, 11 December 1959:

> There are two methods used in selecting candidates...If the 'redbrick man' chooses method one (that is, selection chiefly by written examination) he will find the type of examination set is composed with 'Oxbridge men' in mind and it is completely in tune with the system of examination of the older universities.
>
> If, on the other hand, he chooses method two (or the 'house party system') he will find himself in keen competition with men from Oxford and Cambridge who are, in general, more articulate than himself in expressing their ideas and, consequently, more socially 'presentable'. This is probably the result of an individual tutorial system of teaching. It does not mean that this difference in the two types of candidate would still exist after a few years in the service.[72]

The problems identified by Fitzpatrick existed notwithstanding the anonymity of candidates. As with the academic written examinations, candidates taking the QTs in Method II were identified only by an examination number – this was generally recognised as good practice, not only in the civil service competitions but also for other public and professional examinations. The evidence is that privately some members of the Commission had doubts about the reliability of their provisions for eliminating bias, while publicly insisting that bias did not exist. Allen, as mentioned earlier, accepted in evidence to the 1977 Select Committee on Expenditure, that there was a bias in selection in the statistical sense, but he explained it in this way:

> The way in which the Oxbridge candidates, and I think the same is true of the public school and direct entry people, gain most is on the written examination, the compulsory test at the beginning, which is marked on the basis that the people who do the marking do not know where the people come from. So if the bias...is in the system it arises from the kind of test applied; it is a kind of literacy test – a simple test of that kind.[73]

The difficulty here is that the question of bias at the QT stage may not have been quite as straightforward as Allen thought – and this would have been apparent if Allen had been able to know the thoughts of some of the Commission personnel and others in the civil service who had expressed anxieties about this issue, or even if he had read Fitzpatrick's letter to *the Times*. Some examples illustrate this.

Waterfield knew of the reservations of the Foreign Secretary, Ernest Bevin, on graduate recruitment to the foreign service. Bevin had stressed that he thought the Commission examination was a 'bit too narrow', too academic and he wanted 'more in the shape of personality'.[74] Waterfield was also concerned about the reliability of the QTs. He wrote that he 'had been worried over the evidence that certain candidates who might have been expected, by reason both of their academic record, and their Service record, to succeed in the examination, had nevertheless failed to reach the qualifying mark'. He added:

> I should perhaps add that Mr Fulton of Balliol, whom I questioned the other day, said that as far as he knew, there was no criticism at Oxford of our present examination and no wish to suggest that we were ploughing men who ought to have qualified. It may be, therefore, that the number of failures is not higher than one must expect in any examination system and that we need not worry. I hope this will prove to be the case; but I should like to be fortified by further investigation.[75]

Soon afterwards there were changes in the regulations, giving greater discretion to the Commissioners, lowering the qualifying mark and introducing a pre-board interview to ensure that only candidates with a good chance of success would proceed to the Civil Service Selection Board.

Waterfield was succeeded as First Commissioner by A.P. (later Sir Paul) Sinker, then by L.N. (later Sir Laurence, then Lord) Helsby. In February 1961 Sir George Mallaby, who succeeded Helsby, related to H.A. Needham, then Director of Examinations, his recent experience when dining with Sinker. Sinker said that he thought that the QT stage in the Method II examination (which then consisted of an Essay paper, an English paper and a General paper)[76] was absolutely untrustworthy. Mallaby expressed great surprise and said he thought it was a very well-devised practical intellectual test. Sinker did not dissent from this view, but alleged that the standard of marking between different examiners varied so alarmingly that nobody could have any confidence in the results. Mallaby added that he had been worried by the high failure rate of candidates at modern universities, but he had been an admirer of that type of examination and had not expected to hear such a radical attack on it.[77]

In responding to queries about the QTs, the replies from the Civil Service Commission are revealing. For example, Mallaby explained to Dame Evelyn (later Baroness) Sharp that the examination was designed to keep out those

> who cannot write or reason. It is not in any sense an academic examination, but it is certainly a test of intellectual power. Without it, or something like it, we should be flooded with a great many unworthy and valueless candidates.[78]

In reply to a letter from the University of Glasgow, Needham explained that in the qualifying examination purely academic learning counted for little and much more advantage was derived from breadth of experience and knowledge of human affairs in general. He suggested that Glasgow students might do better if they had a year or two of post-graduate applied work or time for scholarly reflection and travel.[79] This seems to have been, in one sense, a helpful and fair response to the query from Glasgow, though it rather assumed that the students' financial resources would stretch to meeting the cost of acquiring that experience.

A few years later, a paper concerned with the Fulton Committee's comments on recruitment, mentioned that the Commission had some doubts about parts of the qualifying examination.[80] Then, again, in 1968, in connection with the recruitment of principals aged 36–51 years, K.M. Reader commented that he had never been entirely happy about the use of the qualifying examination for older candidates. John (later Sir John, then Lord) Hunt suggested a process of sifting rather than using the qualifying examination, or a combination of the two.[81] Sifting in this context refers to making a qualitative judgment of a candidate on the basis of his record and referees reports and, if strongly supported, passing him on to CSSB even if he achieved below the QT pass mark. Sifting on these lines was used to pass 'near misses' on to CSSB from the mid 1950s.[82] Doubts about the qualifying examination, which in some respects, and on the basis of results, appeared to favour candidates with Oxford and Cambridge backgrounds, continued throughout the rest of the life of the Commission.

Some of these doubts were clearly associated with the age of candidates and this was not overlooked by the staff of the Commission. Reader, for example, wrote in 1966 that he had 'a hunch...that Oxbridge candidates may be a little older than those from elsewhere and our papers may give some advantage to those with a little more maturity and sophistication'.[83] On another occasion he queried whether it had a significant effect on success in a degree course when a student spent a third year in the school sixth form instead of starting straight away at university after 'A' level.[84] He also drew attention to the Greats degree at Oxford which took four years.[85] It was to some extent a response to these concerns that candidates with first-class degrees were later exempted from the QTs; then candidates were also exempted if they had a higher degree.[86] There were, indeed (self-) critical minds within the Commission, but they were not known outside. The attitudes seen from outside were of an institution confident in its procedures and methods, and defensive in the context of its political environment.

Publicity, liaison and visits

After the Second World War the Civil Service Commission paid particular attention to recruitment publicity. Before the war there were plenty of candidates for most competitions; after the war there were often fewer well-qualified candidates than there were vacancies. E.J.D. Warne, an assistant director of examinations 1954–59, was also the Advisory Officer who supplied publicity to, and answered questions from 4,000 schools, 1,000 Youth Employment Offices and 250 Local Education Authorities. In addition, Warne organised civil service representatives to attend careers events. For example, in 1959–60 staff from the Commission, or from its panel of speakers in other departments, represented the Commission at over 200 careers conventions or similar meetings. The Commission was also represented at local careers exhibitions sponsored by Local Education Authorities or by Rotary Clubs. Furthermore, the Commission advertised in the press, participated in sound broadcasting and television and prepared articles for the press and for schools yearbooks. This wide publicity operation covered all types of civil service jobs.[87]

In the early 1950s most of the presentations had been organised by Mrs Olga K. Collett, then Assistant Commissioner and Schools Liaison Officer, and the exhibitions went all over the country. At the exhibitions, the civil service presentations were highly regarded by the organisers, especially the Rotary Clubs: they were attractively presented, well staffed and could be relied upon. Sometimes, however, there were modest surprises for the staff when visiting distant towns, and attitudes revealed in the files were not always consistent with the Commission's public statements. At the Aberystwyth Exhibition in May 1955, for example, an unusual feature was the number of university students who came to the civil service stand for advice. It was evident that the university's careers adviser knew nothing of the civil service and Collett noted that she handed out about 20 sets of papers for the administrative group competitions. She mentioned that she tactfully directed the attention of these students to the Special Departmental Classes (SDC) and to opportunities for graduate entrants to executive class positions rather than to the administrative class.[88] This tactic apparently reflected the general approach in the Commission which did not wish to encourage candidates whom they thought had little prospect of success, and who would create additional work and increase the cost of competitions. Indeed, at about the same time, when the Commission was considering the future of the annual conferences it had been organising for representatives of university appointments boards, W.H. Fisher, Secretary of the Commission, was unsympathetic to their continuation. He wrote: 'We don't want to stimulate the interest of provincial universities in the Administrative Class.'[89] Similarly, in 1960 D. O'Donovan, put the position that staff should adopt when visiting universities like this:

> We want to convey that we really do hope to see more of the best people from the provinces competing, but we do not wish to do anything which will increase the number of hopeless candidates. The line, therefore, seems to be to mention the Administrative Class, but to devote more time to other jobs...The Durham people are taking a very keen interest in the GCE Executive competition.[90]

One of the valuable post-Second World War developments was increasing co-operation with university appointments boards (UABs): these were created in universities to facilitate the distribution of information about career opportunities and to provide advice for students who asked for it. This was advanced by what became annual conferences organised by the Commission for secretaries of UABs. The 1951 conference was Sinker's first as First Commissioner, but afterwards he suggested less elaborate meetings: for a nucleus from Oxford, Cambridge and London, with the others appearing in rotation, say every three years. Collett said this would be unfortunate for the provincial universities because they had such a 'pronounced inferiority complex' and there would be hurt feelings. She added: 'We are looking to the provincial Universities to supply us with our SDC entrants and we do not want their interest generally to grow less keen.' At the Board meeting on 22 June 1951 it was decided to hold the conference every other year (no conference in 1952), but with 'Ad hoc meetings if necessary... with Oxford, Cambridge, London and probably the Scottish universities.' There was, in fact, no regular conference for UAB secretaries for several years after 1951,[91] though they were later resumed.[92]

The Commission's public emphasis on attracting applicants for the administrative group of competitions was slightly different. When Mrs A.K. Ogilvy-Webb was making preparations for a 1959 BBC programme on the foreign service for the 'Facts and Figures' series, Warne stressed that the Commission had no preference for candidates from any particular source, and said that the main reason for the imbalance in the educational background of recruits was that the best pupils from all types of schools went to Oxford or Cambridge if they could. He added: 'there is no bias against candidates from the other universities', and 'we would like to see them competing in larger numbers and securing a larger share of places'.[93] A similarly defensive attitude was adopted by Mallaby when Cledwyn Hughes MP wrote to *The Sunday Times*[94] a letter that would now be regarded as fair comment on a matter of public interest, drawing attention to the dominance of Oxford and Cambridge among entrants into the foreign service. Mallaby reacted, 'Hughes has written an offensive and ill-informed letter', and a reply was sent to the newspaper emphasising the serious efforts of the Commission, Treasury and universities to encourage 'Redbrick' undergraduates to consider a career in the civil service.[95]

It was not just in relation to recruitment to the administrative class that publicity was regarded as important. In the period after the Second World War the Civil Service Commissioners regarded it as part of their duties to stimulate recruitment as and when deficiencies in quality or quantity became apparent.[96] This was especially important when normal recruitment failed to fill all the vacancies. The various First Commissioners contributed their own ideas to further this activity. A particular advance in this respect during Helsby's time as First Commissioner was the creation of liaison officers. He and his Cambridge contacts believed the best stimulus to recruitment was supplied by ex-members of a college who returned after joining the civil service and gave good reports of it to their successors. He therefore thought there was merit in seeking out, within the civil service, fairly young former members of Oxford and Cambridge colleges, and graduates of the newer universities, and giving them the responsibility, as part of their duties, for keeping in touch with their colleges and stimulating the best people of each generation to apply to join the civil service. Helsby mentioned this idea at a meeting in the Treasury on 10 May 1955, and later confirmed it in writing to Sir Alexander Johnston.[97] When the idea was put to Sir Edward (later Lord) Bridges, as Head of the Civil Service, he was supportive and accordingly wrote to heads of government departments about it. Details were later approved by a meeting of establishment officers:[98] the departmental establishment officers then recommended names; the Commission considered the records of the individuals; the universities and the chosen liaison officers were then contacted. Twenty names were approved for Cambridge (one each for 20 colleges); similarly 20 names were approved for Oxford colleges; ten names were approved for all the other universities in England, Scotland and Wales. During the exchanges of correspondence P.T. Sloman (Treasury) recalled to F.L. Howard (Civil Service Commission) that some years previously, under the rather different scheme then in use, he had been encouraged in talks to provincial universities, which did not generally produce members of the administrative class, to emphasise the SDC opportunities and similar openings for graduates.[99]

It seems that the liaison officers not only made themselves available to encourage undergraduates, they also sought to influence young dons who were recognised by staff in the Commission (J.H.T. Goldsmith, for example)[100] as probably the most important recruiting sergeants for the civil service. Mrs M. McArthur, principal psychologist at CSSB, had no doubt that dons were the most useful sources of information for undergraduates (whereas the main function of liaison officers seemed to her to be 'to put unsuitable ideas into unsuitable heads').[101] R.C. Livesey, a principal at CSSB seconded from the Ministry of Transport and Civil Aviation, told the First Commissioner that he thought that 'for Oxbridge the LO system is otiose and for the provincial universities in vain'. Mallaby replied: 'I think it would be better if I did not at this stage commit my own dark thoughts to paper, but if you would like to come and see me...I should very much welcome a discussion with you.'[102]

When the Estimates Committee in 1964–65 focused on recruitment to the civil service it said it was disturbed to learn that after the Treasury had sanctioned two posts of principal level to improve contacts with teaching staff at universities, one of these was to be devoted to improving liaison links with Oxford and Cambridge. The Committee found it difficult to understand why both posts were not allocated to the civic universities.[103] Within the Commission it was felt that the duties being assigned to A.S. Pratley[104] had been misunderstood: they extended beyond liaison work. Nevertheless, a note on a discussion between the Secretary and the First Commissioner stressed: 'We need someone to look after Oxbridge liaison since, rightly or wrongly, this is still our main A.C. recruitment field.'[105]

Other publicity schemes were introduced from time to time. A complement to the work of liaison officers was 'Whitehall visits', where undergraduates could spend a week in a department seeing how it worked. Another scheme was for young dons to spend a couple of years seconded to a department. Although these and other schemes, such as a university representative participating in FSB as a board member, may all have had some effect, there was no attempt to enlist the co-operation of academic public administration specialists in provincial universities (there were hardly any such specialists in Oxford or Cambridge) – though they were often sought out by undergraduates interested in the possibility of a civil service career. By 1962 there were 28 liaison officers for Oxford colleges, 21 for Cambridge colleges, six for London colleges, 13 for all the other English universities, four for Scottish universities, three for Welsh colleges, one for Northern Ireland and one for Eire.[106]

Perhaps of most significance in the matter of special attention towards particular universities were the numerous visits by First Commissioners. They were themselves very well connected with Oxford and Cambridge, both in terms of their own education and in terms of numerous family and social contacts. The most significant example, because of the number of visits he made and his personal approach, was Waterfield, though the others also visited as often as they could. Waterfield set the precedent for this attention, and he set a high standard in terms of devoting time to it probably because he reckoned himself to be underworked.[107] He had plenty of energy and a forceful personality.

Waterfield had been a scholar at Christ Church, Oxford – as was his son John, after the Second World War. His nephew became a student at Corpus Christi. His daughter Jill was a student at Lady Margaret Hall. One of his daughters spent some time working at the Dragon School, Oxford. It seems that Waterfield loved Oxford and took advantage of every opportunity to visit, whether for pleasure or for business – and he was as happy to visit colleges on civil service matters in his own time at weekends as at any other times. He made numerous visits during the Second World War, to advance plans to reform recruitment to the foreign service as well as the home civil service. After the war he applied his energies to telling people, especially in Oxford and Cambridge, about 'the new residential system' of personnel selection. Sometimes Lady Waterfield accompanied him (on Sunday 18 October 1945, when in Cambridge, they called on G.M. and Mrs Trevelyan for tea; on 2 March 1946 the Waterfields had tea in Oxford with John and Mrs Fulton).[108] He was frequently having lunch or dinner as a guest in a college: sometimes he stayed there, for example with R.H. Dundas, Emeritus Student at Christ Church. He also had a large personal correspondence with most of the Heads of Oxford colleges. He tried to make a visit to Oxford for meeting senior figures there at least once a term, and he usually succeeded.

In 1949 Waterfield became very worried about the failure to fill all the vacancies from the administrative competitions, and towards the end of his career 'as an experiment' he, with Sir Reader Bullard (Foreign Office) visited 27 colleges at Oxford and two women's colleges at Cambridge (and at the same time Sir Herbert Creedy and Sir Geoffrey Thompson, on behalf of the Foreign Office, visited 17 colleges at Cambridge). Around this time Waterfield also spoke at the London School of Economics and University College, London.

The nature of these particular visits was as important as their number. At Oxford the meetings where he spoke were informal and intimate, taking place in the private rooms of the Head of College. The audience was gathered by invitation of the Head of the College. It was made only to those who, in the opinion of the Head of the College, would be suitable applicants for administrative posts, whether or not they had themselves given any indication of being interested in a civil service career. Waterfield invited those who attended his meetings to inform him personally, in writing, whether they proposed to apply for the administrative/foreign service examination, and, if not, to give him their reasons for their decision. He received 53 letters from his Oxford meetings. At Cambridge he used the same tactics, but received only two letters. At University College, London, 25–30 students attended his meeting and he received five letters.

From Waterfield's visit to Oxford in December 1948 there were some especially interesting developments. During his various talks, at Balliol, Christ Church, New College and Brasenose, he received support for two ideas. One was to improve the system of obtaining referees reports on candidates. The other was to draw up a panel of dons to sit on FSB.

The people Waterfield saw agreed that the referees requests (initially for the reconstruction competitions, but later the procedure was applied to other competitions and continued for many years after Waterfield's retirement) would be sent not to the referees nominated by the candidates but to the Head of College. He felt this would be an improvement because he found that at Balliol, for example, the Master had the complete record of each undergraduate and could also assess the comments made by the tutors. Once Waterfield had the agreement of his small group of Heads, he wrote to all Heads of Colleges, seeking their agreement, then to Vice-Chancellors of other universities. Generally, as with J.S. (later Sir James) Duff (Durham) they fell into line and agreed, for whatever reason, but some respondents felt that the tutor named by the candidate as best acquainted with his work should write the report. Sir Philip Morris, Vice-Chancellor, University of Bristol, however, was one of a few to express clear reservations:

> I regard it as a matter of principle that a man who has appointed his own referee should stand by his decision and that what the referee he had appointed has to say about him should reach the appointing body in the form in which it is written.[109]

Waterfield's other proposal was for a panel of universities to sit on FSB: he was thinking of 18 names – six from each of Oxford and Cambridge, three from London and three from the Scottish and provincial universities. His reasoning was that the distribution should reflect the number of candidates for the civil service from the various universities. Sir John Stopford, University of Manchester, replied that he had discussed Waterfield's suggestions with his colleagues and they felt that the proposed representation on the interviewing board would not be helpful to them:

> We are not...satisfied with the proposed constitution of the panel... which seems to us to be unsatisfactory. It appears to be based on the distribution of the successful candidates in recent competitions and if these proportions are retained a vicious circle is perpetuated since a preponderance of representatives from the older universities on the selection panel is likely to mean that a large proportion of successful candidates will be selected from the older universities.[110]

Stopford suggested that a fairer basis of representation would be the number of students in the various universities, which would give Oxford and Cambridge three each, three for London, five for English provincial universities, two for Scotland and one for Wales.

Waterfield responded:

> I could not possibly accept your argument that the basis of representation should be the total number of students at each University rather than the number of candidates: still less the suggestion which frankly shocks me – that 'a preponderance of representatives from the older universities on the selection panel is likely to mean that a large proportion of successful candidates will be selected from the older universities'.[111]

Nevertheless Waterfield must have given the matter further consideration because two days later he proposed two members from the university panel on each board, one from Oxford or Cambridge, and one from 'the rest'. In a further letter to Stopford he expressed the hope that the modification would go some way to meet his objection to the over-weighting on the panel of the views of the older universities.

Stopford replied:

> We all think that the new representation is distinctly better than the old and a step in the right direction...It has been suggested to me that I should tell you that we are surprised that you are shocked by a statement in my earlier letter and I think it is only right to inform you that this statement is not a personal opinion but the considered opinion of a number of responsible people here who have experience in several universities, including the older ones. It is not an irresponsible and unconsidered remark but does represent a view which is widely held in this and, I believe, other universities.[112]

Waterfield may have set a high standard for making such a large number of visits to Oxford and Cambridge in a very short period of time, but this did not mean that other First Commissioners made little effort. In their visits, however, they tended to target more specifically College Heads and Senior Tutors. Mallaby, for example, regarded it as his duty to stimulate interest in the public service. On one occasion he said: 'I do what I can to foster it in all Universities by making personal visits and chatting away to all the people who think themselves important.'[113] He was a member of the Senior Common Room at Merton (his college) and, as he put it himself, 'a constant visitor to Oxford'.[114]

'Bias' in selection

As Goldsmith wrote on one occasion, 'it is always impossible to prove absence of prejudice.'[115] The allegations of bias in selection have been widespread and frequent. There have been many people who have accused the Commission of bias in favour of candidates from Oxford and Cambridge or from the upper classes generally[116] and it has not been possible here to consider and evaluate the large literature on the topic. Much depends on the definition of 'bias' as explained at the beginning of this chapter. Even where a 'statistical bias' is accepted as a statement of fact the problem is not resolved because most people take the word to include prejudice and/or to mean that decisions are being made on irrelevant or unacceptable criteria.

From its inception the CSSB criteria of selection were based upon a job evaluation study of the qualities found in a sample of assistant secretaries – because assistant secretary was regarded as the minimum grade a successful candidate recruited by the administrative competition was expected to be able to achieve. That seemed an acceptable basis for developing selection criteria in the 1940s and would generally have been regarded as a responsible and valid procedure in personnel management. It may be, however, that the qualities evident in a successful assistant secretary in, say, 1945, included educational and familial elements different from the qualities that might be regarded as important in recruits in a different decade, or for a career in a civil service within a system of government that has changed over the years. Perhaps some fundamental re-consideration of qualities should be considered in the context of allegations of bias in selection.

Among qualities to be considered, the age of candidates should not be overlooked. Worldly experience of life in almost any context is important for senior positions in the civil service. Therefore the upper age limits for candidates is of considerable relevance because older candidates are likely to have acquired more experience and self-confidence. Candidates at Oxford and Cambridge have generally been older than candidates from other universities – but it is not always possible for experience to be gained without expenditure or, at least, loss of earnings. Moreover, many students may feel obliged to earn their living as soon as possible, and once embarked on a career it may be easier to stay in it rather than reconsider options after a few years. Much, therefore, may depend on wider aspects of the employment prospects for graduates.

What may have been unhelpful over many years and in many contexts have been the assertions that there is no weighting of the scales in favour of Oxford and Cambridge candidates – without considering all the relevant factors. Similarly, it seems complacent to reiterate that the 'base of Oxford and Cambridge entry has radically widened to embrace students of every social origin on the basis of merit and ability'.[117] The factors affecting a student's choice of university, and especially the re-emphasis that Oxford and Cambridge are best, seem more complex than may at first appear to people who are themselves products of Oxford and Cambridge.

Some of the evidence in the files must be seen against general attitudes of their times: it would be unfair to impose contemporary criteria on practices or attitudes of a previous period; time differences can make evidence appear starkly unacceptable to people in a later period. Nevertheless, the evidence is, as this chapter has shown, in some respects more surprising than might have been expected. There were critics asking questions in the past: but often with inadequate factual material their questions tended to be inadequately informed and could be dismissed by officials indicating that outsiders did not know the facts or could not sufficiently appreciate the issues. In these circumstances outsiders could be ignored or treated as tiresomely interfering. It is, perhaps, not surprising, that Kelsall, whose book was bought by the Civil Service Commission, but then lost,[118] told the Estimates Sub-Committee that he had had no approach from the Commission to discuss the contents of his book.[119]

Given, however, the criteria and the selection system that existed, discussions about bias in selection during the life of the Civil Service Commission may need to be re-focused. The words bias and selection are used in a variety of ways and this should be more widely recognised. This chapter has demonstrated that, from the perspective of the Commission, attention should be directed to a number of important factors that have not previously been central to the allegations. There is no evidence of bias in the sense of intended and explicit favouritism or patronage in the normal sense of those words; but as time passes the statements of selectors, and their attitudes in earlier times, the educational system, and various facets of recruitment publicity appear in a different light. Even when there is no intended and explicit favouritism, evidence exists (in this and other chapters of this book) of social attitudes that did not move with the times, and of complacency and a lack of rigour in dealing with allegations about bias and in reviewing existing procedures. Taken together, these factors may result, in practice, in as much bias in selection as would occur if intended preference towards candidates with certain social and educational backgrounds was the policy in recruitment. There is a need to review all such factors, as well as to consider afresh such evidence as is available, in a context of greater openness than has generally existed in the British system of government.

Notes

1 Expenditure Committee, *Eleventh Report from the Expenditure Committee, Session 1976–77, The Civil Service Vol. II (Part II) Minutes of Evidence taken from 25 October 1976 to 9 May 1977*, HC 535 – II (London: HMSO, 1977), Q. 1,982.
2 For example, R.K. Kelsall, *Higher Civil Servants in Britain from 1870 to the Present Day* (London: Routledge & Kegan Paul, 1955); Peter Kellner and Lord Crowther-Hunt, *The Civil Servants, An Inquiry into Britain's Ruling Class* (London: Macdonald & Jane's,

1980); Social Survey of the Civil Service: Memorandum submitted by A.H. Halsey and I.M. Crewe, *The Civil Service Vol. 3(1) Surveys and Investigations: Social Survey of the Civil Service* (London: HMSO, 1969).
3 Expenditure Committee, *Eleventh Report*, 1977, Q. 1,982.
4 *Royal Commission on the Civil Service, Minutes of Evidence* (MacDonnell Commission), 26 March 1912–19 April 1912, Cd. 6210 (London: HMSO, 1912), QQ. 334–7.
5 MacDonnell Commission, *Minutes of Evidence*, 10 October 1912–13 December 1912, Cd. 6740, Q. 21,214.
6 Ibid., Q. 21,678.
7 Ibid., Q. 21,835.
8 Ibid., Q. 20,795.
9 *Royal Commission on the Civil Service 1929–31, Report and Minutes of Evidence* (Tomlin Commission), Cmd. 3909 (London: HMSO, 1931), Q. 1,259.
10 MacDonnell Commission, Cd. 6740, QQ. 20,909, 21,004.
11 Ibid., Q. 20,309.
12 Ibid., Q. 20,384.
13 MacDonnell Commission, Cd. 6210, Q. 374.
14 Ibid., Q. 375.
15 Ibid., Q. 579.
16 Ibid., Q. 583.
17 Ibid., Q. 715.
18 Ibid., Q. 715.
19 MacDonnell Commission, *Minutes of Evidence, 25 April 1912–2 August 1912*, Cd. 6535, Q. 5,544. Other reference works indicate that he was not knighted until 1919.
20 Ibid., Q. 5,784.
21 MacDonnell Commission, Cd. 6740, Q. 20,535.
22 Ibid., Q. 20,536.
23 Tomlin Commission, Q. 1,388.
24 Ibid., Q. 1,420.
25 Ibid., Q. 1,419.
26 *Ninth Report from the Select Committee on Estimates, Session 1947–48, The Civil Service Commission, together with Minutes of Evidence taken before Sub-Committee D*, HC 203, 205 (London: HMSO, 1948), QQ. 1,885–6.
27 MacDonnell Commission, Cd. 6740, Q. 20,313.
28 Ibid., Q. 21,306.
29 MacDonnell Commission, *4th Report*, Cd. 7338, Ch. 3, para. 50.
30 D.V. Glass, *Social Mobility in Britain* (London: Routledge & Kegan Paul, 1954).
31 Kelsall, *Higher Civil Servants in Britain*, p. 62.
32 Ibid., p. 71.
33 Ibid., p. 75.
34 *Memorandum by the Civil Service Commissioners on the use of the Civil Service Selection Board in the Reconstruction Competitions* (London: HMSO, 1951).
35 Kelsall, *Higher Civil Servants in Britain*, p. 85.
36 Tomlin Commission, QQ. 1,155–60.
37 For example, a series of articles and correspondence in *The Spectator*, September and October 1955.
38 PRO/CSC5/581.
39 PRO/CSC5/1515.
40 PRO/CSC5/253, H.A. Roberts to R.S. Meiklejohn, 25 January 1932.
41 PRO/CSC5/253, R.S. Meiklejohn to H.A. Roberts, 28 January 1932.
42 MacDonnell Commission, Majority Report, Cd. 7338, Ch. 3, para. 42, p. 39.
43 See J. Donald Kingsley, *Representative Bureaucracy: An Interpretation of the British Civil Service* (Yellow Springs, OH: Antioch Press, 1944), Ch. 4.

44 PRO/CSC3/355.
45 PRO/CSC5/343, E.H. Ritson to A.P. Waterfield, 20 April 1942.
46 PRO/CSC5/343, A.P. Waterfield, note of meeting 3 July 1943.
47 PRO/CSC5/343.
48 Tomlin Commission, Q. 1,249.
49 Ibid., Q. 1,259.
50 PRO/CSC5/281.
51 PRO/CSC5/281, Helen Darbishire, Principal of Somerville College, to Secretary, Civil Service Commission, 14 May 1934.
52 PRO/CSC5/281, Will Spens, letter 30 July 1934.
53 PRO/CSC5/281, James Rae to Will Spens, 2 August 1934.
54 PRO/CSC5/281.
55 PRO/CSC5/281, Memorandum, apparently by C.G. Nelson, 30 October 1934; Note by L. Blaikie, 1 November 1934.
56 PRO/CSC5/282.
57 PRO/CSC5/282.
58 PRO/CSC5/281.
59 PRO/CSC5/281, G.G. Mennell to Douglas Veale, 21 November 1934.
60 PRO/CSC5/281, W.R. Fraser to G.G. Mennell, 12 January 1935.
61 PRO/CSC5/282, responses from the universities on the draft new regulations.
62 307 HC Deb., 5s., col. 1416 (16 December 1935).
63 PRO/CSC5/281, W.S. Morrison to Sir Arnold Wilson, 7 January 1936.
64 PRO/CSC5/341.
65 Tomlin Commission, QQ. 1,061–2.
66 Ibid., Q. 1,172.
67 Ibid., Q. 1,248.
68 PRO/CSC11/95. See also Eunan O'Halpin, *Head of the Civil Service: A Study of Sir Warren Fisher* (London: Routledge, 1989).
69 PRO/CSC11/260.
70 Richard A. Chapman, *Leadership in the British Civil Service* (London: Croom Helm, 1984).
71 PRO/CSC5/282, letter from Will Spens, 22 December 1936.
72 Copy in PRO/CSC5/1092.
73 Expenditure Committee, *Eleventh Report*, 1977, *Evidence*, Q. 1,982.
74 Ernest Bevin, speech at the Labour Party Conference in Bournemouth, 12 June 1946. Copy in PRO/CSC5/327.
75 PRO/CSC5/327, A.P. Waterfield to Director of Examinations, 14 June 1946.
76 For specimen examination papers see Appendix 4, *The Method II System of Selection (for the Administrative Class of the Home Civil Service). Report of the Committee of Inquiry, 1969*, Cmnd.4156 (London: HMSO, 1969).
77 PRO/CSC5/1092.
78 PRO/CSC5/1092, G. Mallaby to Evelyn Sharp, 6 February 1961.
79 PRO/CSC5/1092, H.A. Needham to A.B. Webster, 4 November 1964.
80 PRO/CSC5/1270.
81 PRO/CSC5/1502.
82 PRO/CSC5/742.
83 PRO/CSC5/1307, K.M. Reader to F.J.R. Bartlett, 7 January 1966.
84 PRO/CSC5/1273, Memorandum by K.M. Reader, 21 December 1966. See also PRO/CSC5/1144.
85 PRO/CSC5/1273.
86 PRO/CSC5/1307.
87 PRO/CSC5/1066.

'BIAS' IN SELECTION

88 PRO/CSC5/535.
89 PRO/CSC5/502, note dated 2 December 1954.
90 PRO/CSC5/839.
91 PRO/CSC5/502.
92 PRO/CSC5/940.
93 PRO/CSC5/947.
94 *The Sunday Times*, 7 July 1963.
95 PRO/CSC5/1065.
96 PRO/CSC5/546, L.N. Helsby, at a meeting in the Treasury, 10 May 1955.
97 PRO/CSC5/547, L.N. Helsby to A. Johnston, 20 May 1955.
98 PRO/CSC5/546, 28 July 1955.
99 PRO/CSC5/547, P.T. Sloman to F.L. Howard, 28 July 1955.
100 PRO/CSC5/832.
101 PRO/CSC5/832.
102 PRO/CSC5/1049, R.C. Livesey to G. Mallaby, 6 December 1961; G. Mallaby to R.C. Livesey, 7 December 1961.
103 *Sixth Report from the Estimates Committee, Session 1964–65, Recruitment to the Civil Service*, HC 308 (London: HMSO, 1965), para. 67.
104 PRO/CSC5/1172.
105 PRO/CSC5/1149.
106 PRO/CSC5/1049.
107 PRO/CSC5/399, A.P. Waterfield to Henry Wilson Smith, 20 March 1943.
108 PRO/CSC5/341.
109 PRO/CSC5/415, Philip Morris to A.P. Waterfield, 24 January 1947.
110 PRO/CSC5/415, John Stopford to A.P. Waterfield, 24 January 1947.
111 PRO/CSC5/415, A.P. Waterfield to John Stopford, 1 February 1947.
112 PRO/CSC5/415, John Stopford to A.P. Waterfield, 14 February 1947.
113 PRO/CSC5/1186.
114 PRO/CSC5/1180, G. Mallaby to J.O. Prestwich, 27 August 1962.
115 PRO/CSC5/1238, Minute of 20 October 1962.
116 PRO/CSC5/947, Correspondence between E.J.D. Warne and Mrs Ogilvy-Webb.
117 From a brief by Brian Gilmore for Nigel Fisher, Under Secretary of State for Commonwealth Relations and the Colonies, for the House of Commons debate on 29 July 1964, on the proposed combined Foreign and Commonwealth Diplomatic Service: PRO/CSC5/1145.
118 PRO/CSC5/1186.
119 *Sixth Report from the Estimates Committee, Session 1964–65*, QQ. 375–6.

Part III

THE CIVIL SERVICE COMMISSION IN BRITISH PUBLIC ADMINISTRATION

12

THE CIVIL SERVICE COMMISSION

A bureau biography

One of the intentions in creating the Civil Service Commission in 1855 was to mitigate the evils which resulted from the fragmentary character of the service.[1] The creation of the Commission was not the only element in the development of a unified civil service, but it was, without doubt, the most important element. Nor was its contribution to this development achieved simply by the creation of what became a department of government dedicated to the recruitment of staff in accordance with specific principles – for the process of creating a unified civil service took some time, required continuous attention, and some of the characteristics of the unified service changed over the years. Before 1855 there was no unified civil service: after 1991 there was also no unified civil service. The Civil Service Commission existed from 1855 to 1991.

The term 'unified civil service' in this British context refers to recruitment in accordance with specified principles and procedures (usually by a central department responsible for recruitment); to a service with allegiance to the monarch as head of state, not to a partisan government; to work in a democratic context, involving accountability to the elected government within a parliamentary framework; and consequently to an ethos or ethic characterised by an emphasis on public service.

The Civil Service Commission – a central department for recruitment

Before 1855 the usual method of appointment to the civil service was, as William Robson put it in 1922, 'by patronage, unchecked and uncontrolled; and as a result corruption and inefficiency were rampant'.[2] The details of the Northcote–Trevelyan Report, intended to rectify this condition, have been explained in chapter 2. The report recommended recruitment by open competition, accompanied by tests of age, health and character, together with reform to distinguish between routine and intellectual work. The Commissioners appointed to ensure that these qualities were properly assessed began mainly to test by limited competitions candidates nominated by the heads of the various departments. Some departments, however, quickly chose to recruit by open competition; open competition became the norm from 1870; and the issue of a certificate of competency gave the Civil Service Commissioners recognition of their importance because the Superannuation Act of 1859 made this certification from the Commissioners a condition for receiving a pension. Although certificates were issued to departments, not to the individuals examined, certification became the major element for initiating officials into what became the unified civil service. Moreover, pensions were non-contributory, given by grace, and entitlements were not transferable to employment outside the civil service; nor could they be claimed by individuals who left before the completion of their service; therefore certificated civil servants could not leave without losing valuable benefits of a sort that were not often available elsewhere.

Although from the early days of the Commission recruitment was often to individual positions in particular departments, these posts were, to an increasing extent, grouped into classes for convenience of recruitment, and the classes were given similar conditions of service and pay structures. These arrangements were generally the responsibility of the Treasury, because they were matters of recruitment policy, but the Commission always worked closely with the Treasury and therefore in practice contributed to developments in the sphere of policy through being responsible for recruitment in practice. The Commission's role in recruitment policy making was limited but it made significant contributions to the unified civil service.

One of the reasons for the Civil Service Commission's particular role in this context was its relations with ministers and the constraints on it and its staff from the political environment in which it worked. The Commissioners had an independent role because they were appointed by Orders in Council; the staff of the department were, however, part of the regular civil service for grading, conditions of service, and potential for transfer elsewhere in the civil service. The independent role of the Commissioners became particularly important from time to time when ministers wished to influence or enquire into decisions of the Commissioners on individual candidates – as is clearly illustrated from the examples given of Lord Palmerston, in chapter 6, and Michael (later Lord) Heseltine in chapter 4.

These, however, were examples of political sensitivity at the highest level and in relation to individual candidates for posts in the civil service. In more general matters of its own departmental policy making and recruitment practice, members of staff at all levels in the Commission were just like any other civil servants. They were constrained by requirements of accountability to ministers even though there was normally no minister in the government specifically designated to answer questions on civil service recruitment: instead such matters were dealt with by the Prime Minister or one of the Treasury ministers. This is well illustrated by the controversy in 1948 concerning Sir Percival Waterfield's speech in Oxford, that led to the debate in the House of Lords: the government was represented by Lord Pakenham who was then Chancellor of the Duchy of Lancaster.

From time to time the importance of the Commission, and the need for a department dedicated to recruitment by fair and open competition, was questioned, but the advantages of maintaining a central department responsible for recruitment were generally accepted. The Interim Report of the Committee appointed to enquire into the Organisation and Staffing of Government Offices is an example of this. It argued in 1918 that considerable waste and inefficiency would result from competition between departments in the recruitment of temporary staff. Applicants to a department where there was no vacancy, it said, could not be expected to go the round of the other departments, and it was natural that they should take up private positions and be lost to government service. The committee also argued that departmental recruitment, combined with different rates of pay, led to employees of one department being attracted away to similar posts in other departments. In addition, when there was a shortage of qualified candidates, the co-ordination of recruitment in the hands of a single independent authority became more necessary. The committee concluded that 'whatever the advantages which direct recruitment may have for individual departments, the disadvantages from the point of view of the Service as a whole clearly outweigh them'.[3] This helped strengthen the position of the Commission after the First World War.

The alternative view prevailed after the Second World War, and from that time there was increasing devolution of recruitment to individual departments, especially in the regions away from London. These views concerning devolution should not, however, be considered in isolation from other factors relevant to the ethos of the civil service. In the nineteenth century and the first half of the twentieth century civil servants were encouraged to put the interests of the department before, or at least give equivalent standing to, their own – an example of this is outlined in chapter 5, where the Foreign Office said that a quality to be required in its staff was that 'they should take such an interest in the Office as to consider its credit and reputation as their own'.[4]

The attitude towards the ideal of public service generally changed after the Second World War and by the late 1970s R.W.L. Wilding, then in charge of the Management Group in the Civil Service Department, put his view of the professional ethic of the administrator quite differently. He said it was necessary to distinguish energy from commitment: 'It is absolutely necessary to pursue today's policy with energy; it is almost equally necessary, in order to survive, to withhold from it the last ounce of commitment.'[5]

In the light of such a statement – understandable, perhaps, in the context of changes in the elected government – it may not be surprising that some ministers, both Labour and Conservative, increasingly felt the need for specialist advisers on a recognised and at least quasi-permanent basis. Such advisers were chosen because they were unrestrained in their commitment to ministers. It is similarly not surprising that politicians of all persuasions should have supported the creation of agencies to deliver government policies, with managers 'prepared to show real qualities of leadership'[6] and 'commitment to change'.[7]

In the specific context of the Civil Service Commission, these new approaches to public administration resulted in both institutional and procedural changes: the

Commission became part of the Civil Service Department; the Recruitment and Assessment Services agency was created; and there was increased emphasis on departmental recruitment. It seems unlikely that the unintended consequences of these changes were adequately appreciated before the most significant change of them all was introduced and the Commission, as a department of government, was abolished in 1991. The decision to abolish the Commission was made by ministers without any official or public inquiry into the matter; nevertheless there was no significant public reaction to its demise. Indeed, as far as is publicly known, there has not been any proper study of the consequences of the decision: no comparative study (before and after) into the costs of civil service recruitment; no inquiry into the satisfaction, efficiency and effectiveness of the service provided under the new recruitment arrangements; and no consideration of the implications of the duplication of personnel recruitment services in over 3,000 units of recruitment.

The important decision to create the Recruitment and Assessment Services agency from the Commission was a consequence of the then government's policy to create agencies. As a result of that policy officials increasingly thought of themselves not as belonging to a unified civil service but as belonging to particular departments or agencies. Sir Peter Kemp told the Treasury and Civil Service Select Committee in 1991 that agency staff 'do not feel they are in the Civil Service, they are working in this Agency'.[8] The unified civil service was being undermined.

The emphasis behind the creation of agencies was to achieve better value for money and to develop steadily improving services. It was part of the Conservative government's general approach to make government more efficient, according to an ideology which regarded business values, and business methods, as the most productive and preferred ideology. This approach, championed by Margaret (later Baroness) Thatcher, was continued by her successor as Prime Minister, John Major, who referred in his Citizen's Charter to next steps agencies as 'part of the drive towards more businesslike and decentralised delivery of services'.[9] That there was little opposition in Parliament or elsewhere to this approach may have been at least partly because the proposals for the creation of agencies was along similar lines to the proposals for accountable management and 'hiving off' in the Fulton Report – proposals which had been accepted by the then Labour government.

The important part played by the Civil Service Commission in creating a unified civil service cannot be doubted: there is plenty of evidence in the earlier chapters of this book. Sir Robin (now Lord) Butler, when Head of the Civil Service, was confident in 1989 that 'a unified but not a uniform' civil service had been retained.[10] Some may still argue that the civil service is unified, because the higher civil service appears to be unified and broad principles of public service are still expected, but it is a view difficult to sustain in view of the demise of the Civil Service Commission, the devolution of pay and conditions of service, the introduction of performance-related pay and the continuous and increasing emphasis on business-like methods (assumed to be superior in the private sector) for dealing with customers rather than citizens. People who still regard the civil service as unified, or hope that it is, stress that there are distinctive codes and procedures, loyalty, impartiality, fair and open competition in recruitment and promotion on the basis of performance and merit.[11] It is, however, very difficult to argue that a unified service still exists if the staff do not believe they belong to one. This history of the Civil Service Commission shows the importance of a common admissions experience as a contribution to that ethos and feeling of belonging.

In the early years of the twenty-first century there have been signs of a new interest in the importance of a unified public service. Jocelyne Bourgon, President of the Canadian Centre for Management Development, argued the case strongly at the 2002 Biennial Conference of the Commonwealth Association for Public Administration and Management. Two of the characteristics of a unified public service mentioned by her were 'a *political leadership* willing to state the importance of political process, government and public sector institutions' and 'a *strong sense of public sector values*, acquired over time, and the importance of serving the collective interest and the public good, which guide the actions of public servants at all levels'. Her conclusion was that a unified public service was not a sufficient condition but '*a necessary condition for good government*'. She asked herself the question 'Does it matter?' and replied 'I should say so!'[12] It may be that some of the lessons from Commonwealth experience and practice are now worth reconsidering for the United Kingdom. At the very least there should be a review of civil service recruitment practice to ensure that it is consistent with the expectations of a civil service in the twenty-first century. Much was achieved by piecemeal adaptations in the twentieth century: but there have been changes in the institutions of government, their ways of working and the expectations and attitudes in the social and political environment.

Recruitment: examinations and competitions

The Civil Service Commission made its mark in civil service recruitment by being one of the first government departments anywhere in modern times to have a major impact on civil service personnel management. It did this by energetically developing new examinations and methods of assessment for an exceedingly large and varied number of positions in public service. Although its procedures for the recruitment of graduates often attracted public attention it should not be forgotten that the number of candidates it assessed was enormous and the variety of its examinations was very considerable. It should also be remembered that it examined for the Royal Military Academy at Woolwich, the Royal Military College at Sandhurst, the Royal Air Force College and for a large number of other governments and agencies, including the India and Ceylonese Police Forces, the Ceylon Civil Service and the Gibraltar Civil Service. In 1947 it received 909,878 letters and despatched 1,193,812.[13]

Some of the achievements for which the Commission was admired were very significant in the modern context (the development of the Method II system of selection is an outstanding example) but others of its procedures were practised in ancient times in other civilisations. Wolfgang Franke,[14] and others referred to by him, showed that the origins of regular civil service examinations in China can be traced back to the Han dynasty (210 BC–AD 8), and manifested the Confucian attitude that moral qualities and not technical abilities were decisive criteria for official appointments. Later, the supplying of candidates for recommendation and examination (that is, what in the modern British context was termed nomination for examination) became the privilege of certain influential families. Some of the procedures applying in ancient times were, in practice, lost until re-invented: for example, candidates were known by numbers so that examiners did not know whose paper they read, and, to further prevent identification by handwriting, papers had to be copied by special copyists and only the copies were seen by the examiners. Nevertheless there were weaknesses in the system because only someone who had grown up in the scholarly tradition could hope to compete successfully: consequently a family or clan background was important for success. From the eleventh-century to the nineteenth-century thousands of candidates in China were competitively examined at any one time and bonds developed, linking together cohorts of candidates who passed the examinations. The Chinese examination system attracted admiration in Europe and, perhaps because of the emphasis on classical studies in nineteenth-century British education, Chinese experience influenced the development of the examination systems in Britain and India.[15] Not everything that was regarded as a credit to the Civil Service Commission was therefore as new as was sometimes thought; and sometimes weaknesses observed in the ancient world reappeared in somewhat different guises. It therefore seems that allegations of 'bias' in selection and the advantages of privilege arise in the experience of different examination systems at different times. Such allegations may not matter in business management contexts but they can be of major importance in the public sector. How they are resolved can also be of some importance.

One aid to resolving these problems is to focus on the system of examinations and assessment. This was certainly done by Edgar Anstey and his colleagues in the Commission, who were concerned with research in the period after the Second World War. Earlier experience should not be disregarded because, as mentioned in chapter 3, new methods of assessment after the First World War included the use of intelligence and other tests developed mainly by occupational psychologists. Nevertheless the experience of the 1940s seems more relevant to the present discussion. The point here is that before criteria necessary for a job are agreed (to form the basis for a procedure for recruitment) it is necessary to analyse what the job entails. It may also be an advantage to study employees who are apparently doing the job well, to consider how their qualifications and attributes are relevant for a profile for selection.

While this procedure may appear to be a matter of common sense, it also brings with it potential dangers. Intelligence tests may or may not measure what people believe to be intelligence: much depends on definitions, and the tests may simply measure what intelligence tests can measure (which may, nevertheless, be relevant and useful). Similarly, one of the difficulties with job analysis is that it places a premium on current experience: the qualities of individuals in post at the time of job analysis may become the basis for further selection, without radical re-consideration of what the job requires. It is then easy to perpetuate not only personal qualities and educational requirements but also non-essential social or cultural characteristics. It should therefore be no surprise that there are concerns about favouring certain types of candidate: bias is not just a preference for candidates with one type of education or syllabus; it may also be a preference for 'our kind of people' (with similar social skills, contacts, expectations and assumptions). This is not necessarily a matter of wilfully favouring particular individuals or groups – those involved in such selection may have been doing their best to be fair to candidates and have had at heart the best interests of, say, the civil service. Nevertheless, the lesson emerges that what may be unquestionable at one time or in one place, and in the context of particular standards or environments, may be quite different or challengeable in other contexts.

There is plenty of evidence in earlier chapters to show how this happened; it illustrates aspects of the administrative culture, and this administrative culture is particularly apparent in the official attitudes towards academics, especially social scientists. Observers from other countries (academics, journalists or whoever) sometimes express surprise at the absence of co-operation between scholars in the social sciences and practitioners in British government. In some areas, involving technical expertise, there is good co-operation, leading to constructive, mutually beneficial results, but these beneficial consequences are much less common in more generalist areas. Examples in earlier chapters illustrate this well – including the official attitudes towards the work of William A. Robson (chapter 8), Edwin Bock (chapter 10), Peta Rickerd (chapter 10) and some of the comments by Waterfield (reported in various chapters). There are complex reasons for this, including the strong background of higher civil servants educated at Oxford and Cambridge universities, where they studied history or classics but very little political science, public administration or sociology. For such senior officials, who often demonstrated personal attributes of confidence and superiority, it was easy to make light of the jargon of newer academic disciplines and to draw attention to the apparent lack of relevance in work that was intended to assist in the practice of government. It is also easy to make disparaging comments about research that may have a long time scale, where results are presented long after the problems it was intended to address have ceased to be pressing or fashionable. It is therefore not surprising that in 1969 Sir William Armstrong, when Head of the Civil Service, could say that he did not know of any case of a teacher or student of public administration being asked to advise on a question of administration, of administrative processes or of administrative organisation in this country.[16]

Partly, this may be because it is not easy for such academics to access official information – they may work on what they can get and then concentrate on asking questions that they think are important. Asking such questions can be valuable, but it can also be easily derided if the questions indicate a lack of complete command of the information or issues. This was, for example, sometimes the case when academics raised questions about allegations of bias in selection – and it was easy for Waterfield to be genuinely shocked by the attitude revealed by Sir John Stopford (see chapter 11). Nevertheless it should be remembered, to Waterfield's credit, that he did look into the questions raised and took action he deemed relevant. In that incident it may not have been an issue of alleging lack of integrity but of different types of experience and integrity being out of harmony. The contrast in a comparative perspective was perceptively put by C.H. Sisson when he said that the British administrator travelling abroad is shocked to discover that many countries are administered by men who read books about public administration.[17]

One example of a civil servant in the Treasury who was seconded specifically to consider this sort of question was Peter V. Dixon. Dixon was a not untypical administrative class civil servant: educated at Radley College, then King's College, Cambridge, where he read classics and law. He became an assistant principal in the Treasury in 1955 and was seconded to the Civil Service Selection Board 1964–65. In 1965 (and perhaps on other occasions as well) he spoke about careers in the civil service to pupils at Marlborough College.[18] In 1969 Dixon wrote an important and perceptive paper on 'The Civil Service as a Profession', in which he drew attention to a number of ethical problems.[19] He said that the Fulton Report was largely based on the assumptions that the abuses which led to the nineteenth-century reforms were no longer with us. He argued that it was 'quite wrong to suppose that because one set of moral issues is largely behind us (which one hopes to be true), that the Civil Service is free of ethical problems today. The dilemmas to be found are often considerable'. He then listed eleven examples of ethical problems that could face a professional civil servant. Courage and honesty seemed to emerge as virtues relevant to dealing with the issues he outlined – but he noted that neither of them were qualities listed on personal assessment forms. These, however, are not measurable and not normally regarded as relevant in civil service selection. The issues raised by Dixon do not seem to have received much attention at the time or since: they are, however, very relevant to the recruitment of individuals expected to rise to the most senior posts in the civil service and to the continuing assessment of individuals. These issues were therefore central to an important and sometimes controversial part of the work of the Civil Service Commission. In the twenty-first century one wonders what Dixon would have made of advertisements for civil service posts (such as Leasing Adviser in the Inland Revenue) that draw attention to the advantage of experience gained in civil service work for subsequent careers in the private sector.[20] One also wonders how he would have reacted to the revelations in 2003 about recruitment consultants acting on behalf of departments. It was found that out of 30 departments of government using recruitment consultants, only 11 departments provided them with the job specification, only five with the person specification/attributes, only four with details about the body and only three about the service levels expected.[21] Because Dixon was concerned with ethical problems and the accountability of the civil service, reference to his paper may be used as an introduction to some of the wider perspectives of accountability, as they emerge from this study of the Civil Service Commission.

Perspectives of accountability: the social and political environment

The history of the Civil Service Commission is, in some senses, a history of increasingly specific but increasingly narrow interpretations and practice of accountability. Originally the Commission was created to eliminate the defects of recruitment to the civil service by patronage, but it should be remembered that the intentions of patrons were not necessarily and wholly bad. Indeed, for some senior politicians, patronage was a time-consuming duty that they carried out conscientiously. Patronage was part of political activity: this is seen, for example, in the Gladstone papers in the British Library and the Palmerston papers in the Hartley Library. In general, patrons in the early and mid nineteenth century were looking after their own interests, widely interpreted, when making nominations, and they were unlikely to knowingly nominate individuals who they thought would be unsuitable or who would bring them discredit. The essential difference between patronage and open competition was that patrons did not have the interests of the state or the public interest uppermost when making their nominations. In similar vein, more than a century later, it might be revealing to examine the modern use of patronage in the appointment of the numerous special advisers in government.

Another aspect of civil service recruitment requiring more detailed examination in the twenty-first century is delegation. It could be argued that widespread delegation of recruitment to a very large number of recruitment units has encouraged the appointment of people who may have the abilities necessary for a particular job, but not necessarily (if at all) the appointment of people whose qualities inspired confidence for a successful long-term career. The overall purpose of the appointment procedure changed during the time of the Commission. In the second half of the twentieth century individuals were thinking less of spending their working lives with one employer; consequently some of the qualities being sought in selection were different: the nature of the civil service was different. Seen in this way, it is possible to agree with Sir Andrew Turnbull, the present Head of the Civil Service, that in the twenty-first century there is still a permanent civil service but there are no longer permanent civil servants.[22]

The history of the Commission is, to a large extent, a history of the sensitivity of a department of government to the social and political environment in which it operated. During this period there was continual change in that environment, but one of its characteristics, more apparent at some times than at others, was the scrutiny by individual elected representatives and the institutions through which they worked. In the British system of government, from time to time these individuals and institutions make themselves felt in public and in private. Public occasions became well known – such as the 1948 debate in the House of Lords, or the requirement to give evidence to commissions and committees of inquiry (examples include the Reports from the Select Committees on Estimates in 1948[23] and 1965,[24] and the committee chaired by J.G.W. Davies which inquired into the Method II system of selection for the administrative class).[25] The day-to-day impact of the political environment and the significance of accountability in this context has, however, been much more complex and comprehensive than at first appears. A minor incident leading, for example, to a parliamentary question may have a long-lasting effect on all aspects of the work of an official and will condition his or her everyday work for the rest of his or her civil service career. Accountability in this context therefore influences all aspects of public sector management: it is not simply a matter of a rare occasion leading to a ministerial resignation. Accountability in the British system of government is an essential element of democracy, but it may also be the cause of bureaucratic procedures and attitudes of mind: accountability in business can be quite different, representing other interests and can be observed through different manifestations.

As has already been explained, the Civil Service Commissioners were appointed by Order in Council and therefore were independent of civil service terms and conditions of service. In the last resort they were accountable to the head of state and this gave them strength when dealing with ministers in matters of questionable propriety. In other respects they were accountable to the Public Accounts Committee for matters of public expenditure. For most of the Commission's life the department was also accountable to the Treasury because the Commission was one of its subordinate departments. In its quasi-judicial work, involving recruitment on a basis of fairness, equality and open competition, and work culminating in certification, it had to adhere to legal principles. In more modern usage of the concept of accountability the Commission demonstrated its special relationship to candidates, educational institutions and other departments of government.

The complexity of accountability relationships and the work arising from this experience are illustrated by the administrative culture, not only within the Commission but also more generally in the civil service. This is seen, for example, in the links the Commissioners had with educational institutions. Sir Laurence Helsby and others recognised that the advantages of a public school education included the acquisition of self-confidence – a self-confidence that became a particular asset in the Method II system of selection and that could also be observed in successful senior civil servants. The Commission had numerous links with public schools and universities and some of these were explored in chapter 11. In 1884 Theodore Walrond, for example, became a governor of Rugby School, where he had been a pupil and a master.[26] Waterfield cultivated Westminster (where he had been a pupil).[27] It was known that some schools were particularly well represented at senior levels and in particular departments (for example, Foreign Office schools were Eton, Winchester, Rugby, Harrow and Marlborough).[28] The Commission kept in touch with all these educational institutions, mainly because they had provided good candidates in the past and could be expected to provide similarly good candidates in future, if they were encouraged to do so. The representation of individuals with such backgrounds was sometimes regarded as a healthy feature in the educational world of competition between institutions. When S.M. (later Sir Stanley) Leathes was appointed Secretary to the Commission in 1907 he wrote that he was very glad that Cambridge was to have its proper place on the Commission (and Lord Francis Hervey shared his feelings).[29] In 1964 Sir George Abell, who had been a pupil at Marlborough, was concerned that fewer successful candidates for the administrative class and foreign service were coming from the 'leading schools' which had provided successes in the past. He wrote: 'Cheltenham, of which I am Governor, has had no candidate of any kind for either competition in the last five years.'[30]

These relationships were important not only because they were part of the administrative culture but also because they were part of the accountability relationships: and the Commission sometimes saw particular schools and universities as customers in a business relationship. In the context of the Commission, however, these attitudes and experiences seem, strangely, to have existed alongside surprise about expressed criticism of bias in recruitment. As the 1985 Annual Report put it: 'until more non-Oxbridge candidates apply and are successful, there is little chance of correcting the self-fulfilling myth that our procedures are biased in favour of Oxbridge'.[31] As with a biography of a person, the story of an important institution in government may include anomalies and contradictions. This may be a natural phenomenon, and it may not be unhealthy, but it may also mirror a phenomenon in British society worth further consideration.

Bureau biography

The initial expectations of a bureau biography are that it is the life story of a living being, based on office records. Usually a biography is of an individual, and biographies endeavour to present as complete a picture as possible: consequently evidence is gathered together from wherever it may be found. In the case of an individual this evidence often includes family documents and recollections, but usually a person worth writing about has a record of achievements outside the family, often through work, and often of a national or international standing. It is the work or leisure achievements that provide the momentum or challenge to the writer of a biography. In the case of many of the best biographies the enthusiasm or admiration of the writer is evident to the reader, even when a character is not totally unblemished and the blemishes have to be recorded to provide as complete a picture as possible. Indeed, there must always be some sort of impetus motivating a successful biography. In the case of outstanding civil servants in the British system of government most of the raw material for study is in the files because the files on which civil servants work are public records and there is usually very little other evidence available. There are various reasons for this but mainly they revolve around the anonymity and political accountability of officials, and the limited scope (particularly the limited leisure time outside work) that they have for other major activities.

Biographies, however, are not exclusively about individuals. Just as the evidence in the files can sometimes provide enough resources for the biography of an individual, so can the files provide material for the biography of a government department. This is illustrated by the opening sentence of the history of the Civil Service Commission of Canada which begins: 'This is the story of an Act, the people who created and changed it, the organisation vested with responsibility for administering it, and the evolution of procedures designed to implement the objectives adumbrated in the Act.'[32] As with the biography of an individual, all available resources are used to provide as complete a picture as possible. These resources include legislation, publications of the department including annual reports and the various writings about cases, procedures and work programmes but, most important of all, the official papers which are often the best source for understanding the life of the institution.

The biographer of a public institution may have certain advantages over the biographer of a private institution. The work of a government department has to be based on the files, the official records, because of the requirements for political accountability. The twin pillars of the British system of government, as A.V. Dicey explained in the nineteenth century, are parliamentary sovereignty and the supremacy of the rule of law. Parliamentary sovereignty means that the supreme power in the community is vested in Parliament: officials are ultimately accountable to ministers, ministers are accountable to Parliament and Parliament is accountable to the people. To ensure that such accountability is effective (though there are always cases that prove the point) records are kept more meticulously than they need to be kept in private organisations. There is therefore often more time and effort spent on making and keeping records than would be necessary in the private sector. Also there has to be continuous sensitivity, by everyone who works in a government department, towards the political environment within which department activities take place. As far as the rule of law is concerned, the firm base for all government activities is legislation – departments do what Acts of Parliament require and their activities are constrained by the powers specifically vested in them. This is a significant difference between public sector management and business management.

Furthermore, public records tend to be more meticulously kept than records elsewhere because in a democracy the people have some entitlement to know what is done (and how it is done) in their name. This does not mean that all records are kept for ever. As explained in chapter 1, only a very small proportion (about 1 per cent) of records are preserved and there are constraints on access to them. Nevertheless the general principle applies: public records are kept not only for efficient administration but also for reasons of accountability. In addition, these reasons of accountability contribute to the administrative culture, and an appreciation of the culture of an organisation is at least as important for understanding how the organisation actually works as appreciating its constitution, legal requirements or terms of reference.

All these elements contribute to understanding how a government department works and to assessing its importance. In the case of the Civil Service Commission they are particularly important because there are fewer constraints on access to its records than would apply in other departments. Its annual reports (and the files on them) provide a great deal of basic information; very little is affected by the rules for extended closure; and in any case the Commission, as a department of government, ceased in 1991.

Practical constraints on public administration research and writing are also less burdensome than they previously were. At their most extreme these constraints were illustrated by official attitudes towards the Whitehall Series and the New Whitehall Series of books on government departments, as outlined in chapter 1; the continuation of some of these attitudes is also illustrated by official attitudes to the work of social scientists (see chapters 9 and 10). Attitudes towards the social sciences, in British society generally, but especially within the official bureaucracy, have become more relaxed in recent years. Making official files available after 30 years instead of after 50 years has helped, and in some areas of work files have been made available after less than 30 years.

The Civil Service Commission, it should again be stressed, was important for developing a unified civil service and creating respected standards and procedures for recruitment. It was much more than a subordinate operational or technical department. It may have lived mainly in the ambit of the Treasury, and been accountable usually through Treasury ministers, and for practical purposes it may have been a 'central agency'[33] providing services within government, but it was also in some respects independent, and without doubt it had a personality of its own. Indeed, during its lifetime it was a bulwark of liberal democracy. When the Recruitment and Assessment Services agency was sold Lord Beloff, in the House of Lords, referred to the sale as 'a major constitutional issue'. He added 'to privatise this core element of government is like privatising the Grenadier Guards'.[34]

This bureau biography of the Civil Service Commission is both a record of a very significant department in British administrative history and a contribution to the much wider understanding of how public administration actually works. Unlike books in the Whitehall Series and the New Whitehall Series, which were written by serving or former civil servants, there have been no constraints on this author to avoid anything controversial. Indeed, matters of controversy are shown to have been valuable because records of them are more detailed and more revealing than matters of routine, but they must be seen in their context, their significance has to be interpreted cautiously and they must be assessed against the mass of uncontroversial routine work that is carried out efficiently and without attracting public attention. Without proper accounts of what actually happened in public administration, including indications of what was thought important (and why) at the time, and as far as possible with evaluations from as independent a perspective as possible, it is neither easy nor consistent with the expectations of the highest standards of social science research to reach conclusions that will advance the study of public administration. The intention in writing this book has been to contribute to advancing that study. Its insights from the past may, however, also be relevant to current and future policy not only on staff recruitment, but also on wider issues of public administration practice.

Notes

1 *Report on the Organisation of the Permanent Civil Service, presented to Parliament February 1854* (Northcote–Trevelyan Report) (London: HMSO, 1854), 'Summary of our recommendations'.
2 William A. Robson, *From Patronage to Proficiency – the Public Service* (London: The Fabian Society, 1922), p. 7.
3 *Interim Report of the Committee appointed to enquire into the Organisation and Staffing of Government Offices*, Cd. 9074 (London: HMSO, 1918), para. 6.
4 PRO/CSC5/155, Hammond to Mann, 25 June 1855. See also chapter 5.
5 R.W.L. Wilding, 'The Professional Ethic of the Administrator', *Management Services in Government*, 34(4), 1979, 184.
6 Efficiency Unit, *Improving Management in Government: The Next Steps, Report to the Prime Minister* (Ibbs Report) (London: HMSO, 1988), para. 35.
7 Ibid., para. 15.
8 *Treasury and Civil Service Committee, Seventh Report, Session 1990–91, The Next Steps Initiative*, HC 496 (London: HMSO, 1991), Q. 326.
9 *The Citizen's Charter: Raising the Standard*, Cm. 1599 (London: HMSO, 1991), p. 36.
10 *Treasury and Civil Service Committee, Fifth Report, Session 1988–89, Developments in the Next Steps Programme*, HC 348 (London: HMSO, 1989), Q. 320.
11 *Treasury and Civil Service Committee, Seventh Report, Session 1990–91*, Q. 343 (Evidence of Sir Angus Fraser).
12 Hon Jocelyne Bourgon, 'A Unified Public Service: Does it Matter?', Speech to the CAPAM Biennial Conference 2002, *Commonwealth Innovations*, 9(1), 2003 (Toronto: CAPAM, 2003).
13 PRO/CSC5/521.
14 Wolfgang Franke, *The Reform and Abolition of the Traditional Chinese Examination System* (Cambridge, MA: Harvard University Press, 1963). See also E.N. Gladden, *A History of Public Administration, vol. 1, From the Earliest Times to the Eleventh Century* (London: Frank Cass, 1972).
15 Franke, *The Reform and Abolition*, Ch. 1.
16 Sir William Armstrong, 'The Tasks of the Conference', *PAC Bulletin*, No. 6 (May 1969), p. 2.
17 C.H. Sisson, *The Spirit of British Administration* (London: Faber, Second edn. 1966), p. 28.
18 PRO/CSC5/1238.
19 PRO/BA19/22.
20 See advertisement in the *Financial Times*, 8 May 2003.
21 *OCPA Review on working with Recruitment Consultants in the Public Appointments Process, Stage 2: Report* (London: Office of the Commissioner for Public Appointments, 2003).
22 BBC Radio 4, *Today*, 5 May 2002 and *The Times*, 1 May 2002.
23 *Ninth Report from the Select-Committee on Estimates, Session 1947–48, The Civil Service Commission*, HC 203, 205 (London: HMSO, 1948).
24 *Sixth Report from the Estimates Committee, Session 1964–65, Recruitment to the Civil Service*, HC 308 (London: HMSO, 1965).
25 *The Method II System of Selection (for the Administrative Class of the Home Civil Service), Report of the Committee of Inquiry, 1969*, Chairman Mr. J.G.W. Davies (Davies Report), Cmnd. 4156 (London: HMSO, 1969).

26 John Curgenven, 'Theodore Walrond: Friend of Arnold and Clough', *Durham University Journal*, 44, 1951–52, 56–61.
27 PRO/CSC5/475.
28 PRO/CSC5/475.
29 Cambridge University Library, Add. MS. c. 36,24.
30 PRO/CSC5/1238, First Commissioner to Secretary, 14 August 1964.
31 *Civil Service Commission, Annual Report, 1985* (Basingstoke: Civil Service Commission, 1986) p. 12.
32 J.E. Hodgetts, William McCloskey, Reginald Walker, and V. Seymour Wilson, *The Biography of an Institution: The Civil Service Commission of Canada 1908–67* (Montreal: McGill – Queens University Press, 1972) p. ix.
33 Colin Campbell, *Governments Under Stress: Political Executives and Key Bureaucrats in Washington, London and Ottawa* (Toronto: University of Toronto Press, 1983).
34 HL Deb., 6s., vol. 574, cols. 1557–60 (25 July 1996).

APPENDIX
Civil Service Commissioners 1855–1991

This list of Civil Service Commissioners continues up to 1991 the list published (up to 1979) in the book by K.M. Reader. The source for the appointments after 1979 is the Annual Reports of the Civil Service Commissioners. After the Civil Service Commission was abolished as a department in 1991 the Office of the Civil Service Commissioners continued some of the duties previously the responsibility of the department, but in recent years the number of part-time Commissioners has expanded greatly: in 2003, for example, there were 14.

The office of First Commissioner was created in 1862, and from then on the name of the First Commissioner is given first. An asterisk indicates a part-time Commissioner.

Date of relevant Order in Council

21 May 1855	Rt Hon Sir Edward Ryan J.G. Shaw Lefevre CB Edward Romilly
26 April 1862	Rt Hon Sir Edward Ryan Sir Edward Walker Head KCB Hon Edward Turner Boyd Twistleton
5 February 1870	Rt Hon Sir Edward Ryan George Webbe Dasent
10 December 1875	John Somerset, Baron Hampton GCB George Webbe Dasent Theodore Walrond
28 June 1880	George Henry Charles, Baron Strafford (Viscount Enfield) Sir George Webbe Dasent Theodore Walrond
15 September 1887	George Henry Charles, Earl of Strafford Sir George Webbe Dasent William John Courthope
18 August 1892	William John Courthope Lord Francis Hervey
12 August 1907	Lord Francis Hervey Stanley Leathes
10 January 1910	Stanley Leathes H.W. Paul

APPENDIX

5 February 1918	Sir Stanley Leathes David Beveridge Mair (Director of Examinations) Lawrence Courtney Hamilton Weekes (Secretary)
20 December 1927	R.S. Meiklejohn David Beveridge Mair (Director of Examinations) Lawrence Courtney Hamilton Weekes (Secretary)
16 March 1933	Sir R.S. Meiklejohn R. Blaikie (Director of Examinations) G.G. Mennell (Secretary)
9 March 1939	A.P. Waterfield CB G.G. Mennell (Secretary) C.G. Nelson (Director of Examinations)
18 April 1946	Sir A.P. Waterfield CB W.P. Barrett (Secretary) F. Milner (Director of Examinations) Dr C.P. Snow (Scientific) Col J.R. Pinsent DSO (Civil Service Selection Board)
25 July 1947	Sir A.P. Waterfield CB F. Milner (Director of Examinations) A.H.M. Hillis (Secretary) Dr C.P. Snow (Scientific) Col J.R. Pinsent DSO (CSSB) Major A.T. Sumner MC (Engineering)
13 September 1948	Sir A.P. Waterfield CB A.H.M. Hillis (Secretary) F. Milner (Director of Examinations) Dr C.P. Snow CBE (Scientific) Col J.R. Pinsent DSO (CSSB) Major A.T. Sumner MC (Engineering) Sir Austin Earle CB CBE
4 March 1949	Sir A.P. Waterfield CB A.H.M. Hillis (Secretary) C.J. Hayes (Director of Examinations) Dr C.P. Snow CBE (Scientific) Col J.R. Pinsent DSO (CSSB) Major A.T. Sumner MC (Engineering)
28 April 1951	A.P. Sinker CB W.H. Fisher (Secretary) C.J. Hayes (Director of Examinations) Dr C.P. Snow CBE (Scientific) Major A.T. Sumner (Engineering) J.H.T. Goldsmith (CSSB)
3 June 1954	L.N. Helsby CB W.H. Fisher (Secretary) J.H.T. Goldsmith (CSSB) C.J. Hayes (Director of Examinations) Dr C.P. Snow CBE (Scientific) Major A.T. Sumner MC (Engineering)

APPENDIX

29 July 1955 Sir L.N. Helsby CB
W.H. Fisher (Secretary)
J.H.T. Goldsmith (CSSB)
C.J. Hayes (Director of Examinations)
Dr C.P. Snow CBE (Scientific)
P.H.L. Thomas (Engineering)

3 August 1956 Sir L.N. Helsby KBE CB
J.H.T. Goldsmith (CSSB)
C.J. Hayes (Secretary and Director
  of Examinations)
Dr C.P. Snow CBE (Scientific)
P.H.L. Thomas (Engineering)

13 December 1957 Sir L.N. Helsby KBE CB
J.H.T. Goldsmith (CSSB)
Dr H.A. Needham (Director of Examinations)
D. O'Donovan (Secretary)
Sir C.P. Snow CBE (Scientific)
P.H.L. Thomas (Engineering)

28 July 1959 Sir G. Mallaby KCMG OBE
J.H.T. Goldsmith CBE (CSSB)
Dr H.A. Needham (Director of Examinations)
D. O'Donovan (Secretary)
Sir C.P. Snow CBE (Scientific)
P.H.L. Thomas (Engineering)

20 November 1959 Sir G. Mallaby KCMG OBE
Sir F. Brundrett KCB KBE (Scientific)
J.H.T. Goldsmith CBE (CSSB)
Dr H.A. Needham (Director of Examinations)
D. O'Donovan (Secretary)
P.H.L. Thomas (Engineering)

23 July 1962 Sir G. Mallaby KCMG OBE
Sir F. Brundrett KCB KBE (Scientific and Engineering
  Adviser)
J.H.T. Goldsmith CBE (CSSB)
Dr H.A. Needham CBE (Director of Examinations)
J.C. Seddon (Secretary)

28 February 1964 Sir G. Mallaby KCMG OBE
Sir F. Brundrett KCB KBE (Scientific and Engineering
  Adviser)
Dr H.A. Needham CBE (Director of Examinations)
J.C. Seddon (Secretary)

27 May 1965 Sir G. Abell KCIE OBE
Sir F. Brundrett KCB KBE (Scientific and Engineering
  Adviser)
J.C. Seddon (Secretary)
K.A.G. Murray (CSSB)
K.M. Reader (Director of Examinations)

APPENDIX

10 October 1967	J.J.B. Hunt J.C. Seddon (Secretary) K.A.G. Murray (CSSB) K.M. Reader (Director of Examinations)
(12 April 1967)	Sir C. Cawley CBE (Scientific and Engineering Adviser)
6 May 1969	J.J.B. Hunt CB
(26 August 1968)	S.W.C. Phillips CB (Second Commissioner) J.C. Seddon CBE (Secretary) K.A.G. Murray (CSSB) K.M. Reader (Director of Recruitment) Sir C. Cawley CBE (Scientific and Engineering Adviser)
29 April 1970	J.J.B. Hunt CB S.W.C. Phillips CB (Second Commissioner)
(22 October 1969)	Dr F.H. Allen (Scientific and Engineering Adviser) K.A.G. Murray (CSSB) K.M. Reader (Director of Recruitment) J.C. Seddon CBE (Secretary)
25 May 1971	K.H. Clucas CB Dr F.H. Allen CB (Scientific and Engineering Adviser) K.A.G. Murray (CSSB) K.M. Reader *S.W.C. Phillips CB
23 October 1972	K.H. Clucas CB Dr F.H. Allen CB K.A.G. Murray (CSSB) K.M. Reader
7 February 1974	Dr F.H. Allen CB K.M. Reader K.A.G. Murray (CSSB) G.R.R. East
26 February 1975	Dr F.H. Allen CB K.A.G. Murray (CSSB) K.M. Reader G.R.R. East D.G. Daymond
17 January 1977	Dr F.H. Allen CB G.R.R. East *D.G. Daymond (part-time from March 1977) C.E.H. Tuck (CSSB)
21 December 1977	Dr F.H. Allen CB G.R.R. East *D.G. Daymond C.E.H. Tuck (CSSB) S.D. Light

APPENDIX

9 February 1978	Dr F.H. Allen CB C.E.H. Tuck (CSSB) S.D. Light *D.G. Daymond
24 October 1978	Dr F.H. Allen CB *D.G. Daymond C.E.H. Tuck (CSSB) S.D. Light *Miss M.P. Downs
20 December 1978	Dr F.H. Allen CB *D.G. Daymond C.E.H. Tuck (CSSB) S.D. Light *Miss M.P. Downs
19 October 1979	Dr F.H. Allen CB *D.G. Daymond C.E.H. Tuck (CSSB) S.D. Light *Miss M.P. Downs *Mrs M.E. Sunderland
19 December 1979	Dr F.H. Allen CB *D.G. Daymond C.E.H. Tuck (CSSB) *Miss M.P. Downs *Mrs M.E. Sunderland E.J. Morgan
31 July 1981	A.M. Fraser TD C.E.H. Tuck (CSSB) *Miss M.P. Downs *Mrs M.E. Sunderland E.J. Morgan
23 June 1982	A.M. Fraser CB TD C.E.H. Tuck *Mrs M.E. Sunderland E.J. Morgan (CSSB) *N. Johnson
16 March 1983	D.J. Trevelyan CB C.E.H. Tuck E.J. Morgan (CSSB) *N. Johnson *Dr J.S. McFarlane
19 October 1983	D.J. Trevelyan CB E.J. Morgan (CSSB) *N. Johnson *Dr J.S. McFarlane N.B.J. Gurney

APPENDIX

12 February 1986	D.J. Trevelyan CB E.J. Morgan (CSSB) *Dr J.S. McFarlane N.B.J. Gurney *D.P. Hornby
7 April 1987	D.J. Trevelyan CB *D.P. Hornby *Miss D.M. Whittingham
18 May 1987	D.J. Trevelyan CB *D.P. Hornby *Miss D.M. Whittingham J.K. Moore (CSSB)
23 March 1988	D.J. Trevelyan CB J.K. Moore (CSSB) *D.P. Hornby *Miss D.M. Whittingham B. Walmsley
22 June 1988	D.J. Trevelyan CB J.K. Moore (CSSB) *D.P. Hornby *Miss D.M. Whittington B. Walmsley *G.L. Dennis
16 May 1989	J.H. Holroyd J.K. Moore (CSSB) B. Walmsley *G.L. Dennis *Miss D.M. Whittington *D.P. Hornby
24 July 1990	J.H. Holroyd J.K. Moore *Miss D.M. Whittington *G.L. Dennis *Ms U.K. Prashar
5 October 1990	J.K. Holroyd J.K. Moore *G.L. Dennis M.D. Geddes (RAS) *Ms U.K. Prashar
16 October 1991	J.H. Holroyd J.K. Moore *G.L. Dennis M.D. Geddes (RAS) *Ms U.K. Prashar *Mrs J.C. Rubin

BIBLIOGRAPHY

Public records

The main source for this book is the official files and papers in the Public Record Office (now the National Archive). The Civil Service Commission files are the most important, but it is sometimes necessary to refer to related records; these are often files in the Treasury class (especially the establishment files in T1, T162 and T199) but sometimes also the files of other departments. The papers of the Fulton Committee on the Civil Service, for example, are in BA1. These records have provided a great deal of background material for understanding and seeing the context of particular issues.

Within the Civil Service Commission records references in this book are most frequently to the following:

CSC2	Volumes of Correspondence (65 volumes)
CSC3	File Series I (pieces 1–364)
CSC4	Annual Reports of the Commissioners (bound volumes)
CSC5	File Series II (pieces 1–1840)
CSC6	Regulations, rules and memoranda for open and limited competitions
CSC8	Commissioners' Minute Books for the period 1855–1962
CSC10	Examinations, tables of marks and results of competitions
CSC11	Recruitment and Establishment: individual cases
CSC13	War files (relating to 1937–41)

In the endnotes to each chapter references to PRO sources are given as PRO, followed by the class and series number, then the box or file number.

Private papers

The following private collections were also consulted:

Creech Jones papers	Rhodes House Library, Oxford
Gladstone papers	British Library
London County Council records	London Metropolitan Archives
LSE Council records	British Library of Political and Economic Science (LSE)

Palmerston papers — The Hartley Library, University of Southampton
Robson papers — British Library of Political and Economic Science (LSE)
Stanley Leathes papers — Trinity College Library, Cambridge
Trevelyan papers — The Robinson Library, University of Newcastle upon Tyne

Official publications

The most important published source is the Reports of the Civil Service Commissioners. These reports were usually annual but occasionally they covered periods of more than a year, and during the Second World War publication of the report was suspended. Although there are copies of these reports in the Public Record Office (in CSC4, together, generally, with background papers and drafts), the reports are also in major reference libraries such as the British Library of Political and Economic Science (LSE) and the Mitchell Library, Glasgow.

In addition to the Reports of the Civil Service Commissioners there are publications arising from royal commissions and committees of inquiry. Most of these are Command papers but submissions to the commissions and committees have often been published independently – often with the intention of raising public awareness on particular issues or matters of concern. Together with the reports of commissions and committees there are often published submissions from departments of government and minutes of evidence taken from witnesses representing government departments, or other witnesses with specialist experience relevant to the inquiry. The MacDonnell Royal Commission on the Civil Service (1912–14) was probably the most generous in the quantity of oral and written evidence it published.

Another major source is the papers published by the House of Commons and the House of Lords. These include the reports of debates in both Houses (HC Deb and HL Deb) and the reports of parliamentary committees (together with minutes of written and oral evidence received from various sources).

The most significant official publications, in date order, are:

Reports of Committees of Inquiry into Public Offices and Papers Connected Therewith (London: HMSO, 1854.
Report on the Organisation of the Permanent Civil Service (Northcote–Trevelyan Report) (London: HMSO, 1854).
The Indian Civil Service, Report to the Right Hon Sir Charles Wood by T.B. Macaulay and others (Macaulay Report) (London: W. Thacker and Co, 1955).
Second Report of the Royal Commission to inquire into the Civil Establishments of the different Offices of State at Home and Abroad, with Minutes of Evidence, Appendices etc. (Ridley Report), C. 5545 (London: HMSO, 1888).
Appendix to the First Report of the *Royal Commission on the Civil Service, Minutes of Evidence* (MacDonnell Commission), Cd. 6210 (London: HMSO, 1912).
Appendix to the Third Report of the *Royal Commission on the Civil Service, Minutes of Evidence* (MacDonnell Commission), Cd. 6740 (London: HMSO, 1913).
Royal Commission on the Civil Service: Fourth Report of the Commissioners (MacDonnell Report), Cd. 7338 (London: HMSO, 1914).

BIBLIOGRAPHY

Report of the Committee appointed by the Lords Commissioners of HM Treasury to consider and report upon the scheme of examination for Class I of the Civil Service (Leathes Report), Cd. 8657 (London: HMSO, 1917).

Interim Report of the Committee appointed to enquire into the Organisation and Staffing of Government Offices, Cd. 9074 (London: HMSO, 1918).

Report of the Committee on Recruitment for the Civil Service after the War (Gladstone Report), Cmd. 34, 35, 36, 164 (London: HMSO, 1919).

Report from the Select Committee on the Civil Service (Employment of Conscientious Objectors), together with Minutes of Evidence and Appendices, HC 69 (London: HMSO, 1922).

Royal Commission on the Civil Service 1929–31, Report and Minutes of Evidence (Tomlin Report), Cmd. 3909 (London: HMSO, 1931).

First and Second Reports from the Committee of Public Accounts, together with the proceedings of the Committee, Minutes of Evidence, Appendices and Index, HC 45, 144 (London: HMSO, 1936).

Recruitment to Established Posts in the Civil Service during the reconstruction period, Cmd. 6567 (London: HMSO, 1944).

The Scientific Civil Service: reorganisation and recruitment during the reconstruction period, Cmd. 6679 (London: HMSO, 1945).

Ninth Report from the Select Committee on Estimates, Session 1947–48: The Civil Service Commission, HC 203, 205 (London: HMSO, 1948).

Memorandum by the Civil Service Commissioners on the use of the Civil Service Selection Board in the Reconstruction Competitions (London: HMSO, 1951).

A Handbook for the New Civil Servant, Issued by HM Treasury, Fifth Edition (1952) (London: HM Treasury, 1952).

Her Majesty's Civil Service Commissioners, A Note on their duties and history (London: HMSO, 1952).

Royal Commission on the Civil Service, 1953–55 (Priestley Report), Cmd. 9613 (London: HMSO, 1955).

Control of Public Expenditure (Plowden Report), Cmnd. 1432 (London: HMSO, 1962).

Sixth Report from the Estimates Committee, Session 1964–65: Recruitment to the Civil Service, HC 308 (London: HMSO, 1965).

The Civil Service, Vol. 1 Report of the Committee 1966–68 (Fulton Report), Cmnd. 3638 (London: HMSO, 1968).

The Civil Service, Vol. 2 Report of a Management Consultancy Group (Fulton Report), Cmnd. 3638 (London: HMSO, 1968).

The Civil Service, Vol. 3(1) Surveys and Investigations (Fulton Report), Cmnd. 3638 (London: HMSO, 1969).

The Civil Service, Vol. 3(2) Surveys and Investigations (Fulton Report), Cmnd. 3638 (London: HMSO, 1968).

The Civil Service, Vol. 4 Factual, Statistical and Explanatory Papers (Fulton Report), Cmnd. 3638 (London: HMSO, 1968).

The Civil Service, Vol. 5(1) Proposals and Opinions (Fulton Report), Cmnd. 3638 (London: HMSO, 1968).

The Civil Service, Vol. 5(2) Proposals and Opinions (Fulton Report), Cmnd. 3638 (London: HMSO, 1968).

The Method II System of Selection (for the Administrative Class of the Home Civil Service), Report of the Committee of Inquiry, 1969, Chairman: Mr J.G.W. Davies, OBE (Davies Report), Cmnd. 4156 (London: HMSO, 1969).

CSD Report: First Report of the Civil Service Department (London: HMSO, 1970).

CSD Report 1970–71: Second Report of the Civil Service Department (London: HMSO, 1971).

Eleventh Report from the Expenditure Committee, Session 1976–77: The Civil Service, HC 535 I and II (London: HMSO, 1977).

Report of the Committee on the Selection Procedure for the Recruitment of Administration Trainees (Allen Report) (Basingstoke: Civil Service Commission, 1979).
Report by Sir Alec Atkinson, Selection of Fast Stream Graduate Entrants to the Home Civil Service, the Diplomatic Service and the Tax Inspectorate: and of Candidates from within the Service (Atkinson Report) (London: Management and Personnel Office, 1983).
Twenty-sixth Report from the Committee of Public Accounts, Session 1983–84: Fraud in the Property Services Agency; The Wardale Report; System Controls in District Works Offices, HC 295 (London: HMSO, 1984).
Fifth Report from the Defence Committee, Session 1984–85, The Appointment and Objectives of the Chief of Defence Procurement, HC 430 (London: HMSO, 1985).
Efficiency Unit, *Improving Management in Government: The Next Steps, Report to the Prime Minister* (Ibbs Report) (London: HMSO, 1988).
Treasury and Civil Service Committee, Fifth Report, Session 1988–89, Developments in the Next Steps Programme, HC 348 (London: HMSO, 1989).
The Citizen's Charter: Raising the Standard, Cm. 1599 (London: HMSO, 1991).
Treasury and Civil Service Committee, Seventh Report, Session 1990–91, The Next Steps Initiative, HC 496 (London: HMSO, 1991).
Civil Service Commissioners' Recruitment Code (Basingstoke: Office of the Civil Service Commissioners, 1992).
Open Government, Cm. 2290 (London: HMSO, 1993).
Select Committee on the Public Service, House of Lords, Session 1995–96, First Report, *The Government's Proposals for the Privatisation of Recruitment and Assessment Services (RAS), with evidence*, HL 109 (London: HMSO, 1996).
Civil Service Fast Stream Recruitment Report 1999–2000 (London: Cabinet Office, 2000).
Civil Service Fast Stream Recruitment Report 2001–2002 (London: Cabinet Office, 2002).
OCPA Review on working with Recruitment Consultants in the Public Appointments Process: Report (London: Office of the Commissioner for Public Appointments, 2003).

Books and articles

K.M. Reader wrote a short history of the Civil Service Commission 1855–1975. It was originally intended as a publication to mark the 100th anniversary of its creation, but it was not made generally available. It was later updated and published in 1981 in the Civil Service Studies series. The text is only 71 pages but the valuable appendices include a reprinting of the Northcote–Trevelyan Report; the Order in Council of 21 May 1855, creating the Civil Service Commission, with a statement of its duties; examples of certificates of qualification; and a list of Civil Service Commissioners from 1855 to 1979.

Other books and articles read in the preparation of this book:

Annan, Noel, *Our Age: Portrait of a Generation* (London: Weidenfeld & Nicolson, 1990).
Annan, Noel, *The Dons: Mentors, Eccentrics and Geniuses* (London: Harper Collins, 1999).
Armstrong, Sir William, 'The Tasks of the Conference', *PAC Bulletin*, 6 (May 1969), 1–7.
Balogh, Thomas, 'The Apotheosis of the Dilettante', in Hugh Thomas (ed.), *The Establishment* (London: Anthony Blond, 1959).
Bird, Dennis L., *The Civil Service College, 1970–1995* (London: HMSO, 1995).
Blunt, Sir Edward, *The ICS: The Indian Civil Service* (London: Faber & Faber, 1937).
Boulton, David, *Objection Overruled* (London: McGibbon & Kee, 1967).
Bourgon, Jocelyne, 'A Unified Public Service: Does it Matter?', *Commonwealth Innovations*, 9(1), 2003, 3–6.

BIBLIOGRAPHY

Bridges, Sir Edward, *Portrait of a Profession: The Civil Service Tradition* (Cambridge: Cambridge University Press, 1950).

Bridges, Lord, *The Treasury* (London: Allen & Unwin, 1964).

Campbell, Colin, *Governments Under Stress: Political Executives and Key Bureaucrats in Washington, London and Ottawa* (Toronto: University of Toronto Press, 1983).

Cape of Good Hope, *Report of a Commission Appointed by His Excellency the Governor to Enquire into and Report upon the Existing Condition and Regulations of the Civil Service in this Colony*, G100–'83 (Capetown: W.A. Richards & Sons, 1883).

Castle, Barbara, *The Castle Diaries 1964–70* (London: Weidenfeld & Nicolson, 1984).

Chapman, Brian, *British Government Observed* (London: Allen & Unwin, 1963).

Chapman, Richard A., 'Profile of a Profession: The Administrative Class of the Civil Service', Memorandum No. 2 in *The Civil Service, Vol. 3(2), Surveys and Investigations, Evidence Submitted to the Committee under the Chairmanship of Lord Fulton 1966–1968* (London: HMSO, 1968), pp. 1–29.

Chapman, Richard A., 'The Rise and Fall of the CSD', *Policy and Politics*, 11(1), 1983, 41–61.

Chapman, Richard A., *Leadership in the British Civil Service* (London: Croom Helm, 1984).

Chapman, Richard A., *Ethics in the British Civil Service* (London: Routledge, 1988).

Chapman, Richard A., 'The Demise of the RIPA: An Idea Shattered', *Australian Journal of Public Administration*, 52(4), 1993, 466–74.

Chapman, Richard A., *The Treasury in Public Policy-Making* (London: Routledge, 1997).

Chapman, Richard A. and Greenaway, John, *The Dynamics of Administrative Reform* (London: Croom Helm, 1980).

Cohen, Emmeline, *The Growth of the British Civil Service, 1780–1939* (London: Allen & Unwin, 1941; reprinted by Frank Cass, 1965).

Cooke, C., *Biography of an Ideal: The Diamond Anniversary of the Federal Civil Service* (Washington, DC, US Civil Service Commission, 1959).

Critchley, T.A., *The Civil Service Today* (London: Victor Gollancz, 1951).

Curgenven, John, 'Theodore Walrond: Friend of Arnold and Clough', *Durham University Journal*, 44, 1951–52, 56–61.

Dale, H.E., *The Higher Civil Service of Great Britain* (London: Oxford University Press, 1941).

Eaton, Dorman B., *The Civil Service in Great Britain* (New York: Harpers, 1880).

Elliott, Sir Ivo (ed.), *The Balliol College Register 1833–1933* (Printed for private circulation, 1934).

Ellis, Roger, *Who's Who in Victorian Britain* (London: Shepheard Walwyn, 1997).

Evans, Dorothy, *Women and the Civil Service* (London: Pitman, 1934).

Faber, Geoffrey, *Jowett: A Portrait with a Background* (London: Faber & Faber, 1957).

Fabian Society, *The Reform of the Higher Civil Service: A Report by a Special Committee for the Fabian Society* (London: Fabian Publications in conjunction with Victor Gollancz, 1947).

Fabian Society (A Fabian Group), *The Administrators: The Reform of the Civil Service*, Fabian Tract 355 (London: Fabian Society, 1964).

Foss, Michael, *The Royal Fusiliers* (London: Hamish Hamilton, 1967).

Franke, Wolfgang, *The Reform and Abolition of the Traditional Chinese Examination System* (Cambridge, MA: Harvard University Press, 1963).

Franks, Sir Oliver, *The Experience of a University Teacher in the Civil Service* (London: Oxford University Press, 1947).

Fry, Geoffrey K., *Statesmen in Disguise* (London: Macmillan, 1969).

Fry, Geoffrey K., *Reforming the Civil Service: The Fulton Committee on the British Home Civil Service 1966–1968* (Edinburgh: Edinburgh University Press, 1993).

Gladden, E.N. *Civil Services of the United Kingdom 1853–1970* (London: Frank Cass, 1969).

Gladden, E.N., *A History of Public Administration* (2 vols) (London, Frank Cass, 1972).

Glass, D.V., *Social Mobility in Britain* (London: Routledge & Kegan Paul, 1954).

BIBLIOGRAPHY

Graham, John W., *Conscription and Conscience: A History 1916–1919* (London: George Allen & Unwin, 1922).

Greaves, H.R.G., *The Civil Service in the Changing State* (London: Harrap, 1947).

Griffith, Wyn, *The British Civil Service 1854–1954* (London: HMSO, 1954).

Halsey, A.H. and Crewe, I.M., *The Civil Service, Vol. 3(1), Surveys and Investigations: Social Survey of the British Civil Service* (London: HMSO, 1969).

Hamilton, Sir H.P., 'Sir Warren Fisher and the Public Service', *Public Administration*, 29, 1951, 3–38.

Harris, José, *William Beveridge, A Biography* (Oxford: Oxford University Press, 1977).

Hart, Jenifer, 'Sir Charles Trevelyan at the Treasury', *English Historical Review*, 75, 1960, 92–110.

Heath, Sir Thomas, *The Treasury* (London: Putnam, 1927).

Heclo, Hugh, and Wildavsky, Aaron, *The Private Government of Public Money* (London: Macmillan, 1974).

Hennessy, Peter, *Whitehall* (London: Secker & Warburg, 1989).

Hill, C.E. (Compiled by), with a preface by G.W. Jones, *A Bibliography of the Writings of W.A. Robson*, Greater London Papers No. 17 (London: London School of Economics and Political Science, 1986).

Hodgetts, J.E., McCloskey, William, Walker, Reginald and Seymour Wilson, V., *The Biography of an Institution: The Civil Service Commission of Canada 1908–1967* (Montreal: McGill-Queen's University Press, 1972).

Hughes, Edward, 'Civil Service Reform: The Trevelyan Report', *Manchester Guardian*, 23 November 1953.

Hughes, Edward, 'Civil Service Reform 1853–5' *Public Administration*, 32, 1954, 17–51.

Hutchinson, Horace G. (ed.), *Private Diaries of the Rt Hon Sir Algernon West GCB* (London: John Murray, 1922).

Keeton, G.W., *Trial by Tribunal* (London: Museum Press, 1960).

Kellner, Peter and Crowther-Hunt, Lord, *The Civil Servants: An Inquiry into Britain's Ruling Class* (London: Macdonald and Jane's, 1980).

Kelsall, R.K., *Higher Civil Servants in Britain, from 1870 to the Present Day* (London: Routledge & Kegan Paul, 1955).

Kingsley, J. Donald, *Representative Bureaucracy: An Interpretation of the British Civil Service* (Yellow Springs, OH: Antioch Press, 1944).

Laffin, John, *Brassey's Battles: 3,500 Years of Conflict, Campaigns and Wars from A–Z* (London: Brassey's Defence Publishers, 1986).

Lee, J.M. *Reviewing the Machinery of Government 1942–1952: An Essay on the Anderson Committee and Its Successors* (London: J.M. Lee, 1977).

Lowell, A. Lawrence, *The Government of England* (New York: Macmillan, 1908).

Mallaby, George, *From My Level: Unwritten Minutes* (London: Hutchinson, 1965).

Mallalieu, J.P.W., *Passed to You, Please: Britain's Red-Tape Machine at War* (London: Victor Gollancz, 1942).

McKechnie, Samuel, *The Romance of the Civil Service* (London: Sampson Low, Marston & Co., no date – 1930?).

Meynell, Dame Alix, *Public Servant, Private Woman: An Autobiography* (London: Gollancz, 1988).

Milner, Frederic, 'Recent Developments in the Work of the Civil Service Commission', *Public Administration*, 25, 1947, 61–70.

Monck, Bosworth, *How the Civil Service Works* (London: Phoenix House, 1952).

Moore, R.J., 'The Abolition of Patronage in the Indian Civil Service and the Closure of Haileybury College', *The Historical Journal*, 7(2), 1964, 246–57.

Moss, Louis, *The Government Social Survey: A History* (London: HMSO, 1991).

Newsom, Sir Frank, *The Home Office* (London: Allen Unwin, 1954).

BIBLIOGRAPHY

Numa Minimus, *Vox Clamantis* (London: Macmillan, 1911).
O'Halpin, Eunan, *Head of the Civil Service: A Study of Sir Warren Fisher* (London: Routledge, 1989).
O'Toole, Barry J. and Jordan, Grant (eds.), *Next Steps: Improving Management in Government?* (Aldershot: Dartmouth, 1995).
Part, Antony, *The Making of a Mandarin* (London: Deutsch, 1970).
Pellew, Jill, *The Home Office, 1848–1914: From Clerks to Bureaucrats* (London: Heinemann, 1982).
Pinney, Thomas (ed.), *The Letters of Thomas Babington Macaulay* (Cambridge: Cambridge University Press, 1981).
Pirotta, Godfrey A., *The Maltese Public Service 1880–1940: The Administrative Politics of a Micro-State* (Malta: Minerva Publications, 1996).
Rae, John, *Conscience and Politics: The British Government and the Conscientious Objector to Military Service 1916–1919*, (London: Oxford University Press, 1970).
Reader, K.M., *The Civil Service Commission, 1855–1975* (London: HMSO, 1981).
Richards, Peter G., *Patronage in British Government* (London: Allen and Unwin, 1963).
Robson, William A., *From Patronage to Proficiency – the Public Service* (London: The Fabian Society, 1922).
Robson, William A. (ed.), *The British Civil Servant* (London: George Allen & Unwin, 1937).
Robson, William A. (ed.), *The Civil Service in Britain and France* (London: Hogarth, 1956).
Roseveare, Henry, *The Treasury: The Evolution of a British Institution* (London: Allen Lane, The Penguin Press, 1969).
Royal Institute of Public Administration, Report of an RIPA Working Group, *Top Jobs in Whitehall and Promotions in the Senior Civil Service* (London: Royal Institute of Public Administration, 1987).
Sampson, Anthony, *Anatomy of Britain* (London: Hodder & Stoughton, 1962).
Sayers, Dorothy L. (ed.), *Great Short Stories of Detection, Mystery and Horror: Second Series* (London: Gollancz, 1931).
Scrutator, 'The Civil Service Commission', *O and M Bulletin*, December 1945, pp. 3–7.
Sheriff, Peta, *Career Patterns in the Higher Civil Service* (London: HMSO, 1976).
Sisson, C.H., *The Spirit of British Administration* (London: Faber, Second edn, 1966).
Society of Civil Servants, *The Development of the Civil Service: Lectures delivered before the Society of Civil Servants 1920–21* (London: P. S. King & Son, 1922).
Thain, Colin and Wright, Maurice, *The Treasury and Whitehall: The Planning and Control of Public Expenditure, 1976–1993* (Oxford: Clarendon Press, 1995).
Thatcher, Margaret, *The Downing Street Years* (London: Harper Collins, 1993).
Trevelyan, G.O., *The Life and Letters of Lord Macaulay* (London: Longmans, 1883).
Troup, Sir Edward, *The Home Office* (London: Putnam, 1927).
Vernon, P. E., 'The Validation of Civil Service Selection Board Procedures', *Occupational Psychology*, 24, 1950, 75–95.
Wheare, K.C., 'The Machinery of Government', *Public Administration*, 24, 1946, 75–85.
Wheare, K.C., *The Civil Service and the Constitution* (London: Athlone Press, 1954).
Wilding, R.W.L., 'The Professional Ethic of the Administrator', *Management Services in Government*, 34(4), 1979, 181–6.
Wilson, N.A.B., 'The Work of the Civil Service Selection Board', *Occupational Psychology*, 22, 1948, 204–12.
Wright, Maurice, *Treasury Control of the Civil Service, 1854–1874* (Oxford: Clarendon Press, 1969).

INDEX

Abbott, Elizabeth 197
Abell, Sir George 96, 176–7, 182, 259
Aberdeen 35, 134
Aberdeen University 225
Aberystwyth 235
absolutists 55
accommodation 95
accountability 257–9 *see also* political accountability
accountable units 83
accounts 73
Adams, E.V. 81
administration group 75
administration trainee 76
administrative class 42–5, 50, 58, 63, 67, 75, 107, 135, 172, 175, 185, 188, 190, 214, 222, 226–7, 230, 235, 237, 258–9
Administrative Class Follow-up (1966) 177
administrative culture 5–6, 102, 113, 125, 138, 172, 191, 194–5, 230, 255, 258–60
administrative group 228, 235
administrative reform 70
Administrative Reform Association 16
Admiralty 22, 34, 113, 132, 206
agencies/agency approach 82, 84, 251
Air Force 106, 118
Air Ministry 163
Alfred, A. Montague 79
Allan, Miss Dorothy Spece 198
Allen, Dr F.H. 80, 204
Allen, Sir Douglas (Lord Croham) 220, 232
Allen, Sir Philip (Lord) 179, 181
analogous tests 54
Anderson, Sir John (Lord) 2, 222
Anglo Iranian Oil Company 54
Annan, Noel 104, 203
Anstey, Edgar 177, 182, 213, 254
Anti Slavery Society 151
appeals 84
Appeal Tribunal 144, 146
appointment of Commissioners 95
aptitude tests 67

armed forces 68
Armstrong, Sir Robert (Lord) 78
Armstrong, Sir William (Lord) 180–1, 183–5, 255
Army 56, 105–6, 114, 118, 131, 141, 150, 153; funds 55; reforms 27; selection of officers 53
Army Directorate for Selection of Personnel 182
Army Pay Corps 47
Ashburton, Lord 13, 103
Ashley, Professor W.J. 224
assignments 73
assistant principal 76
assistant secretary 54
Association of Certified and Corporate Accountants 115, 117
associations of teachers 106
Athenaeum 172
Atkinson, Sir Alec 81
Atomic Energy Authority 59, 180
Attlee, Clement (Lord) 209, 217
Australia 36, 105, 159, 161–2
Austro-Hungary 36

Bacon, Francis 20, 205
Bailey, A.M. (Sir Alan) 181–2
Baldwin, Stanley 49, 196
Balfour, A.J. 21
Balliol College, Oxford 14, 19, 22–3, 45, 229, 233, 239
Balogh, Thomas (Lord) 70, 175
Bancroft, I.P. (Sir Ian/Lord) 210
Bangor, University College 221
Bank of England 182, 188
Barker, E. (Sir Ernest) 50, 231
Barlow, Sir Alan 58
Barnes, Sir Thomas 120
Barrett, W.P. 57, 205
Barrington, C.G. 125–6
Barstow, G.L. 147–8
Barton, F.P. 104, 134

INDEX

Basingstoke 73, 83
Belfast 104, 134
Belgium 36, 160
Beloff, Lord 261
Bengal 14, 17, 35, 50
Benson, Sir Arthur 189
Berkeley, Arthur Mowbray 131–2
'bestness' 69
Beveridge, Lady *see* Mair, Mrs (Lady Beveridge)
Beveridge, Sir William (Lord) 158, 229
Bevin, Ernest 150, 203, 233
'bias' in selection 6, 42, 54, 74, 80, 171, 179, 183, 186, 191, 196, 200, 202, 220, 231–2, 236, 241, 254–6, 259
'Bill of Rights' 204
Bird, Dennis 2
Bird, James 150
Birmingham University 221–2, 224
Blackman, Harold 151
Blaikie, L. 19, 118–19, 229–30
Board 197; meeting(s) 150, 159–60, 229, 236
Board of Agriculture and Fisheries 148
Board of Control 13
Board of Education 44, 50, 195
Board of Inland Revenue 209
Board of Ordnance 15
Board of Trade 15, 36, 142
Bock, Edwin A. 211–13, 217, 255
Bourgon, Jocelyne 253
Brasenose College, Oxford 239
brewing 222
Bridges, Sir Edward (Lord) 2–5, 66, 157, 159, 164, 167–71, 173, 205, 209, 216, 237
Bristol 142
Bristol University 239
British Broadcasting Corporation 62
British Columbia 36
British Psychological Society 207
Brittain, Vera 150
Britton, H.S. 152
Brodrick, J. 115
Bryan curves 61
Buchan, O.M.C. 110
Buckfield, Sgt J. 117
Bullard, Sir Reader 238
Bunker, A.R. 101–2
bureaucracy 230
Burlington Gardens 62, 73, 158
Burma 156, 203
Burt, Cyril 48
Burton, R.N. 111, 183, 185–8, 190–1
business: management 260; methods/values 82
Butler, G.G. 19
Butler, R.A. (Lord) 107, 156
Butler, Sir Robin (Lord) 252

Cabinet Office 66, 80–5, 208, 210
Caine, Sir Sydney 109–10
Cairo, Egypt 36, 54
Camberwell 145
Camberwell Trades Council and Borough Labour Party 143
Cambridge, Duke of 131
Cambridge Modern History 43, 204
Cambridge University: attended by recruits 29, 80, 127, 221, 226, 255; attracts best students 242; 'bias' towards 220, 234, 241; Christ's College 59; consultation with 230, 236; Corpus Christi College 45, 228, 238; discussions (in 1930s) 50, 229; discussions (in 1940s) 52; dons at 204, 212; early interest in reforms 104; evacuation to 62; on FSB 239; geography at 116; Helsby comments 169–70; King's College 45; Leathes' familiarity 222; Padmore comments 168; post First World War recruits 46; represented on CSC 259; represented on CSSB 225; represented on Davies Committee 191; social strata 166; syllabuses 224, 231; Trinity College 43, 62; Warren Fisher visits 228
Cambridge University Appointments Board 180, 182, 225, 228
Campbell-Bannerman, Henry 43, 216
Canada 36, 67, 159, 161–2
Canada, Civil Service Commission of 3, 260
Canadian Centre for Management Development 253
Capita Group plc 85
Capita RAS Ltd 85
Cardwell, Edward 27
careers exhibitions 235
careers officers 107
Carr-Saunders, Sir Alexander 212
case examiner(s) 97, 99
Case Examiners' Manual 97–8
Caserta 54
Castle, Barbara 217
Cecil, Lord Robert 196
Census Office 19
Central Africa 161
Central Interviewing Board 53
Central London Recruiting Depot 143
Central Office for Labour Exchanges and Unemployment Insurance 142
Central Probation Board 60, 209
Central Tribunal 55, 143–7
certificate(s) of qualification: after probation 137; CSC powers dependent on 128; evidence and assignments branch 32; exceptions to 77–8, 81; for permanent appointments only 74–5; found insufficient/unreliable 136–7; independence of CSC 93; Levene's appointment 79; medical examinations 49; on probation

INDEX

17–18, 25, 52; requirements 111;
Superannuation Act (1859) 22, 33, 76, 250;
Treasury requirement 24
certification 18, 21, 23, 71–2, 112, 258;
recertification 113; replaced by 'written approval' 83
Ceylon 156, 159, 161–2, 203
Ceylon Civil Service 253
Ceylonese Police Force 253
Chalmers, Sir Robert 149
Chamberlain, Neville 50
Champion, Mrs 133
Chapman-Andrews, E.A. 200–2
Chapman, Brian 70, 175
Chapman, Richard A. 3
Charter Act (1833) 23
Cheltenham Ladies' College 259
Chester, D.N. (Sir Norman) 157
Chichester Secondary School for Girls 106
Chief of Defence Procurement 77
Chiesman, Dr W.E. 97–8, 101
China 36, 130–1, 156, 254
Christ Church, Oxford 45, 50, 238–9
Christopherson, D.G. (Sir Derman) 184
Christ's College, Cambridge 22, 59
Church, D.G. 118
Churchill, Winston 209, 217
Civil Service Code 84
Civil Service College 190
Civil Service Department 71, 73, 75, 80–1, 102, 163, 177–8, 186, 188, 190, 251–2
Civil Service Management Board 85
Civil Service Reconstruction Committee 52
Civil Service Selection Board (CSSB) 32, 53–4, 60, 81, 83–5, 157, 166–7, 170–1, 176–7, 179–87, 189, 201–2, 205–7, 212–13, 216, 224–5, 231, 233–4, 237, 241, 256
Clapham, J.H. 45
Clare College, Cambridge 184
Class I 26, 29, 42–3, 45, 50–1, 108, 195–6, 221
Class II 26–7
clearing house 34
clerical assistant 56, 67, 77
clerical class 58, 75, 226
clerical officer 56, 67, 77, 106
Clerk of the Furniture 112
Clerk of the House of Commons 114–15
Clerk of the Parliaments 114–15
closed politics 5, 52, 99
Coal Board 180
codes of conduct 194, 208, 217
Codling, Sir William 119
Cohen, Emmeline 2
Cole, G.D.H. 164
Colebrook, Sir Edward 14
Collett, Mrs Olga K. 235–6

Collins R.J. 127
Colonial Land and Emigration Office 15
Colonial Office 15, 20, 150, 160
Colonial Service 172, 189, 226
Commissioners of Works 112
Committee of Vice-Chancellors and Principals 52, 74, 184
Commonwealth Relations Office 159–61
competition(s) 25, 34, 72, 127
competitive examinations 26, 42–3, 45
conscientious objectors 54–6, 148
consortium *see* Customer
consultation 230
Consultative Committee 44
Cooke, Charles 3
Cooper Brothers/Coopers and Lybrand 71, 75, 84
Copyright Act 119–20
copyright issues 115, 118–20
Cork 134
Cornell University 59
Corporation of Accountants Ltd 117
Corpus Christi College, Cambridge 45, 228, 238
corruption 137, 249
Council of Women Civil Servants 197
County Councils Association 106
County of London Appeal Tribunal 143
Couper, Sir George 129
Courthope, W.J. 20, 107, 114, 116, 204, 227
Court Martial 146–7, 149
Cousins, D.C. 50, 231
Craig, J.H.M. (Sir John) 196–7
crammer(s)/cramming 106, 221, 224, 227, 231
Crane, Professor F.R. 80
Cranfield School of Management 84
Creedy, Sir Herbert 238
Crewe, Ivor 186–7
Crimean War 16
Critchley, T.A. 2, 157–8
Crombie, J.I.C. 230
Crookshank Committee/Report 60–1
Crookshank, Harry 60
Cross, Lord 153
Crossman, R.H.S. 164
Crown Agents 142
Crowther-Hunt, Lord 2, 176, 180–1, 183, 185, 189–90
Crystal Palace 61
Customer Consortium 84–5
Customs Department 27
Customs and Excise 58, 148, 152
Customs Service 117

Dasent, Sir George 20, 131
Davidson, Strachan 22–3
Davies, J.G.W. 73–4, 180, 182, 184–8, 191, 258

279

INDEX

Davies Committee/Report 74, 76, 175, 185–6, 188, 190–1
Davis, H.W.C. 45
Day, A.J.T. (Sir Albert) 156
Deakin, W. 110–11
delegation 68–9, 71, 74–5, 80, 82, 84, 97–8, 257
Delhi 54
Dell, Miss 165–6
'departmental view' 216
Department of the Environment 79
Department of Health and Social Security 82
Department of Practical Science and Art 15
devolved recruitment 82
Dicey, A.V. 260
Diplock, Miss 172
direct entry assistant secretaries 70, 213
direct entry principals 69, 213–14, 234
Director General of Military Education 105
director of research 190
disabled candidates 115
dispersal 73
Dixon, P.V. 256
Dominions Office 203
Downham, Lord *see* Hayes Fisher
Downs, Miss M.P. 80
Dragon School 238
Dublin 27, 42, 104, 127, 134
Ducat, Col C.M. 46
Duff, J.S. (Sir James) 239
Dulwich 142
Dulwich College 184
Dundas, R.H. 238
Dunk, W.E. 159
Durham University 109, 173, 184, 221, 239

Eastern Cadetships 29
East India Company 12, 13, 25, 112
Eaton, Dorman B. 17
economical and convenient 230
economy 103, 197–8
Eden, Sir Anthony 51
Edinburgh 27, 35
Edinburgh University 189, 222
Educational Reform Council 106
educational system 220, 226–30
Edwards, P.L. 36
effective(ly) 126, 252
efficiency/efficient (including inefficiency) 59–61, 85, 98–9, 103, 125–6, 131, 136–7, 221, 230, 249, 251–2, 260
Efficiency Unit 82
Ellenborough, Lord 25
embarrassed/embarrassment 5
equality/equal opportunity 103, 134, 194, 216, 226, 258
ethical implications of examining 232
ethos of public service 5, 6, 79, 249, 251–3

Eton College 21, 43, 45, 105, 258
Eustace, Rev J.M. 131
evacuation 62
evidence branch 73, 99, 135
Exchequer and Audit Department 106, 142
Exchequer Office 18
executive class 58, 67, 75, 226, 235
Executive Class Follow-up Survey 177
executive officers 69
executive search consultants 82, 84
exemption 140–1, 143–4, 147–8, 150–1, 153
Exeter College, Oxford 176, 189
Exeter University 173
expediency 208

Fabian 70, 163, 173, 175
Factory Acts 12
fair/fairness: Central Tribunal 143; changes over time 255; cramming 106; Davies Committee 76, 191; in delegation 69, 77; emphasis by CSC 35, 134–5, 138, 194, 216, 224, 250; Fulton unfair 181; implementation 29; Levene's appointment 78; Method I 74, 231; Method II 186; in personnel management 59–62; quasi-judicial judgments 258; in reconstruction 48; remuneration 128; response to Glasgow 234; responsibility of CSC 80, 103–5; unfair to history/Oxford 108–9; in speeding up 75; unified civil service 253; women candidates 196
Farrer-Brown, Leslie 161
Federation of British Industries 54
Federation of Rhodesia and Nyasaland 159
Federation of University Women 197
Federation of Women Civil Servants 197
Fiji 161
Final Selection Board 54, 84–5, 179, 182, 184–6, 200–2, 231, 238–9
Finer, Herman 44
First Division 42, 113
First World War 5, 29, 33, 43, 45, 53–5, 58, 61, 67, 132, 140, 151, 163, 195–6, 204, 230, 251, 254
Fisher, Sir Warren 1–2, 5, 49, 55, 228, 230–1
Fisher, W.H. 97–9, 212–13, 235
Fitzpatrick, Raymund 232–3
Foreign Office 51–3, 130–1, 200–1, 238, 251, 258
foreign service 57, 107, 196, 200–1, 216, 225, 230, 233, 236, 238, 259
France 56, 132, 160, 185
Francs case 208
Franke, Wolfgang 254
Franks, Oliver 2
Fraser, Sir Ian (Lord) 118
Fraser, W.R. (Sir Robert) 55, 196–8, 229

280

INDEX

fraud 132, 137
Freeman, Roger 84
Fry, Geoffrey K. 2, 189
Fry, P.J.M. 72
Fulton Committee: appointment of 71, 175; implementation of recommendations 102; on recruitment 234, 252, 256; report of 6, 73, 85, 103
Fulton, John (Lord) 233, 238
functions of CSC 32

Galway 134
General Certificate of Education 68–9, 106, 227, 235
German experience 53
German Universities Commission 156
Germany 57–8, 117, 156, 160
Gibraltar Civil Service 253
Girton College, Cambridge 197
Gladstone, Viscount 45
Gladstone, W.E. 14–15, 18–19, 22–3, 137, 257
Gladstone Committee 45, 195
Glasgow University 221–3, 234
'Glorious Revolution' 204
Goderich, Lord 26
Goff, Mr 181
Gold Coast 156, 160
Goldsmith, J.H.T. 62, 165–6, 172, 212, 237, 241
Gordon, George S. 52
Gordonstoun 35
Government Geological Survey 58
Government Hospitality 159
Government Organisation Committee 102, 158
Gow, Dr J. 106
Graduate Tax Inspectors 81
Greats 14, 23, 50, 179, 222, 224, 229, 234
Greaves, H.R.G. 2, 212
Greece 35, 160
Grenville, Lord 12–13
Griffiths, R.C. 162, 165
Gubbins, F.B. 129
Guillemand, Sir L. 152
Guppy, S.J. 143, 145

Hacket, Dorothy C.L. 57
Haileybury College 12–14, 129, 132
Haldane Report 195–6
Halsey, A.H. 183
Halsey Report 185–7
Hamburg 156
Hamilton, W.A.B. 159
Hammond, E. 130
Hammond, J.L.LeB. 22
Hancock, C.J. 176
Hanscombe, R.N. 119
Hardman, E. 117
Harrison and Sons, Messrs 133
Harrow 258

Harvard University 59
Hawtrey, R.G. (Sir Ralph) 140
Hayes, C.J. (Sir Claude) 57–8, 97, 160–6, 169–73
Hayes Fisher, W.Y. 31
Headlam, Edward 19
Headmasters' Committee 105
Headmasters' Conference 106–7
health declaration(s) 69, 75, 98–9
Heath, Sir Thomas 148, 150
Heclo, Hugh 2
Hedley, T.L. 31
Helsby, L.C. (Sir Lawrence/Lord) 60, 72, 97, 109–10, 159–60, 164–7, 169–73, 176–7, 209–10, 233, 236–7, 258
Hennessy, Peter 2
Herdman, Miss E. 117
Hertford College, Oxford 20, 22
Hervey, Lord Francis 20, 22–3, 259
Heselden, G.C. 98
Heseltine, Michael (Lord) 77–9, 84, 250
Heygate, A.C.G. 45
Hillis, A.H.M. 57, 99–101, 157, 160–2, 205
HMSO see Stationery Office
Hodgetts, J.E. 3
Hoff, H.S. 59
Holmes, David 214–15
Home Office 56, 157, 179, 203
Hopkins, R.V. (Sir Richard) 53, 208
Horn, Holloway 118–20
Hornby, Dr James J. 105
Horne, Sir Robert (Viscount) 196
Hounslow Barracks 145, 147, 149
House of Commons 141
House of Lords 18, 70, 84, 157, 188, 206, 250, 258, 261
Houston, Fred H. 134
Howard, F.L. 200, 237
Howell, R. 36
Howlett, Richard 20
Howorth, R.H. 109
Hughes' Civil Service Academy 104
Hughes, Cledwyn 236
Hughes, M. 104
Hungary 36
Hunt, J.J.B. (Sir John/Lord) 96, 102, 179–88, 191, 234
Hunt, Norman see Crowther-Hunt, Lord

Iddesleigh, Lord see Northcote, Stafford
immoral see moral
impartiality 35
Imperial Chemical Industries (ICI) 61–2, 181
Imperial Defence Committee 62
Inch, P.G. 119
Incorporated Society of Auctioneers (and Landed Property Agents) 115–16
Independent Labour Party 143

281

INDEX

India 36, 129, 156, 159–62, 203, 254
Indian Civil Service (ICS) 11–15, 17, 23, 26, 28–9, 34, 42–3, 51, 103–4, 118, 128–9, 132, 204, 231
Indian languages 118
India Office 34, 115–16, 118, 132
India Police Force 253
Indonesia 160
inefficiency *see* efficiency
influence 85, 99
Inland Revenue 27, 54, 82, 142, 256
inspector of taxes 58
Institute of Chartered Accountants 117
Institute of Cost and Works Accountants 115
Institute of Municipal Treasurers and Accountants 117
Institute of Public Administration *see* Royal
Institute of Quantity Surveyors 115
integrity 125, 130
intellectual aristocracy 203–4
intelligence tests 48, 67
Inverness 35
Investigating Section (Treasury) 99
Ireland 134
Isle of Lewis 35
Isle of Skye 35
Italy 58, 117

Jamaica 28
'Jamboree' 158
Japan 156, 160
Japanese camps 58
Jenkin, Patrick 79
J.L. and E.T. Daniell, solicitors 142
job analysis/evaluation 54, 171, 241, 254–5
job specification 25, 256
Johnston, A. (Sir Alexander) 158–9, 209, 237
Jones, Arthur Creech 6, 55, 140–53; Colonial Secretary 140, 172
Jones, Douglas 131
Jones, G.W. 164
Jowett, Benjamin 13–14, 16, 18–19, 103–4
justice 35, 44, 57, 62, 126, 134, 169, 172

Keble College, Oxford 173
Keeling, Desmond 183
Kellner, Peter 2
Kelly, W.F.C. 46
Kelsall, R.K. 70, 166, 212, 224–5, 242
Kemp, Sir Peter 252
Keynes, John Maynard (Lord) 163
King's College, Cambridge 45, 256
Kneller Hall, Twickenham 18

Labour Exchanges 32–3, 42, 44, 195
Labour Exchanges Act 32, 41
Lady Margaret Hall 238
Lambeth Police Court 145
Lancaster University 109

Land Registry 69
Lansdowne, Lord 13
Laski, Harold J. 70
Law Officers of the Crown 21
Lawrence, Miss M.A. (Dame Maud) 198
Law Stationers 22, 24, 27
Lear, Gilbert E. 142
Leasing Adviser 256
Leathes, S.M. (Sir Stanley) 20–2, 33, 42–5, 48–9, 116, 149, 196–7, 204–5, 222, 259
Leathes Committee/Report 33, 41–5, 50, 63, 224
Lee, J.M. 3
Leeds University 221
Lefevre, John G.S. 13, 17–18, 103, 126
Leicester University 110
Levene, Peter (Lord) 77–9
Lewis, Sir George Cornewall 18–19
liaison officers: for authors 157; for universities 107, 234, 236–8
Liberal Christian League 143
Limerick 134
Lindsay, A.D. 45
Lingen, R.R.W. 23
Lisbon 58
Literae Humaniores see Greats
Liverpool 42, 132
Liverpool University 110, 221
Livesey, R.C. 237
Local Advisory Committee 143
Local Education Authorities 235
Local Tribunal 143–4
Lockhart, J.S. 20, 31
Lodge, Professor Richard 222
London 27–8, 68, 73, 83, 104–5, 127, 132, 134, 142, 169, 199–200, 222, 228–9, 236; (external) students 110
London Association of Certified Accountants Ltd 117
London Clerical Recruitment Unit 81
London County Council (LCC) 62, 150
Londonderry 104, 134
London Gazette 112
London School of Economics 109–10, 116, 163, 165, 211–13, 224–5, 229, 238
London University 52, 183
Lord Chancellor 21
Loughnane, Mary 176
Lowell, Professor Lawrence 93
Lower Division 28, 104
Lucking, Mrs R.A. 198–9
Lucy, Lieut 146

McArthur, Mrs M. 166, 237
Macaulay, T.B. (Lord) 13, 17, 43, 103, 116, 204
Macaulay Committee/Report 13, 34, 43, 104, 111, 126, 128, 130, 227
McCosh, Dr James 104

282

INDEX

MacDonnell Royal Commission/Report 11, 33, 41–5, 195–6, 204, 220, 222, 224, 226
McDowell, C.M. 132
McGill University 215
Mackenzie Davey, D. 80
Mackinder, H.J. 116
Maclean, Brigadier 53
Magdalen College 52
Mair, David Beveridge 22, 48–9
Mair, Mrs (Lady Beveridge) 22, 229
Maitland, John G. 20, 95, 125–6, 133
Major, John 252
Malaya 161
Mallaby, George 3, 108–9, 208–10, 217, 233, 236–7, 240
Mallalieu, J.P.W. 70
Malmesbury, Earl of 130
Malta 14, 36
Management and Personnel Office 80–1
Manchester University 239
Mann, Horace 19–20, 22, 94, 130, 133
Marchant, Sir James 1
Marlborough College 256, 258–9
Marshall, T.H. 229
Max Factor Group and Company 80
Meadows, Thomas T. 130
medical examination(s) 49, 69, 75, 97–9, 127, 196, 198–9
Medley, Professor Dudley J. 221, 223
Meiklejohn, R.S. (Sir Roderick) 49, 96, 147–8, 151–2, 158, 222, 225–6, 228–31
Melville, Henry 13, 103
Memorandum by the Civil Service Commission *see* White Paper
Mennell, G.G. 20, 49, 51–2, 118, 158, 228–30
merit(s) 136, 138, 194, 216
Merton College, Oxford 208, 241
Mesopotamia 132
Method I 51, 74, 108, 110–11, 186, 223, 231
Method II 41, 49, 52–4, 63, 67, 69–71, 73–4, 135, 185–7, 223, 227, 231–3, 253, 258
Methodist Church 143
Metropolitan Police 68
Meynell, Alix 3
Michie, Sgt T. 117
Middlesex Appeal Tribunal 151
Military Representative 153
Military Service Act(s) 55, 140, 144, 146, 148, 152–3
Mill, John Stuart 25
Milner Barry, P.S. 165
Milner, Frederic 56, 157
Mines Department 163
Ministry of Civil Aviation 163
Ministry of Defence 208–9
Ministry of Fuel and Power 163
Ministry of Health 52, 113, 208
Ministry of Information 62
Ministry of Labour 46, 53, 176

Ministry of Labour and National Service 54, 57, 59
Ministry of Pensions 152
Ministry of Transport 184
Ministry of Transport and Civil Aviation 237
Minute Book of Board Meetings 136
Monck, Bosworth 70, 157
monitor 83, 113
Moore, John 183–4
morale 179–81
moral issues/qualities/tests 26, 42, 103, 105, 129, 135, 164, 198–9, 254, 256–7
More O'Ferrall, Patrick 14
Morris, Sir Philip 239
Morrison, Herbert (Lord) 156
Morrison, W.S. 230
Moss, Louis 2
Mountbatten, Lord Louis 35
Municipal Corporations Act 12
Murray, John 45
Murray, K.A.G. 176–7, 179–82, 186, 213, 225
museum posts 75
Myers, Dr C.S. 48

Nairn, Rev J.A. 43
Namur 149
Natal 36
Nathan, Sir Matthew 152
National Association of Auctioneers, House Agents, Rating Surveyors and Valuers 116
National Health Commission 151
National Institute for the Blind 118
National Institute of Industrial Psychology 48–9, 182–3, 205
National Insurance Act 41
National Research Council of Canada 59
National Service 57
National Trust 208
National Union of Docks, Wharves and Shipping Staffs 150
National Union of Societies for Equal Citizenship 197
National Whitley Council 53, 58
Navy 118
Needham, H.A. 110, 172, 233–4
Nelson, C.G. 22–3, 49, 230
networks 120–1
New Bodleian 117
Newby, L.J. 147
New College, Oxford 239
new public management 115
New Whitehall Series 1–2, 6, 261
New York 161
New Zealand 36, 159, 161–2, 208
'Next Steps' agencies/initiative 80, 82, 252
Nigeria 160
Nigerian Civil Service 68
No Conscription Fellowship 143

283

INDEX

Nomico, Constantine Joseph 35
nomination 17, 25, 34, 71–2, 112, 114, 127, 130, 249, 254
Norman, H.C.H. 212
Northcote, Sir Stafford 15
Northcote-Trevelyan inquiry/Report 14–18, 29, 34, 36, 126, 128, 130, 134–5, 156, 163–4, 178, 204, 226–7, 249
Northern Ireland 162
North-West Frontier Province 162
Norway 36
Norwood Committee 227
Norwood, Sir Cyril 227
Nottage, Raymond 162, 169
Nuffield College, Oxford 183
Nuffield Foundation Home Civil Service Fellowship 160–1, 173

Oakeshott, Professor M.J. 110
O'Brien, Sir Leslie (Lord) 183
Occupational Psychology 206
O'Donovan, D. 235
Office of the Civil Service Commissioners 103
Office of the Minister for the Civil Service 82
Office of Public Service 85
Office of Works 15, 31
Official Secrets Act(s) 133, 210, 213
Ogilvy-Webb, Mrs A.K. 236
Old Age Pensions Act 41
Olivier, Sir Sydney 148
open competitions 24, 48, 54, 68, 76–8, 80, 104, 112, 130, 138, 194–5, 216, 224, 230, 249–50, 253, 257–8
openness 224, 242
operational work 189
Order of St John of Jerusalem 117
Orders in Council: (1855) 17–18, 23–4, 72, 93, 111, 135; (1862) 20; (1870) 20, 23–4, 26–7, 29, 34, 104, 137; (1871) 137; (1876) 24, 28; (1890) 28; (1892) 114; (1897) 114; (1905) 114; (1918) 45; (1956) 74, 77; (1969) 77; (1978) 77–8, 80; (1982) 78, 81; (1991) 82–3; (1995) 84
Organisation and Methods 67–8, 75, 97, 100–1
Organisation and Staffing of Government Offices, Committee on 251
Ottawa 156
Owen, David (Lord) 78
Oxford and Cambridge Club 110
Oxford and Cambridge Schools Examination certificates 106
Oxford Military College 131
Oxford University: attended by recruits 29, 80, 127, 220–1, 255; attracts best students 242; Balliol College 45; 'bias' towards 191, 212, 220, 234, 241; Christ Church 50; consultation with 228–30, 236; Corpus Christi College 238; Crowther-Hunt 190;

discussions (in 1930s) 50, 226; discussions (in 1940s) 107; dons at 212; early interest in reforms 104; on FSB 239; geography at 116; Helsby comments 170; historians unfairly treated 108–9; Leathes' familiarity 222; Magdalen College 52; Nuffield College 183; Padmore comments 169; post First World War recruits 46; Queen's College 108; Red Cross 117; reforms of nineteenth century 204; represented on CSSB 225; social strata 166; St John's College 50; syllabuses 110, 224, 231; Warren Fisher visits 228; Waterfield's discussions 52; Waterfield's speech (1948) 70, 250; Waterfield's visits 240

Padmore, T. (Sir Thomas) 96, 98, 157–8, 167–9, 171, 184, 205–6, 209, 217
Padmore Committee 98, 101–2
Pakenham, Lord 250
Pakistan 156, 159–62
Palmer, Sydney 151
Palmerston, Lord 19, 23, 26, 125–6, 250, 257
Parker, H. 209
parliamentary sovereignty 260
Part, Antony 3
Partington, Frederick William 132
part-time Commissioners 80
patronage 11–12, 16, 33, 72, 85, 99, 198, 224, 242, 249, 257
Paul, Herbert W. 22, 204
Paul, S. Cassan 31
Paynter, Reginald H. 133
Pearson curves 61
P-E International plc 83
Pellew, Jill 3
pension(s) 16, 21, 72, 76, 141, 151, 199–210, 250 *see also* superannuation
Perham, Margery (Dame Margery) 151
permanent appointments 74
personation 132
Perth, Australia 36
Peru 156
Petch, Louis (Sir) 190
Phillips, E. 148
Pinsent, Col J.R. 53–4, 61, 200
Pit Ponies Protection Society 151
Playfair Commission 12, 24, 28, 41–2, 195
Plowden Committee 175
Police Court 146
Police, recruitment for 180
policy communities 120
policy making 189
political accountability 260
political environment 250
Poor Law 12
Poor Law Board, investigation into 15

INDEX

Post Office 15, 27–8, 30, 43, 67, 74, 106, 151, 180, 195, 200
Practitioners' Guide 83
Pratley, A.S. 213–14, 237
pre-interview 57, 233
preliminary test examination 26
Prestwich, J.O. 108–9
Preventive Officer 117
Priestley Royal Commission 71, 176
Prince Philip 35
Princeton University 59
Principal Civil Service Pension Scheme 76–7
'prior options' 84
prisoners of war 115, 117
Privy Council Office 15
probation 15–17, 25, 29, 52, 60–1, 76, 135–8, 227
professional ethic 251
projection tests 54
promotion 112–13, 135, 138
Property Services Agency 79
propriety 125
psychological tests 48, 54
psychologist(s) 32, 49, 53, 55, 60, 180, 206–7, 225, 254
Psychologists Committee 115
Public Accounts *see* Select Committee
publications by officials 203–10
public interest 103, 107, 120–1, 125, 137, 187, 195–6, 216–17, 220, 236, 257
publicity 234
public opinion 141
Public Record Office 3–5
public records 259
Public Records Act (1967) 4
public school(s) 29, 220, 225, 227, 258
public sector management 260
public service 103, 121, 130, 136, 150, 173, 197, 216, 226, 240, 253
Public Trustee 195
Publishers' Association 120
Punjab 162

Quaker meetings 147
qualifying examination(s)/tests 45, 54, 76, 85, 187, 231–4
quasi-judicial role 61, 121
Queen Elizabeth House, Oxford 151
Queen's College, Belfast 104, 134
Queen's College, Oxford 108
Queen's University of Ireland, Dublin 104
Queen Victoria 35

Radley College 208, 256
Rae, Sir James 49, 95, 228–30
Railway Executive Police 68
Ramsay, Sir Malcolm 46
Reader, K.M.: advantage of age 234; article on the CSC 156; brief for Helsby 110, 165, 172; Davies Committee 186; on fairness 135; Fulton recommendations 179; history of CSC 2, 68, 71, 159–60, 162–3; on Method I 109; qualifying examinations 234; on Robson 171; on Treasury/CSC relations 177–8
Reading University 52
reconstruction 45, 51, 53–4, 57–8, 63, 67, 167, 200, 239
record department (of CSC) 133, 212
Recruitment and Assessment Services (RAS) 83–5, 252, 261
Recruitment Code 83–4
Recruitment Handbook 82–3
Recruiting Office 145
recruitment policy 73–4, 82, 250
Recruitment Research Unit 67
Red Cross Society 57–8, 117–18
referees requests 239
Reform Act (1832) 12
regional development 73
registered writers 24
Register of Writers 27
Registrar General 195
Reichel, Sir Henry 221
Reid, William 14
relationships 94
Remington Company 30
Rendel, G.M. (Sir George) 51, 107
Representation of the People Act (1918) 151
Research Division (of CSD) 67, 76
Research Unit (of CSC) 67
Reserve Forces Act (1882) 145
Reynolds, Philip 109
Rhodes James, Robert 210
Richards, Peter G. 12
Richardson, F.E. 133
Rickerd, Peta 211, 213–15, 217, 255
Ridley Commission 28, 41–2, 195
Ritson, E.H. 227
Ritson, Miss 198
Roberts, Dr 99
Roberts, H.A. 225
Robertson, Sir Malcolm 51–2
Robinson, Ernest 148
Robson, William A. 2, 163–73, 249, 255
Romilly, Edward 17, 22
Rose, Kenneth 210
Roseveare, Henry 2
Ross, P.S. 178, 213–14
Rotary Clubs 235
Royal Air Force 163
Royal Automobile Club 184
Royal Commission on Civil Establishments 20
Royal Commission on Military Education 27
Royal Flying Corps 163
Royal Fusiliers 145, 149
Royal Geographical Society 115

INDEX

Royal Institute of Public Administration 2, 158, 162–3, 169
Royal Irish Constabulary 27, 133
Royal Military Academy *see* Woolwich
Royal Military College *see* Sandhurst
Royal Navy 35
Royal Ordnance Factories 113
Rugby School 258
rule of law 260
Ruskin College, Oxford 151
Russell, Dr A.E. 49
Russell, George F. 142
Russell, W.H. 16
Ryan, Sir Edward 17–19, 23

St Andrews University 42
St Dunstan's 118
St John's College, Cambridge 19, 182
St John's College, Oxford 50, 227
Salisbury, Marquis of 104
Sampson, Anthony 2, 204
Sandhurst 27, 106, 114, 131, 133, 253
San Francisco 161
Savile Row 73
Sawyer, D.W.G. 57
scholars, work of 211
School Certificate 106, 227
schools 103, 127
scientific civil service 41, 58–9, 67, 71
Scotland 222
Scott, Sir David 201, 203
Scott, R.R. (Sir Russell) 197, 208
Scottish Board of Health 198
scrutiny 81, 257
Sebastopol 17
Second Division 28
secondments 75, 77–9
Second World War: administrative reform 70; case-examiners 97; conscientious objectors 55–6, 150; copyright issues 115, 120; Foreign Service reforms 107; health declarations 198; Method I 108, 231; Method II 231; post-war clerical recruitment 106; post-war consultation 96; post-war delegation 251; post-war publicity 234, 236; post-war research 254; pre-war recruiting difficulties 113; pre-war selection 63, 222; prisoners of war 117; reconstruction 5, 41, 45, 67; recruitment during war 69; regular recruitment suspended 50; scientists in government 58–9; Robson, W.A. 163; Sharp, E.A. 199; Waterfield visits Oxford and Cambridge 238
security services 4
Sedburgh School 173
Seddon, J.C. 72, 176, 178–9, 186, 213
Select Committee: Treasury and Civil Service *see* Treasury and Civil Service

Select Committee on the Civil Service (Employment of Conscientious Objectors) 141–2
Select Committee on Civil Service Appointments (1860) 26
Select Committee on Estimates: (1946) 157; (1947–8) 70, 99, 223, 258; (1964–5) 71, 242, 258; (1965) 175–7, 237
Select Committee on Expenditure (1977) 80, 232
Select Committee on Public Accounts 79, 157, 258
Select Committee on the Public Service 84
self-declaration 198
Selwyn College, Cambridge 184
'semi-celibate way of life' 204
senior branch (foreign service) 54
Sex Disqualification (Removal) Act 216
Shackleton, Lord 183–4, 187–8
Shanghai 130
Sharp, E.A. (Dame Evelyn) 57, 118, 199, 233
Shaw, George Bernard 163
Sheldon, Robert 79
Siam 36
Sibley, Sir Franklin 52
Sidney, Elizabeth 182–3
sift(ing) 234
Simon, Sir John (Viscount) 49–50
Simon, Lord (of Wythenshawe) 164
Simons, Michael 176
Simpson, J.R. (Sir John) 99–102
Simpson, R.J. 98
Sind 162
Sinker, A.P. (Sir Paul) 67, 96–9, 158–62, 167, 212–13, 233, 336
Sisson, C.H. 256
Sloman, P.T. 237
Smellie, Professor K.B. 110
Smith, A.L. 45
Smith, Miss Alice 197–8
Smith, Goldwin 19
Smith, W.H. 20
Smyth, Miss D. 197
Snow, C.P. (Sir Charles/Lord) 59, 164–5, 210
Snowden, Philip 222
Society of Accountants and Auditors 117
Society of Authors 120
Somerset House 152
South Africa 14, 36, 159, 161–2
Southampton 133
Southampton University 184
Southern Rhodesia 162, 203
South London Federal Council against Conscription 143
Southport 62
Spearman, Professor C.E. 48
special advisers 71, 75, 77, 190, 251, 257
special departmental class(es) 54, 235–7

INDEX

Spedding, James 20, 94–5, 125, 204
'speeding up' inquiry/review 188, 190
Spens, Will 45, 228
Spielman, Miss Winifrid 49
Spottiswoode, William 22
Stalag Luft 1, 117
stamps 27
Stanley, A.P. 19
Stanley, Lord 26
Stationery Office 119–20, 132, 161–2
Stephenson, Sir John 203
Stoke D'Abernon 54, 74
Stopford, Sir John 239–40, 256
Storey, G. Johnstone 104
Strafford, Lord 22, 131
structure of Commission 32
Strutt, H.A. 157
Sudan 161
Sumner, Major A.T. 164–5
Sunderland, Miss M.E. 80
'Sunningdale Conference' 176
superannuation 16
Superannuation Act (1859) 21–2, 33, 250
Supplementary Clerkships 127
Sweden 160
Swindale, John 225
Syracuse University 213

Tancred, Peta *see* Rickerd
Telegraph Learner 28
telephone(s) 30–2
Temple, Rev Frederick 18–19
temporary appointments 74–5, 77
Thain, Colin 3
Thatcher, Margaret (Lady) 80–1, 252
The Political Quarterly 163–4, 166, 170, 172
Thomas, Major T.W. 149
Thomas, W.B. 208
Thompson, Sir Geoffrey 238
Thwaites, Brian (Sir) 184
Tidman family 144, 146, 150
Tomlin Royal Commission 222, 225, 228, 231
Tonbridge School 182
transfer 112
Transport and General Workers 150
Transvaal, South Africa 36
Treasury: advice 152; and India Office 116; ambit 5, 141, 152, 258, 261; appointments to selection boards 45; appoints MacDonnell 42–3; approval 19, 24–5, 34, 93, 112, 119–20, 125, 128, 206; attitude 140; bombed 62; and Central Interviewing Board 53; Circular(s) 27, 40, 60, 141, 150; contacts with 6; Civil Servant's Guide 158; on civil service practice 152; Clerkship 125; conscientious objectors rules/memorandum 55–7, 147–8, 151, 230; consultation 51; CSC accountable to 258; employment of blind persons 118; encourages liaison officers 237; encourages 'Redbrick' undergraduates 236; Establishment Officers' Circular 117; functions transferred to 81; group of departments 66, 93–4, 125, 177; Hillis in 161; investigation into 15; Investigating Section 99; Leathes' appointment 20–1; liaison with 108; medical examinations (women) 199; Meiklejohn in 49; Minute(s) 30, 43, 133, 141; More O'Ferrall in 14; O and M division 67, 97, 99; Oxford and Cambridge proposals 228–30; policy on publications/research 207, 209, 213; preliminary test examination 26; procedures with CSC 23; pressures from 53; recruitment policy 73–4, 82, 250; regulations 58; relations with CSC 178, 189; Smith, W.H., First Lord 20; standardisation of examinations 29; typewriters/typists 30–1; Waterfield's appointment 49
Treasury and Civil Service Committee 252
Treasury Establishment Report 96–7
Treasury Medical Adviser/Service 97–101
Treasury Solicitor/Treasury Solicitor's Department 21, 77–8, 119–20
Trend, Sir Burke (Lord) 210
Trevelyan, Sir Charles 13–15, 18–19, 23, 94–5, 127
Trevelyan, G.M. 227, 238
Trinity College, Cambridge 14, 17, 19–21, 43, 62, 227
Trinity College, Dublin 127
Turnbull, Sir Andrew 257
typewriters 30
typists 43, 49, 67

unified civil service: after 252–3; conditions before 128; CSC role 6, 11, 36, 58, 68, 103, 249–50, 261; development of 4, 249–50; role of Order in Council (1870) 23–4
Uniform Efficiency Rating System 60
Unilever 183
United Nations 151
United States 36, 67, 161–2
United States Federal Civil Service 3, 48, 60
universities 103
University Appointments Boards(s) 74, 106, 235
University College, London 238
university expansion 70, 113
University Grants Committee 110, 180
university reform 14

Veale, Douglas 52, 229
Vernon, P.E. 206–8, 216
Victoria, Australia 36
visits 234, 238

INDEX

viva voce examinations 42, 44, 50–1, 228
Vox Clamantis 43, 204–5

Wade and Phillips 177
Wales, University of 42
Walrond, Theodore 19–20, 23, 131, 133, 258
Wandsworth Prison 147
War Cabinet *see* Cabinet Office
Wardale, Sir Geoffrey 79
Wardale Report 80
Warne, E.J.D. 234, 236
War Office 34, 53, 114, 142–3, 206
War Office Selection Board (WOSB) 53–4, 182–3
Waterfield, John 53
Waterfield, Sir Percival: on bias 256; centenary celebrations 158; conscientious objectors 56–7, 148; consultation 230; doubts on selection process 45; on educational system 227; employment of blind persons 118; foreign service; wives 201–3; Hayes' comments on 161; on interviews 223; life 3; on Mallaby 209; medical examinations (women) 199; Method II 49–53; Ministry of Information 62; Oxford speech 70, 250; on publications 157, 205–8, 210, 217, 255; reform of foreign service recruitment 107; on relations with Treasury 96, 115; retires 5, 41, 66, 233; tour of North America 156; and Treasury Medical Adviser 97, 100–1; and Treasury O and M 100–1; and Treasury Solicitor 120; visits 238
Watford 53–4
Waverley, Lord *see* Sir John Anderson
Weekes, L.C.H. 55–6, 143–4, 146–9, 196
West, C.S. 127
West Africa 161
West Bengal 162
Westfield College, London 184
West Germany 180
West Indies 161
Westminster School 50, 106, 258
Weybridge 133

Wheare, K.C. 2
Whitehall Series *see* New 'Whitehall visits' 237
Whitehead, J.E. 157
White Paper (Memorandum) on reconstruction recruitment 58, 117, 157, 167, 206
Whitgift Middle School 184
Whitley Council 168, 182
Whyatt, Woodrow 210
Wightman, W.E. 109, 215
Wildavsky, Aaron 2
Wilding, R.W.L. 176–9, 183, 185, 251
Wilson, A. (Sir Arton) 57
Wilson, Arnold (Lieut Col, Sir) 230
Wilson, A.T.M. 182–4
Wilson, Harold (Lord) 175, 189–90
Wilson, N.A.B. 205–6, 216
Wilson Smith, Sir Henry 52, 57
Wilson, Sir Horace 50, 52
Wilson, T.A. 127
Winchester College 54, 184, 258
Winnifrith, J.D. (Sir John) 101, 165
woman, as Commissioner 196
Women Citizens Association 197
women, employment of 31, 42–3, 53, 67, 195–203, 216, 220
Women's Political and Industrial League 197
Wood, R.S. 50
Woolf, Leonard 163
Woolley, Rev Dr J. 22
Woolwich 27, 106, 114, 253
Woolworth, F.W. and Co Ltd 80
Workers Education Association 151
Workers' Travel Association 150
Wormwood Scrubs 146–7, 149
Wren's 224, 231
Wright, Maurice 2–3
writers/writerships 24–5

Young, G.M. 12, 162
Young, Miss 198

Zante 35